D0221129

DT LIBRARY RENEWALS 458-2440

DATE DUE

WITHDRAWN
UTSA LIBRARIES

Public Housing That Worked

Public Housing That Worked
New York in the Twentieth Century

NICHOLAS DAGEN BLOOM

PENN

University of Pennsylvania Press

Philadelphia

Copyright © 2008 University of Pennsylvania Press

All rights reserved. Except for brief quotations used for purposes of review or scholarly citation, none of this book may be reproduced in any form by any means without written permission from the publisher.

Published by
University of Pennsylvania Press
Philadelphia, Pennsylvania 19104-4112

Printed in the United States of America on acid-free paper

10 9 8 7 6 5 4 3 2 1

Library of Congress Cataloging-in-Publication Data

Bloom, Nicholas Dagen, 1969–
    Public housing that worked : New York in the twentieth century / Nicholas Dagen Bloom.
        p. cm.
    Includes bibliographical references and index.
    ISBN 978-0-8122-4077-1 (alk. paper)
    1. Public housing—New York (State)—New York—History—20th century. 2. New York City Housing Authority—History—20th century. 3. City planning—New York (State)—New York—History—20th century. 4. New York (N.Y.)—Social conditions—20th century.   I. Title.

HD7288.78.U52N726 2008
363.5'85097471—dc22   2008006013

**Library
University of Texas
at San Antonio**

For Brenna Roxie Bloom and Leanne Bloom

Contents

Introduction

Is it possible to say anything new about public housing? After hundreds of sobering studies and thousands of desultory newspaper articles it is difficult to imagine that any uplifting lessons can be salvaged from this country's tragic public housing experience. Almost all these studies have been informed by a sense that public housing inevitably fails no matter the intentions of administrators or tenants.

The story of the New York City Housing Authority (NYCHA)[1] reveals such important differences from other cities that urban historians, sociologists, journalists, and designers should never have generalized about public housing's essential nature without wrestling with America's largest and most successful public housing system. *Public Housing That Worked*, by enumerating the factors that led to New York's survival, offers a renewed historical framework for American public housing history generally. The reader of this book will come to realize that, as in New York, public housing could have been built and maintained to a decent standard; tenanted with a wider range of income groups; and policed in a systematic fashion.

It is distressing that much American subsidized housing turned out to be not much better, and arguably worse in some extreme cases, than traditional slums. Too little attention has been paid to management deficiency as the principal factor in this widespread failure. Dedicated housing advocates rarely prospered at America's mismanaged, patronage-ridden big-city housing authorities. Where patronage was not rampant, housing administrators often lacked the necessary skills and staff to manage multi-family housing.

Architects and planners were the first to lump together public housing and urban ills. Idealistic designers had promoted public housing in the first place, but by the 1950s they were blaming tall buildings and modernist superblocks for mounting social disorder. Critics became so obsessed with the negative influence of design on behavior, however, that they rarely factored in growing evidence of basic housing management failure. Sociologists in the 1960s and after linked public housing to a growing crisis of an urban underclass trapped in America's inner cities. Because of their obsession with exposing broader social injustice, they also downplayed housing administration as a factor in public housing disorder.[2]

As the years passed, public housing's increasingly distressing story became the domain of historians. In the 1980s, the historian Arnold Hirsch gave a name to the perversion of the public housing concept: the "Second Ghetto." Hirsch reminded historians that in Chicago, as in other cities, public officials unceremoniously dumped poor residents displaced from urban renewal and highway projects into nightmarish public housing projects concentrated in existing, poverty-stricken black neighborhoods. A second ghetto was thus born on top of the first. Hirsch and many of those who have followed in his footsteps at most acknowledged management problems, but their own liberal political instincts stopped them from attributing widespread failure to glaring governmental deficiencies. Did this second ghetto, however, have to be as horrific as it became in Chicago, St. Louis, or Newark?[3]

NYCHA's history illustrates that housing management practices, broadly defined, are the most important factors in the long-term shape of public housing communities. NYCHA has operated under many of the same stresses that bedeviled other housing authorities, but its success has illustrated that constant vigilance can sustain concentrations of high-rise superblocks in second ghettos. NYCHA's current deputy general manager for operations, Robert Podmore, believes that even today in New York within three or four days there would be a "serious impact on quality of life" should maintenance standards falter at the authority's many developments. Very few other housing authorities had any sense of urgency to their management operations and most failed to address serious defects either on a daily or even yearly basis.[4]

Indeed, New York has not succeeded in the long term simply because its job is easier than that of other housing authorities. First, it is a tower-block system with almost all of its twenty-six hundred buildings six stories or higher. Many NYCHA developments, housing a high percentage of very poor tenants and concentrated in the poorest sections of the city, remain under siege. Aluminum flashing is often stolen, tenants inexplicably urinate in hallways and elevators, security systems are frequently sabotaged, garbage is dumped from windows every day, graffiti is constantly applied to glazed brick, and shockproof glass is frequently shattered. Not long ago a tenant was even mangled by an adolescent tiger he kept as a pet![5]

Good management not only means remedying these physical defects but also arresting criminals, controlling tenancy, and collecting rents. Vigilance also means keeping patronage to a minimum, holding employees and tenants responsible for their behavior, seeking private sec-

tor help where necessary, and using politics to build and protect housing rather than destroy it. NYCHA's success, and continuing effectiveness, should in no way be considered inevitable.

The results of this watchfulness are evident today. During my visits to
a great many NYCHA housing developments in every borough, I have
found well-maintained brick buildings, mature plane trees and green
lawns, active community and recreation programs, and first-class play
equipment. Developments also frequently adjoin city parks and public
transportation. During the day these public housing developments have
significant numbers of staff cutting grass, fixing elevators, cleaning graffiti, and collecting trash. That 9,640 of the authority's 13,687 employees
(2006) remain in operations, the division engaged in daily management, is immediately evident on a visit to NYCHA developments.

These clusters of towers, housing over 400,000 tenants, may not be environments that middle-income families would like—apartments are
small, lobbies and hallways of glazed tile and steel are institutional,
crime and vandalism are frequent, and elevators are slow—but the price,
location, and management level compensate for these deficiencies.
Poverty and its attendant problems have not been used as an excuse for
neglect. New York may have a tighter housing market than many cities—
a factor that helped keep public housing popular—but administrators
have made clear choices that determined the outcome.

Administrators made the right choices not only because they wholeheartedly endorsed the notion of public housing, in contrast to the situation elsewhere, but because their housing system emerged from a long
tradition of multi-family housing management in New York. Apartment
buildings existed in other cities, but large multi-family apartment complexes were rare. New York might have been one of the worst cities imag-
inable for tenement dwellers, but the vast number of well-managed
apartment houses for middle- and upper-income New Yorkers offered
an instructive model for NYCHA. New York's public housing administrators knew that similar high standards would be essential to ensure that
their buildings did not become tenements. They knew that the most important difference between a tenement and a decent apartment building was management quality.

From the beginning NYCHA has imitated the apartment management
methods of middle- and upper-class buildings for its poor and working-
class populations. What might have seemed like luxury in other cities,
heavily staffed and closely managed low-income projects, seemed less remarkable or controversial in New York because of this multi-family tradition. Furthermore, the massive growth of government employment
across the board in New York from the Great Depression onward helped
normalize NYCHA's emphasis on heavy staffing.

Administrators in other cities seemed to think that the creation of a new building would be enough to end the problems associated with slum living. They lacked the context, experience, or desire to make the right management decisions or build large, competent staffs. Problems multiplied when cities such as St. Louis and Chicago switched from low- or medium-rise projects to high-rise towers modeled on New York's. Having never mastered multi-family management in the first place, they showed almost no talent for the towers in the park: their buildings quickly became unlivable. Even the low-rise housing projects in most cities suffered from decades of neglect.

The popular and scholarly image of public housing has been little touched by the New York experience. Rather, public housing's abysmal reputation in the United States has been most powerfully shaped by the experience of cities such as St. Louis, Chicago, Baltimore, Cleveland, Newark, and Philadelphia. For most journalists and academics, a growing list of failed projects nationally—from Pruitt-Igoe in St. Louis to the Robert Taylor Homes in Chicago—sufficiently confirmed the essential impracticality of public housing as a whole. Growing problems in Europe's once fabled social housing estates have only added to the chorus of public housing doubters. The physical evidence of anarchic public housing elsewhere, and its subsequent demolition in so many cities, *is* an important and legitimate source of public housing's unsavory reputation, but it is not the whole story.

Administrative incompetence was widespread enough to raise doubts about the wisdom of the Housing Act of 1937, which placed the responsibility for public housing in local hands. Local politicians and housing management appears to be, in most cases, a dangerous combination. With weak administrative controls in place, authorities across the country acted ineffectively to arrest disorder. The New York story provides a fresh perspective on familiar stories of housing failure by showing that, rare as it may be, a housing authority dedicated to everyday management can maintain housing even under trying conditions. What appeared as endemic problems of public housing, particularly its high-rise expression, looks more like local, albeit widespread, administrative failure.

Failure to highlight evident public housing success in New York has been a tremendous oversight, an omission that has excessively tainted the history of U.S. public housing and allowed failure to appear inevitable. Given NYCHA's comparatively tidy grounds and twenty-six hundred well-maintained high-rise buildings, often in densely concentrated public housing districts, one could argue that tower-block housing has been a smashing success in the United States; after all, at this point NYCHA not only accounts for over 10 percent of all public housing nationally but almost all extant high-rise public housing in the United States. Even without overly praising NYCHA, the New York example throws a monkey wrench into the well-oiled gears of public housing history and criticism.

In spite of its scale and demonstrated competence, there has not been a comprehensive study published on NYCHA even though New York's was one of the first authorities, quickly became the largest in the nation, and accounts for almost all of the country's public housing high-rise towers. Somehow, the story of public housing in the United States barely touches New York. NYCHA has become the elephant in the room in fields such as urban history, sociology, and architectural history.[6]

Why has New York's public housing history remained at the margins? Not only is the authority's scale intimidating, but also its policies can appear arbitrary and paternalistic to those with an interest in urban poverty. In an age when either citizen activists or business interests are considered to be the proper sources of all wisdom in terms of planning and community life, NYCHA appears to be a dated model of intrusive, big-government social control. But is its story really without value in social policy and historical debates? America sorely needs new models of public sector competence if it is to maintain, and possibly enhance, its long-term investment in urban infrastructure. New York, for this reason, is still an exception that matters.[7]

NYCHA's policies can be grouped into three major ideological trends. The first era stretched the longest, from 1934 to 1968. During this time NYCHA was an institution dedicated to the idea of *model housing as a municipal service.* Model housing meant replacing slums with tightly managed, high-quality housing projects. NYCHA's era of model housing lasted much longer than in other cities, and this helped it to survive the second, more challenging phase, which stretched from 1968 to the 1990s: *welfare-state public housing.* During this difficult era the authority faced, and survived, most of the strains that broke housing systems in other cities. The final phase, which stretches from the 1990s to the present, can be considered a return to early management principles, with a twist. The authority now maintains public housing to a high standard because of its vision of public housing as *affordable housing* rather than welfare housing, a subtle but important difference. While other cities implode or redevelop their public housing from the ground up, NYCHA has been able to reengineer its existing system for the working poor.

In the era of *model housing as a municipal service* government housing became one of the keys to a modern city by clearing the slums *and* providing model housing in place of the tenements. Mayor Fiorello La Guardia (elected in 1933) became the force for what would one day become a vast program. Housing for the poor and ill-housed, according to

NYCHA's founders, was not a social program but an exercise in progressive government not that different from public water supplies or publicly owned mass transit. New York looked to European housing programs as a model, and housing advocates helped to popularize the European vision of housing as a tool of civic and humanitarian uplift. NYCHA quickly pioneered the use of eminent domain for public housing construction and pressured the federal government for larger programs in these years. It was, in fact, New York's housing advocates who, in large measure, pushed through federal housing programs in 1934 and 1937.

By the end of the 1930s New York had also developed high-rise methods of construction and design that would permit its administrators to combine model tenements with slum clearance in central sites. Housing developments thus rose close to existing municipal services (transit, education, health care, and so forth). The pared-down towers that New York built looked superficially like those later erected in other cities; in fact, however, New York's towers were sturdier and have stood the test of time. Early NYCHA leaders, while cutting the frills, also landscaped the projects with an eye to long-term beauty and staffed their buildings on the model of better apartment buildings. This foresight, which started in the 1930s but expanded during the postwar boom, helped set New York on the road to better-quality public housing in the long term. These high-rise towers became the model, though seldom duplicated in quality, for all high-rise public housing in the United States after World War II. Other cities, who had built mostly low-rise housing before the war, failed to comprehend the more complex management system essential to tower living.

Consistent with this vision of *model housing* was the housing authority's search for model tenants. Tenants at Harlem River Houses and other early developments were carefully selected and few tenants on public relief or welfare found a berth. These methods endured, in one form or another, until 1968 and made NYCHA tenancy comparatively less troubled. The authority also divided its developments racially in the early years in order to build political support for a mass program, even though this meant acquiescing to racial prejudice common at the time. New York's racial policies in this era paralleled those in other cities, but a city such as Chicago actually oriented public housing to minority needs even before World War II, thus racializing public housing from the outset.

NYCHA's broad vision of municipal housing clashed in the 1930s with the United States Housing Authority's view that public housing should be only for the poorest families. Federal officials had to be careful that public housing would not even appear to compete with the private sector—either by its luxuriousness or by serving more comfortable families.

At Red Hook Houses (1939) and Queensbridge Houses (1940), NYCHA not only demonstrated how cheaply public housing could be built (leading to the pared-down, high-rise, slum-clearance projects of the future) but also stared down federal officials in order to avoid a higher welfare tenancy. Other American cities pursued careful tenant selection in the 1930s and 1940s as well, but even in this period they acquiesced more easily to federal demands for very low income, often welfare, tenants in their housing. They also largely had abandoned their tenant selection systems by the 1950s, whereas NYCHA maintained its selectivity until the late 1960s.

Because federal officials favored public housing as welfare housing, resisted slum clearance, and provided limited funding compared to New York's grandiose dreams, NYCHA had to build its own housing and did so using entirely separate city- and state-funded housing programs. New York could draw on three programs by 1940 whereas other cities failed to develop alternative sources of funding. These city and state programs allowed New York to get a quick start in housing after the war. The passage of the Housing Act of 1949 quickened New York's tempo, but NYCHA relied heavily on city- and state-funded programs to build its housing during this time. These programs permitted slightly higher income levels and, in the case of city-funded housing, more attractive developments. By 1965, only 41 percent of NYCHA developments had been built with federal funding, as opposed to 37 percent from state funding and 22 percent from city funding. (See Appendix A.) Most American cities moved slowly to build any housing and were so dependent on federal dollars that they built only for the poorest citizens.

Robert Moses, New York's legendary city planner, eagerly used NYCHA during the 1940s and 1950s as a putative destination for slum clearance tenants displaced elsewhere. Slum clearance by the authority in poor areas during the postwar era also reached staggering proportions, but NYCHA also built housing projects on vacant land. Even in the Moses era, New York continued to build decent structures and maintain its towers to a high standard. NYCHA's employees, selected through civil service tests, proved far more competent than their peers in other cities. The lack of civil service protections and the presence of patronage problems plagued housing management in other cities during this era.

NYCHA used the war years and the postwar housing crisis to maintain its vision of public housing as a city service that could serve a wide range of the city's families. Higher-income black and white tenants dominated in the immediate postwar period, many of them veterans' families, and they paid surcharges to stay. NYCHA quietly achieved a remarkable level of integration in all of its different housing programs in the first decade after World War II. Many higher-income white families still moved out faster (voluntarily or because they exceeded income limits) than they could be replaced. By the late 1950s, the authority's tenancy had become majority minority.

Robert Moses made much of public housing as a destination for New Yorkers uprooted to make way for his many redevelopment projects, but in reality he allowed the authority to reject tenants who likely would have been accepted in other cities. As higher-income families left public housing, and additional site tenants from urban renewal projects filtered in, managers noticed more problem families than before and adjusted their policies; in other words, they refused to turn model public housing into a poorhouse. In 1953 NYCHA put in place twenty-one moral factors such as single motherhood and irregular work history that kept welfare families comparatively sparse in number even as the minority population grew. NYCHA also created the nation's first public housing police force to help control disorder. In contrast most other cities used public housing as a dumping ground for urban renewal site tenants and allowed screening to falter. They also failed to develop competent police forces to control growing problems.

By the late 1950s New York had tired of Moses' and NYCHA's vast slum clearance techniques; worse, surprisingly few site tenants had been directly accepted in public housing from Title I and other clearance projects because of low income limits for admission and high behavioral standards. What had been good for NYCHA—tight tenant selection— had been bad for the reputation of Moses. Mayor Robert Wagner, Jr. purged NYCHA of Moses' men in 1958. New leadership arrived that promised to reduce the size and scatter new developments as well as stem growing racial concentration. The new managers, inheriting an essentially sound organization, re-energized the management programs and provided steady leadership well into the 1960s, even though they failed to reverse the shift to mostly minority tenancy. Nor did they abandon high-rise construction or slum clearance.

The dramatic shift to *welfare state public housing* came in 1968. The combination of federal policies, local incompetence, and other factors had already steered most public housing in the United States in this direction. In New York pressure had been growing on NYCHA because its tenancy as a whole, while more than half minority, featured half the welfare tenancy of the national average. The welfare department had been complaining for some time and finally won a new policy—by the early 1970s the welfare percentage had doubled at NYCHA. Though welfare numbers never reached the level of other authorities, certain developments became dangerously concentrated. NYCHA faced growing disorder, including drugs and antisocial behavior, at the same time that legal challenges to eviction inhibited a tough approach.

NYCHA also temporarily became an overt tool for racial integration. So-called scatter-site programs designed to send black residents to traditionally white areas mostly failed to launch in the 1960s. The experiment fully ended, however, in the early 1970s at Forest Hills, where NYCHA expended much of its political capital on a controversial public housing project. Excessive humanitarian concern further undermined the ability of NYCHA and other housing authorities to maintain their housing stock. The notorious Brooke Amendment capped public housing rents nationally at 25 percent of income but effectively raised the rent on the working poor by making 25 percent the new minimum. Congress then regularly failed to provide an adequate subsidy to make up for lost rental income.

NYCHA may have been one of the more successful representatives of the social potential of public housing in the 1970s, but even it suffered from growing problems. Other cities, in contrast, had far worse experiences with welfare concentration, corruption, shoddy construction, and social disorder in public housing. New York's budgetary shortfalls, and high energy and labor costs undermined, but did not eliminate, NYCHA maintenance and security. NYCHA also began what it called the Tier Program to encourage income mixture in its projects. The best news during this time was HUD's performance modernization funding (rewarding NYCHA for its good management with extra funds) and the Transfer Program of city and state projects to federal status that allowed for large-scale renovation. The authority also fought back against drugs in the 1980s with the help of new laws and tough techniques that eventually yielded measurable improvements.

Today, NYCHA's good management practices have preserved high-rise public housing in New York when it has failed elsewhere. Even an economic renaissance in a city such as Chicago, with a return of population to the center city, failed to reverse decades of public housing mismanagement. Most American cities have gladly adopted the federal Hope VI program of replacing their troubled projects, high-rise and low-rise, with mixed-income communities. Public housing in New York, in contrast, has started to seem again like a valuable reservoir of affordable housing in a pricey global city.

In the most recent phase of NYCHA history, the authority's managers, like others in the modern nonprofit housing field, deny that subsidized housing should serve only the very poor. Under its *affordable housing* philosophy NYCHA has sought out tenants who can afford to pay a reasonable rent and comport themselves better than the welfare dependent. Evidence of this management style can be seen in the success of New York's "working family preferences," which jump working families to the head of the waiting list and in recent years have accounted for approximately

50 percent of new tenant families. In 2006 welfare families accounted for less than 20 percent of tenants whereas working families counted for more than 40 percent. By keeping its housing to a higher standard, New York has been able to pursue income diversification in its existing buildings—at great cost savings to the city and federal government compared to Hope VI redevelopment.

The New York City authority began with many advantages, but like all of America's public housing authorities, it has had to overcome challenges to its existence. Administrators have had to make difficult choices in a variety of management fields, but what united these diverse efforts was a commitment to professional housing management. It was not the case that other authorities failed because it was impossible to succeed. Managing large, complex, urban systems such as housing or transit is an essential and feasible task for cities that wish to compete on a regional, national, and international scale. Public housing may be dying as a social institution nationally, but NYCHA's long-term demonstration of the power of good public management deserves far greater attention in the broad analysis of municipal activities.

Part I
Model Housing as a Municipal Service

Chapter 1

Defining a Housing Crisis

Tear down the old. Build up the new. Down with rotten, antiquated rat holes. Down with hovels. Down with disease. Down with crime. Down with firecraft. Let in the sun. Let in the sky. A new day is dawning. A new life. A new America!

—Fiorello La Guardia, 1944[1]

New York City had tolerated its tenement districts for decades, and even modest forms of tenement regulation amassed a dismal record. The Great Depression, however, weakened New York's inviolate traditions of private property. Housing reformers, in this moment of crisis, reinvigorated the Progressive-era notion that tenement districts (Figure 1) threatened the health and long-term welfare of the city as a whole. These zealous activists used the mass media, exhibitions, and public forums to sell public housing as the most enlightened means of comprehensive urban reconstruction. For the first time in New York's history, the notion of replacing tenements with housing built and managed by the government began to seem reasonable.

What eased the selling of public housing in New York, and the founding of NYCHA in 1934, was not only the promise of thousands of jobs but also the seductive model of European public housing developments. Idealized visions of European housing projects became a key ingredient in New York's sales pitch. New social housing, on a European scale, would be paired with an expanded array of New Deal–funded municipal public works that would usher in a more enlightened urban age. New York would thus end the private sector monopoly on low-rent housing by establishing public housing as a new municipal service that both cleared slums and built model housing in its place.

In the years before the Housing Act of 1937 and the state housing programs approved in 1938, NYCHA built little, but its leaders laid the groundwork for what became America's largest housing program. The housing authority secured its legal right to condemnation for public

Figure 1. Tenements, typical of those that once covered much of the city, on the site of what became Amsterdam Houses (1948). La Guardia Wagner Archive/NYCHA Photograph Collection.

housing projects and began instructive experiments under the Public Works Administration. The new authority also heightened the sense of crisis by feverishly demolishing tenements and artificially enhancing a local housing shortage. These years of planning and talking initially seem less important than subsequent decades because of the limited amount of construction actually achieved, but it was during this time that New York laid the groundwork for all of its future endeavors.

New York City, normally a whirlwind of activity, had slowed to a crawl by the early 1930s. The Depression was an authentic crisis that threatened the social fabric of the city and the nation. Unemployment reached record levels as business activity slumped. The city appeared to be spiraling out of control as shacks sprouted in Central Park, foreclosures soared, and socialists called for an end to capitalism itself. Housing reformers now seemed mild in their prescriptions for a renewed, more humane city.[2]

The context of high unemployment provided the most immediate and persuasive justification for the public housing program. Langdon Post, the authority's first chairman and a dedicated housing reformer, made clear in a 1934 radio address that "housing reaches deeper down into the pool of the unemployed than does any other branch of this [construction] industry." He estimated that in many branches of the construction trades, unemployment had reached 90 percent, of which about 50 percent were on relief. Government-funded housing projects he promised, would absorb 75 percent of those workers on relief and might in short order employ nearly ten thousand workers. Post had started to make noise; these were dramatic, if unrealistic, estimates.[3] It was not, Post admitted, a "humanitarian change of heart on the part of our legislators, but the fact that the administration in Washington, under economic stress, is compelled to spend money to relieve distress."[4]

The immediate problems of unemployment catalyzed housing programs in New York, but activists used the crisis to redefine New York's slums as an equally vexing and imminent threat to urban welfare. One of the first major projects of the authority in 1934 was a citywide property inventory that both answered the need for employment in a suffering city and gave NYCHA precious ammunition. The eight-month survey by six thousand employees of the Civil Works Administration found that most of the city's older multi-family buildings were "firetraps, breeders of crime and disease," and covered seventeen square miles of the city. The authority figured that approximately half a million families with one million children lived in housing of this type.[5] Reformers claimed that these slums "bred tuberculosis, crime, juvenile delinquency, immorality," and "a general breakdown of social morale." Tuberculosis rates seemed particularly alarming in slums, with a rate approximately twice as high as the citywide average.[6]

A different formulation of the crisis perspective came from those with a less humanitarian bent. These urban advocates, including figures such as Robert Moses, were less concerned about the million left in the tenements than they were about the image and liabilities of a city full of tenements. Suburban hinterlands, both those within the city's boundaries and outside, had swelled in the 1920s as a broad segment of families rode trains and cars to new homes. Albert Mayer, a prominent architect who completed housing studies for NYCHA, found that the tenement districts, rather than being upgraded, seemed to take a turn for the worse as a result of decentralization: "residential urban areas lost population; owners could not afford to keep up their properties, which consequently deteriorated; poorer classes of people took possession; properties deteriorated still further, and hence new slums were created."

The city's leaders, thought Mayer, had to create "a way of life that can compete with suburbs."[7]

These convergent visions of crisis—substandard housing as both a humanitarian and civic threat—focused on the old-law tenements. That the old-law tenement, a mix of subdivided single-family homes and purpose-built congested walk-ups, remained a staple of the New York housing scene frustrated housing reformers. Frontal assaults on the tenement evil in the form of Tenement House Laws from 1867 and 1879 had little improved the state of New York's tenements. Housing created under these laws (so-called old-law, or dumb-bell tenements) often lacked indoor plumbing and central heating, and, because they were very nearly built out to the lot line, sufficient air or light. Windowless rooms were all too common. Reformers in 1900 counted eighty thousand tenement buildings that housed over two million unlucky denizens. The 1901 reforms, adopted in an era of Progressive reform, set higher standards of air, sanitation, and light, including much enlarged central courts. The "new-law" tenements that resulted from the legislation sprouted uptown in Manhattan or in the outer boroughs rather than in the crowded tenement neighborhoods. The Multiple Dwelling Law of 1929 finally mandated what could be considered modern standards of light, construction, and hygiene, but the Depression muted the law's impact by halting almost all new construction.[8]

Direct regulation of existing old-law tenements had proved equally unsatisfying. The Tenement House Department, a result of the 1901 legislation, had been designed to supervise new construction and improve existing housing by requiring updates such as indoor toilets, new windows, and fireproofing. Many indoor toilets and windows had been installed, but the department's inspectors had limited success confronting the city's squalid tenement districts. The 1901 law, after all, grandfathered existing old-law tenements; enforcement of violations proved time consuming; machine politicians interfered; funding was inadequate; and business interests whittled away at the department and its underlying legislation. Government action threatened what was likely the city's most lucrative industry. One of the key figures in the department, Lawrence Veiller, became frustrated by the painfully slow progress in upgrading slums, but he, like many others in his generation, viewed public housing as inimical to American values.[9]

Tenement districts thus remained in the 1930s an easy target for reformers with a grand vision. Old-law tenements might have suffered from a 20 percent vacancy rate by 1933, but large segments of New York's poor obviously still lived in the 80 percent still occupied. They endured irremediable infestations, substandard or nonexistent sanitary facilities, drafty windows, and tiny courtyards that barely permitted air circulation. Tenants generally used coal as a heating source, and most tenement apartments were firetraps that annually harvested their share of victims. It was, in fact, "a rash of fatal fires" in the early months of the La Guardia administration that further "dramatized the dangers of substandard housing."[10]

The idea of replacing tenements with model housing had a long history in New York, but from the perspective of housing advocates previous experiments had been as grand a failure as the tenement laws. Forty years of philanthropic building, for instance, had yielded units for only 3,588 families by 1910. Examples of philanthropic housing in New York are the Tower Buildings (1879) and Dunbar Houses (1928). Philanthropists not only tended to favor the cream of the ill-housed poor, but "the volume of even pure philanthropic housing had to be limited by the limitations of the philanthropy itself. They could be demonstrations and experiments" at best.[11]

Limited-dividend experiments, combining profit and philanthropy, had blazed the trail toward public housing. The City and Suburban Homes Corporation, for instance, built a number of attractive complexes across the city and returned dividends of almost 5 percent annually between 1899 and 1936. The corporation provided good-quality housing for those of moderate income but, like others in the business, grew slowly because a sufficient number of investors could not be found to create a mass movement.[12]

Government subsidy of limited-dividend projects seemed to solve the problem of limited capitalization—and was based on Europe's tremendous success using the very same means. The indefatigable reformer Mary Simkhovitch, the founder of the pioneering settlement house known as Greenwich House, convinced Governor Al Smith in 1926 to create a state program that granted tax exemption for low-cost housing for twenty years. The legislation limited investors to a 6 percent return and a monthly rental maximum of $12.50 per room. Labor unions constructed some of the best of this housing for their members, particularly the Amalgamated Tenements in the Bronx (1927). Private developers, unfortunately, showed little interest, and most other labor unions lacked Amalgamated's vision of worker housing. By 1936 only eleven state-funded limited-dividend projects had been completed.[13]

President Hoover's Reconstruction Finance Corporation (RFC) limited-dividend projects, announced in 1932, attempted once again to drive forward new projects while at the same time relieving the malaise in the building trades. The loans, funneled through the State Housing Board and overseen by Robert Moses, were distributed to private industry in a pattern similar to that of the state-funded projects that preceded them. The RFC-funded (later PWA-supervised) projects were all estimated to rent monthly at between eleven and twelve dollars per room. New York, with its tradition of model low-cost housing, actually gained approval for two projects. Under this program, the Fred French company built Knickerbocker Village (1933), a high-rise slum clearance project on the Lower East Side; the future federal administrator and wealthy philanthropist Nathan Straus Jr. built Hillside Homes (1935) in the Bronx. Both of these developments proved to be important, if different, precedents for NYCHA (see Chapter 3).[14]

Few New Yorkers believed that limited-dividend or philanthropic housing like these would make much of a dent in New York's housing deficiencies. Limited-dividend programs would have seemed much more impressive had they been on a scale to rival programs in Europe. By 1905, London's limited-dividend corporations had built housing for 123,000 people. London's municipal corporation, the London County Council, had even built 15,000 public housing units before World War I. In the interwar years publicly subsidized housing in Europe became a mammoth operation. Why not New York?[15]

European Envy

> *Housing is the one field where private enterprise and individual initiative have notoriously failed. . . . For reasons inherent in our political thinking, the State has not interfered in private housing in this country and the State housing reforms which have played so large a part in the mitigation of European slums are here unknown.*
>
> —*Editors of Fortune, 1932*[16]

Many New Yorkers had lost patience with demonstration projects; they now envisioned a government housing program as a powerful tool of humanitarian and civic transformation. Mary Simkhovitch took the housing lawyer Ira Robbins aside one day in 1933 and informed him that "this business of trying to improve conditions in old-law tenements is all right . . . But we ought to do what they did in Vienna." What they, the socialists, did in Vienna was to create some of the most attractive public housing developments the world had ever seen—and on a tremendous scale. Langdon Post, the first chairman of NYCHA, also believed that because "practically every country in Europe has accepted" a role in low-cost government housing, "for the first time the slums of Europe are really being cleared." New York housing advocates had obviously tuned their program to the European one.[17]

America and New York had dithered in housing because before the 1930s no sense of crisis existed on the American urban scene. Few Americans before the Great Depression honestly believed that America would not redevelop its old housing in due course. As a nation engaged in constant acts of creative destruction—and blessed by abundant land around its cities—excessive concern about housing quality reflected a lack of faith in American social and geographic mobility. The Depression weakened this confidence and many worried that the country, and its older cities, had shunted into a permanent decline. It looked as though Americans might finally have to plan and upgrade older urban areas. In the context of diminished expectations the European model of urban reconstruction took on new meaning. A country such as Great Britain, in obvious economic decline, had somehow still managed to clear slum districts and rehouse large segments of its populace.[18]

Americans had made frequent pilgrimages to leading examples of good planning in the late nineteenth and early twentieth centuries, whether Birmingham, Frankfurt, London, or Paris. There they found not only new boulevards and grand public buildings but also more practical innovations such as zoning, abundant recreational facilities, public markets, public baths, and improving sanitation. Even more astounding, and somewhat unsettling, was the discovery of low-cost housing, in both city centers and the suburbs, partly subsidized by city governments. America's municipal reformers made significant progress in areas such as public water, public markets, schools, sanitation, parks, zoning, and occasionally public transit, but otherwise American reformers could do no more than gaze longingly at European municipal reforms in areas such as town planning and housing.[19]

During the 1920s the distance between Europe and the United States grew, particularly in terms of municipal housing. Even before World War I, a few European municipalities directly built a few thousand housing units of low-cost housing; quite a few cities also subsidized an impressive volume of low-cost housing undertaken by a mix of philanthropists, building societies, cooperatives, and limited-dividend corporations. The left-leaning interwar years, however, were notable for vast programs of low-cost housing, according to the historian Daniel Rodgers: "In all, between 1919 and 1933 some six million new dwellings were built in Europe, three million of them outside the framework of the private housing market."[20] Vienna's famous public housing projects may have been designed as the vanguard of a new social order that would destroy capitalism, but municipal housing in this period did not require Vienna's extreme version of municipal socialism. Council housing authorities in Britain alone, for instance, had built one million homes by 1938.[21]

Many New Yorkers who later played leading roles in public housing, such as the housing lawyer Louis Pink, Nathan Straus Jr., and the socialist leader B. Charney Vladeck, had toured European social housing developments and collected their impressions on paper for the American public. Beautifully illustrated texts such as Louis Pink's *A New Day for Housing* (1928) and Catherine Bauer's much lauded *Modern Housing* (1934) raised expectations about the power of public housing by celebrating European housing success.

Pink's *A New Day for Housing* highlighted the many versions of social housing in Europe by the 1920s. In London Pink discovered minimal but still attractive model tenements that had transformed slum neighborhoods: "the typical Council tenement is five stories high, but two rooms deep, has no central heat, but does provide a bath . . . There is plenty of light and air." Pink was also impressed, as would be many others, with the garden-city low-cost housing estates in London's suburbs: "They have winding streets and courts, attractive stucco and brick cottages with red tiled roofs, gardens, hedges, trees, flowers, playgrounds, and schools."[22]

Catherine Bauer most admired the modernist continental developments that she featured in her forcefully written, well-illustrated book. Like many reformers of the time she preferred subsidized housing on the city's edge because decentralized housing would be less expensive while still providing maximum air, sunlight, open space, and opportunities for community planning. This new way of living was perhaps best exemplified in Frankfurt's modernist housing developments (Figure 2), but Bauer also endorsed traditional-style dwellings. Bauer was most impressed that European reformers had committed to "finding a new way to house everybody" and celebrated that housing had become "a Public Utility" in Europe much like sanitation, fire fighting, and education.[23]

New Yorkers had the opportunity throughout the 1930s to learn, without travel or reading, of the many advantages that public housing had brought to European cities. Bauer's popular housing exhibit at the Museum of Modern Art in 1934 contrasted tenement conditions with streamlined European housing projects. European housing experts also frequently spoke in New York City to prominent civic organizations. To say that these various sources of information painted a flattering portrait of European social housing is no exaggeration.[24]

American housing advocates liked to argue, misleadingly, that mass support for public housing in Western Europe revealed its essentially apolitical nature. The tireless housing pioneer Edith Elmer Wood, for instance, viewed European public housing as an investment in social health rather than socialism: "European experience justifies belief that in a few years the death rates, sickness rates and delinquency rates of a transplanted slum population would approach the city average." That the Ministry of Health in Britain oversaw the public housing program lent credence to such an interpretation.[25] In a "Letter to a Banker,"

Figure 2. European public housing in Frankfurt am Main of the type that inspired housing advocates in the United States. La Guardia Wagner Archive/NYCHA Photograph Collection.

Langdon Post assured Americans that subsidized units built in England had not only provided a stimulus to private building but had resulted from "the policies of a frankly conservative government."[26]

These American advocates consciously overlooked the degree to which public housing either originated in leftist proposals or was agreed to by conservative figures fearful of growing socialist power. Only a few connected the dots in public. Helen Alfred, a housing reformer with socialist tendencies, remembered that for some time "municipal housing smacked of Socialist Vienna, Red Moscow; hence was dangerous, *defendu*."[27] The actual leftist connections could create qualms for the liberal minded. Ira Robbins remembered that he faced an uphill battle convincing New York's democratic Governor Herbert Lehman to go along with public housing because the "Vienna example, as convincing as it was, was 'tinted red' by its sponsors."[28]

In spite of these liabilities, and in the leftist New York context, local government officials ultimately found European examples a handy precedent to justify their unorthodox use of public power. At the dedication of First Houses in 1935, Governor Lehman even felt comfortable alluding to the fact that "students of housing have been well acquainted with the great programs" in Europe. He reminded his listeners, "Over twenty years ago in cities abroad, local communities undertook to serve the housing needs of those families who found it impossible to provide for themselves homes of modern standards."[29] Mayor La Guardia in 1934 "declared that Vienna, Berlin, Liverpool and other European cities have done more to improve housing than any American city."[30] When launching what he envisioned as a massive, city-funded housing plan in 1938, La Guardia again cited Europe: "The Mayor said he claimed no originality for his plan, since it had already succeeded in Great Britain and Holland. The London County Council, he added, had erected thirteen square miles of new buildings in 200 different units, providing accommodations for 350,000 persons." This casual statement likely sent shivers through the spine of many a New York property holder.[31]

This enthusiasm for European public housing had practical consequences. New York was not sailing into terra incognita but into its own version of a proven vision. European housing projects were an attractive reality that contrasted sharply with American tenements. They were vital evidence that could be conveniently cited for what was, in reality, a controversial program in the American context.

Diffusing the Opposition

There is a tendency to overstate unanimity on the issue of public housing in New York, but even in the depths of the Depression there existed significant opposition to government meddling in the housing market. A fair number of real estate interests supported public housing for its potential role in slum clearance (either adding value to their properties or taking real estate albatrosses from around their necks), but a municipal housing program represented the most comprehensive assault on private property the city had ever seen. Many property owners simply refused to accept the vision of humanitarian or civic crisis dramatically illustrated by public housing advocates. Nor did they see anything in European housing except socialism and unfair competition with private enterprise.[32]

Developers and owners of property understood how large the New York public operations could become because they alone knew how many people put up with substandard housing; it might be impossible to put the genie back in the bottle. E. A MacDougall, the developer of the upscale, segregated cooperative community of Jackson Heights, condemned the many efforts to bring government into the housing business. He believed that European housing conditions truly threatened public health whereas New York's old tenements had "emptied out" and would be redeveloped in due course. He called even limited-dividend projects "a semi-socialistic enterprise" that, through use of tax exemption, represented unfair competition with existing private accommodations.[33]

Others believed that the condition of New York's tenements had been grossly misrepresented in both scale and quality. One gentleman even went so far as to argue that "during the five years preceding 1901 many of the very best tenements in this city were built." He boasted that "many of them have two toilets on each floor and many of them have individual toilets."[34] Opinion like this generally revealed the callousness of the city's landlords. Some business interests carefully shifted their focus to calls for state-sponsored rehabilitation of private housing, and renovation remained the preferred solution for many progressive business leaders. A few ridiculed the oft-repeated assertion by housing advocates that the housing they intended to build, at prices of $5 per room per month, would not compete with either new or old housing in the city as a whole.[35]

Some housing supporters believed that real estate interests' opposition was slowing the formation of government agencies to create housing, but opponents did not bring housing to a halt. Opponents lacked unity, and monied interests during the Depression had lost much of their prestige and social power. Many small-scale tenement owners, for instance, had already lost or sold their properties to richer investors.[36] Ira Robbins, who later became a NYCHA administrator, delivered a broadcast in 1934 infused with class criticism. "If you read through the list of wealthy owners of tenements," he began, "you will think you are reading the social register."[37] By 1937 Langdon Post would even alarmingly admit that public housing would "to some extent . . . compete with existing old-law tenements in the city and with obsolete buildings."[38]

Opponents of public housing in this era now found themselves in the position that had long stymied reformers: they lacked an alternative vision. With few new houses under construction in the Depression years, and many more being lost to decay, real estate interests could scarcely compete with a dazzling vision of new hygienic housing featured in books, articles, editorials, talks, and exhibits. Refusing to accept that a genuine crisis in housing existed left them effectively on the sidelines. Opponents would reemerge during the postwar boom when suburban private housing again came within reach of the region's working-class population, but by then the public housing programs had become well established.

Institutionalizing Housing

European precedents proved essential in selling housing, but a genuine talent for lobbying shown by housing reformers closed the sale. A new generation of reformers and political figures demanded a level of government action that in another age had been taboo. They were so good at their business that they managed to convince a reluctant Roosevelt administration to go along with a comparatively daring national public housing program.

Public housing received a boost locally from New York's leftist tint. Labor leaders such as Sidney Hillman of the Amalgamated Clothing Workers of America encouraged the city to build housing for the jobs it would yield. B. Charney Vladeck, one of New York's socialist leaders and a founding member of NYCHA's board, boldly claimed, "There could be no adequate rehousing in the country until the time when the 'hold' of the real estate interests on urban America 'is completely broken.'" The municipal socialist Paul Blanshard of the powerful City Affairs Committee effectively lobbied the city government for new housing.[39] A massive labor rally in 1934 even called on the city "to recognize housing construction and maintenance as a 'public enterprise' in the same category as transportation and education."[40]

The socialist tradition made a difference at the local level and often smoothed the way for government action. Many tenement neighborhoods, with strong leftist traditions, devoted significant political capital to the early competition for housing projects. Brownsville community activists, according to the historian Wendell Pritchett, desired public housing in the 1930s because "unlike other working-class groups that opposed any type of 'socialistic programs,' Brownsville Jews believed that government should intervene when the market failed." Leftist support like this, operating on a local and citywide basis, bolstered New York's program and is different from lukewarm or hostile reaction to public housing in other cities.[41] Mainstream liberal organizations such as the Welfare Council of New York, the League of Mothers Clubs, the New York League of Women Voters, and the Women's City Club lent their considerable weight to the cause as well.[42]

The founding of the Public Housing Conference at Greenwich House in 1932 drew together a wide range of the city's leftist and liberal housing reformers. The conference's seemingly prosaic goal, from the outset, was to achieve a monthly "rental of approximately $7.50 a month a room" for "wage earners" rather than relief recipients. The organization, while supportive of limited-dividend projects, sought to create a "Housing Authority similar in scope to the Port Authority, with powers to supervise slum clearance in the city" and build housing. Notable members of the conference included Paul Blanshard, Mary Simkhovitch, Helen Alfred (an "obstreperous and flamboyant" housing advocate[43]), Edith Elmer Wood, the architect Clarence Stein, Rabbi Steven Wise, the socialist Norman Thomas, Louis Pink, Lilian Wald, Representative Fiorello La Guardia, and the social critic Lewis Mumford.[44]

The conference's members each had his or her own ideas about the ultimate role of housing in modern life, but the organization carefully framed its support of municipal housing on a number of progressive principals: public health; a shortage of decent, affordable housing; the failure of limited-dividend projects to reach the lowest-income renters; and employment possibilities. Public housing would be a tool for building a better city; socializing a segment of the housing market was a mere side effect of finally realizing progressive goals. The Public Housing Conference began to lobby the city to set up a housing department and sought $25 million in funding from President Herbert Hoover's Reconstruction Finance Corporation to build housing that could rent monthly at $8 per room. From their efforts came Knickerbocker Village, Hillside Homes, and a few other limited-dividend efforts.[45]

The besieged mayor, Jimmy Walker, a product of the Tammany political machine, was no fan of public housing, but he mildly endorsed housing in 1932 as a public works project should the federal government buy the city's bonds. The interim mayor, John O'Brien, the Tammany stalwart who followed Walker, however, gave a lukewarm response to the many calls for a municipal housing agency, even when faced with intense lobbying.[46] Because of Tammany's resistance to housing programs, the mayoral candidate Fiorello La Guardia in 1933 could provocatively link together "model multiple dwellings" with the more practical goal of making "Boss rule . . . a thing of the past."[47] Tenement crowding and misery seemed to serve Tammany well by keeping the poor dependent on local politicians. Eliminating the slum would not only improve the city's health and welfare but might also weaken patronage. As a congressman, La Guardia had associated himself with the fight for housing and during his mayoral campaign would remind liberal forces that "he had long been an advocate of municipal housing projects." La Guardia's commitment to action contributed to his victory over the machine in 1933.[48]

As mayor-elect that November, La Guardia announced that he immediately sought to create a city housing commission. He couched his haste in concern that New York would be beaten out by other cities and thus lose "jobs for the unemployed." Answering charges that the high vacancy rate in city apartments obviated the need for public housing, he retorted that the housing he had in mind "will be in competition not with real estate, but with disease and poverty."[49] His belief that low-cost "housing would become exclusively a function of government . . . because of its important relation to governmental control of public health" led ultimately to a European-scaled program.[50] Nor did La Guardia's choice for tenement house commissioner, Langdon Post, shy from activist government. The way Post saw it, "State operation of bridges, tunnels, parks, canals, health institutions and schools" was "implicit in our State constitutions" and for this reason "the construction and operation housing . . . is merely a perfectly logical extension of this recognized principle."[51]

La Guardia and Post, and those who supported them, had an advantage shared by very few other housing advocates. The historian John Buenker has documented that New York State during the 1920s had been "an island of progress and reform" by pursuing "new frontiers in labor and welfare legislation, education, housing and public power." Governors Al Smith and Franklin Roosevelt had not pioneered public housing, but they had used the governorship to pursue progressive platforms, including limited-dividend housing. The Depression-era sense of crisis accentuated the state's potential role in ameliorating social problems.[52]

In 1933 a bill had been prepared under La Guardia's direction (by the lawyers Ira Robbins, Charles Abrams, and others) for the creation of state housing authorities and, after much revision, it passed in January 1934 with Governor Lehman's strong support. Its passage reflects both the political skills of proponents and the sense of urgency related to unemployment woes. Lehman's support, it should be added, developed only after intensive lobbying. Seeing the potential employment benefits of the program, he came around with the Public Housing Conference's nudging.[53]

The creation of an authority was an unorthodox solution to housing reform but featured Progressive-era advantages that helped mute opposition. Because good-government reformers had legitimate concerns about giving so much power to machine politicians, the bill insulated housing programs from local patronage politics. Authorities, after all, had tax exemption, could issue debt, collect data, hold hearings, build housing, and even condemn land through eminent domain. New York State's housing authorities, including NYCHA, were to have an unsalaried board of five members appointed, on a rotating basis, by the mayor. Mayors were supposed to pick only the initial chairmen; the authority boards would assume responsibility for selecting subsequent leaders. With power in the hands of a technical and professional elite, an authority such as NYCHA operated more like European cities where the business classes and an elite bureaucracy dominated municipal government.[54]

In 1934 La Guardia named Langdon Post as chairman and Mary Simkhovitch, the Reverend Robert Moore, B. Charney Vladeck, and Louis Pink as board members. As La Guardia lightheartedly admitted in 1935, "Where can you find a housing board to equal it; an idealist on housing [Pink], a social worker [Simkhovitch], a Catholic Priest [Moore] and a Socialist [Vladeck]."[55] A board of such devoted housing experts and advocates could be counted upon to develop a broad and positive approach to public housing. New York's administrative ethos, it turns out, already had diverged from that in other cities. The urban historian John Bauman found that none of the first appointments to Philadelphia's authority, for instance, "won the unqualified endorsement of Philadelphia housing reformers." Real estate interests often dominated boards in Philadelphia and other American cities.[56]

First Lessons

At first glance it looks as though the New York City Housing Authority in these early years had limited success. On closer examination, however, it becomes clear that Langdon Post and those around him began shaking up the economic and legal framework of New York City. The federal government may have approved only two projects before the Housing Act of 1937, and the state and city programs were not approved until 1938, but NYCHA undertook vitally important research and initiatives.

The notion of crisis received a powerful boost from Post's determination to clear tenement houses from congested neighborhoods. Such a dramatic program required little money but would both eliminate sub-standard housing and create pressure among the working class for pub-licly subsidized housing. Post, it appears, single-handedly "revived the long disused power to vacate buildings found to be unfit for human habitation."[57] In his dual role as head of the Tenement House Commis-sion, Post began work on slum clearance projects that replaced con-gested tenement blocks with new park space.[58]

Post aimed to pressure owners to comply with forceful amendments to the multiple dwelling law made in 1935. He "estimated that nearly half of the 65,000 old-law tenements would be unable to comply" with the new laws that would go into effect beginning 1 January 1936. Tene-ment owners, now redefined to include mortgage holders (and the banks held many more mortgages than normal as a result of the Depres-sion), appeared unwilling to pay the high costs of renovating tenements long past their proper expiration date. Post openly paired this enforce-ment to building pressure for public housing because he frankly ac-knowledged that those displaced from this housing would not "be provided by private initiative" because of their low income levels. He ar-gued, instead, that "government subsidies are the only way."[59]

Between 1934 and 1936 the authority demolished 1,100 old-law tene-ments, which represented ten thousand dwelling units.[60] Another forty thousand apartments were lost to abandonment by property owners in-dignant over the new city regulations.[61] In 1936, Post predicted that "demolition of old houses and the condemnation of others as unfit for human habitation would contribute to the housing shortage." As he himself said, "The only way to get action [on public housing] is to cre-ate the need."[62] When many banks and other property owners initiated mass evictions from substandard buildings, Post offered a temporary stay on criminal liability for building owners. During this crisis he called again for a "long term public housing program."[63] Even a housing advo-cate such as Harold Riegelman had to acknowledge that "from excellent and humane motives we have thus accelerated the housing shortage . . . if we keep on this course we shall have the highest housing standards in the world, while a third of the population sleeps on park benches."[64]

Post had, in fact, achieved his goals of turning the housing authority into a powerful organization with the ability to shift the city's political economy. NYCHA would remain an authority dedicated to slum clear-ance until the 1960s. Clearing slums for parks and other public uses, however, remained distinct from clearing slums for public housing. It was the experimental First Houses (1934) project that created this pow-erful combination.

First Houses, NYCHA's first project, might be forgotten today were it not for its being first and a test case for the power of housing authorities

Figure 3. This modern image of First Houses (1936) illustrates both its modest scale and its integration with the surrounding neighborhood. Photograph by Seth Knudsen.

(Figure 3). NYCHA had launched First Houses to demonstrate the potential for tenement renovation, favored by real estate interests, without replacing potential federal support for new housing projects. First Houses was built with labor donated by the Federal Emergency Relief Organization using WPA labor. The authority partly acquired the property, on the Lower East Side, by exchanging authority bonds for slum properties Vincent Astor wished to relinquish. The philanthropist Bernard Baruch bought authority bonds to help finance the project. NYCHA also sold salvage materials, gleaned from its clearance projects, to raise funds for its operations.[65]

First Houses remains one of NYCHA's most attractive complexes, but it turned out to be very expensive per room because of high labor costs, poor planning, low densities, and high quality materials (see Chapter 3 for details). These high costs turned out to be more of a public relations problem than a practical setback because the federal government's donation of labor and material permitted rents of only $6 per month per room. By achieving low rents the authority could claim success. First Houses also, according to Post, firmly established "the marketability of Housing Authority bonds" and the "Authority's right of condemnation." These were, indeed, two very important principles. NYCHA would, over the decades, raise billions through bond sales for both short-term and long-term needs.[66]

The legal basis of the authority's operations, established in *New York City Housing Authority v. Muller*, proved central to public housing not only in New York but also in the nation as a whole. NYCHA records from the 1930s indicate that Andrew Muller, one of the property owners of what would become the First Houses site, "contended that the Municipal Housing Authorities Laws, as well as the State Housing Law, violated the constitutions" of both the federal and state governments. He believed "that the taking of his property was for a private use" and the municipal housing laws "for the benefit of a class." Like many others at the time, he thought that the police power constituted the extent of government power over private housing.[67]

NYCHA's counsel, Charles Abrams, composed the 1936 brief that placed America's public housing program on a solid legal basis. Abrams employed a historical argument by dividing the history of New York State housing law into three periods: "Purely restrictive legislation [tenement house laws] . . . Constructive legislation [limited dividend] . . . [and] Constructive legislation through public low-rental housing."[68] The historian Scott Henderson believes Abrams's legal strategy effectively demonstrated that "these stages suggested a progressive increase in public activity," thus housing authorities could be seen as a legitimate expression of this trend.[69]

In 1936 the New York Court of Appeals accepted his logic and upheld a lower court decision in NYCHA's favor by arguing in a similar fashion that the police power of the state had proved inadequate to the task of remedying slum conditions. The court, in a fit of sociological jurisprudence, argued that to end the "evil" of slums and offer low-cost housing it was necessary to create "large scale operations . . . under direct control of the public itself." Such operations were not designed to benefit a certain class but to "safeguard the entire public from the menace of the slums." The state's interest in slums was buttressed by the loss of taxes and the high cost of services. Government housing was no different from the city's assumption of "many activities formerly and in some instances still carried on by private enterprise."[70]

The decision established the legality of NYCHA's operations and opened the way to an expansion of its activities in future years. Its language also lent credence to Post's and La Guardia's definition of public housing as a legitimate municipal service. Because the Public Works Administration (PWA) had failed in the courts to build public housing directly (in *United States v. Louisville*, 1935), it was logical that local housing authorities, based on the *Muller* decision, would not only be able to condemn land but ultimately be entrusted with the design and construction of public housing.[71]

What NYCHA Learned from the PWA

Not only had the PWA housing programs failed to pass judicial muster, but problems quickly mounted as local and federal officials struggled for power. NYCHA learned from its experience with the PWA that construction had to be both decentralized and much more economical. Many instructive lessons, after all, are negative ones.

In the spring of 1934 the PWA initiated a small federal public housing program. New York's liberal senator, Robert F. Wagner, had tweaked legislation at Mary Simkhovitch's urging in 1933 to include low rent housing in the National Industrial Recovery Act. The Depression-era political "mobilization of urban working class constituencies" that brought an increasingly liberal Congress allowed Wagner's plan to move ahead. The PWA, under the direction of Harold Ickes, the secretary of the Interior, became the vehicle for federal housing action through both direct action and partnership with local authorities.[72]

As late as March 1934, however, Post found that in contrast to the Roosevelt administration's speed in other areas, at the federal level "no definite plan had been worked out" for public housing.[73] In May 1934, the PWA's Housing Division finally announced the Williamsburg (1937) project, with projected monthly rents of between $6.00 and $7.50 per room. NYCHA moved ahead with land assembly in Williamsburg even though Post admitted it did not have final approval.[74]

At first it seemed that the PWA would primarily supervise and finance the project; in time, the PWA nudged its way into a more direct role.[75] Evans Clark, NYCHA's financial advisor, condemned Ickes's leadership of the PWA because "even the smallest detail of housing business in the PWA office became enmeshed in a tangle of checks and counter-checks" and "contractors jacked up their estimates 10 to 20 percent."[76] Lines of authority had become so blurred that "Post . . . discovered NYCHA and PWA were both collecting option agreements from the 700 property owners on the Williamsburg site." Apparently Ickes, like many reformers of his era, lacked any faith in local officials. In the context of what happened to housing in other cities, his skepticism seems more reasonable today. Williamsburg, an attractive low-rise development, turned out to be too expensive to serve as a true model for housing in New York.[77]

Harlem River Houses (1936) raised further doubts about the PWA's management. The overcrowding of Harlem, a result of the Great Migration and housing segregation, had by the 1930s become a serious and distinct social issue that NYCHA might address. Harlem's population had exploded from 83,000 in 1920 to 204,000 in 1934. In the 1930s Harlem replaced the Lower East Side as New York's most overcrowded tenement district. Harlemites faced higher-than-average rates of unemployment, disease, and rents—and became outspoken that the government relieve their misery. Langdon Post had assured black leaders that "Harlem [was] not being neglected" in plans for public housing,[78] but a riot on 19–20 March 1935 in Harlem led to NYCHA assurances of imminent action. The authority's planners had previously considered land costs too high in crowded Harlem for anything but small projects, but the second PWA project, announced in 1934, became Harlem River Houses. Harlem River Houses remains a darling of architecture critics, but like Williamsburg Houses and First Houses it was constructed at a very high cost per unit.[79]

High development costs meant that the low rents paid by tenants of these early projects resulted from elevated levels of government subsidy rather than economical construction. Even staunch housing advocates such as Loula Lasker believed the PWA had lost "sight of the main problem . . . to provide adequate though not necessarily ideal accommodations for low-income families." NYCHA and the PWA negotiated hard over interest rates for the final loans, which allowed them to charge an average monthly rent of $7 per room, and more fundamentally over the future course of public housing management.[80]

Secretary Ickes took the position that "he preferred to keep administration of low-cost housing construction, so far as possible, in the hands of the federal government." Post, La Guardia, and many housing reformers sought the empowerment of local housing authorities, as in Great Britain's successful program, because "the Federal Government will be hamstrung in its efforts to push forward a really large-scale program."[81] Post and others won the battle for local control (with the Housing Act of 1937; see Chapter 2), but the PWA story, and perhaps Ickes's philosophy, looks better from a long-term perspective. It may be true that the PWA created housing that seemed too nice for its intended population, but this was intentional.[82]

The PWA had its faults, but the developments it painstakingly sponsored are today considered some of the finest American public housing because PWA housing, in the words of the historian Gail Radford, represented "the most thoroughgoing challenge to a market-based housing system ever attempted in the United States." Most of the public housing that followed under the federal acts of 1937 and later would be designed with the very poor in mind. Local authorities, outside New York, also underperformed.[83]

New York housing advocates, in spite of the PWA setbacks, always aimed for a program that far exceeded anything else dreamed of in the United States. NYCHA's Chairman's Committee on Long Range Programs, led by the planner Albert Mayer, in 1935 had recommended a $150 million annual budget as part of a long-range $1.5 billion program that would one day house hundreds of thousands of New Yorkers. The scale of the recommended projects was shocking: one was projected to cost $73 million alone and yield 55,000 rooms on 350 acres. New York's political classes and NYCHA's board liked the scale of the plans, but Washington never gave its assent. These plans nevertheless remained at the heart of NYCHA's mission during the 1930s. New York would eventually build a large system, but only by drawing on non-federal sources of aid.[84]

Mayor La Guardia even had the temerity to ask in 1935 for $150 million in loans from the federal government as part of his long-term plan. This request was made in spite of the fact that New York had already received a disproportionate amount of the small funds for housing then available. Post and La Guardia, promising housing for thirty thousand families and approximately forty to fifty thousand jobs, acted as though the money would be forthcoming from the president. Approximately $100 million seems to have been approved by the president in 1935, but before the Housing Act of 1937 New York received funding only for First Houses, Williamsburg Houses, and Harlem River Houses.[85] Roosevelt awaited further Senate action in 1936 and rejected further housing projects for the moment because housing projects did not appear to "give employment to large numbers of needy persons. . . . They require much preliminary work and after construction of the buildings has started require a large number of skilled workers, few of whom are now to be found on relief rolls."[86]

In spite of the fact that New York had built very few apartments by 1937, the authority and those who supported it had made substantive progress shaping both public opinion and administrative powers. Advocates had effectively enhanced a sense of crisis in the city, redirecting a concerned public from short-term economic concerns to more elaborate humanitarian and civic goals. The public and politicians had been goaded, in particular, by appeals to European housing accomplishments. Chairman Post had spotlighted slums and his enforcement of strict laws had increased demand for public housing projects. NYCHA also had in hand judicial approval of the replacement of slum clearance with model tenements. What looked like a flailing authority, embarrassed by criticism of its methods and expensive housing projects, was in fact well on its way to becoming a powerful city-wide organization.

Chapter 2

Three Programs Are Better Than One

Without New York City's pressure for a large federal housing program in the 1930s the federal Housing Act of 1937 would not have come into existence. To turn experimental tools into a housing program to rival the power and scale of European cities would demand more than small demonstration projects by a public works program. In spite of the fact that New Yorkers birthed the United States Housing Authority (USHA), the federal agency resulting from the 1937 act, the New York City Housing Authority would within a few years use the state and city housing programs to chart a far more independent course. New York would thus draw on three programs for support rather than just one. This combination became a key element in the scale and long-term management success of the New York program.

The implementation of the three programs at the local level did not, however, glide on a perfectly smooth track. Tensions grew between federal and local officials as New York demonstrated its determination to build public housing with the form, tenancy, and location of its own choosing. New Yorkers, after all, had sought in the comparatively decentralized USHA a release from the straightjacket of the PWA. The potential scale of the program also created local power struggles between NYCHA's chairmen, the mayor and Robert Moses.

What makes New York's conflicts stand out from those in other cities is that controversy over implementation did not undermine near unanimity among leaders (and the liberal public that supported them) that public housing was a positive and potentially transformative force in the city. What is more, the public housing program generally benefited from conflicts that pitted members of the loyal opposition against each other. By debating issues and shifting staff New York moved forward.

At the national level, New York's leadership proved essential in the Housing Act of 1937 primarily because Senator Robert Wagner (a Democrat representing New York) believed, in his own words, that "partially subsidized housing, like free schools, free roads, and free parks, is the next step that we must take to forge a better order."[1] Wagner, like many in his liberal circle, admired European housing developments and in 1936 had taken the time to visit and inspect them.[2] Inspired by both his travels and his deeply held beliefs, Wagner argued forcefully that "the power of government could be used to ameliorate the kind of conditions every urban lawmaker had encountered firsthand."[3]

Not everyone agreed. Wagner had started work on the legislation as early as 1935 and yet only through political negotiation and clever legislative footwork by Catherine Bauer and other housing specialists did he overcome the opposition's resistance to an unprecedented and questionable use of federal power. The passage of the Wagner Steagall Act in the fall of 1937 was in large measure due to Senator Wagner's fight for public housing.[4]

President Roosevelt, for instance, in 1936 had "pointed to the one third of the nation that was 'ill-housed, ill-fed, and ill-clothed,'" but he thought remediation of these conditions might be achieved by harnessing the private sector through the FHA or a similar program rather than through the creation of multi-unit housing projects. Roosevelt at heart "believed families should have individual homes . . . however modest." The Roosevelt administration, under pressure from housing reformers and labor leaders, finally backed the act in 1937 because of housing's potential role in economic recovery. By 1936 Wagner and others had documented that the economy had partially rebounded while employment had not. Technological improvements that reduced the need for employees seemed to point the way to massive, long-term government programs.[5]

Catherine Bauer and congressional leaders steered and finessed the legislation through years of legislative wrangling, but New York housing leaders shaped the legislation to bolster their own programs. The New York housing lawyer Ira Robbins, at the behest of the National Public Housing Conference (which had grown out of New York's Public Housing Conference), had drafted the initial national legislation in 1935. Langdon Post proved successful in gaining higher construction costs per unit for large cities such as New York. As the head of the newly created American Federation of Housing Authorities, he lobbied Wagner and others for a program that would supercede Ickes's control. Mary Simkhovitch also lobbied the president and the first lady for their support of the Wagner bill. In 1937 the city's liberals launched a coordinated push for public housing that included mass rallies and housing exhibits across the city. That New York was such an important part of Roosevelt's political base meant that pressure from New York mattered.[6]

The new United States Housing Authority, the signature accomplishment of the act, was specifically designed to succeed where the PWA had failed.[7] Under pressure from conservative interests, the USHA strenuously avoided all competition with the private sector. The PWA's high quality developments and flexible income limits had meant that its developments competed with private housing. The 1937 act thus emphasized the lowest income groups and much lower costs per unit—even though the exact levels were left up to future federal administrators. Nor did the USHA subsidize limited-dividend or cooperative housing efforts that might have generated higher-income housing. Above all, the federal government abandoned the direct management style of the PWA for both legal and practical reasons. Nathan Straus Jr., who became the first head of the USHA, believed that the PWA experience "showed that the complexities of public housing could not be mastered except by means of a decentralized program."[8]

The new USHA now lent funds to local housing authorities to build the housing plus an annual subsidy to lower rents in the future. The Congress at the time, according to the urban historian Bradford Hunt, did not realize the scale of its long-term commitment because the "annual subsidy of three and one-half per cent of the cost—about equal to interest and amortization charges"—lasted over an approximately sixty-year span. By 1939 some congressmen realized what had transpired and began to pressure Nathan Straus to drive down costs. The subsidy would also become a subject of considerable debate in future decades as the federal government tried to restrict its support of public housing.[9]

The USHA and the New York City Housing Authority

The USHA represented a tremendous commitment of federal funds and power to local public housing authorities. By late 1937 Mayor La Guardia was not feeling secure that Langdon Post, and the authority generally, could be counted upon to drive the program forward. La Guardia was apparently displeased with Post's overzealous crackdown on slum landlords. He was also unhappy with housing construction that was so expensive that it had become a political liability during his reelection campaign. La Guardia thought that he had "a lousy Housing Authority," saying, "I want to get rid of the whole bunch." He dreamed of "another Bob Moses who could take hold . . . and get things done."[10] Nor was La Guardia necessarily on good terms with Nathan Straus by this time. La Guardia's close connection to Interior Secretary Ickes, who had favored another candidate to head the new agency, may have soured that relationship.[11]

The first to fall was NYCHA's counsel, Charles Abrams. La Guardia "forbid" city officials from attending a conference with Straus because Straus was waiting until 1 January to accept applications from local authorities; La Guardia thought that there was no more need for "star gazing conferences." Even before the ban on the conference La Guardia had apparently tired of Abrams, whom he called a "pettifogging lawyer." Abrams, however, was eager to attend the conference because Straus would define his vision for implementing the new, complex legislation. Beyond practical concerns, the order by La Guardia, according to Abrams, "underlies the very formation and existence of the NYCHA, its status, independence, non-partisan and non-political." Abrams did attend, but he resigned from the authority before doing so.[12]

La Guardia kept the heat on Straus, demanding that the administrator approve funding for New York and promising to get "damn rough" if no action was forthcoming. Again Straus invited NYCHA representatives to a conference, this one a follow-up of the earlier one Abrams attended. Straus had not taken well New York's absence from that conference, and certain policy decisions, different from those favored by La Guardia, had been approved. Straus snottily chastised New York: "possibly if the New York City Housing Authority had participated in the conference last week . . . your wishes as to this matter of policy might have prevailed." He pointedly rejected housing proposals sent by New York because they appeared to be too expensive for the new, strict cost limits.[13]

Post, who also thought La Guardia was attempting "to exercise political control" that would be a "grave deterrent to public support of the entire housing movement," decided to attend the Straus conference—which La Guardia had also boycotted. Post stated that although he was resigning (and he had already overstayed his term), he only expected to be replaced by La Guardia when his successor was in place. Post had intentions of attending the conference as NYCHA's chairman. La Guardia played hardball and began immediately referring to Post as the "former chairman of the Authority." Nor did La Guardia budge on sending a representative to Straus's conference.[14]

La Guardia swore in his secretary, Lester Stone, as the new chairman in order to push Post from power. La Guardia claimed the appointment would only last a few days. When reminded that the mayor lacked the power to make such an appointment (because only the NYCHA board could do so), he made a serious, but empty, threat: "They'd better elect him or there will be a new board." Post thought the mayor was throwing "monkey wrenches" into Straus's plans and that Straus was "absolutely right in procedure." Better to develop policy in consultation with authorities than arrange affairs "behind closed doors."[15] Post would later write, "It may be that Mayor La Guardia's benevolent dictatorship of the New York City Housing Authority will do no immediate harm. . . . The fact remains that, in the case of New York City, the action is in direct conflict with the spirit and intent of the state law."[16]

When Straus initially announced the first distribution of money, New

York's portion was noticeably absent—internal bickering seemed to be costing New York. The mayor thus personally submitted revised plans for the Red Hook and Queensbridge projects and quickly assured the public that "Mr. Straus and I are just like that."[17] By mid-December Straus and La Guardia had obviously patched things up, but it was noticeably now La Guardia negotiating directly with Straus over the Queensbridge and Red Hook projects rather than the authority.[18] Straus approved a total of $18 million by late December and New York's program was firmly underway. (A supplemental appropriation raised the total for the two projects in April 1938 to approximately $30 million.)[19] In retrospect, the bickering had cost New York very little. And if the program was going to be under mayoral control, at least the mayor was La Guardia, who had a genuine interest in building quality housing and finding the best administrators for the job; not many cities were so lucky.

The proof that the conflict had not mortally damaged the authority, and in my opinion greatly aided it, was the appointment in late December 1937 of the new chairman, Alfred Rheinstein. La Guardia's choice for successor was an experienced private developer who set a business tone for the authority. Setting some distance between himself and more idealistic housing advocates, he thought it was vitally important "to develop a type of low cost structure and a technique for replacing slums . . . to show the way to private enterprise which must ultimately be enlisted if widespread benefits are to be achieved." The conservatism of Rheinstein has been overplayed in light of comments like this that stressed the potential role of the private sector. Not only did he see it as the authority's job "to clear as much of our seventeen square miles of slums and erect as many projects on these cleared areas as is possible with the money available," but also like traditional housing advocates he claimed that "slums breed crime, disease and degeneracy." He even believed that "socialized medicine is a splendid idea and should be worked out" so that it, like other social services planned for public housing, served not just tenants of public housing but all those in the surrounding areas.[20]

The ultimate proof of his commitment to housing was his willingness to create immense new housing projects using his private enterprise experience. Without Rheinstein's genius for building, NYCHA would likely have failed to move from expensive experiments to mass low-cost housing. Rheinstein impressively beat bare bones federal cost requirements at the enormous Red Hook and Queensbridge projects (approximately three thousand units each). These six-story elevator buildings featured room costs half as high as those at the PWA projects and permitted monthly rents of $5 per room (compared to an average of $7 in PWA projects) with a comparatively modest subsidy. These projects were not built on high-density slums, but the very low costs attained gave confidence that the city could finally embark on true slum clearance, the real goal of both Rheinstein and many of New York's housing advocates.[21]

Pioneering the State and City Programs

The Housing Act of 1937 had provided enough funding for most American cities; in fact, any public housing at all in many cities would be counted as a great victory. New York housing advocates, however, were by no means content to rely solely on the federal government. New York officials, including Mayor La Guardia, set to work to find more money even before the ink had dried on the Housing Act of 1937. New York used the liberal pressure on both parties, created by the Depression, to push through America's only large state-funded housing program. La Guardia also gained permission from the state government for a locally funded city housing program, the only one of its type in the United States.[22]

Housing proposals had been drifting aimlessly around the state legislature for years, but in 1938 Governor Lehman convinced the legislature to take action. Democrats and liberal Republicans ultimately envisioned a $300 million program, but state law required such an unprecedented program to be passed twice by the legislature and then submitted to the voters—a process that would take at least two years. In order to expedite housing and guarantee its legality the New York State Constitutional Convention of 1938 took up a similarly scaled housing program. Housing advocates overcame remaining Republican opposition to public housing through organized Democratic leadership and "Republican turncoats such as Robert Moses and Harold Riegelman." Moses, in fact, took credit for drafting the legislation and in the 1940s and 1950s he picked most of the sites for the state developments that came out of the convention.[23]

The convention ultimately passed a housing amendment, thus making New York State the first in the country to do so.[24] The proposed housing amendment (including a total limit to the state program of $300 million) also included the potential for *municipally* funded public housing. The plan, at La Guardia's urging, allowed the city a 2 percent debt increase in order to finance what might become millions of dollars worth of public housing.[25]

The amendments, collected together, were put to voters in November 1938 with broad support from Governor Lehman, socialists, liberals, and the *New York Times*. Voters ratified the amendments and other liberal social amendments that year. Even business interests, some of which might benefit from public spending, mostly lined up in support. The Republican leadership in the state legislature authorized the start of the state program in 1939. State-sponsored housing projects, with more flexible income levels and rules, would give NYCHA more latitude in tenant selection. Large state developments such as Fort Greene Houses (1944), with its 3,501 units, became the leading edge of NYCHA's and later Robert Moses' ambitious urban reconstruction.[26]

The city program, approved under the state plan, arose from La Guardia's general frustration with the pace and scale of federal public housing. As La Guardia pointed out, up to that time only 2,318 public housing apartments had been constructed in the city. An approximate $30 million limit on New York's share of the federal program meant that the city was unlikely to dent the demand for better quality, low-cost housing. The funds for the city program were derived from an Occupancy Tax on all city renters and actually got off to a slow start in the 1930s and 1940s. By 1953, city-subsidized public housing (known as City I) included only five relatively small developments. The "unsubsidized" city program (City II and III), launched after World War II, would, in contrast, be much larger than the subsidized program, and by 1953 it included twenty large developments (Appendix A).[27]

The city projects, in the long term, offered an important counterweight to the welfare-oriented federal programs by creating quality apartments *and* significantly higher income levels. The scale of the program, and the attractiveness of the developments spread widely across the city, indicates that city leaders worried little about pushing the private sector out of the lower-cost housing market. The dispersion of these projects in a great number of neighborhoods also helped preserve the authority's political support.[28]

By late 1938 NYCHA had powers and funds inconceivable in other cities, but in the short term it still waged battles with the federal government. Evident city success in building very low cost housing in central sites under New York's federal program began to challenge the dearly held ideals of the USHA administrator Nathan Straus. Straus remained devoted to building garden city, low-rise public housing similar to Hillside Homes and decentralized housing estates in Great Britain. He aimed to use the lever of land price acquisition limits to encourage low-density public housing across the United States. The authority, by pioneering high-rise public housing, defied Straus because its methods showed that, even under tight budgetary controls, it was possible to achieve slum clearance and model housing at costs comparable to vacant land sites at the city's fringe. Alfred Rheinstein believed that the only important figures in public housing were the final costs per unit. What difference did land costs make if the housing that emerged could be rented with low subsidies?

Rheinstein expected to be rewarded by Straus with greater autonomy but found himself stymied. A temporary truce arranged at a "Woodpile" conference at the Red Hook Houses construction site did not hold. Straus kept returning to a $1.50 per square foot limit on site land purchases and Rheinstein became outspoken in his criticism of Straus; he demanded more local autonomy and land price flexibility. In time, La Guardia abandoned Rheinstein, who had also battled Straus to gain higher income levels in Red Hook Houses, and Rheinstein stepped down.[29] (See Chapter 3 for more details on the battle over site location.)

Having played an important role in the recent passage of the state program, realizing how much money was at stake, and sensing disarray at the authority, Robert Moses tried to step in the breach. In August of that year he had made a diplomatic request to La Guardia "to put all the city work under one man," or at least a committee he could dominate, but La Guardia did not budge.[30]

In November, shortly after the passage of the state-housing amendments, Moses invited leading civic leaders and businessmen to the Museum of Natural History for a presentation on his internally produced $245 million housing program. He envisioned ten "genuine slum clearance" projects that would be partly financed with a tax on cigarettes. He thought that sites should be announced in advance, that housing funds should help pay for adjoining parks, and that private limited-dividend projects should also be subsidized. He recommended that a new board be composed of officials representing "vitally affected" departments. Showing nothing but disdain for the authority, he warned that "the public will not long tolerate management of such an enterprise by well-meaning amateurs."[31]

Mayor La Guardia, who admired Moses in so many ways, was not impressed. He not only cut off Moses' broadcast on WNYC (unbeknownst to Moses) but also wryly observed that "the plan is a beautiful printing job . . . but apparently he isn't thoroughly familiar with housing problems."[32] Behind the scenes, according to Moses' biographer Robert Caro, La Guardia also made sure that Moses' plans lost traction in a housing committee the mayor had created. Until 1941 La Guardia continued to make "sure that Moses never knew what new public housing project was being planned until the planning was completed." In 1942, however, he actually turned to Moses for a vast postwar public housing plan.[33]

In December 1939 the mayor appointed Gerard Swope, the former president of General Electric, as NYCHA's new chairman. The talent that La Guardia could draw from the private sector illustrates the relative prestige of the position as well as La Guardia's magnetism. As La Guardia noted, "When you get a man like Mr. Swope to assume the responsibility on a non-salaried basis I think we have good ground for rejoicing." As Swope frankly admitted, "I have not the remotest idea of policy," but he had served on the Board of Managers of Greenwich House. It is possible that Mary Simkhovitch, the longtime head of that settlement house, played a role in recruiting him.[34]

Under Swope's leadership, New York began to show signs of becoming a public housing thoroughbred. The different versions of public housing funding available to the city began to complement each other. Notable projects underway at this time include Vladeck Houses (1940), the first true slum clearance, city-sponsored project; East River Houses (1941), the first development with buildings above six stories; and Fort Greene (1944), the first state-funded project. At the time Fort Greene was America's biggest project, with 3,501 apartments in 39 buildings. La Guardia called it "the most daring housing project ever attempted by this or any other city in the country." He was right.[35]

Rheinstein had estimated that by 1940 the authority would have completed housing for 15,000 families. Indeed by 1942, even with the loss of funding and supplies for the war effort, New York had twelve projects finished with housing for 13,180 families. Nathan Straus estimated that by 1940 New York had absorbed 10,000 of 50,000 apartments in the federal program.[36] Because a total of only 55,465 housing units of any kind were built anywhere in New York City between 1934 and 1941, the planner Peter Marcuse believes public housing "was important because of its relative" share of total construction during the Depression years.[37] Housing reformers could also take heart that the program appeared on its way to becoming a partly self-supporting public utility. As early as 1942, NYCHA could boast that "revenue from tenants covers 71% of total operating costs, including debt service and rent payments" to the USHA.[38]

During World War II New York City may have gained little from the Lanham Act, which provided funding for defense housing, but New York would begin large-scale, permanent public housing construction even before the Housing Act of 1949.[39] The authority, for instance, launched large projects during the war years that would utilize previously approved and primarily state funds, including Lilian Wald Houses (1949), Jacob Riis Houses (1949), Brownsville Houses (1948), Marcy Houses (1949), and Abraham Lincoln Houses (1948). As indicated by the completion dates for these projects, most of these may have been planned and authorized during the war, but because of material shortages they took much longer to complete. La Guardia admitted that "the exigency of war has put a complete stop on all new construction." NYCHA did use the war years, however, to quietly acquire sites for future housing projects.[40]

Public housing by the 1940s looked different in New York because of the ambitious goals and mixture of funding sources designed to realize an extensive program. Other cities gingerly dipped their toes into the field of social housing, but New York plunged headfirst. The goal was no longer to create a few model projects but to launch a European-scale authority with the funds and legal powers both to rescue the poor and to redevelop the city along modern lines. Even power struggles had sharpened the program by bringing good leaders such as Alfred Rheinstein and establishing New York's independence. New York had not immediately realized grandiose dreams, but the ingredients for a gigantic program sat ready for better days.

Chapter 3

High-Rise Public Housing Begins

Within its first decade of operation the New York City Housing Authority invented America's version of high-rise public housing. It seems inevitable with hindsight that New York, a vertiginous skyscraper city, would embark on high-rise housing, but just the opposite is true. High-rise elevator buildings in New York before the 1930s served the better off in society rather than the poor or the working class. The New York City Housing Authority's first three projects, in fact, were walk-ups.

New York tilted to high-rise public housing in the late 1930s because of overlapping ideological and cost concerns. In seeking to house large segments of the city's working class in low-cost, hygienic, light-filled convenient developments—and clear the slums in the process—New York had to take the radical step of housing poor people in elevator buildings. Buildings grew higher, room size decreased, and internal finishing of apartments was redesigned or eliminated to save money.

What distinguished New York from the housing authorities that later adapted New York's high-rise style was administrators who understood the difference between *low-cost* and *shoddy* high-rise housing. New York's high-rise projects were basic, but they were also durable and built to high standards. An independent engineering and design analysis in 1945 "found no criticism of the projects built by the Housing Authority. They are, in our judgment, well built and in accordance with good current construction practice." The evaluation did note, "They have been built economically." These decently constructed buildings, when paired to sound practices of daily management, have stood the test of time.[1]

The difference between wise and false economies is also evident in the early years of site and landscape design. Cost cutting did not have to mean barren open spaces; landscaping installed in these early years compensated for the dreary architecture as the trees eventually provided greenery and shade. Today, public housing grounds in New York feature towering trees, bushes, and large lawns in large measure because of sound planning in the 1930s and 1940s.

Nor did economizing mean finding the cheapest land; in fact, NYCHA had to fight federal officials in order to buy the central lands that it thought would make the best housing and achieve the most slum clearance. These developments were not placed on inconvenient, low-cost land but in relatively central neighborhoods convenient to the center city (by transit) or nearby industry. Comparatively good sites that included accessibility to employment, transit, and educational and social institutions meant in the long term that many of New York's projects remained popular with tenants.

Searching for the Minimum

The decision to break with the philanthropic past proved central in New York's ability to build its immense housing system. Public housing in New York might have had a strong tradition of model housing on which to build—New York by the 1930s had the greatest concentration of philanthropic housing projects in the United States—but this housing could hardly be considered low cost. Philanthropic and limited-dividend housing, unlike most NYCHA superblocks, remains some of New York City's most physically attractive housing for any class of tenants. NYCHA selectively drew upon precedents as it formulated its own methods of low-cost design and construction.

The garden apartment developments of the City and Suburban Homes Company in Brooklyn known as Homewood Apartments (1920), for instance, featured four-story buildings surrounding a courtyard and luxury details. Its architect, Andrew Thomas, included sunrooms, large windows, iron balconies, and Romanesque entries.[2] One observer accused philanthropic projects such as this of succumbing to City Beautiful aesthetics, "which lost sight of the social function of the housing."[3] Thomas later pared down the flourishes and details in his Metropolitan Life Insurance Company Project (1924) in Long Island City. The small apartments, "massive brick volumes," and lack of decoration likely set important precedents for NYCHA projects.[4]

Privately built, RFC. (and subsequently PWA aided) limited-dividend projects offered very different options for the future of public housing in New York.[5] Clarence Stein, the architect responsible for the path-breaking Sunnyside Gardens and Radburn garden city, linked his Hillside Homes (1935) design to the New York garden apartment tradition by placing moderate height courtyard buildings on only 32 percent of the site, yielding a generous ten acres for gardens and recreational space. All of the apartments, surrounded by such generous open spaces, featured light and cross-ventilation rarely found in tenement districts. All of this luxury was possible because one of Hillside's sponsors, Nathan Straus Jr., sold his land at $.70 per square foot, a philanthropic gesture that furthered his vision of decentralized, low-rise, garden-city style

Figure 4. New York housing advocates at first disliked Knickerbocker Village (1934), but they adopted its high-rise approach when cutting costs. La Guardia Wagner Archive/NYCHA Photograph Collection.

housing. Queensbridge Houses (1940), one of NYCHA's first projects, can be considered to be a cut-rate version of Hillside. The influence of Hillside is, however, most noticeable in the six- to eight-story, city-funded, postwar projects in the outer boroughs.[6]

Knickerbocker Village (1933), an RFC. project on the Lower East Side, proved far more controversial than Hillside because its high-rise (twelve story), courtyard apartment buildings on only 46 percent of the land replaced former slum properties acquired at $14 per square foot. Even with its impressive height, the expensive land, high standards of construction, and open spaces yielded high monthly rents of approximately $12 per room (Figure 4). NYCHA chairman, Langdon Post, worried that the high-rise model established by Knickerbocker might lead to "a new type of slums. Manhattan does not need residential skyscrapers for the masses."[7] Post and other chairmen would, however, quickly drift back toward the Knickerbocker model as costs skyrocketed in the first low-rise projects. Authority administrators would figure out how to reduce amenities and add subsidies to make low-cost high rises a realistic public housing option. Knickerbocker's pioneering of high-rise housing, while delayed a few years at NYCHA, became a much more influential model than Hillside Homes.[8]

Practical experience in apartment design, beyond limited-dividend and philanthropic projects, proved useful in drawing up New York's plans. The architectural historian Richard Pommer documents the notable fact that New York possessed "a large corps of Beaux-Arts and commercial architects skilled in apartment house and low-cost housing layout." Quite a few of these designers would take a turn designing NYCHA projects. Their intimate knowledge of the basic requirements of apartment house living played an important role in creating livable buildings even after many of the luxuries, initially adopted from better apartment buildings, were cut for reasons of economy.[9]

Nor were New York designers unfamiliar with important planning concepts pioneered in garden-city developments such as Sunnyside Gardens or modernist European public housing projects in Germany and Great Britain. NYCHA would take its own path to superblocks and towers in the park, but the growing currency of modernist concepts internationally helped justify what could be seen as outrageous plans for the housing of the city's poor citizens.

At first glance, New York's first public housing project, First Houses (1936), appears unrepresentative of public housing in New York as a whole, but when it is examined more closely it reveals hints of the future NYCHA style. Anxious to get any public housing at all in motion, NYCHA publicized First Houses to the general public as a tenement house renovation project because federal officials initially favored this less controversial form of public intervention in the housing market. NYCHA officials also hoped that they, unlike housing reformers before them, could demonstrate an innovative method of tenement rehabilitation that might interest the private sector.[10]

First Houses remains a popular small complex today and feels human in scale because it is only five stories high and covers only 45 percent of its site. The development housed new tenants at only 160 persons per acre; followed the footprint of selected existing tenements on the block; and boasted twelve stores that connected the complex to the neighborhood streetscape. First Houses proudly featured quality oak floors and brass light fixtures that have stood the test of time; the small but carefully designed public spaces, framed by mature plane trees, remain equally attractive.[11]

NYCHA chairman Langdon Post boasted of First Houses that unlike the limited-dividend projects that did not serve the poor First Houses "are the first dwellings which are predicated upon the philosophy that sunshine, space and air are minimum housing requirements to which every American is entitled, no matter how small his income." Beauty, then, would be measured in hours of sunlight, breezes, and sanitary conditions rather than architectural innovation. This new city service might not deliver architectural beauty, but it would be a conduit of hygienic living.[12]

Compared to earlier philanthropic and limited-dividend housing projects, with the exception of Metropolitan Life's Long Island City project, First Houses represented a new type of low-cost urban dwelling. The individual red brick buildings are exactly alike in terms of scale and appearance and the facades are flat, unornamented brick. Window surrounds and entrances are plain. First Houses was certainly designed to *look* inexpensive. The *New York Times* welcomed the homely appearance: "Recent urban housing plans sound real because the architect's drawings are not too pretty. . . . Too many slum clearance prospects have striven to combine the best features of a Harkness quadrangle at Yale with the charm of an old Tudor mansion." It lauded First Houses because they were "walkups, somewhat barrack-like in appearance, with lots of windows, and will try to rent for $5 a room."[13]

Had First Houses really been cheap construction, its barebones appearance would have been more justifiable. First Houses was and still is often portrayed as a tenement renovation project when it actually, and almost surreptitiously, became new construction. Reporters discovered that because workers demolished alternating structures, "the walls of those left" began to "sway alarmingly. . . . The final result was that all four units along Avenue A were demolished, together with two on Third Street. Of the three not entirely torn down only parts of the side walls and floor beams are left." In the end, "only a few of the old foundation supports" could be salvaged.[14]

The renovation plan had defied the advice of the State Board of Housing and NYCHA's technical advisor, Frederick Ackerman, a leading authority on low-cost multi-family housing, who believed that "new buildings could be erected for a like cost, but it was pointed out in reply that work-relief funds could not be obtained for new buildings."[15] The authority had to stand behind its renovation story and plan for political reasons, but the reality was mostly new construction. As one sharp observer noted, the method employed was "analogous to creating a cripple artificially and then supplying him with a crutch."[16]

First Houses turned out to be surprisingly expensive government work ($3,653 per room) in large measure because it was not a true rehabilitation project, it involved high-quality interior materials, it boasted inflated payrolls, and it was too small to spread costs across a large number of units. Very low monthly rents ($6 per room) could be charged only because of the more generous subsidy provided.[17] Even the *New York Times* admitted that First Houses as built could scarcely serve as a future model for public housing because hidden labor and material costs meant that "each dollar of investment will have been saddled with three dollars of subsidy, a ratio no government would be able to apply to slum clearance work . . . without going bankrupt." Post even acknowledged that "First Houses cost too much."[18]

In this early period, NYCHA developed its own technical division, which was led by Frederick Ackerman, who worked with the local architectural societies to create committees to coordinate NYCHA's overall design effort.[19] The architectural direction for both Harlem River Houses (1937) and Williamsburg Houses (1938), built by the PWA, came from NYCHA because the authority provided the early financing to pay the designers employed as part of the Williamsburg and Harlem River architectural teams (or "associations"). The PWA preferred local teams because "private architects were more likely to provide for regional variations in design." The PWA agreed to move ahead with construction only in late 1935 and NYCHA's early preparation of the Harlem River and Williamsburg plans allowed it to beat President Roosevelt's postponement of public housing projects that took effect after 16 December 1935.[20]

The authority may have selected the design teams, but it did not impose a singular vision. Harlem River Houses, for instance, designed by architects with extensive multi-family experience, integrated lessons learned in limited-dividend and RFC-sponsored projects such as Hillside Homes (Figure 5).[21] The historian Gail Radford praises the complex for its integration with "the surrounding community" by means of carefully

Figure 5. Harlem River Houses (1937) represented the Public Works Administration's impressive if unrealistic answer to housing the urban poor. La Guardia Wagner Archive/NYCHA Photograph Collection.

structured courts and passages. Additionally, the architects, by lining up the edges of buildings parallel to the street, "observed enough of the city's traditional design conventions that their creation fit comfortably into the neighborhood around it."[22]

The complex—four-story walk-up buildings of reinforced concrete—included attractive landscaped courtyards and 32 percent ground coverage. Compared to later NYCHA complexes, Harlem River's low buildings did not block sunlight or create a menacing skyline; Art Deco rustication along the base of the buildings added a little visual interest. The landscape designer Michael Rapuano cleverly subdivided the cobblestone-paved courtyards for intensive use. Like First Houses, however, Harlem River Houses featured mostly flat brick facades of uniform height. The notion of a superblock, apparent but not dominant at First Houses, became more notable at Harlem River. Tenants now had their own special landscaped spaces and the buildings float in the complex. No one at the time seems to have realized the danger of sealing off minimalist low-income housing from the urban fabric, primarily because model tenants would live in these barracks. Keeping out nonresident riffraff seemed to be the greatest challenge at the time. Harlem River Houses, while integrating some stores and lined up to surrounding streets, stood out as a low-income housing complex.[23]

Costs soared again at Harlem River Houses not only because it was a low-rise development with modest ground coverage (the land cost a relatively high $3.40 per square foot), but also because the buildings featured high-quality construction, including soundproof tiles between units, metal trim, and bronze hardware. The wooden kitchen cabinets, closet doors, enamel tubs, china toilets, tiled bathroom floors, and plaster walls doubtless pleased tenants more than accountants. Stairhalls featured glazed terra cotta even though hall floors were cement. Hallways, with only four apartments per landing, reduced anonymity.[24] The NYCHA Management Division, when negotiating for final NYCHA control with the PWA, stated frankly that "the houses were built without specific relation to construction costs to the rent-paying ability of the prospective tenants."[25]

By 1937 Post had painfully referred to Harlem River Houses as a "model" rather "than as an answer to the acute housing needs" of the black poor in Harlem.[26] New York Times editorialists believed that Harlem River was no more than a "fragment of that low-rental Utopia" because "these accommodations could not be multiplied . . . without an expenditure of more billions of dollars than all the public agencies in the country could handily rake together."[27] Tough negotiation by the city in its lease agreement with the PWA made possible of, rents on average, $7 per room per month, but lacking this subsidy it was estimated that tenants would have had to pay $14 per room per month.[28]

Figure 6. The modernist designs of Williamsburg Houses (1938) laid the groundwork for revolutionary public housing. La Guardia Wagner Archive/NYCHA Photograph Collection.

Both Harlem River Houses and First Houses, with their barracks appearance (if not interior specifications) and superblock concepts, reflected a new notion of low-cost housing. They were, however, only partially realized as new architectural and planning concepts. Both featured high-quality interiors and structured public spaces, and both loosely followed the lot lines of their respective blocks—they were similar in many respects to the limited-dividend experiments before them and did not represent a radical break with the past. Williamsburg Houses (1938), also built by the PWA with NYCHA's aid, is widely viewed as a sharp break with past design that augured the future direction of New York public housing.[29]

Richmond Shreve, the head of the Williamsburg architectural committee, selected William Lescaze to bring a modernist touch to NYCHA projects. Lescaze, who had designed the ground-breaking PSFS skyscraper in Philadelphia, was a major force in the translation of European modernism into an American idiom. Williamsburg thus featured the abstract geometrical massing and industrial styling characteristic of European housing projects (Figure 6).[30]

Williamsburg's planning layout also reflected a new direction for New York superblocks. Lescaze, according to leading architectural historian Richard Plunz, favored the *Zeilenbau* planning method that floated strips of buildings in open space. Lescaze, some years later, proudly claimed responsibility for Williamsburg's "site plan, which was the first one that did not put buildings parallel to the street lines. This was done in order to get better orientation of the apartments and wider open spaces between them." Some scholars have noted that the Williamsburg project still loosely followed a courtyard model, but residual nods to apartment house traditions were superficial in light of the emphasis on the free-floating building.[31]

NYCHA did provide over fifty shops at Williamsburg (see Chapter 7 for problems with these), but the superblocks there and at later projects, which generally had far fewer stores, transformed a mixed tenement neighborhood into a primarily residential zone. This distillation of a city into different, largely separate zones aligned not only with the growing popularity of planning concepts such as zoning but also with the plans of the leading modernists Walter Gropius and Le Corbusier. Gropius's essay that accompanied Catherine Bauer's 1934 Housing Exhibition at the Museum of Modern Art is one of many sources pointing the way to the Williamsburg superblock. He thought it was "disgraceful to let children play in the street or in dark inner courts"; he believed that grass should be "as near as possible to the dwellings"; and he thought that "the tall apartment house gives us the possibility of building widely spaced, airy, green cities." Catherine Bauer promised that a superblock "makes a pleasant place to live in and bring up children."[32]

Williamsburg's modernist designs offered a machine aesthetic but did not achieve industrial-scale economies. These four-story walk-ups, like their peers at Harlem River Houses, allowed ground coverage of 32 percent, but costs escalated because the low heights did not at that point balance out the high land costs. Glazed brick stair hall exteriors, high ceilings in the apartments, wood floors, closet doors, and commodious kitchens raised expenses. Each building also had up to eight stairwells with only two apartment entrances at each landing. Williamsburg, like the early projects, looked cheap but was comparatively expensive.[33]

Some people within the authority tried to distance themselves from the high costs, holding the federal government responsible, but the close relationship of the two groups, however acrimonious, would not permit such a neat division. First Houses finished at $3,653 per room; Williamsburg at $2,266 per room; Harlem River Houses at $2,103 per room. The worship of open space had contributed to the problem. While luxury Upper East Side apartment buildings of twenty stories or so achieved densities of 1,500 people per acre, Harlem River Houses topped out at 150 per acre and Williamsburg at 185 per acre. Such low numbers might be acceptable in a low-rise city and made more sense in Brooklyn, but they did not aid the creation of a mass program that would also include slum clearance.[34] By 1937, even Post was promising that future housing projects would be less "pretentious" than Williamsburg, and he envisioned "six-story elevator apartments" that would reduce "land cost per room."[35]

New Yorkers had discovered that American public housing would have to be further simplified and higher density. Americans poorly understood the public housing they so admired in Europe. Not only did Americans face higher labor costs than their European peers, but European governments had created economical, not luxury, housing. Some of the finest housing projects of interwar Vienna, for instance, may have had lovely grounds, eye-catching architecture, and community amenities, but many of the tiny apartments lacked private baths and central heat. Britain's low-rise council estates in the suburbs featured mass-produced, minimum housing (mostly lacking central heat) primarily for the better off sector of the working class. American public housing advocates could hardly omit private bathrooms, central heat, or open space because they found the slums lacking in these very qualities, but they definitely had to cut frills.[36]

Langdon Post's successor at the authority, the businessman and developer Alfred Rheinstein, made it his mission to cut costs on public housing projects even below the new, low, federal maximum of $1,250 per room set by the newly appointed housing administrator Nathan Straus Jr. As Rheinstein admitted, "I have always felt that Government Housing would be a failure . . . unless low cost of construction and operation were achieved."[37] He slashed costs in the planning phase of the projects in early 1938. The total projected costs for both projects—Red Hook and Queensbridge—fell from an estimated $40 million to a trim $18 million. A supplemental appropriation raised the total in April of that year to $30 million, but the increased funding expanded the number of units rather than their quality.[38]

Rheinstein began to emphasize economy by eliminating the bloated payrolls of the PWA and the WPA. The chairman now took advantage of private sector efficiency to build the projects. Private contractors overseen by NYCHA staff replaced relief labor in his projects. The system of competitive bidding served the authority well for decades and in that time billions of dollars ultimately flowed to local contractors with little apparent controversy or malfeasance. Government support of the building trades, of course, extended the political support for the program.[39]

Rheinstein dramatically reduced construction costs at Red Hook Houses (1939). He started frugally with the site itself. The land costs at Red Hook started low (approximately $1 per square foot) because the site, while relatively central, was lightly populated and of little economic value.[40] Rheinstein oversaw the shift to higher buildings that had been in the works. In a 1938 memorandum Frederick Ackerman found that in many areas foundation costs would be so high that "there [would] seem . . . to be no reason for continuing the program of building three and four-story walk-ups."[41] The schematic plans for the high-rise projects came from a team of architects and planning experts who simply added two stories and an elevator to the four-story buildings they had been building. They had found that "the savings in construction and land costs of a 6-story building more than compensated for the cost of maintenance of a special type of elevator developed for these projects, which stops on the 1st, 3rd and 5th floors only."[42]

Indeed, in six-story steel and concrete buildings, tenants at Rheinstein's Red Hook now had the benefit of elevators (a luxury not seen at First Houses, Harlem River Houses, or Williamsburg), but the small elevators made stops only on the fourth and sixth floors. The greater height cut costs for NYCHA by allowing for taller buildings and more apartments per floor (four as opposed to only two at Williamsburg), yet *seemed* to avoid loss of convenience for tenants. Small "skip stop" elevators would become a common feature in even much higher NYCHA buildings and in public housing towers elsewhere. In order to save additional money, the planners repeated plain, brick-faced, "cross-shaped buildings" across the whole site. The towers opened up land at the same time that they increased density. Red Hook Houses topped out at 240 persons per acre but was still 75 percent open space. If it was lower than Manhattan densities, it must be remembered that Red Hook was in Brooklyn. Even today Red Hook Houses is much taller than other housing in its immediate area.[43]

Cost cutting affirmed the importance of the superblock because the open space surrounding the towers remained one of the primary benefits to tenants and the city as a whole. Chairman Rheinstein believed that "super-blocks eased congestion, facilitated the flow of traffic, provided larger outside areas for residential dwellings and made it possible to utilize larger spaces for recreation."[44] The Building Trades Employers Association, in contrast, thought the new buildings were "surrounded by far more recreational space than can ever be practical" for such a comparatively small population. The association also worried that NYCHA was sacrificing apartment size for open space, when in fact "the government renters would prefer more living, and less play room."[45]

The association might have been on to something. Tenants may have been bathed in open space and greenery, but the interiors sent a different message. Rheinstein believed that he could eliminate details (such as wood floors or closet doors) that might damage the success of market rentals: "the public housing authority is relieved from the restrictions of competition and profit and, therefore, should obtain results which more truly reflect the real needs and the appropriate standard."[46]

Contractors at Red Hook cast piping into floors, the concrete floors became the ceilings of apartments below, only one closet per apartment had a door, and sidelights replaced ceiling lights. Room size also decreased. NYCHA apartments featured very small rooms until the late 1950s. Costs dropped to only $1.50 per square foot in part because of these economies, low land costs, and greater height. The final room cost of $850 came out even lower than the $1,250 USHA limit and was less than half the cost of the earlier projects. Tenants were not necessarily thrilled with these choices. The City-Wide Tenants Council, representing tenant opinion, would complain that the lack of closet doors had become "a serious annoyance to tenants, making necessary dust-catching draperies and making it almost impossible to keep dust out of the closets."[47]

Rheinstein likewise scrubbed Queensbridge Houses of luxuries in its three thousand apartments set in twenty-six six-story buildings (Figure 7). The land, mostly vacant, again came cheap to the authority (approximately $1 per square foot) and provided a fine start to economizing.[48] Repetition, in particular, saved a great deal of money. The Y site plan configuration used at Queensbridge was "found to offer unusual possibilities for economical construction, privacy and adequate light and air

Figure 7. The model of the Queensbridge Houses (1940) illustrates the grand scale of economized, six-story public housing. La Guardia Wagner Archive/NYCHA Photograph Collection.

for all rooms." As at Red Hook, elevators skipped floors on these six-story buildings. Queensbridge lacked basements, the concrete slab served as both the ceiling and the floor, and closet doors were reduced to a bare minimum. The population density was not as high as Red Hook's, but it was still better than earlier projects, achieving a top number of 195 persons per acre.[49]

Queensbridge's redeeming qualities are its outdoor spaces—a series of outdoor rooms that have become leafy, parklike oases—and the central shopping and community district that provides a focus for the community in a primarily industrial area. That William Ballard, the chief architect, had participated in the Hillside Houses project may help explain a temporary return to the courtyard emphasis. The combination of so many Y-shaped structures, however, according to Richard Plunz, did not provide a fully legible interior plan and the complex (like many that followed) suffers from wasted open space at its edges that was created by rotating the structures away from the lot line. The Y-shaped structures also made the complex stand out that much more from the rest of the city.[50]

The combination of increased height and minimum amenities opened a new chapter in NYCHA's history—the pairing of slum clearance and housing projects. Costs had slipped so low that the authority felt confident paying for higher-cost slum land in the Lower East Side at what became the six-story Vladeck Houses (1940), a mixed federal and city project (Figure 8). Before Vladeck, only First Houses had been built in a high-density tenement district. Other sites had been a mix of decaying industrial buildings and comparatively low-density slums. In contrast to the Queensbridge and Red Hook projects, where land costs equaled about $1.00 per square foot, the land for Vladeck Houses cost $3.76 per square foot. Yet Vladeck's room costs remained relatively low—$1,175— even with higher land costs. Vladeck, like its predecessors, was a series of six-story plain brick buildings, but its generous open spaces yielded a density only between 151 (federally funded section) and 187 (city-funded section) persons per acre.[51]

High-rise construction paired to economies of great variety provided the magical elixir that allowed the authority under Rheinstein and his successors to build low-cost housing wherever and whenever it chose— cost criticism would become a thing of the past. The authority's board, in fact, agreed in 1940 that "there could be no objection at this time to buildings higher than six stories as long as density is not increased."[52] The high-rise East River Complex (1941) in Harlem, built at a remarkable $711 per room, mixed six-, ten-, and eleven-story buildings and covered only 22 percent of the land with a respectable density of 211 persons per acre (Figure 9). In the high-rise buildings architects divided

Figure 8. Vladeck City Houses (1940) was New York's first city-sponsored slum clearance housing project. It pointed the way to large-scale postwar slum clearance. Photograph by Nicholas Dagen Bloom.

Figure 9. East River Houses (1941) represented the irresistible destination of NYCHA designs once administrators realized the costs savings possible in high-rise buildings. Photograph by Nicholas Dagen Bloom.

the elevators to serve higher and lower floors and grouped eight apartments at each landing. Even though East River replaced an industrial slum rather than high-density residential slums, its bottom-barrel costs pointed to the stunning cost advantages of high-rise construction. The low land coverage was an extreme response, but experts knew that "the space between buildings must be increased in direct proportion to the height of the buildings" in order to achieve more sunlight and airflow than tenements did.[53]

With these projects, New York moved closer to modernist concepts, but cost concerns more than ideology drove these innovations. New York helped pioneer an American version of what would become a commonplace modernist building style, the "tower in the park," the car-free superblock combined with high-rise buildings.[54] Examples of high-rise public housing towers could be found across Europe by this time, but there is no evidence that NYCHA designers drew inspiration from them. European high-rise designs such as the sixteen-story modernist towers in Drancy (France) or the Karlmarxhof in Vienna reflect distinct architectural ideals; NYCHA's plain brick towers, at most the expression of housing as a basic municipal service, resist architectural categorization.[55]

Frederick Ackerman had endorsed this tilt to high-rise superblocks. While reviewing the early stages of the East River project he pushed the authority "to abandon anything in the nature of enclosed courts and long rows" to maximize air circulation. In addition, he wrote to Rheinstein, "We should push the efficiency of elevator and public halls up to that maximum which has been pretty well established by experience as reasonable."[56] East River's large superblocks ultimately followed *Zeilenbau* styling by turning away from both the courtyard tradition and the New York grid. Today, thick mature trees have given the central area a sense of enclosure, but flat red-brick facades, large open grounds, and a barracks appearance gave a stark appearance to East River Houses that set another precedent for postwar projects.[57]

Such a direction, it should be noted, preceded Robert Moses' control over authority policy. Moses is not to blame for introducing the "tower in the park" superblocks in New York City, although he did much in the late postwar years to multiply their number. Moses, in fact, wrote to the authority's director in 1940 recommending more sensible alternatives to the low land coverage NYHCA sought at the time: "I think you should consider a coverage of as much as sixty per cent, which is considerably below what is required of speculative builders of apartment houses." He also suggested that NYCHA include stores and garages.[58] Stanley Isaacs, then the president of the Borough of Manhattan, admired the authority's cost-cutting measures, but he doubted the wisdom of NYCHA high-rise planning: "I am very sorry to see the drift to higher buildings . . . I just cannot be convinced that these lofty elevator apartments are sound for the type of tenant you are reaching."[59] The authority would continue to build six- and seven-story buildings in the outer boroughs where land costs were lower but largely ignored its critics.

A few sharp staff members of the authority, however, understood that building high rises for family groups might prove troublesome; the high-rise superblock was, after all, an untested type of low-income neighborhood. Catherine Lansing, NYCHA's executive director of community planning, saw the potential dangers of height in 1943. The Fort Greene Houses (a mix of six- and thirteen-story buildings comprising 3,501 units) worried her.[60] Lansing found that "the stairhalls were dirty, the front doors were marked, scratched and the windows in the doors and around the doors were broken. Shrubbery, even when well located, had been destroyed in the areas close to the 13 story buildings." She made a number of suggestions that NYCHA would one day adopt out of desperation:

My recommendation would be that if we continue to build 13 story buildings we consider them frankly as institutions and change our whole type of design to reflect the institutional character. If glass is required by law, it should be protected by a grill. . . . Materials both inside and out used for walls should be highly glazed so that they cannot be written on. . . . The lobby size should be increased and/or the speed of elevators increased or better yet, the 13 story elevator buildings should be abandoned for the purpose of housing families with children. . . . It is my opinion that everything is wrong with this job."[61]

Lansing lacked the power to alter design policy, but many of her particular suggestions, including faster elevators and more institutional hardware, would become formal policy during the 1950s as the towers in the park came under siege. Fort Greene, for instance, has undergone at least two major renovations since it opened. Even today NYCHA managers freely acknowledge that system-wide high-rise buildings (above six or seven stories) are more difficult, but not impossible, to manage.[62]

Most observers during the late 1930s seemed more excited about the possibilities revealed by economy than its long-term effect. The *New York Times* welcomed the cost cutting, noting that "lowered construction costs are tremendously encouraging" and would "make our Federal, State and city loans and subsidies go much farther and build more houses."[63] Rheinstein himself believed that the "simple six-story apartment structures" of Queensbridge and Red Hook would "have a 'vital influence' on architecture of the future." His prediction proved to be right on target.[64]

In these early years of the public housing program other cities built quality public housing, but all of their housing projects were low rise. New York, however, was already gaining experience with high-rise public housing construction and management before World War II, experimentation that would prove invaluable once the decision had been made to scale up public housing after the war. Other cities adopted high-rise methods after the war but failed to build decent housing in the first place or manage it well in the long term, and often some dismal combination of the two.

Estates for the People: Landscaping Public Housing

Most housing authorities across the United States forgot about their grounds and their buildings floated in dust bowls or asphalt that enhanced the stigma of government housing. NYCHA, in contrast, invested in greenery for its benefits to the city as a whole. Hundreds of acres of new lawns, playgrounds, and trees in former slum districts would be the new lungs of the city, an essential element in a modern, hygienic New York. Again, New York understood the difference between basic and shoddy.

NYCHA designers had a rich tradition of landscape ideals and concepts at hand. New York's concerns for parks and their social purpose can be traced to the revolutionary work of Frederick Law Olmsted, who viewed his parks as carefully constructed exemplars of natural beauty in the city *and* as potential sites for behavioral training of the urban masses. He was followed by a great number of progressive reformers, including those in settlement houses, who cared less for scenic beauty and more for "wholesome play facilities" in tenement neighborhoods that would both provide healthful exercise and channel youthful energy.[65]

Robert Moses placed an even stronger emphasis on active recreation space during the 1920s and 1930s. Moses' Depression-era parks program increased expectations of what could be achieved in the way of open space in the modern city, and both his parks and personality strongly influenced NYCHA's landscape designers.[66]

Of a different but equally important nature were the fine common spaces at famous elite courtyard apartment developments in Jackson Heights as well as moderate-cost developments such as Sunnyside Gardens, Dunbar Apartments, and Hillside Homes. Open spaces in these housing developments primarily served as an envelope of passive green space that would soften the urban environment—but some did provide small play areas. Catherine Lansing, who played a leading role in NYCHA's community planning, visited Hillside Homes in 1935 and admired the wading pools and "remarkably fine recreation space planned."[67]

A third influence, parallel to these local examples, came from European low-cost housing of the 1920s. Photographs of these, illustrating books and articles on public housing, portrayed a variety of generous courtyard spaces with wading pools, gardens, play furniture, and grassy lawns. Public housing designers in the United States would have found it impossible to avoid European examples because they were featured in MOMA's housing exhibitions and in influential books such as Catherine Bauer's *Modern Housing* and Louis Pink's *A New Day for Housing*. NYCHA planners and the architectural groups associated with NYCHA during this time had collections of photographs from Europe and American limited-dividend projects.

The first public housing projects, built to high standards, successfully mimicked the thickly landscaped American and European apartment precedents. At First Houses and Harlem River Houses, the authority's design teams not only planted lines of mature trees and shrubs but carefully structured and landscaped the grounds. Areas not planted they paved in a mixture of pavement and Belgian blocks. Designers studded this landscaping, which was primarily for passive enjoyment, with lines of benches, small playgrounds for children, and small sculptures. Harlem River's superblocks, attributed to the noted landscape designer Michael Rapuano, featured changes of grade and materials that broke up its larger open spaces into manageable sections. A slightly raised masonry barrier delineated the sunken play areas and a wading pool closely imitated the water features found in European public housing developments.[68]

Williamsburg, in contrast, presaged future problems related to modernist planning concepts. There the landscapers wrestled with and did not seem to have overcome a more abstract and unfamiliar planning and architectural style. Designers surrounded Williamsburg's free-floating buildings with convoluted pathways that led to cow paths in actual practice. Nevertheless, with its dense planting, mature trees, and four-story buildings arranged in courtyards it still preserved a sense of enclosure. Nor did the first economized projects, while stripped of ornament and frills, lack for landscaping. Queensbridge (1940), for instance, may have been built to the most basic standards, but it still had a strong sense of enclosure, lines of trees, and thickly planted green spaces.[69]

Chairman Alfred Rheinstein, the force behind economized building, nevertheless endorsed simplified landscaping because of its positive influence on the city at large. He believed that the pleasant grounds of public housing could help reconcile those resentful citizens not lucky enough to gain access to housing projects if "certain benefits, such as playgrounds, nurseries, assembly rooms and other recreational facilities, [were] available to the entire neighborhood." Furthermore, "The landscaped uncrowded area should ventilate the neighborhood." A more clear and direct articulation of the notion of housing as a wider municipal service, designed to benefit the city as a whole as well as tenants, is difficult to find.[70]

A finely tuned landscape program had been developed, according to Rheinstein, to reach these goals: "Throughout, restrained and simplified mass planting of small trees and shrubs will be used to differentiate areas. . . . The effects will be unpretentious, consistent with a low-rental housing project." Shade trees would be found in "secluded brick bays, ideal sitting places" and benches would be "placed at intervals along the walks." Low-income housing had proper plants, too: "The plant varieties will be compact and restrained in form, of good foliage character, stout branched or occasionally armed with thorns, and hardy under city conditions." Public housing might not be beautiful, but it would not be barren.[71]

The demands of landscaping for low-income housing early occupied the authority's thoughts and it learned from experience what worked to create green spaces in such environments. Crowded or polluted urban sites (Vladeck, East River, Queensbridge, and Red Hook) demanded a careful horticulture: "Years of experiment has shown that plane or sycamore trees, pin oaks, red maples, gingko trees, and similar varieties are most likely to live." And "hardy varieties of shrubbery like privet and barberry, which can withstand city locations, are also planted." The thousands of towering plane trees and many shrubs lining NYCHA developments, the result of good planning in the early years combined with long-term maintenance, still provide shade and green space across the city.[72]

In the first decades of NYCHA's growth it primarily devised a landscape for passive enjoyment. The grounds, open to the public, were beachheads of green in a crowded, polluted environment. Designers provided small playgrounds on the grounds of every development and paved areas ideal for informal play, but NYCHA viewed its superblocks as housing complexes rather than city parks. Private housing managers, after all, provided limited recreational facilities and NYCHA would do the same. If children needed active parks they could go elsewhere. As NYCHA's community planners reminded Alfred Rheinstein, "In view of the fact that the city has assumed the responsibility of public recreation, schools, police and fire, for the community as a whole, there is no reason why housing should bear the costs of providing these facilities."[73]

There was, of course, one powerful man who disagreed with NYCHA's recreation spaces and who rarely saw a park space that could not serve as active recreation space: Robert Moses. Throughout the 1930s Moses characterized NYCHA grounds as "landscaping" not parks. Generally NYCHA worked well with Moses to make sure that new developments adjoined new city parks as at Red Hook, Harlem River, and

Queensbridge.[74] Moses nevertheless warned the authority in 1940 that "the operation of interior or border playgrounds in a public housing development, where the boundaries are not definite and where the tenants have prior rights and claims, is no substitute for properly operated independent playgrounds under the Park Department open to the general public."[75]

As with most of his sniping at the authority, Moses' criticism had evaporated by the late 1940s, when he gained more control of the authority's policies. In 1948, for instance, Moses defended the city's record in Harlem: "Every one of the public housing projects has play facilities within the project and additional playgrounds operated by the Park Department." Moses' efforts to link parks with public housing is, in fact, evident across the city to this day; an impressive number of well-equipped active recreation parks adjoin public housing developments.[76]

Moses and his associates exercised direct influence on NYCHA landscaping of the era; the lines of benches and fences echo his preferred park designs at the time. Gilmore Clarke, the other half of the leading landscape firm of Clarke and Rapuano, and a favorite of Moses, designed the grounds of the Kingsborough project; its lines of benches to protect planted areas, large mature trees, central paved mall, and closely planted shrubs along project walls are reminiscent of city parks at the time. In 1940, Allan Harrison of the authority recorded that "on other projects Mr. Clark[e] has approved the landscape drawings for the Park Department."[77] In 1941, George Spargo of Moses' staff also reported to Moses, for instance, that the authority "amended the Brownsville plan to agree with [the] recommendations" by Moses' staff.[78]

The authority may have resisted recreation at first, but its growing inventiveness did earn it a temporary national reputation in playground design. NYCHA's early playgrounds featured "slides and swings [that] proved to be somewhat hazardous, and . . . were not too stimulating to the children's imaginations" as indicated by the "way in which they took to the bushes, and began climbing the young trees.[79] At Red Hook Houses NYCHA staff member A. J. Moffat invented play equipment designed to stimulate imaginative play. Having noted "the attraction of partially demolished buildings for children," he fashioned out of concrete blocks a four-foot-high, E-shaped wall called the dodger, and children "soon swarmed all over it."[80]

Many NYCHA employees then built varieties of these structures, including logs, pipes, mushrooms, shelters, boats, airplanes, and railroad tracks (Figure 10).[81] Some within the authority found this mania for experimental equipment less impressive. By 1944 at Fort Greene an experimental playground equipped with dodgers, jungle gyms, tunnels, and pyramids did not attract as many children as hoped. Only the jungle gyms proved really popular. The dodger, in particular, was "not used often. The children walk and climb over this equipment and then walk away." A few of the large concrete pipes and other remnants of this era's play equipment remain, mostly because they are too difficult to remove.[82]

The landscape planning of these early years reflected an attention to detail rarely achieved in other cities. NYCHA administrators realized that large open spaces alone were unlikely to be viewed by tenants, or neighbors, as amenities that improved life in the city. Accordingly, they thickly planted these spaces, carefully considered and maintained appropriate plants, and invented play structures—even as they cut costs across the board on other details. Robert Moses even did his part to provide first-class parks adjoining many of these new complexes. The notion that open space would be landscaped and maintained became a key feature that distinguished New York's towers from those in other cities.

Rethinking Slum Clearance

Site selection remains a touchy subject in public housing history. Arnold Hirsch and those who have followed in his footsteps have provided ample evidence from cities such as Chicago and St. Louis that postwar slum clearance and high-density public housing represented a conscious strategy by white city officials to restrict the growth of black neighborhoods by rehousing poor blacks in black neighborhoods. Urban renewal, often benefiting wealthier people or individuals, would only continue if it did not send dispossessed blacks into all-white neighborhoods.

A corollary of this story, which can be tracked back to early housing advocates such as Catherine Bauer, is that concentration of poor, displaced people in these towers led inevitably to public housing failure. Some analysts believed, and many do today, that decentralized and dispersed sites would have led to diffusion of poverty and less troubled housing. The federal government's contemporary Hope VI program is, in part, based upon this notion of decentralization.[83]

The notion of public housing as a tool of racial segregation is compelling for cities such as Chicago and New York both before the war and after, but the second element of the tale, that decentralized public housing would have been much better in the long term, is more an article of faith than anything else. New York's story, beginning in the 1930s, raises fundamental questions about this species of opinion. Centralized projects in New York, often in racially segregated areas, remain full and relatively popular. At the same time, many garden-city-style, low-rise public housing complexes—in cities such as Baltimore and New Orleans—have

Figure 10. Experimental play equipment, including the Dodger and the Airplane, at the James Weldon Johnson Houses (1948) in East Harlem. La Guardia Wagner Archive/NYCHA Photograph Collection.

experienced many of the same pathologies as high-rise public housing in cities such as Chicago.

Quite a few of New York's reformers, those more concerned about civic revival than humanitarianism, at first only envisioned slum clearance as a tool for gentrification of tenement districts below 96th Street.[84] Others, such as Langdon Post, plainly desired to clear slums and build model tenements in central crowded districts but believed that "the price of land in . . . Manhattan slums is utterly fantastic" and "out of proportion to its real value."[85]

As NYCHA chairman, Post planned to use public housing on the periphery to reduce land costs in the center of town. He revealed that the authority "intends to carry on some of its building on the periphery of the city with the definite purpose in mind of breaking fictitious metropolitan land values." Not only would the authority be adding low-cost housing that would compete with existing slum housing, but Post aimed to recast the political economy of the entire city. That he envisioned a program that would eventually house hundreds of thousands of people gives some indication of the long-term impact public housing might have on urban land values.[86]

Federal policy makers at the PWA had equally complex positions. Robert Kohn, the first director of the PWA's Housing Division, preferred low-rise, low-density housing only possible on cheap, vacant lands. Interior Secretary Ickes, in contrast, supported slum clearance and tried to emphasize this direction after Kohn resigned in 1934. Court decisions blocking the PWA from condemnation nevertheless favored vacant land sites after 1935 and nationally led to more vacant land projects than Ickes ideally wanted.[87] Conflicting agendas at the federal level essentially allowed New York, in its early years, to steer its own course. As the PWA admitted in 1934, "Washington might feel justified in paying $8.00 for a 100% slum and only $4.00 for a 50% slum."[88]

The great majority of Williamsburg tenements, for instance, lacked hot water, steam heat, and private baths or toilets, but it was not a district of densely packed old-law tenements of the type long targeted by housing reformers. The Williamsburg site quickly drew criticism from Washington in 1934 as a poor match for public housing. NYCHA successfully defended the choice to the PWA administrator because "there are no worse slums anywhere, at the price."[89] The authority openly admitted, too, that the Harlem River project "will not actually be slum clearance, since the site is vacant" but "it is on the edge of slums and will offer to many families . . . a new type of housing."[90]

Industrial and low-density residential sites in the outer boroughs took on even greater importance during the 1930s in light of housing destruction elsewhere. By 1938 the authority was facing growing criticism that it had cleared old-law tenement housing inhabited by approximately 250,000 tenants but had built only a few thousand units as replacements.[91] In 1938 Alfred Rheinstein admitted that while he also favored slum clearance, the lightly populated Queensbridge and Red Hook sites provided new housing without destroying many existing homes. That industry had already started to abandon these areas offered an opportunity that the housing authority could exploit. The Publicity Division did suggest, however, concealing a photograph of the East River site that "shows clearly that the buildings are chiefly industrial—rather than slum tenements."[92]

Quite a few observers disliked NYCHA's initial strategy. Robert Moses rightly judged Harlem River as "not slum clearance at all. It represents the building up of the only large vacant area in the terribly congested Negro section of Harlem."[93] Advocates of Chelsea slum clearance believed that NYCHA's "present policy of launching all public housing projects in boroughs other than Manhattan is unsound in that it is costly to the city."[94] As NYCHA would soon begin work on low-cost slum clearance public housing projects such as Vladeck Houses (1938), this criticism could be discounted. By then, however, a more formidable foe had emerged, one actually dedicated to *stopping* NYCHA's growing interest in slum clearance.

Nathan Straus, the new director of the USHA, had been a proponent of vacant land use even before becoming the administrator of the USHA. He was the codeveloper of Hillside Homes and in his travels had been impressed by the vacant land, peripheral low-density public housing estates of Europe. London's Becontree estate, for instance, was built on farmland after World War I and provided twenty-five thousand picturesque cottage-style row houses with garden spaces.[95]

Straus's preference for decentralization had solid ideological support within New York reform circles. In the 1920s leading figures such as Clarence Stein and Lewis Mumford (both individually and as part of the Regional Plan Association) believed "the metropolitan future . . . lay in towns planted in regional 'greenbelts' where there was room for a new communal civilization."[96] Catherine Bauer, in *Modern Housing*, called London's slum clearance projects "greatly inferior in quality, both of the dwellings themselves and of surrounding environment, to the outlying developments." Bauer served as Straus's special assistant between 1938 and 1940 and during this time the USHA's policy documents and guidelines overwhelmingly favored vacant land *Zeilenbau*.[97]

Straus's resistance to slum clearance for new public housing could also be made in terms of fairness. Concern about the high costs of slum land reflects the long-held repugnance of housing reformers for encouraging speculation by falsely inflating the price of slum land. New York's progressive zoning law of 1916 was so permissive, for instance, that property owners logically anticipated vast sums in the future even if their property was temporarily derelict. Straus did not believe that federal money should be used to prop up these inflated prices and preferred that cities should enforce their housing laws (and thus reduce the value of slum land) or buy and donate land to be used for public housing. As the USHA administrator, Straus favored proposals that included "two-story houses for two to four families, on large sites in new outlying areas where land was comparatively cheap." He saw this type of housing as the potential "backbone" of public housing in the nation. The USHA was thus flexible in judging how authorities met the act's requirements for slum clearance (that is, slum clearance anywhere could be counted toward the requirement).[98]

In order to enforce his preferences, Straus set a new maximum cost for land, even in New York, of $1.50 per square foot. Chairman Rheinstein was "deeply disappointed in Washington's determination to make cheap land the chief factor in location."[99] He worried that Straus's limit of $1.50 per square foot on the price available for land "would mean that blighted areas in the more congested sections of Brooklyn would be ignored in any future plans." He predicted public housing would only be built in Queens and Staten Island because of low land costs there. Sites like those for Queensbridge and Red Hook were not in abundance.[100]

Rheinstein favored clearing slums if it could be accomplished economically. He believed that vacant land projects invited high public costs without solving the problem of the "festering sore of the slums."[101] Central public housing would also be of greatest convenience to future tenants who would not have to endure overlong commutes and substandard or nonexistent public services. The chairman shared in a body of opinion every bit as influential as advocates of garden cities. Among those who shared his vision was the real estate expert Clarke Dailey, who believed that decentralized public housing would demand new infrastructure in a city already "staggering under the load of the debt service for subways which have siphoned the population to outlying parts of the city." Figures such as Robert Moses shared Dailey's concern for preserving central property values and controlling governmental costs.[102]

In a revealing memo to the chairman of the State Housing Board, Rheinstein articulated a sensible alternative to the requirement of low land acquisition costs for New York City, arguing without ideological rancor that the "cost of land per room is far more important than cost per square foot and total cost per dwelling unit is a far more accurate gauge of economy than either of the others." This philosophy of economy, rooted in construction costs rather than land prices, kept alive the possibility of slum clearance in New York. It also pointed the way to high-rise towers in cleared neighborhoods.[103] With the economies at the Red Hook project in hand, Rheinstein estimated that "this savings undoubtedly will permit slum clearance which, in the past, was a doubtful prospect because of the high cost of land in New York City."[104]

The authority seemed to have worked out a compromise with Straus that allowed it to continue to acquire developed sites (for more than $1.50 per square foot) at a "woodpile conference" at which Mayor La Guardia, Senator Wagner, Nathan Straus, Comptroller McGoldrick, and Rheinstein "ironed out difficulties of rent price as they sat on a pile of lumber" at the Red Hook construction site.[105] It was apparently Wagner who deserves the credit for the resolution, but Rheinstein's "having whittled costs to an amazingly small minimum" put paid to promises of moderate cost public housing no matter the land costs. Straus waived the rules so that construction could continue although he obviously was not happy to do so.[106]

Vladeck Houses, as it became known, was the first federally sponsored slum clearance job on the Lower East Side after the "woodpile" agreement opened the door to land price flexibility. Vladeck Houses was hailed in 1938 "as a triumph for Mr. Rheinstein's insistence that slum clearance projects should be in congested slum areas" even though at that time it was unclear what the terms of the actual agreement had been.[107] The *New York Times* later explained that the high land costs at Vladeck (more than twice that of the $1.50 limit) had been circumvented by the city's agreement to "erect a park in the middle of the development [in essence closing the streets] and to finance the construction of another project immediately adjacent," what became Vladeck City Homes.[108]

Everything seemed to be moving along swimmingly, but the principle remained unresolved and federal/local tension never cooled. The conflict reached a head in October 1939. Rheinstein penned a critical article in *Harper's* on Straus's $1.50 policy, calling it unfair to cities such as New York. Straus suddenly and spitefully demanded $1.50 land costs or a city contribution to make up the difference on a project in Bedford Stuyvesant that he had previously approved at higher land costs—and made it clear that he was finished working with Rheinstein. This seemed unreasonable, undemocratic, and capricious to Rheinstein and he quit his position when Mayor La Guardia failed to come to his defense. With Rheinstein gone, Straus again relented, claiming that token payments had been arranged with the city. Projects, in spite of land costs that often exceeded $1.50, moved forward. Straus would approve more slum clearance projects as well that December.[109]

Straus had relented, but the high-density, slum clearance direction of NYCHA always irked him. At East River Houses' groundbreaking, for instance, he warned, "you must beware lest you overcrowd human beings in even such a wonderful project as this."[110] In 1941, at the dedication of low-rise, peripheral Clason Point Houses (which he had promoted), he boasted, "It combines unique features with soundness in planning—a veritable garden city within an urban center." Low land costs, approximately $0.35 per foot, had made this utopia possible.[111]

By December 1939, after Rheinstein's departure, NYCHA officials could still claim that "selection of sites within certain limits as to land costs has been left a local function. Protests by the NYCHA on the land cost limit policies of the USHA, have resulted in a considerable increase in this limit." The authority also highlighted the good news that Vladeck, South Jamaica, Bedford Stuyvesant, and the Navy Yard projects "are true slum clearance jobs."[112] To build in these slum areas a variety of arrangements had been worked out with federal officials, including city land donations (acquired by closing streets) to reduce total land costs. During this time a novel form of reporting land costs by the authority satisfied federal officials. Land costs from vacant and slum land were, by 1941, being "lumped together to satisfy the requirements of the Federal Authority."[113]

The authority never gave in to Straus; it not only paid more for slum clearance sites but ignored calls for decentralization or use of vacant land. During these years it also paid close attention to transit lines, existing educational institutions, and parks when planning site acquisitions for its many housing projects. Only Clason Point (1941) and Edwin Markham Houses (1943) followed a low-rise, peripheral model (Figure 11). By 1945, as part of its postwar planning, the authority had razed 7,900 units of housing solely in preparation for future public housing. The degree to which NYCHA leadership was committed to slum clearance is evident. In the rest of the United States, where land costs were lower and leaders more pliant, Straus's preferences carried more weight. By 1940, for instance, two- and three-story row houses comprised 62,639 of 90,436 units approved under the USHA program.[114]

New York's dogged pursuit of central-city slum clearance projects would look worse today if the authority had not adequately managed its towers over the decades. That they did meant that residents could benefit from the existing services and conveniences of central-city residence. The characteristically American notion that decentralization is inherently superior to concentration, which still conditions the field of public housing history (and public policy as represented by Hope VI), is not supported by the New York experience in these early years or in the decades that followed.

By the early 1940s NYCHA's design philosophy included all the elements that would be applied in its sweeping postwar program. Administrators had pioneered the minimum, but also well-constructed, high-rise

Figure 11. Clason Point (1941) is one of NYCHA's few low-rise housing projects. Photograph by Nicholas Dagen Bloom.

brick tower set in open superblocks. The system of design and construction for these towers in the park proved so economical, at least in New York, that it could be applied to expensive slum clearance sites. An emphasis on central sites in the long term helped retain the popularity of NYCHA projects and focused the authority on its role in civic improvement. The authority also developed landscape designs that were closely keyed to public housing environments and greatly enhanced the minimal brick towers. New York had become an important model for public housing, but the lessons learned in these early years did not translate well in other cities. High-rise housing in other cities after the war, superficially based on those of NYCHA, became a gruesome caricature as sloppily constructed and maintained towers destroyed the promise of public housing.

Chapter 4

Model Tenants for Model Housing

If only model tenants are chosen, nothing is accomplished and nothing proved. But First Houses is in a measure an experiment, an opportunity to see how known methods will work in New York. . . . If the system is to succeed it must pay its way. This has meant an initial preference for families of steady earned income.

—Catherine Mackenzie, New York Times, *1935*[1]

The notion of building public housing for the "families of steady earned income" was a controversial idea. Were such families truly in need of subsidized housing? The New York City Housing Authority's founders believed, however, that the working class was as often ill housed as the dependent poor in the City of New York. Tenements housed a range of income groups, and a housing system that failed to acknowledge this fact would quickly lose popularity. Equally important, working families would pay their way. As Senator Wagner emphasized in 1937, "This, after all, is a renting proposition, not a complete gift." Were the developments to become full of dependent people, public housing might become a political liability to housing supporters. Indeed, this is exactly what happened in many other American cities.[2]

NYCHA was well aware that it could fill its towers with welfare tenants but it simply chose not to. Without its conscious strategies of resistance to federal guidelines and construction of projects under more flexible state and city rules, NYCHA's consistently long waiting lists would have been meaningless: only the poorest, and mostly welfare, tenants would have been admitted. Welfare families, in the Depression years and after, could have filled all of NYCHA's units. Cities such as Chicago, for instance, placed an emphasis on housing the poorest and by the 1940s found its share of welfare tenants skyrocketing. NYCHA, which managed to delay this process until the 1960s, benefited longer from a tenancy that while still poor was less troubled.

A strong dividing line separated the poorhouse from philanthropic, limited-dividend, and public housing that antedated the NYCHA experiment. Philanthropic housing in London at the turn of the century, for instance, closely screened its tenants for good behavior. The vast public and publicly aided cooperative and limited-dividend projects both before World War I and after in Britain and Germany, according to the historian Daniel Rodgers, were "for skilled workers and the lower middle class; the poor had to make do elsewhere." Only Vienna's socialists reached the pool of poorly housed, unskilled workers. The social democratic ideal and labor union participation surrounding public housing in Europe made the housing of working-class families, rather than the destitute, less controversial. As this housing, by and large, did not serve as an almshouse, it not only looked good in this period but could be operated to a high standard.[3]

America's philanthropic housing had been equally choosy. Not only did the tenants ultimately have to carry a higher cost of building maintenance than later public housing tenants, but also the sponsors wanted their housing to be a model type of housing. Housing experts celebrated the fact that managers at New York's Lavanburg Homes, for instance, had rejected ninety families for their "low standard of living." Careful selection might seem unjust but had led to unequivocal success: "In spite of the fact that most of the tenants came to the Lavanburg Homes from abysmally poor and unsanitary districts, the building has not suffered from vandalism or carelessness."[4]

Public housing could be very selective in its first years. By March 1935 First Houses had three thousand applicants for the 122 apartments, and the Authority had to stop taking applications. How to choose from such a deep group of applicants? There was much concern at the time that housing would, like much of the rest of New York's coveted government benefits, be distributed through political machines. Langdon Post in early 1935 allayed fears of patronage: "Political influence would have nothing to do with the choice of tenants." NYCHA did in fact develop an objective system to block political influence, but this system was in its other details by no means value neutral.[5]

May Lumsden, NYCHA's director of tenant relations, recommended a point system that would yield tenants ideally suited to benefit from and take care of this ideal housing. Such a system, she said, would use "mathematical impartiality" to "protect . . . against the eloquence of sad-eyed mothers, the recommendations of interested persons and their [the tenant selection staff's] own human sympathies."[6]

The point system adopted for First Houses had seven categories (income, family, employment, present accommodations, previous residence, rent habits, and social background). *Income* (higher within limits was best and tenants got points for working, being debt free, and having insurance and savings accounts) and *present accommodations* (with an emphasis on substandard quality and health-threatening conditions) received the greatest number of potential points. The authority in its point system thus aimed for the working poor who had incomes that were not to exceed four or five times the rent and who were stuck in substandard housing.[7]

Lumsden acknowledged English influence on the system, but claimed that she had designed her own version. She did admit that the selection system derived partly from "budget figures approved by private social agencies, [and] credit reference schemes employed in high-class apartment houses." That a public housing system could be tracked to such elite precedents is significant and became a key element in NYCHA's management success.[8] Research of tenants after initial applications included verification of employment, and research of juvenile behavior and family histories with the Social Service Exchange. The selection staff actually visited the homes of 3,100 families who had applied to live at First Houses. Even after passing the home visit, potential tenants still had to endure an interview "by the Committee on the Selection of Tenants" that included management personnel and outside community specialists.[9]

It was to no one's surprise that the tenants yielded by the point and investigation system fit the profile desired—the cream of the poor in substandard housing. At First Houses, 75.8 percent of the families came from apartments lacking private bathrooms and a majority also had lived without private toilets and steam heat. At the same time, skilled labor fields dominated the employment profile of breadwinners. The effectiveness of the point system seemed to be justified by some of the first tenants selected, who, according to Catherine Lansing, "appeared to us to be highly desirable tenants. They made a very fine appearance, were intelligent and cooperative and delighted to hear of their new homes."[10]

Similar high standards of tenancy were pursued at Harlem River Houses and it was expected by leading members of the community that the "select among Harlem's poor" would get in while the "teeming slum thousands" would not.[11] The Harlem Housing Committee, for instance, which included black welfare and civic workers, gave greatest weight to being "legitimately employed."[12] High-income Harlemites "in illegitimate employment" could not be allowed in because "it would enable them to exploit the tenants from within." Such care had to be taken to avoid the potential "failure of this project [which] will be taken as evidence that the residents of Harlem are not ready for low rental government housing." [13]

Reflecting the limited labor opportunities of African Americans, Harlem River tenancy was a mix of "unskilled workers and semi-skilled

workers, such as porters, cleaners, and janitors. Other large groups include[d] domestic servants, [and] elevator operators." Average family
income at Harlem River was nevertheless an impressive $1,340.[14] At
Williamsburg, too, investigations would make sure that "only those in
the deserving low-income group are accepted."[15] First Houses, Harlem
River, and Williamsburg had a combined relief and WPA tenancy between only 5 and 8 percent in 1940, an intentional outcome of such a restrictive tenant selection system. It was little surprise that these early
housing projects experienced few social problems and nearly perfect
rent collection.[16]

The combination of such a small amount of government housing with
high standards generated a mass of disgruntled New Yorkers. The leftist
City-Wide Tenants Council worried in 1938, for instance, that the point
system "appeared to discriminate against families with the lowest incomes," and particularly disliked points given for assets, insurance, and
other trappings of middle-class life.[17] In an earlier response to criticism
like this, Lumsden had claimed that NYCHA tenants actually represented "a fair cross-section of low income families" and the three projects then in operation (1937) had a majority of unskilled labor.[18]

More damaging was some evidence that the point system seemed to
be selecting tenants from new-law housing. In response, Lumsden had
already reduced "the standards which [the authority] would have liked
to maintain with regard to living quarters from which the future tenants
came."[19] Lowering standards, probably in reference to housekeeping,
must have made some difference because Alfred Rheinstein could claim
by 1938 that the majority of Harlem River tenants "came from old-law
tenements in dilapidated conditions."[20] By 1938 the general policy had
become that "if it is a new-law house, the family automatically is disqualified" whereas "if it is an old-law house with violations . . . or if it is in a
slum area," the tenant was invited for an interview.[21] Lumsden made it
crystal clear what the new policy meant:

Truly the worst shall be first. The worse the place you are living in now, the better your chances are for getting into Red Hook or Queensbridge. If your family is crowded into an apartment meant for half that many people—if you are
sleeping and living in rooms that have no windows—if you are forced to share
a community toilet—and your only bathtub is the kitchen sink, and it has only
cold water . . . take heart, this message is addressed to you.[22]

NYCHA's system had other controversial results. It was so selective that
it dramatically reduced the chances of entry for site tenants cleared for
the project itself. At Williamsburg, for instance, of 1,300 families displaced, 439 applied for housing and 341 were accepted. A city councilman disliked the excessive selectivity that penalized both the very poor

by evaluating "social desirability" and the lower middle class, which was squeezed by low income limits; it seemed "by the very act of furnishing model housing . . . literally to throw the middle class in the streets."[23] In 1939 the NYCHA annual report admitted that most site tenants had incomes too high for public housing. Answering criticism that existing housing projects up to that time had restricted site tenants, Mayor La Guardia promised that in future projects "we hope that a larger number of the good people who actually live in this neighborhood will be able to avail themselves of the improved housing conditions."[24]

The Red Hook Row

The broader notion of public housing as a municipal service, rather than a social welfare program, crashed into an emerging federal emphasis on public housing as housing for the poorest Americans. NYCHA administrators had to fight for working tenants because they ultimately wanted to clear giant slum districts that then housed a wide range of the city's tenants. Not only would developments be more difficult to manage with more relief clients (from a financial and behavioral standpoint), but political support would evaporate once it became clear to the city's working poor, often suffering in tenements themselves, that they would have no place in the future housing program.

Federal officials such as Nathan Straus did not necessarily seek to turn public housing into welfare housing, but the emphasis on creating housing for the lowest income groups—so as to avoid competition with the private sector—had the same result across the nation. Straus tried to force New York, his largest partner in housing, to accept his, and what he considered Congress's, definition of income limits as developed under the 1937 law. NYCHA fought hard and actually won concessions through political pressure and publicity. This compromise was one of many delaying tactics the authority developed in order to slow the flow of welfare tenants into its projects. New York would in the long run have to build projects without federal aid—as it also began to do during this time—in order to realize fully its goal of rehousing a wide cross section of tenement dwellers.

May Lumsden, in the spring of 1939, wrote to Straus that she and NYCHA staff objected to Straus's belief that "preference should always be given to those having the lowest annual net income." She worried that these limits "might tend to limit occupancy to relief families" and in New York, at least, "the lowest annual income does not necessarily indicate the greatest need for re-housing." NYCHA officials such as Lumsden had by 1939 grown accustomed to rather flexible, and high, income limits.[25] Officials of the PWA, who had encouraged these flexible income limits, frankly admitted that their high-quality projects were "too expensive for the very poor" and worried that a poverty-oriented program would make "them more susceptible to budget cuts." They also claimed, "Participants are often stigmatized."[26]

The top family income limits for entry had ranged from $1,680 at First Houses to $2,184 at Williamsburg. While most admitted families had incomes below these levels, because they were smaller and/or made less money, these relatively high top limits provided NYCHA with significant freedom of choice. The head of the USHA, Nathan Straus Jr., did not, however, budge from his new entry limit of $1,400 (later $1,399) for a seven-person family. Such a level, based on a statistical analysis of who constituted the lowest one-third nationally in terms of income, had been established according to Straus expressly to "weight the scales more heavily in favor of families in the lowest income groups." He believed that the USHA was limited to funding housing for the poorest Americans. The authority agreed, under duress, to try the limit for ninety days.[27]

By the end of June the effect of Straus's new rule could be seen in NYCHA's rejection of thirty families previously accepted under the authority's liberal interpretation of the federal legislation, "which permits the acceptance of tenants whose income does not exceed five and, in some cases, six times the amount of rent to be paid." The authority had welcomed higher-income families that fit under this maximum because it endeavored "to keep a balance between the percentage of relief families" and the working poor. According to the *New York Times*, Chairman Rheinstein reminded the public that "in the past . . . the ratio of relief tenants has been 15 or 20 percent [it was actually lower]. He expressed fear that under the new ruling the percentage of relief families would rise to about 50 per cent." So many relief families would include those "who are not problems for a housing authority, but for the Department of Welfare or other social and correctional institutions."[28]

Why did NYCHA fear welfare tenants? As an experienced builder, Rheinstein realized that very low-income tenants would not be able to support annual maintenance costs: "we think it is harmful to the whole movement of housing if we collect such low rents that the taxpayer will be called upon to make further contributions."[29] Other objections put forward by NYCHA administrators seem equally prescient: "Such a system would put a premium on sheer lowness of income. It acts as a positive deterrent to all attempts to increase the family income."[30] NYCHA was also concerned that isolation of the relief tenants would deprive the poor of the "beneficial effect of contact with families who are self-supporting." It would take longer in other cities for administrators to realize these important principles; by the time they did, it was often too late to resist the welfare tide.[31]

NYCHA's supporters also understood what was at stake in this new ruling. At the Red Hook opening ceremony Mayor La Guardia remained defiant: "We must necessarily abide by the rules of the [USHA]," he admitted, "which kept thirty families out. . . . Because of this ruling, city authorities believe that at least half the tenants will be on relief. . . ." La Guardia let it be known, however, "Personally, I believe that rule is susceptible to amendment." With its high cost of living and particularly nasty slum conditions, "New York City should not have to accept average income levels from other cities."[32] The *New York Times* agreed with both La Guardia and NYCHA: "Public housing cannot be a form of relief and still maintain its financial structure. Relief must take up the job where the Housing Authority has to leave off."[33]

Straus remained unbowed: "The limitation is based upon my profound conviction as to the purpose and meaning of the [USHA] as passed by the Congress, a conviction reinforced day by day as I appear before Congress." He cleverly argued that if NYCHA, after the ninety-day period, really failed to find tenants, then there might not be a need for subsidized housing in New York at all. He was sure, however, that the authority would find tenants if it abandoned "the method of tenant selection based upon a philosophy of housing not embodied in the [USHA]." Straus could even identify two hundred thousand New York families who would qualify under his limits, indicating that while New York had a tight housing market such a market did not preclude filling projects with very low-income tenants.[34]

Far left opinion, in partnership with the City-Wide Tenants Council, took the side of Straus. The *New York Post* found 250,000 families with incomes low enough to qualify for housing. It contrasted this number with the 168 that Alfred Rheinstein had found. It also reported that many poor families were now coming forward because they previously thought that high standards would automatically preclude them. The *Post* sent its reporters to visit 5,000 potential families, interviewed 4,000, and of that number created a list of 500 it thought actually met the standards. In response the authority conducted its own investigation of the same 500 and found that only 64 actually qualified for housing *according to its standards*. Notably, its study found "a great number which do not want public housing and are opposed to it."[35]

The previously rejected higher-income tenants from Red Hook, accepted under higher NYCHA limits, appealed directly to President Roosevelt for a rule change. Straus finally budged in September, but only a little. By that time the ninety-day trial had run out, so "Straus . . . announced in Washington that the top limit would remain at $1,399 for persons seeking six and one-half-room apartments, but that increases ranging up to 30 percent would be sanctioned in the maximum income levels for smaller families." He made it clear that this change was not to be viewed as a retreat from his earlier policy, but would only allow flexibility in smaller units.[36] Red Hook by 1940 thus featured "about 25 per cent of the families . . . on home relief or WPA at least part of the time," about half of what it would have been had NYCHA not fought Straus for a change.[37]

The principle of federal fallibility had been established whether Straus admitted it or not. As NYCHA would boast by December, "NYCHA, when faced with arbitrary determinations from Washington, refused to proceed" under them; the authority was "able to convince the USHA to agree to new limitations, which have proven satisfactory."[38] The USHA agreed in 1940, for instance, to use Red Hook income limits as a guideline for South Jamaica Houses and Queensbridge Houses.[39]

The new chairman, Gerard Swope, and the NYCHA board voted unanimously in 1940 that while the authority would not absolutely limit relief clients, "it consider[ed] the danger mark the percentage at Red Hook, i.e. 30%."[40] NYCHA also tried to balance welfare recipients among the different projects. By 1941, NYCHA limited the proportion of assistance families (including both WPA and relief) in particular projects to between 20 and 30 percent. This was a figure much higher than the early projects but lower than federal policy might have generated.[41]

That NYCHA now considered 30 percent as a cap on welfare tenancy can equally be read as a successful, if partial, assertion of federal power. Whereas First Houses, Harlem River, and Williamsburg had a combined relief and WPA tenancy of between 5 and 8 percent; Red Hook, Queensbridge, South Jamaica, and Vladeck (federal) had rates between 22 and 29 percent. (Relief considered separately compared in similar proportions, 2–3 percent in the former projects versus 10–13 percent in the latter ones.) The fact that only 9 percent of tenants in all projects depended upon welfare hid the growing concentration in newer federal projects. As administrators reported, "We are getting into a different group of tenants in Queensbridge. Because of the low income, you get into a case work group."[42]

That NYCHA's welfare numbers could go up so easily simply based on alterations in tenant selection policy undermines familiar arguments that New York's tight housing market accounted for relatively less impoverished public housing populations. That higher-income tenants wanted to live in public housing had something to do with tight conditions, but the Red Hook experience revealed that New York possessed vast numbers of welfare tenants who would have flooded in to the comparatively small number of units available had NYCHA not consciously shaped its own policies.[43]

The only way to guarantee that public housing would not become welfare housing in New York was for NYCHA to build its own projects. New York did not build its own public housing in order to avoid federal income limits, but the broader housing goals of Mayor La Guardia that encouraged municipally funded public housing conveniently eliminated meddling federal officials.

The new Vladeck City Houses, for instance, was designated from the beginning for transfer applications from those with incomes too high for Red Hook and Queensbridge. The authority's board aimed, with Vladeck, to "show that public housing can be made partially self-liquidating."[44] Vladeck City Houses in 1940 would, in fact, have only 3.3 percent total of relief and WPA tenants (and only 0.4 percent of relief alone). NYCHA viewed Vladeck policies as a precedent for future city projects. The newly approved state program likewise allowed for greater flexibility, permitting "occupancy to continue up to a 50 per cent increase of income above the five-times and six-times ratio" for entry. These programs would become essential to maintaining a lower rate of welfare tenants in the system as a whole.[45]

As employment rebounded during the 1940s, owing to the war, NYCHA found itself not only with a problem of admission limits, but what now seemed like exceedingly low continued occupancy limits. NYCHA faced potential mass evictions of its carefully chosen tenants, many of whom now exceeded maximum income limits. At first a few hundred tenants left, opening up space for many who lingered on NYCHA's long waiting lists. Pressure from the Public Housing Conference, Citizens Housing Council, labor unions, tenant associations, and local politicians began to grow for relaxed standards of continued occupancy. Evidently the rest of the city's nonprofit leadership shared NYCHA's expansive view of public housing tenancy. I would argue that NYCHA needed little convincing.[46]

At first, temporary deferments of eviction were granted to those families with draftees but during 1942 about 4 percent of NYCHA's 13,180 tenants moved out because of high income levels. In December 1943 the authority raised its admission levels modestly at Williamsburg, Harlem River, and First Houses, but at Red Hook, Queensbridge, South Jamaica, and Vladeck (federal) it raised the admission levels "to the statutory limits of 5 or 6 times the rent because the original limits, approved by Washington, were proved too low." Such a change could be justified because of wartime emergency, but NYCHA had long sought a relaxation in income limits.[47]

During the war years the authority even more dramatically shifted rules on continuing occupancy with the permission of the federal government (the Office of Price Administration). In 1942 it raised continued occupancy limits to $2,300, in 1943 to $3,000, and by fall of 1944 found that, with permission of the OPA, it had to waive continued occupancy income maximums *entirely* as high wages and limited housing meant that 55 percent of tenants exceeded the existing income limits. The authority also created a new priority for service men and veterans, many of whom had higher incomes.[48]

In order to justify housing higher-income tenants, the authority had, beginning in 1942, charged surcharges on top of rents. Because the federal government still demanded that each tenant "pay at least ⅕ to ⅙ of his income for rent . . . until the ceiling rent [a market-based rent] is reached," the surcharges recreated this balance between rent and income. The Federal Public Housing Authority accepted the plan in 1943. By 1947, 68.3 percent of tenants paid surcharges. Admission policy also favored higher-income tenants. By 1950, 43 percent of all tenants admitted to NYCHA projects gained their apartments through the grace of higher, continued occupancy levels used for admission (in order to clear sites more rapidly). The city-sponsored no-cash subsidy programs even had admission levels of nearly $5,000.[49]

The authority might have wanted higher-income tenants, but even it knew it had crossed a credibility line by having so many higher-income tenants. Chairman Butler in 1947 announced "progressive evictions" for 2,770 families whose income exceeded $3,000.[50] By 1949 the city was preparing for the eviction of 600 families with income over $5,000 and considering the eviction of 2,000 families with income between $3,600 and $5,000 (the official continued occupancy rate by this time was $3,500).[51] NYCHA tempered the policies only slightly by encouraging transfers to higher-income, city-sponsored developments.[52]

New York had in this period demonstrated some very provocative and potentially dangerous precedents. NYCHA had confirmed that it was possible to find working poor families from among the population and keep welfare families at a manageable percentage. Working-class and even middle-class families, it also turned out, would apparently live in basic, low-cost housing for surprisingly long periods of time. As long as the rent was decent, many seemed determined to make public housing a permanent residence. This represented a threat to the private housing market and led both nationally and locally to eviction pressures. Within a few years, many in New York would wonder why NYCHA and the federal government had been so determined to push out higher-income tenants; the pendulum would quickly swing back in the other direction in the 1950s.

The Complexion of Housing

Back in the 1930s it had been the goal of NYCHA, in keeping with its ambitious plans, to create a public housing system that mirrored the city as a whole. NYCHA administrators intuitively understood that should public housing only serve the minority population, public support, in a white majority city, would fade. The authority also sensed that directly challenging racial divisions in the city would prove costly from a political standpoint. NYCHA drew an intentionally blurry line on race and as late as 1947 could claim, "The Housing Authority has never released a public statement on racial policy. Our experience with bi-racial occupancy, has . . . been highly satisfactory." The history is more complicated and one could argue that policies existed, official or not.[53]

Chairman Philip Cruise, looking back from the vantage point of the 1950s, would admit that NYCHA created Williamsburg for whites and Harlem River for blacks, but that under some pressure it pursued token integration at each. Integration of later projects became standard but in order to maintain white public support, "the proportion was kept in general conformance with the pattern prevailing in the surrounding neighborhood."[54] NYCHA administrators in 1940 had decided, for instance, that new housing in South Jamaica would be primarily minority because "this project is located in a neighborhood having a preponderance of colored people."[55]

The black community was well aware of NYCHA's racialist, if not racist, program.[56] The executive secretary of the NAACP welcomed the South Jamaica project, which targeted slum clearance in a predominately black area and was designated for black tenants, but still hoped that "future developments [would] fulfill the true meaning of democracy by admitting all citizens regardless of race." The NAACP wanted the USHA administrator, Straus, in 1939 to take a stand against "certain so-called Negro projects, which seem to be contrary to the institutional pattern of New York City." Straus at first responded that this was a local issue, but one month later he assured black officials that NYCHA's policies "will be in accord with sound democratic principles." In November of that year NYCHA officials reported integration in all projects and a color-blind admissions policy while also continuing sensitivity to "existing community patterns."[57]

NYCHA continued to manage its projects by race. A complaint from the City-Wide Tenants Council in 1941 documented that black families felt that it was almost impossible to get housing anywhere but Harlem River Houses. The NYCHA administrator, F. M. Didisheim, did admit, internally, that racial steering was policy: "We have colored families in Red Hook and Queensbridge, but cannot deny that selection of these has been more exacting than is the case for white families."[58] Even though state law prevented discrimination in public housing by 1939, token integration seemed to have been used to avoid any direct challenge.[59]

The most frank discussion of NYCHA racial policy took place in a board and staff meeting with NYCHA's Harlem Advisory Committee in 1939. Harlem members inquired if "you are basing the percentage on population. Is that true?" Didisheim responded that it was, "both on population and proportion of the colored and white population that is living in substandard housing." NYCHA, seeing that blacks were worse off in housing conditions, increased total black tenants from 4.7 percent (as it was in the actual population in 1930) to 6 percent. The black population of New York after all had increased from 327,706 in 1930 to 458,444 in 1940. Mary Simkhovitch sharply reminded her visitors, however, that the "overwhelming population in New York City is white. We don't want to act in such a way and do this thing in such a way that it will deter white people from going into projects." Simkhovitch, and the other board members, believed that social perfectionism would have to be distinct from NYCHA's grand municipal vision:

You may say it is up to the white population to receive the colored people in equal numbers everywhere because that is justice. But you know very well we haven't arrived at that condition of social justice that we should. And though we should do certain things, and the best things we can, we don't want to kick over the whole business of housing. We have to think first of housing. . . .

Even more bluntly, she let them know that "we must stick to our guns. We are not missionaries." The Reverend Moore seconded these statements by explaining the larger context of their decisions: "A long time back we thrashed that whole principle out and decided that we were in the business for housing fundamentally, and not for experimentation."[60]

The practice of separation thus continued. By 1940 the authority could boast that blacks now occupied 12.4 percent of units in comparison to a city-wide black population of 6 percent, but these laudable figures obscured the racial divisions. By 1941, First Houses still had no black families; Williamsburg had 1 black family and 1,621 white families; Red Hook had 32 black and 2,513 white; Queensbridge had 52 black and 3,097 white; Vladeck (federal) had 17 black and 1,514 white; East River had 126 black and 1,044 white; and Vladeck City had only 1 black and 239 white. In contrast, Harlem River had only black families; South Jamaica had 312 black families and 136 white; and Kingsborough had 437 black and 729 white families.[61]

The system began to break down not because of policy but because of shifting demand. The black population was poorly housed to begin with and restricted from most neighborhoods. At the same time, low income levels in federal projects favored black workers who had suffered employment discrimination during the war years. Between the initial opening of Red Hook (1939) and 1943, the black population went up most dramatically, of the different projects, from 31 to 106 black families. The black percentage went up more modestly in all but the Vladeck (federal) and Kingsborough developments. Managers at many individual developments found that they could not maintain what they considered to be ideal percentages of minorities versus whites. According to the manager of South Jamaica Houses in 1943, it was impossible "to keep racial distribution of families at the percentage current."[62]

NYCHA would have experienced a more dramatic racial shift at this time had it not held apartments vacant, a practice that belied NYCHA's claim that it had abandoned racial steering. Queensbridge by the fall of 1943 had seventy vacant apartments and Red Hook had sixty-five. An investigator "found that none of the projects had a waiting list of white applicants in any size apartments." East River had become so imbalanced that black applicants were deferred.[63] The manager of Fort Greene referred to "a theoretical percentage of about 17% [that] was suggested on the basis of neighborhood estimates. Our renting records indicate that we have signed leases with 15% colored. However, between the time of leasing and moving, cancellations have increased this percentage to 19%."[64]

In 1945 Mary Simkhovtich denied that NYCHA discriminated and cited as proof the fact that "over 15% of [the authority's] tenants [are] Negroes, which is more than double the percentage of Negro to White in the city." However, she was defining segregation at the admission door as opposed to that at the project level. Even she admitted that "the projects reflect the population of the area where they are situated." Because whites made up approximately 85 percent of the tenant population, most of the projects remained majority white.[65]

Today it is easy to condemn the racial insensitivity on the part of NYCHA's founders, but their insistence on the maintenance of proportionality meant that their system would grow far larger, and in far more neighborhoods, than those in other cities. As soon as public housing became perceived as minority housing, it lost broad political support.

Early Mistakes Elsewhere

Cities such as Boston and St. Louis developed restrictive methods of tenant selection in these early years that were in many respects similar to those in New York. Changes made after the war, including mass evictions for high-income tenants, would help send these cities on a downward spiral. Chicago's initial strategies of social management, in contrast, actually laid the groundwork for failure. The woeful tale of Chicago's early missteps is chronicled in the urban historian Bradford Hunt's dissertation (and forthcoming book), relevant sections of which are summarized below.[66]

The Chicago Housing Authority's executive director, Elizabeth Wood, viewed public housing, at different moments, as welfare housing, black housing, a tool for neighborhood integration, and a path to idealistic community planning. The first low-rise PWA housing projects in Chicago, as in New York, were primarily full of carefully chosen, working-class families who appreciated the low-scale attractive developments, relatively tight management controls, and community programs. Even in the 1930s, however, Wood sought the lowest possible income tenants in line with the same USHA policies that New York bitterly resisted. Chicago during these early years even deliberately set its income limits significantly *below* already low federal regulations.[67]

NYCHA's May Lumsden, who designed New York's rigorous system, wrote to the USHA that Chicago's emphasis "if worked to its logical conclusion . . . will mean 100% relief or sub-relief tenantry." The CHA went so far as to cut maintenance to the bone in 1939 in order to make rents more affordable to the very poor, but in so doing it not only undermined project attractiveness, but had to evict one quarter of its tenants because their incomes now exceeded statutory requirements. By 1940, 36 percent of CHA tenants had been or were then on relief. Unlike New York, Chicago even resisted higher-income tenants during wartime and continued to rent open apartments to a majority of relief families. In a desperate attempt to keep a mixed population the CHA started raising its income levels postwar, but Wood found few takers. Even so, the CHA preserved admission limits lower than New York and continued aggressively to evict tenants whose incomes were too high.[68]

Chicago also blundered in race relations. Unlike New York's liberal leaders, Elizabeth Wood took as her "primary goal the relief of appalling housing conditions experienced by the city's African Americans. As a result, 80% of the units planned between 1939 and 1945" were for blacks even though in 1945 they accounted for only 15 percent of the city's total population. Wood and Chairman Robert Taylor became civil rights heroes but created an adversarial position with the Chicago City Council that later undermined their integration efforts. By the mid-1950s, with some justification, "the average Chicagoan [thought] the projects were built purely to house Negroes." The CHA thus failed to gain approval for many vacant land projects, unlike NYCHA, because of its having so thoroughly united race and public housing. The Chicago City Council, responding to white fears, worked successfully over the decades both to restrict public housing to black neighborhoods and to maintain quotas on black residents in the few white projects. By the 1960s most public housing, with the exception of senior towers, was for blacks in primarily black neighborhoods.[69] Good intentions thus failed to prevent ghettoization in Chicago, and in other cities too, a pattern that stymied the growth of a larger public housing system.[70]

NYCHA used tenant selection policies during its founding years to engineer a housing system that could succeed in the long run. The point system generated working, two-parent families of both races that would be able to pay rents then and in the future. Thses rents, in turn, would be used to fund sizable maintenance operations. These families also seemed to understand that municipal housing was a privilege, not a right. They would control their behavior and thus make this housing look good to the city as a whole. Federal policy undermined NYCHA policies, but New York showed that local resistance could be effective, either by forcing changes in policies or by constructing public housing without federal aid. NYCHA also used racial steering in this era to make sure that public housing would be accepted in white and black neighborhoods, while using the notion of proportionality to mollify both civil rights activists and racists. NYCHA administrators knew that in order for the housing program to become as large as they envisioned it was essential that it not become black, poor housing in a majority white, working-class city.

Chapter 5
Tightly Managed Communities

New York City Housing Authority administrators may have believed that eliminating slums and building model housing would reduce disease and fire, but their faith in the transformative potential of public housing did not preclude a strong managing hand. Unlike an older generation of Progressive reformers, and naïve reformers in many cities who believed better housing inevitably led to better people, NYCHA administrators held a somewhat dim view of human nature. Even the carefully selected tenants it had painstakingly unearthed would have to be watched.[1]

Social control, broadly defined, would be the only way to ensure that the public housing environment met the goals of housing reformers. NYCHA had to prove to the general public and its political masters that it could eliminate the city's slums, not simply create new slums under public control. To this end, NYCHA adopted not only the daily management methods of middle-income apartment houses, radical in itself and not imitated in other cities, but also experimental methods of tenant organization and community programs. By the 1940s NYCHA had established important precedents that remain a part of the authority's operations to this day. Administrators also found that certain overly paternalistic measures had to be significantly rethought.

New York, as an apartment city, possessed an advantage in the creation and maintenance of apartment housing. By the time NYCHA opened its projects, New York had decades of experience behind it in the field of apartment management. Most tenements, of course, suffered from limited staffing. Tenement owners, both distant and residential, invested what little they could while milking the property for every possible dollar.

Middle-class and upper-class elevator apartment buildings, with large staffs and high standards of tenant selection, had better demonstrated the positive potential of densely built urban housing. The thought of transferring these elite methods to low-cost housing, for some reason, never seemed absurd in New York. NYCHA's adoption of this management style appears more like a reflex action rather than a concerted plan. Cities such as St. Louis and Chicago, which later built high-rise buildings after New York's example, failed to bring NYCHA's management system along with the towers and paid dearly.

Kingsborough Houses (1941), featuring over 1,100 apartments in sixteen, six-story buildings, illustrates the transfer of management practices from better apartment houses to NYCHA. Kingsborough in the year it opened included a staff of approximately thirty-six permanent employees. This total included nine employees in the manager's office and "approximately 27 permanent employees plus additional labor on grounds during the summer, and painters for occasional redecorating. Fourteen porters clean the stair halls and public space and operate the incinerators. The balance of the staff is composed of firemen, maintenance men, watchmen and gardeners." Kingsborough might have been cheap to build ($1,107 per room), but skimping ended when construction ceased. This was no tenement operation.[2]

NYCHA held this staff to a high standard. The civil service provisions of NYCHA diffused patronage that plagued housing authorities in cities such as Chicago. Housing advocates pushed for the adoption of civil service standards at NYCHA in 1938 even though NYCHA had initially aimed to opt out of the civil service in order to recruit top-flight professionals. According to a longtime administrator, because of a fight between NYCHA secretary Wilfred Lewis and Mayor La Guardia, "the next thing, the Housing Authority was part of the Civil Service System, which a lot of people bemoaned."[3] By 1941, 84 percent of NYCHA's 719 employees had been selected through the civil service process.[4] The authority initially lost a certain number of talented provisional appointments, but by the 1950s the authority was benefitting from a high degree of professionalism and minimum patronage. Even today, almost all NYCHA employees must pass civil service exams for their positions.[5]

NYCHA thus backed up its building programs with a large staff with clear responsibilities and skills. Grounds full of workers then and now made New York's public housing notably better in appearance than that in other cities. It might have been controversial outside NYCHA to have so many people on the public payroll, but within the authority there appears to have been no controversy about having well-staffed projects. Leaders such as Alfred Rheinstein cut costs on construction, but even he knew that daily management should not be trimmed. High staffing levels remained the model in the postwar years and led to a total staff, at its height, of fifteen thousand employees.

Nor did the authority in these early years shrink from imposing rules that would make these apartment buildings more like middle-class residences. Early tenants of NYCHA's projects had to agree to a raft of rules that signaled a new era in slum life. Not only were their belongings and furniture fumigated on the way in, but also they lost the use of outdoor fire escapes and back areas for household maintenance. As the authority provided both washing machines and clothes dryers in every complex, it announced that "clothes lines shall not be hung from fire escapes, windows or elsewhere"; "no bed-clothes, rugs, mops, dustcloths, etc., may be shaken or cleaned out of the windows"; and all the garbage had to be taken to the incinerator. The tenants would be charged for any damages to the premises and tenants even lost the right to have pets and boarders—the tenement evil and its attendant habits would be terminated. NYCHA went so far as to provide the blinds, and until very recently only allowed its custom blinds to be used.[6]

NYCHA administrators, even with these rules and staff in place, feared that adjustment from tenements to public housing would prove rocky. Fears of social disorder led NYCHA into one of its less successful, but still instructive, management episodes. The community staff, notably May Lumsden (the director of tenant relations) and Catherine Lansing (the executive director of community planning), based their early rent collection program on the famous social management scheme pioneered by Octavia Hill in late nineteenth-century London. The authority was not the first housing organization in the United States or New York to adapt the system, but as the first *public* entity to do so the authority found itself in uncharted waters.[7]

Hill's system had its powerful supporters among American housing advocates. The National Municipal League, for instance, in 1935 published a short pamphlet by the housing expert Beatrice Greenfield Rosahn that celebrated Hill's successes. Rosahn's brief history of the "friendly rent collector system" reveals that this mothering arrangement grew from Hill's intimate concern for the tenants in buildings she managed. Hill discovered that through superior maintenance of older buildings and the personal touch she could help tenants improve not only their housing, but also their social and health conditions. As her reputation grew she began to train women; later she switched to paid, professional women. Hill eventually supervised over two thousand apartments.[8]

Hill applied her ideas in privately held housing, but her ideas proved popular in municipal housing. Many private and public housing authorities in the 1930s in England still employed women managers following the precedents of Octavia Hill. The most devoted followers of Hill in the United States could be found in Philadelphia, where a number of ladies in 1896 had created the Octavia Hill Association of Philadelphia. They adopted Hill's friendly visitor rent collection method and by 1933 supervised 420 units in the Philadelphia area. The methods were not unknown in New York either. The City and Suburban Homes Company, the manager of 3,450 apartments by the 1930s, claimed to have adapted some of Hill's methods. Lavanburg Homes on the Lower East Side (later taken over by NYCHA) also apparently used the weekly rent collection system.[9]

These are notable precedents, but it must also be noted that the vast majority of American philanthropic housing managers demanded that tenants bring their rents to a central office on a monthly (and sometimes weekly) basis. Perhaps the greatest influence of the friendly visitor system was on the growing field of social work. Progressive-era advocates expected social workers, or caseworkers, to help enforce housing laws in their visits to the slums and, at the same time, develop their role as helpful friends rather than simply agents of social control.[10]

The social aspects of housing fascinated May Lumsden and accounts for her interest in Hill's operations. A Barnard graduate in politics and government, she personally admired Hill's approach "based on the use of trained and experienced women in the dual role of rent collector and friendly adviser."[11] She optimistically testified that in Hill's buildings, "instead of the screaming, fighting and drunken brawls" of typical slums "you could now see sewing classes, singing groups, and other amusement." The Hill system would aid housing management by regulating and improving behavior.[12]

A PWA-sanctioned "brief for paternal control" by Mary Simkhovitch, the national housing expert Edith Wood, and others had already, in 1933, "divided project administration into the management of finances and the physical plant and the protection of tenant health and morals." This brief recommended that "a female assistant . . . be responsible for the latter, which included family case work, child care, recreation and tenant organization." Notably, the document "dismissed any notion of tenant control."[13]

Newly hired at NYCHA in 1935, Lumsden also recommended a NYCHA staff with social skills: "sufficient in number and sufficiently varied in experience to handle all phases of recreation, public health, vocational guidance, child welfare, and home economics, as well as the usual rent collection and maintenance problems." Only such multi-talented staff members through their weekly visiting would be able to aid tenants. NYCHA board member Charney Vladeck, a well-known socialist, disagreed with the proposal, but Lumsden prevailed.[14]

By 1938 the Hill system was in place at First Houses, Harlem River Houses, and Williamsburg Houses. Lumsden boasted of a "two year 100% collection record at First Houses, which uses the personal collection method." Best of all, "the weekly home visits permit the manager or management assistants to learn of tenants' difficulties." Visitors could address family issues and help those tenants "who blew out pilot lights;

who didn't know how to flush toilets that had no chains; who thought the toilet was an incinerator." Lumsden believed that "weekly visits . . . enabled [management] to adjust these matters promptly and tactfully." The six housing assistants at Williamsburg Houses not only collected rent and filed repair slips but also played a role in social service referral, interior decoration, employment aid, and multifarious community activities.[15]

Reflecting Hill's gendered concept, until 1940 the test for housing assistant was open only to women because Lumsden believed that women naturally had a better feeling for family life. The first housing assistants from the 1930s were not necessarily as refined as Lumsden had hoped, but she was, according to an early NYCHA staff member, "stuck with them" and shaped them into a tough rent collection team. Men came on board after 1940 to augment the women, but Lumsden never warmed to them.[16]

One of the first male housing assistants believed that a new kind of paternalism seemed to be substituted for the old: "All that they talked about, not being paternalistic, it was in many, many ways paternalistic because you're really observing the behavior and activities of the tenants." The weekly rent collection had the added benefit of allowing the assistants "to observe what was going on in the apartment, they kept close tabs on the tenants."[17]

Catherine Lansing (who came to NYCHA with experience gained from the Christadora Settlement House) recorded the methods of various rent collectors in the early 1940s and found great variation. Some women had a "nice manner" and knew the families well. Other housing assistants, particularly men, lacked a decent doorside manner. Of one, she said, "no amount of training . . . would offset a shyness and lack of understanding which he evidences." This particular collector had no interest in his families and did not respond to a dirty apartment. Furthermore, Lansing reported, "A number of collections were made without one word being spoken. . . . We might as well have the deaf, dumb, and blind collecting rent."[18]

Lumsden might claim, "We don't snoop around or pry into your private life after you have moved in," but tenants did not necessarily see it this way.[19] The Harlem River Residents Association complained vehemently: "We demand a stop to the notorious system started by Mrs. Lumsden giving permission to rent collectors to enter the tenant apartments in the event the tenants are not home. . . . It violates the principle of 'privacy in your home' and is ILLEGAL." The association reminded NYCHA officials that they lived in a housing project, "not a concentration camp." It demanded that the authority shift to office collection. Racial tensions likely exacerbated the humiliating aspects of the system at Harlem River Houses. The City-Wide Tenants Council, which endeavored to represent NYCHA tenants as well as those in private housing, at first lobbied against the system.[20]

Tenants could be ignored, but Lumsden constantly found herself defending the system to skeptical NYCHA administrators. The policy was a foreign import, an oddity that in spite of its demonstrated management benefits could become another political liability for the authority should its procedures and costs be investigated by the press. In 1938, in response to Chairman Alfred Rheinstein's concerns, Lumsden talked to managers of New York philanthropic properties to get their opinions of the system. She discovered, lo and behold, "There was a unanimous opinion on the superiority of the weekly payments over monthly payments."[21]

The authority again considered changing policies in 1940. The new chairman, Gerard Swope, worried that the system was expensive because of extra staffing; visits increased maintenance complaints; and NYCHA board members thought that it would lead to paternalism. Tenants also seemed to be prepaying their rents, an indication of rising wages during the war years. Lumsden, who remained the system's great defender, was again assigned to look into the situation. As proof of its value, she claimed that NYCHA's rental delinquency rate was half that of the national average. The city's Department of Investigation had found, too, that not only were the "tenants . . . frequently willing to confide in them [the collectors] when they need help," but that NYCHA's excellent rent collection record could be linked to weekly personal collection.[22]

Lumsden's report obviously aimed to justify the system but never demonstrated more than a correlation between collection style and collection rates. The authority's tenants were already so carefully selected that friendly visiting could be viewed as overkill. The authority, against Lumsden's advice, began switching from door collection in 1940 at Williamsburg Houses and Queensbridge Houses. By 1944, the authority reported using a weekly rent collection policy that still yielded high collection rates, even though it now collected rents weekly at the management office. By 1946, the authority had even decided that monthly office collection would suffice. In retrospect, it is hard to believe that the friendly visitor system survived as long as it did.[23]

The Citizens Housing Council appointed a special committee to look into the policy change. The committee's report acknowledged that central office collection was "inescapable if the management assistants are required to collect as many as 500 rents per week" (in new, large housing projects such as Queensbridge Houses), but it still mourned the end of the Octavia Hill philosophy. Adjusting to public housing after the slums would always be difficult and "this reeducation can be accomplished only by an understanding and sympathetic approach." Officials of the CHC still believed that "the slum condition is not changed merely by the provision of better physical shelter. To economize on the management staff charged with the social aspects of housing is to defeat one of the main purposes of subsidized housing."[24] The City-Wide Tenants Council, which had once found much fault with the system, now reported in 1941 that tenants missed the visits by the staff, who would "take an interest in and help solve their problems."[25]

Such heartfelt comments had little effect, but they highlight the alternative that NYCHA declined to pursue. The authority refused to believe that it, as the city's housing service, had the responsibility for social services. The growing size of the projects, in particular, made it difficult to maintain such a fine-grained, high-intensity approach. By the 1980s, however, New York would begin backsliding toward this once discredited model of direct social management, albeit with a narrow focus on troubled families.

The absence of community and social resources has been one of many disappointments associated with public housing in most American cities. With barely enough money to build the projects in the first place, and strict federal limits on spending for community programs, housing authorities could hardly be expected to plan for neighborhood life as well. American cities were not, after all, Red Vienna, whose public housing projects, the vanguard of a socialist utopia, featured everything from childcare to cooperative stores and restaurants. New York, however, began experimentation in community operations in the prewar period that laid the groundwork for the massive postwar boom. New York, in particular, benefited enormously both from expanding city services and from a rich nonprofit context for co-sponsorship.[26]

Even many housing advocates at first rejected an extravagant set of project-based services. The architect Frederick Ackerman wrote to Chairman Langdon Post in 1937 averring that the authority's true function was "to provide habitations of reasonable standards at minimum cost-of-use." Inflated cost "arises out of the current concept that housing should be not only the provision of habitations but it should be also education, recreation, sanitation, medication, disease prevention . . . the whole field of welfare."[27] Others sought to limit community facilities to ensure "that low-income families could live in public housing without becoming a group apart."[28]

NYCHA leaders such as Post knew full well, however, that there were risks to avoiding community programs entirely. How could low-income families not become distinct when their neighborhoods had been designed to be so different? Furthermore, administrators knew that the tenement dwellers had already lacked what many middle-class reformers

considered to be *wholesome* recreational options. Chairman Alfred Rheinstein was not being frank, for instance, when he remarked, "These
families don't have the money to spend on commercial recreation, and
provision of means of relief from the monotony of the type of work they
do is essential for normal life."[29] The chairman knew full well that the
bedrock of working-class leisure in New York had been the saloon, a
community feature conveniently missing from NYCHA's tidy superblocks even though they were built after Prohibition's repeal. These
housing reformers, it seemed, aimed to divert youth and adults perma-
nently from saloons, street corners, penny arcades, and dance halls by
never putting any of these institutions into their projects. So, in the end,
New York pursued community and social programs in spite of many
reservations about their cost and social value.[30]

New York's philanthropic and limited-dividend housing had pioneered an impressive level of social innovation from which NYCHA
could draw. Official NYCHA records attribute credit to Abraham Goldfeld, who had introduced community programs at the philanthropic
project on the Lower East Side known as Lavanburg Houses. It was he
who encouraged early NYCHA managers to establish sports, crafts, and
cultural activities in public housing. Goldfeld had social control in
mind: "Anyone experienced in slum life knows that when the children
in the streets have run through their brief repertory of legitimate play,
they turn to less legitimate forms of expenditure of energy." For adults,
too, he prophesized that "the absence of a chance for decent social in-
tercourse" might lead to more conflict.[31]

The Hillside Homes development equally influenced NYCHA. This attractive development boasted a large auditorium, twelve clubrooms,
craft workshops, a community kitchen, a nursery school, a playground,
wading pools, and smaller play areas. Hillside's sponsors provided these
generous facilities but aimed primarily, in their words, for "a setting for
a normal community life" and did "not presume to dictate . . . community life." They thus provided only one staff person to facilitate tenant activism and let the tenants develop their own programs. The working-
and middle-class families joined a great variety of their own organizations. A community like this, with active parenting (and stay-at-home
mothers) had little need for a true community recreation program.[32]

Langdon Post had fewer reservations about community planning than
many of his colleagues. The *New York Times* reported in 1934 that Post
predicted that "the work of the Municipal Housing Authority will go far
beyond the mere purchase of land and erection of model dwelling structures" to include "the operation and management of the communities
created." Mary Simkhovitch, a great advocate of community activity at
Greenwich House, could also be counted on during this time to lend

support and attract outside agencies to the authority's efforts. The proof of Post's and Simkhovitch's support for community planning can be seen in the power NYCHA gave to remarkable women who undertook the actual creation of programs: May Lumsden (the director of tenant relations) and Catherine Lansing (the executive director of community planning).[33]

Catherine Lansing formulated the compelling domestic ideology that offered a middle route between excessive community planning and no planning at all. Public housing, to Lansing, was more than average city shelter because public "housing seeks to restore in some degree the values lost through urbanization." In the city "the chief losers are children. In the small town, they play in their own yard. . . . In the city, they play in the street." Reflecting the characteristic modernist distaste for the street, she argued that in housing projects supervised "playgrounds are established as a community substitute for the back yard, the climbing apparatus for the trees and hay lofts of a normal childhood."[34] Catherine Lansing had visited Hillside in 1935 and was impressed by the large auditorium, the club rooms, the nursery, and the carefully planned exterior recreation spaces—she would work to bring these to NYCHA projects.[35]

Harlem River Houses reflected the most generous approach to community facilities in the early projects. The architects, reported the *New York Times*, "have planned some novel features such as a fully equipped clinic, a supervised nursery for the care of children, a wading pool, a playground along the waterfront, and an 'amphitheatre' seating 250 persons." In addition, NYCHA provided four community rooms for general use. Mayor La Guardia justified these facilities by associating them with a vision of home: "We are going to give the people who live in this project real homes in a community they can take pride in." The essential elements present at Harlem River became standard in many NYCHA projects—even before administrators fully admitted to taking a more ambitious social position in the 1950s.[36]

Nurseries, a specialized service rarely found in apartment buildings, became a part of NYCHA's early projects, in spite of some initial trepidation that they represented excessive social programming (Figure 12).[37] At Williamsburg Houses a child-care program developed in the 1930s because of actions by an outside agency, the Brooklyn Free Kindergarten Society. The service, which cost a modest five cents per day per child, was well received by the parents and fully subscribed.[38]

The Brooklyn Free Kindergarten Society would expand to other Brooklyn projects such as Fort Greene and Red Hook. The New York Kindergarten Association ran the early programs at Harlem River and East River. By 1943, the authority had twenty-eight children's centers in

Figure 12. NYCHA encouraged the establishment of nurseries at South Jamaica Houses (1940) and in its other developments. La Guardia Wagner Archive/NYCHA Photograph Collection.

city and state projects with a capacity of almost two thousand children. All were operated by private agencies supported by a mix of private, state, and city funds and a small tuition; NYCHA, however, not only provided the space but offered daily cleaning, free rent, heat, and utilities.[39]

Public housing became an ideal place for New Deal experiments in additional health and educational service. Mary Simkhovitch, whose Greenwich House had pioneered an infant welfare clinic in the early twentieth century, strongly urged the authority in 1935 to put a baby health station in First Houses. Indeed, the New York City Health Department, under La Guardia's expanding social priorities, did just that. Health centers then grew in step with the authority. Health officials considered NYCHA buildings superior to derelict, often dangerous, former commercial space. The expansion of health services with public housing made sense from a historical point of view. Revisions in housing law had been in large measure rooted in the notion that poor housing bred disease. Senior services, to provide caring for the quietly suffering elderly in poor neighborhoods, would later be added to project facilities by the city government.[40]

The settlement houses near developments also "cooperated wholeheartedly in offering their facilities to the tenants" because "the settlement workers realize that here at last is a group of people who have a chance to carry home and practice, twenty-four hours a day, the recipes for better living that they learn at the settlements."[41] At Vladeck Houses, for instance, the Henry Street Settlement staff designed "Home Planning Workshops . . . organized around the idea of providing a consumer service for the residents." Facilities included an experimental kitchen, a furniture-refinishing workshop, and a shoe repair shop.[42]

NYCHA steadfastly supported externally sponsored community activities like these. The authority so heavily subsidized external social service organizations at its developments, by offering free space, cleaning, supplies, heat, and utilities, that the independence of these external agencies seems doubtful on close examination. A report from 1945 reflects this broad vision: "While the Authority has limited its responsibility to providing and designing the space in which these programs are conducted, we have tended generally toward broad rather than narrow lines in our interpretation of this policy." The authority not only provided the space and looked after its maintenance, but also furnished the centers with tables, chairs, and outdoor playground equipment. Administrators did, however, draw the line at providing items such as toys, pictures, and books for specific programs. In retrospect, this does not appear to be much of a line.[43]

Early public housing projects featured wide-ranging activities, but they all lacked one element that would come to be a standard furnishing at projects—the free-standing community center. NYCHA constructed its first free-standing community building at the Red Hook Houses (1938) in Brooklyn; before, community facilities had been carved out in basements or assorted rooms. The Red Hook center, however, included "three buildings grouped in a U-shape, the unit is to include a recreation building [with a large assembly hall and numerous smaller meeting rooms] . . . a children's center and a row of eight stores." Queensbridge, its sister project, featured a central plaza with a free-standing community center and nursery school grouped together with a few stores.[44]

This shift to free-standing community center buildings emerged from a number of sources. Administrators acknowledged that community centers in basements had already proved unattractive. Red Hook Houses and Queensbridge Houses, enormous projects constructed in areas bereft of indoor recreational facilities, also needed a community focus. Economizing, of which both Red Hook and Queensbridge were stellar examples, contributed to the shift. Red Hook was built on swampy land and it would have been expensive to build basements; in fact, "part of the cost of building an independent community center in Red Hook will be saved by the fact that there will not be a full basement."[45] The growing scale of the housing projects facilitated free-standing community centers. Federal projects, for instance, allocated funds for community facilities in proportion to the number of total units in the project. Thousands of units per project thus generated ample funding.[46]

Both the state and federal governments nevertheless provided next to nothing for *staffing* of recreation programs. The USHA, for instance, did not allow local authorities "to pay for face-to-face leadership of recreation activities since such expense would increase the tenants' rent, whereas the burden should be on the whole community." This restriction in principle meant that recreation would develop inconsistently, if at all, in public housing developments. The free-standing community center buildings, while understaffed, did increase the scale and identity of community programs; forced NYCHA to pay attention to community programs or face embarrassingly empty buildings; and provided a barometer of the authority's commitment to community life.[47]

A WPA survey of housing programs in 1940 revealed a system with two unequal tracks. On one side were Harlem River, Williamsburg, and First Houses, all of which "had inadequate space and facilities." By 1940 First Houses apparently lacked any recreation program at all. Recreation programs at Williamsburg had shifted to a nearby school where space was better, and Harlem River's programs may have been popular but were cramped. On the other side were the projects with separate community centers run by community associations guided by external social agencies. Red Hook had full staffing, hundreds of participants, many clubs, and its community center building was commodious. Although it too faced a questionable future with the loss of WPA workers and limited grant money, the fact that nine hundred families had registered with its community center made its survival likely. Queensbridge, too, had financial problems, but it boasted "a coordinated and integrated program" and its community space, the only one in its neighborhood, was swamped with participants.[48]

The Queensbridge and Red Hook community centers became the future model of NYCHA community planning, but even they were not shaping up as the authority had hoped. The basic staffing of these nicely provisioned centers proved overwhelming for the independent community organizations set up to run them. Queensbridge tenants complained that "delegating the function of conducting community activities in the projects to private agencies, whose budgets and staffs are not adequate to cope with the needs of project tenants, is not sound."[49] In 1941 the authority decided to subsidize the community associations rather than let them fail. A 1941 internal report thus recommended that nonprofits "be confined to planning, to experimentation . . . to supplementation of the recreational activities of the project and not to routine operation of its facilities."[50]

Robert Moses considered assuming responsibility for recreation in public housing during these difficult times, even though he was opposed to the very idea of special recreational activities for public housing residents. In a 1940 letter to the state commissioner of housing, for instance, he expressed the "gravest doubt as to the necessity and desirability of providing indoor recreation facilities for those who live in the housing projects. This seems to me to involve discrimination against others and almost always means duplication of public facilities in the school or park system or the neighborhood."[51]

Moses' staff nevertheless investigated the state of community centers and found that "the operation and maintenance of the recreational facilities in the housing developments is not comparable to our standards."[52] A later report found that in most projects "tenants . . . don't seem to use the facilities very much."[53] The Parks Department staff recommended that they take over the recreational programs. Catherine Lansing, in obvious frustration, welcomed such a change because of the "difficulties of the Housing Authority in securing private sponsorship in the areas in which they had built their large jobs." Moses, however, would only undertake recreation programs with city funding, which apparently was not forthcoming. The recreation programs, with a few exceptions, thus continued to limp along.[54]

In its early projects NYCHA aimed to stimulate tenant activism, but officials believed just as strongly that such activism should be limited to a narrow range of expression. To the extent that the city's municipal services such as schools, subways, and hospitals were politically neutral, so too would be public housing. NYCHA based its policy on precedents from limited-dividend and philanthropic projects. Hillside Homes, for instance, prohibited sectarian or partisan organizations because of the management's belief that the community was a collection of homes rather than a self-sufficient community. Limited-dividend companies such as the City and Suburban Homes Corporation and the Fred French Company (of Knickerbocker Village) faced well-organized tenant organizing in the Depression that challenged management supremacy.[55]

NYCHA gazed fondly only upon project-based community associations. At First Houses a tenant association formed with the goal of organizing community activities such as holiday parties, a tenant newsletter, and other community recreation. The *New York Times* found that at First Houses the association organized "forums on socialized medicine, nationalism and politics," but the organization did not weigh in on major NYCHA policies, nor was the discussion run to advance a particular political organization.[56]

NYCHA, however, could ill afford to have its housing developments chock full of radical activity; one of the criticisms of European social housing had been its political usefulness to socialist parties. The line between the authority's enhanced progressivism and socialism was fuzzy enough; tenant activism threatened to tip the scales too far. At Vladeck Houses, for instance, the tenant organization seemed to be "conducted on party (that is, communist) rather than on pure neighborhood lines. It was extremely active, held many meetings, and swayed a strong influence."[57] Nor was NYCHA, rooted in traditional Progressive values that emphasized expert opinion, interested in negotiating with tenants. The leftist City-Wide Tenants Council, the self-appointed voice of public housing tenants (although not exclusively a public housing organization), might have believed "citizens who move into housing projects do not thereby sacrifice any of their general rights and obligations," but NYCHA did not agree.[58]

The authority not only refused to deal with the City-Wide Tenants Council as the common voice of tenants but also continued to limit political organizing in public housing. Administrators at Queensbridge Houses in 1941, for instance, singled out and nixed a leftist American Labor Party meeting because, it said, "We do not accommodate religious or political groups."[59] NYCHA administrators only allowed "open meetings for a general interchange of views on political subjects" but thought "it unwise to assign community space to any one political party for a rally or meeting."[60] By reducing partisanship, restrictions on political and religious speech in the housing projects seemed successful to housing administrators, but these limitations made housing projects even more alienated from mainstream American communities.

The 1930s and 1940s taught NYCHA about the possibilities and limits of daily management. The establishment of large, qualified staffs at the new projects was in retrospect a remarkable sleight of hand. Shifting high-class apartment management standards to housing for the working class and poor proved to be an excellent idea. Other cities never made this transition and paid the price in the long term. Nothing less than a high level of staffing and control, still largely in place today, seems to work for preserving public housing. Far less successful was the extreme paternalism of the friendly visitors and so it was abandoned.

NYCHA's developments, in time, also included social service programs sponsored by settlement houses and the city government that indicated broader social concerns. Small community centers, while underfunded, already seemed more successful than the basement rooms in the early projects and would become the postwar standard. It seems doubtful that these centers were better than bars, churches, and informal social clubs when it came to building a strong community, but as a demonstration of the authority's sense of social responsibility they set an important precedent for the more troubled postwar era. Other housing authorities in these early years tended to share NYCHA's interest in tight management and community affairs; alas, very few authorities sustained their efforts in the long term.

Part II
Transforming Postwar New York

Chapter 6
The Boom Years

The contrast between public housing management in New York and other cities became obvious in the postwar decades, in spite of the fact that many cities built projects that superficially resembled the towers that the New York City Housing Authority had pioneered. It was during the postwar period when most housing authorities began the downward spiral that culminated in nightmarish housing projects and the discrediting of public housing. One of the primary reasons that New York, in spite of building ever more high-rise superblocks, remained America's best high-rise housing authority in the 1960s is that its longtime patron, the vilified master builder Robert Moses, had done much to preserve the authority as a large, competent housing organization during the 1940s and 1950s.

Moses directed NYCHA's housing program much as he did almost all redevelopment in the 1940s and 1950s. Compared to his signature work in transportation, urban renewal, and parks, he left little of his personal imprint on the housing authority. Moses certainly picked top executives loyal to him, but he primarily inflated NYCHA's size without changing its internal methods. Moses had, after all, stumbled upon an authority that had pioneered the high-rise, low-cost modern tower-block communities he had come to favor for rebuilding New York as a modern metropolis. The public housing program also, in theory at least, provided a necessary adjunct to his vast urban renewal schemes that displaced hundreds of thousands of New Yorkers. NYCHA was, finally, a relatively efficient civil service public authority of the type that he had long advocated.[1]

Moses did not love public housing and showed little concern for destroying vibrant neighborhoods, but he believed in public sector competence. NYCHA's boom years were better than those in other cities because its projects were better built, the tenants more carefully selected, and the buildings better managed than those in other cities. In most American cities public housing was not only poorly constructed and maintained but became the housing of last resort for those displaced for urban renewal.

Most American cities took a breather from public housing during the war years and before the passage of the Housing Act of 1949. New York, in contrast, did not dally. NYCHA's epic postwar program actually fell into place long before the nation's guns grew cold. Mayor La Guardia's unswerving ambition became the most important pillar of the program. He bragged that in 1942, New York, thanks to Robert Moses, already had in the works "the largest post-war program of any city in the country. . . ." The minute we get material we can start to build," he said.[2] La Guardia preferred to ramp up so many projects that when the war was over, New York would be far ahead of its rivals in New York State. By 1943 he was counting in the postwar program eight state projects and one federal project, "the greatest program ever prepared at one time," and one that would absorb an immodest $108 million in spending. The bulk of postwar planning was, per general agreement between the NYCHA and Moses, focused on low-income tenement districts such as Brownsville and East Harlem.[3]

New York's postwar housing goals paralleled European postwar efforts in replanning and public housing rather than those of its mousey sister cities in the United States. Public housing in New York had become an accepted municipal enterprise that would be part of a new and better city. The historian Fred Siegel believes that Mayor La Guardia aimed "to make New York a living example of social democracy" in the United States through the creation of a "permanent New Deal." The liberal atmosphere of 1940s New York bolstered La Guardia's vision—even after he had left office.[4]

NYCHA could count on support not only from traditional supporters such as unions and the Community Service Society, but also on the Chamber of Commerce of the State of New York, which was eager for economic stimulus. More remarkable was the evaporation of opposition. In an astonishing about-face real estate interests even participated in the Housing Week sponsored by local housing advocates. Through the 1940s and 1950s, in fact, NYCHA—protected by Robert Moses and liberal local voters—largely dodged the public red-baiting that compromised public housing in cities such as Los Angeles.[5]

New York's postwar housing program was closely linked to a general municipal building drive of $680 million that would effect all phases of life and included new schools, hospitals, police stations, airport expansion, sewers, highways, and parks. New York would not only provide employment to returning soldiers but would indeed become the modern city progressives imagined. By 1945 the projected housing program alone had grown to $260 million to be funded by state and federal monies. Mayor La Guardia hoped to double the number of units *in just three years*. State projects included in this plan would indeed move ahead,

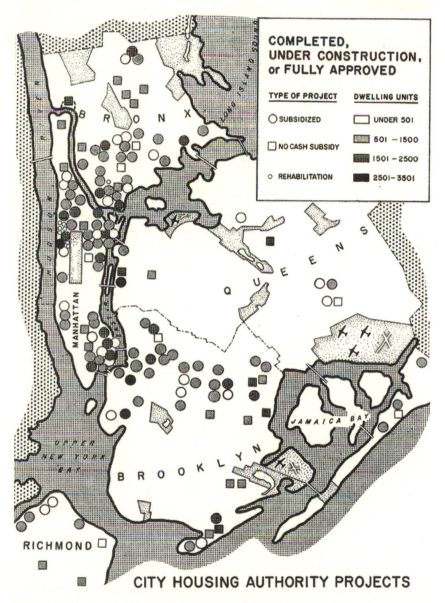

COMPLETED,
UNDER CONSTRUCTION,
or FULLY APPROVED

TYPE OF PROJECT	DWELLING UNITS
○ SUBSIDIZED	☐ UNDER 501
☐ NO CASH SUBSIDY	▨ 501 – 1500
∘ REHABILITATION	▨ 1501 – 2500
	■ 2501 – 3501

CITY HOUSING AUTHORITY PROJECTS

Figure 13. This map illustrates the variety of public housing funding sources in New York. Public housing in New York may have been concentrated in traditional slum areas, but large projects could be found outside these zones too. "No cash subsidy" refers to city-sponsored projects. "Subsidized" includes both state and federal projects. *Department of City Planning Newsletter*, February 1961, Box 89A5, Folder 5, NYCHAR.

but federal projects (accounting for roughly half of the program) would not be approved until 1949 (Figure 13).[6]

Robert Moses emerged as one of the city's greatest housing advocates in this period, particularly once he had installed NYCHA administrators sympathetic to his vision. Moses had spent much of the 1930s accusing NYCHA administrators of incompetence and personally doubted the social wisdom of housing projects, but in truth he found public housing useful for his grand planning. Moses discovered that public housing served two important functions: slum clearance for itself and as projected catchments for those displaced for his other urban renewal projects.[7]

Moses at first resisted a new source of support for public housing, the postwar housing crisis, because he never accepted the reality of a housing shortage in the first place. In 1945, for instance, he remarked that veterans could find housing in summer cottages in the Rockaways or less-than-perfect urban and suburban rooms. This would be preferable to "tents, shacks and other silly devices suggested by hysterical reformers."[8] Most New Yorkers did not agree with Moses and publications across the city and country wondered how America would house its returning veterans in already crowded cities. The postwar housing crisis handed housing advocates, and ultimately Moses, a new justification for housing now that employment remained high.

Liberals viewed the housing crisis as just another example of private sector failure. During the 1930s, while private building had slowly gathered steam, insufficient new housing had been built; wartime rationing and postwar shortages further limited housing construction. By 1945, cities such as New York had what appeared to most observers to be a housing crisis as veterans returned and started families. Housing advocates could now draw on general anxiety about a lack of housing across a much wider cross section of New York society. One figure at the time estimated that in 1945, of 2,255,850 dwellings in New York City, only 2,000 vacancies could be found.[9]

Mayor William O'Dwyer, who was elected in 1945, launched record numbers of housing projects because he believed, as a left-leaning politician, that big government programs could resolve this crisis. O'Dwyer was so successful, according to Fred Siegel, that he would win "reelection in 1949 because of his boast that he had held off economic collapse by building a new school and a new housing project in every month of his term."[10] O'Dwyer could plan for public housing when no other city could because of the existing city and state programs. He even exchanged support for Governor Dewey's New York State Thruway in order to accelerate the city's housing program. In the long term this deal would pay off handsomely.[11]

In 1945 Mayor O'Dwyer made Moses the head of the Emergency Committee on Housing. The report by the committee found that although 23 projects (for 120,000 people) were in the works, a minimum of 150,000 units of public housing might be needed. The committee called for an expansion in state aid to pay for this expanded program. While the committee, essentially Moses, still believed "all groups beyond those of lowest income in theory should be provided for by private or redevelopment capital," it was not confident that private capital would be able to build housing for below $12.50 a room. The committee called for "additional public housing for persons of the upper bracket of the lowest-income group." Public housing for the better-off segment of the working class was not, however, a priority of Moses and would remain unfulfilled for some years.[12]

In the short term, the city was urged to and did move into the creation of temporary housing units for discharged servicemen and their families. The federal government provided temporary housing and Quonset huts for this purpose at locations around the city; NYCHA supervised the housing. By 1947, approximately 8,600 tenants resided in these temporary facilities. The program lasted until 1953, when most veterans had moved into their own housing or into NYCHA's traditional projects.[13]

It was during this housing crisis that Robert Moses gained control over the authority's direction through his many positions. He already exercised great power through his position on the City Planning Commission, but by 1948 he had become the chairman of the Mayor's Committee on Slum Clearance and the coordinator of City Construction, positions that essentially extended his power over all of the city's capital activities. Moses personally selected sites for the state housing program and would eventually sign off on all NYCHA housing projects through the 1950s.[14] Moses' biographer Robert Caro reports that in spite of the fact that one finds "hardly a mention of Robert Moses" in newspaper articles treating NYCHA in the 1950s, "Not a brick of one of those housing projects was laid without his approval."[15]

Moses became so ambitious in housing proposals that authority administrators on occasion had to temper his enthusiasm. By 1946 he was calling for a housing program that through a mixture of private and public efforts would house 1,286,400 people as early as 1949. Maxwell Tretter, the executive director of NYCHA, called Moses' plan "overoptimistic" based on the fact that few projects could actually be completed in such a short period of time. The fact that any federal public housing was at that point only conjectural also dimmed hopes of meeting such a schedule.[16]

Moses continued to trim his sails to match the changing political winds. Mayor O'Dwyer, who was under pressure from veterans and tenant activists, remained more committed than Moses to building for the "lower middle income" and sought city bonds to build higher-end public units on primarily vacant sites.[17] NYCHA chairman, Edmond Butler, had already proposed that the authority move into "unsubsidized" housing using authority bonds and partial tax exemption for rents at $10 per room for "'forgotten' family groups with incomes too high for subsidized public housing but too low for tenancy in privately-built apartments."[18] Moses blinked. He admitted in 1948, "I have certainly changed my mind . . . in regard to partially subsidized or so-called unsubsidized public housing." He "saw no alternative at the moment because of very high construction costs and the plight of those who are ineligible for subsidized public housing."[19] By 1947, the first city-aided program (City Part I), which was funded from the occupancy tax, had built only twenty-five hundred units in four projects; another five more were underway with limited subsidy in the late 1940s (and were known as City Part II). The new and far larger housing program launched in 1948 became known as unsubsidized city-aided public housing, or City Part III[20] (see Appendix A).

NYCHA placed many of these city-backed developments on vacant land in the outer boroughs and they were known for a long time as higher-income, primarily white projects. Lower-rise developments (six to eight stories) like these proved ideal for middle-class neighborhoods already showing resistance to low-income housing (Figure 14). At least ostensibly they also provided Moses with a destination for higher-income site tenants displaced for redevelopment and highway construction. The initial fifteen projects (costing $200 million total) achieved rents estimated at $17 per room per month. In 1952 Moses even suggested six additional developments that were also approved. By 1965 the city housing programs had brought forth thirty-six developments with approximately thirty-four thousand units.[21]

In 1947, lobbying also began for an increase in the amount of money available in the state program, in part because of rising construction costs. A statewide referendum in the fall of 1947 approved $135 million additional dollars and an annual subsidy limit of $13 million. The measure faced some opposition by real estate interests, but it passed nevertheless. By 1947, the city had completed fourteen large state projects for sixty thousand people, eight projects were under construction, and six more were in the planning phase. By 1965 the state program included forty-eight developments with nearly fifty-two thousand units. Although built to lower standards than the city program, state developments initially provided NYCHA with greater income flexibility than the federal program allowed.[22]

Figure 14. Eastchester Houses (1950) in the Bronx, like many city-sponsored projects, was characterized by medium-scale buildings set comfortably in abundant and well-planted open space. La Guardia Wagner Archive/NYCHA Photograph Collection.

Consolidating Power

New York had obviously made great strides in launching a housing program, even with infighting behind the scenes. In 1946, however, Moses demanded that Chairman "Butler be replaced by a full time man. He can't give enough time."[23] Mayor O'Dwyer, acting on Robert Moses' suggestion, aimed for a comprehensive reorganization of the NYCHA board in 1947. The mayor desired to reduce the number of members to three, one of which (the new chairman) would be a full-time salaried expert with a construction background. O'Dwyer admitted that he aimed to "have the cooperation of an agency whose members were his own appointees." In other words, he wanted to purge members of the board picked by Mayor La Guardia.[24]

By March 1947, with a revised O'Dwyer bill set to pass, Butler announced his intention to retire. Significant opposition to the reorganization plan mounted from those who thought that the new chairman's position would be too narrowly defined to construction issues; from financial institutions that worried about mayoral control of such a major organization; and from others who worried that O'Dwyer intended to place Moses in another position. Governor Dewey nevertheless signed the Steingut Bill that gave O'Dwyer the power to appoint a full-time chairman, but the final legislation left the larger board in place.[25]

Mayor O'Dwyer, on Moses' advice, selected Major General Thomas Farrell as chairman in Butler's place. Farrell neatly fit the bill of a seasoned construction professional who knew how to get "big things done without undue delay." He had been the chief engineer of the New York State Department of Public Works before his war service, thus making him an associate of Moses.[26] Farrell immediately began a reorganization of the authority to bring it in line with "the city administration and the State Housing Authority." Say what you will about Farrell as a Moses man, he knew how to move a project forward and presided over a growing public housing boom that brought forth record numbers of bland, solidly constructed buildings.[27]

Few were surprised when Maxwell Tretter, the executive director of the authority, resigned, as did a number of other longtime administrators—Moses had targeted them for removal. NYCHA board members allowed Farrell to make his technocratic, Moses-friendly appointments, including most notably Philip Cruise as secretary. Cruise had worked closely with Moses at the Parks Department and would become chairman in 1951. According to Warren Moscow, who served as the executive director in the 1950s, "Cruise wouldn't go to the bathroom unless he asked Moses first."[28] O'Dwyer finally got majority control of the NYCHA board when Mary Simkhovitch stepped down at the end of her term in

1948. In her place O'Dwyer appointed his loyal friend Thomas Shanahan, a local banker, Tammany stalwart, and associate of Robert Moses. Shanahan, unfortunately, would use his NYCHA connections for personal and political kickbacks.[29]

Under Farrell's leadership the authority launched a record numbers of projects, in spite of upward spiraling costs and strict cost limits. NYCHA only could achieve high numbers with renewed levels of economy. The authority continued its policies of minimal interior furnishings, its towers rose higher, and the design department reproduced architectural plans at different sites. Farrell could claim at the end of 1948 that "more projects to provide homes . . . were started by the NYCHA in the year 1948 than in any other single year since the Authority was organized." That year alone fifteen projects to house sixty thousand people were launched; the city funded ten of the fifteen while the state paid for the remaining five. So much local activity, according to Chairman Farrell, "was made possible by the determination of the City administration to make the fullest use of its housing powers."[30] Nor did the pace slacken in 1949 on state and city projects. By early 1949 projects underway would eventually house a quarter of a million people, or 3 percent of the city's population. NYCHA even got another bump when a referendum authorized $300 million more for the state program in 1949. By 1953, 80 percent of residents in public housing funded by New York State could be found in New York City.[31]

New York's administrators could make do without federal funds, but their ambition far exceeded sources of city and state funding. New York thus became an important force in lobbying for the Taft-Wagner-Ellender bill, which became the Housing Act of 1949, the first (nondefense) federal money for low-income public housing since 1937. Conservative Democrats and Republicans, who were influenced by business interests opposed to public housing and their own antisocialist sentiment, had effectively bottled up public housing after the war. Not even Truman's support could prevail until his surprise re-election in 1948. The legislation that emerged in 1949 was less than many housing advocates wanted, emphasized private-sector redevelopment, and provided funds at very low levels per unit, but it did promise an ambitious 810,000 units by 1955. New York became the largest single recipient of new housing funds from the federal government, receiving $99,464,000 for construction of approximately 60,000 additional units and $4,475,880 in annual subsidies. With the new federal and state programs, New York now planned to house half a million tenants in 135,000 apartments, a target figure that had doubled in just a few years. NYCHA would meet these figures, but it took longer than it planned.[32]

The Cold War suddenly intruded on the planners' dreams. The Korean

War emergency shrank New York's program when Truman slashed housing funds in 1950. Federal projects stalled out between 1950 and 1953
and New York was unable to meet its targets. By one reckoning, the authority built only one-third of the original 60,000 federal units. Nationally the story was much the same. The war took away Chairman Thomas
Farrell, who re-entered the military, and his assistant, Philip Cruise, took
his place in 1951. With Cruise on top, Robert Moses' influence at the authority reached its peak.[33]

New York, unlike other cities, moved ahead during the war years with
planning for federal projects and continued construction on its projects
funded out of city or state sources. By 1952, the majority of NYCHA's
265,000 residents (in sixty-eight projects) lived in state- and city-sponsored
developments. NYCHA bonds remained attractive to investors and by
1955 private investors had invested approximately $965 million in them.[34]

When Congress did release the flow of public housing funds after the
war, NYCHA consumed a remarkable proportion of the total. Of the approximate 35,000 units approved nationally in 1955, for instance,
NYCHA received 8,000. The total federal program remained comparatively small because the Eisenhower administration viewed public housing provisions in the Housing Act of 1954 as a necessary evil demanded
by large-scale urban redevelopment. Eventually the authority would
have its half million residents, but only in the 1960s.[35]

The dominance of NYCHA by a Moses man had become essential because Moses badly needed public housing as an adjunct to his wider development plans. As he would admit to Arthur Hays Sulzberger, "It is
hardly necessary to tell you that I am not a rabid houser. . . . Nevertheless we must have public housing" because "our private capital slum
clearance requires public housing to take care of displaced tenants of
the lowest incomes."[36] Moses' flashy reports for Title I clearance projects
always included a statement by NYCHA chairmen to the effect that relocation of the poorest tenants was being looked after by the authority. For
Title I sites, NYCHA established an estimated "percentage of site families . . . eligible for relocation in public housing." These figures could
range as high as 60 percent of site tenants from a Harlem site to 15 percent for an urban renewal project in Washington Square South.[37]

By the mid-1950s Moses found himself in a public relations disaster
that NYCHA humanitarianism had not diverted. The 15 percent figure
proved to be the more durable estimate for rehousing urban renewal
site tenants in public housing. As Chapter 9 indicates, Robert Moses permitted the housing authority to tighten its tenant selection standards in
1953, a decision that rendered meaningless the often optimistic statistics
on rehousing that Moses included in his Title I publications. Low federal and state income admission limits, as well as the growing public dis-

taste for public housing, also severely limited tenant relocation to public housing. A range of the city's nonprofit organizations (hospitals, universities, and so forth) had benefited from Moses' redevelopment power, but activists cast new doubts. By 1956 the Community Service Society, among many concerned groups, scored Moses for failing to rehouse the displaced.[38] Moses might remind the public that "Title I was never designed to produce housing for people of low-income," but the cost of his redevelopment schemes in terms of lost housing seemed intolerable.[39]

Displacement caused by NYCHA's own bulldozer approach had also grown as the percentage of site tenants rehoused in public housing dropped over the course of the 1950s. By 1955 NYCHA had cleared five hundred slum sites and demolished fifty-five thousand apartments. That year the authority could claim that its thirty-eight projects underway would house double the number of people who had been displaced. Chairman Cruise also claimed (likely restricting his statistics to projects built between 1950 and 1954) that 40 percent of site tenants actually gained admission to public housing. By 1957, however, *all* NYCHA projects built by that time had been able to house only 18.1 percent of site tenants.[40]

The authority's leaders refused to abandon their claim that whether housed in public housing or not, the majority of the uprooted "are much happier in their new surroundings." Administrators believed that most dislocated site residents, helped by a cash bonus, found lower or comparable rents on standard housing.[41] It is difficult to accept that the tens of thousands of citizens relocated were as grateful as they were made out to be by the authority. To reduce happiness to material factors alone reflects the technocratic, insensitive blind spot of the authority that allowed it to destroy whole neighborhoods. The former administrator William C. Vladeck in 1957 speculated that "most of the accommodations they have found are ones which have resulted from the illegal creation of single-room occupancies." Had the city not been experiencing a massive drain to the suburbs in this era, thus opening up older housing to the displaced, the effects would have been far more noticeable.[42]

Not only the poor felt pinched during this time. Many wealthy developers overlooked low-rent projects because they did not compete with private enterprise, but the higher-income city program had the potential to crowd out their own efforts to house the middle class. According to the Real Estate Board of New York in 1954, NYCHA might "eliminate private enterprise from the middle-income field." It counted 22,400 no-cash subsidy units out of a total 69,400 units in NYCHA's inventory that it thought competed with its own products. It did feel, however, that with similar levels of tax exemption it could produce equally affordable housing. Advocates of the poor, on the other hand, had their doubts about public housing for higher-income New Yorkers.[43]

NYCHA nevertheless continued to build higher-cost, no-subsidy housing for a few more years. Mayor Wagner's administration, after all, was eager to balance a growing sense "that with all the public housing projects going to minority populations, they had better do something for their white constituency, too."[44] Warren Moscow, Wagner's trusted associate at NYCHA, was even more blunt when he admitted in 1956, "Yes, we are definitely in the middle-income housing field."[45] Because the rents in the Mitchell Lama projects (initiated in 1955) were on a par with NYCHA city-funded projects and were built by private developers with state aid, many housing advocates wondered why NYCHA felt moved to build anything but low-income housing. Business interests meanwhile continued their opposition. In 1960 Mayor Wagner, under pressure, announced that the city would sell off eight uncompleted higher-income, city-sponsored NYCHA developments as cooperatives.[46]

Harsh Medicine: Prescription for a Moses-Free Authority

The preceding examples indicate that by the late 1950s NYCHA had become controversial. Dissatisfaction surrounded not only the authority's association with Title I, its relocation policies, and its comparatively higher-income target market, but also mounting social problems, lackluster design, and bulldozer methods (detailed in other chapters). In light of the authority's power over so much of New York's destiny, a shake-up was all but inevitable. What actually spurred the reorganization, however, were fears of communism that were partly inspired by the Cold War.

The explosive Preusse report of 1957 emerged as a harsh vaccine to stave off more damaging investigations planned by political enemies of housing in the state legislature and the U.S. Congress. Anticommunism also gained momentum within the authority itself. Vice Chairman Thomas Shanahan, who was angered by Mayor Wagner's attempts to reign in his use of the authority for personal advantage, made an attempt in 1957 to hire a former FBI agent to investigate loyalty at the authority's highest levels. Shanahan's plan was blocked at the state level but helped fuel suspicion.[47]

One longtime manager, Henry Bresky, believes that the internal McCarthyism at NYCHA received further impetus from the resentment of certain project superintendents, ranked just below managers, who were unable to pass open competitive exams for promotion. They used their union to funnel their resentments and accused managers above them of being "Reds and subversives." They even provided material for a sensationalistic series of articles in the *Daily News*, documenting widespread mismanagement. The superintendents fueled the flames by telling lurid tales of "reds in the Authority and how they were damaging the Authority because of their disloyalty. . . ." The Republican-dominated state legislature threatened to investigate the authority, and housing opponents in Congress appeared eager to investigate.[48]

The city government and NYCHA had to address these attacks on both loyalty and competence. In 1957, a comprehensive city-sponsored investigation of NYCHA by the city investigator Charles Tenney snared few communists, however, yielding only four resignations and three dismissals out of fifty-eight hundred employees. Mayor Wagner, at the authority's bidding, in 1957 also appointed his own investigating team, headed by Charles Preusse, to look into management complaints. Preusse and his experts dug deeply into NYCHA operations, with NYCHA's aid, and the final report offered harsh appraisals.[49]

Preusse found "grave management defects that cry for correction. . . . A substantial part of the Housing Authority's management structure will need overhauling." The report, however, identified no outright corruption or any true incompetence. The worse that could be said of its governing board was that the "authority's members had not exercised strong control over the agency's operations"; and that high-ranking administrators rarely inspected projects to determine conditions. The report itself admitted that the authority faced "problems of staggering difficulty and complexity." On a more positive note, the report identified only five projects (out of eighty) as being in serious disrepair while another third simply had growing vandalism problems. Compared to the well-documented problems of housing authorities in other cities by this time, these failings were minor.[50]

NYCHA benefited enormously from the study with a minimum of organizational reform or turmoil. Anti-communist critics were partially mollified, or at least one issue poorer, and a wave of talented administrators flowed into the organization. One of Preusse's constructive recommendations was the end of voluntarism on the board; the board shifted from five members, including the chairman, to three salaried members, one of which would be the chairman. The mayor endorsed Preusse's suggestions and successfully sought state legislation to change the board's structure. As reform legislation went, it was notably mild and mostly encouraged NYCHA to shape up.[51]

Internal reorganization followed on the heels of the report. Current administrators had demonstrated great talent for building housing, but in other areas of management their performance had been lackluster. Both the executive director, Warren Moscow (who had been sent in by

Wagner to attempt reform of the authority), and the general manager quickly resigned. In early 1958, Thomas Shanahan and William Wilson, board members and associates of Moses, also stepped down. Shanahan's departure proved timely. Shanahan was by 1959 embroiled in scandals related to Title I and for at least a decade had used his NYCHA connections to his personal and political advantage. Philip Cruise, the chairman, would also resign after Wagner had named his successor, William Reid, in April 1958. By reorganizing the board and purging many associates of Moses, the city government put space between NYCHA and the growing controversies associated with Title I.[52]

William Reid, a former deputy mayor under Mayor O'Dwyer, brought with him a well-earned reputation for integrity, financial aptitude, and knowledge of municipal management. He also shared the sense that public housing was a legitimate public service: "It's no more socialized than aid to farming, or aviation or the steamship lines. They all receive subsidies. Private enterprise cannot supply low income clients with decent, safe, sanitary housing."[53] To be the executive director Mayor Wagner picked Ira Robbins, by then executive vice president of the Citizens Housing and Planning Council, who was welcomed by the *New York Times* as a "friendly, stimulating critic of governmental policy who now moves to the other side of the firing line." By 1959 Robbins had been promoted to vice chairman (and thus was a member of the NYCHA board).[54]

The new officials rapidly began to sever the authority's ties to Robert Moses. In 1959 Chairman Reid curtly informed a flailing Moses, who was now desperate to dump site tenants in public housing, not only that selection standards would remain, but also that their "experience has shown a rather small percentage of tenants of Title I sites have relocated in public housing projects." Moses stubbornly responded, "We shall proceed with our projects in any event."[55] By the end of 1960, however, the Committee on Slum Clearance was no more, as was Moses' position as coordinator of construction. The Moses era was effectively over at NYCHA.[56]

Reid gave project managers greater judgment over evictions, sold off some of the middle-income projects, enhanced community programs, revised design standards, improved maintenance, and streamlined tenant selection. That the new administrators inherited a large, civil service bureaucracy and an intact management structure—rather than one crowded with patronage appointments as in Chicago—aided reforms. When they went out to visit each of the developments, for instance, they found "*to [their] great satisfaction . . . that the program as a whole, consists of well built, well maintained, well managed, modern structures.*" The new leadership was able to create a focused renovation program rather than attempting an overhaul of the entire system. That they found generally good conditions certainly offers a more positive spin on the Moses-era administration that had built and managed this giant system.[57]

The new board made a point of distinguishing itself from its predecessors. Board members spoke on the radio, met with the community, and visited the projects. Right-wing political pressure had faded and they did not yet have to face the dramatic social and fiscal changes of the 1970s. Just below the surface continuities to the preceding administration were evident. NYCHA had not, for instance, abandoned its role in clearing the old city. Its annual report for 1962 made clear that "public housing is still the most effective single instrument the city has for slum clearance. Urban renewal, school construction, neighborhood conservation and other public improvements would be delayed if housing were not available for the dislocated low-income families."[58] In 1960, for instance, the authority claimed that of the thirty thousand people who had been forced to move that year, one quarter ended up in public housing. By 1961 that ratio had dropped to 16 percent of the twenty-three thousand people who had been forced to move. Without Moses these figures seemed less controversial, but they remained substantial nonetheless.[59]

In its annual report of 1961, NYCHA listed $1.5 billion in assets and annual rent collection of $85,400,000 from 109,216 apartments. Its operating expenses were $66,000,000 and its annual debt service was $48,816,000. Annual subsidies to the authority now reached $35,000,000. As these figures indicate, during this time NYCHA, even with a growing staff of approximately nine thousand employees, still maintained a balanced budget. The authority had become a landlord to approximately 435,000 people in 105 developments. NYCHA had become the vast, partly self-supporting, public utility only dreamed of in the 1930s.[60]

Housing Deceleration

Mayor Wagner had reorganized NYCHA to save it, but like almost all Americans he had growing doubts about public housing's utopian goals: "Once upon a time, we thought that if we could just bulldoze the slums and build shiny new public housing for low income people, all social problems involving these people would virtually disappear. That has turned out to be not so."[61] Wagner, in spite of these reservations, remained bullish on public housing in the early 1960s and intended to dramatically expand the number of units even with rising construction costs and limited federal funds. He announced in 1961 that he planned to spend another one billion dollars on fifty-seven thousand more units that would house another quarter of a million people. These astronomic figures were not met, but the authority maintained a stronger building program than many other cities during the early 1960s.[62]

New funding, it was hoped, would come from the federal government, where Wagner had successfully gained a waiver of limits on New York's federal program. President Kennedy, likely to reward New York for its electoral support, aimed to accelerate public housing construction in New York. In 1962, the authority managed to launch housing for an impressive 13,715 people. William Reid admitted, however, that because of the exhaustion of funds from federal and state sources, the authority would be able to build only approximately five thousand of the seventeen thousand units under study in 1963. New federal limits, which tried to contain skyrocketing total development costs, also pinched the authority's program.[63]

Political support for the housing program seemed to be fading even faster at the state level. Mayor Wagner admitted, for instance, that a "false and distorted picture" of public housing had "resulted in a growing resistance to the construction of public housing projects in some sections of the city."[64] Most of the counties outside New York joined together in an effort to destroy an additional housing bill in 1960; the bill barely passed. Most notably, Richmond (Staten Island), voted against the housing proposition. Middle-class areas had reason to worry that new public housing, in the turn against slum clearance, would end up in their neighborhoods. The publication of Jane Jacobs's *The Death and Life of Great American Cities* in 1961, which raised important questions about the social and planning assumptions girding public housing, likely undercut much liberal support for such projects.[65]

Governor Nelson Rockefeller, too, expressed his doubts about the billion dollars that had been spent by the state on public housing. At a speech in Washington he announced that "his administration was trying 'to get the Government out of low-cost housing'" and encourage private sector solutions to such projects. He appointed a commission to investigate the degree to which public housing had achieved its stated goals rather than simply concentrate poverty and racial groups. The top housing advisor to the governor, James Gaynor, was a former executive director of NYCHA and wondered if the authority "had not already exceeded its optimum capacity."[66]

Governor Rockefeller's committee, in a surprising move, recommended an expansion of the low-income programs but sought liberalization in income levels to encourage socioeconomic diversification; rehabilitation of older private housing; and increased opportunities for local debt to be used in housing. In a revealing statewide vote in 1964, state voters rejected a referendum shaped by the committee and strongly endorsed by the governor. Staten Island and Queens joined state voters in rejecting the referendum while Manhattan, the Bronx, and Brooklyn supported it. This was the first statewide defeat for public housing since the program had been approved in 1938. Some attributed the rejection to well-organized conservative opposition and to the fact that New York City had received the vast majority of state funds (80 percent). A general turn from liberalism to conservatism, and a backlash against the results of public housing, also seemed to be in the air.[67]

Even had NYCHA successfully won the right to build more public housing, there were signs that the old formulas of financing had run their course. In 1962, the Federal Public Housing Administration warned NYCHA that it was headed for difficult financial straits and objected to the "numerous supervisory layers, dual channels of supervision, excessive central office hierarchy and failure to decentralize authority." It believed, too, that rents were out of line with operating costs and debt service. Mayor Wagner's tolerance for collective bargaining, however progressive, raised NYCHA's operating costs at a rate faster than could be covered by the rents from a tenant population lacking equally lucrative employment. The State Housing Commission added its criticism of NYCHA's administration on similar grounds a few days later and thought, like the federal government, that NYCHA's "administrative overhead is excessive."[68]

NYCHA had reached the first of many impossible moments. As criticism of its methods and finances mounted, so too did demands for more housing action. New York City, after all, still had impressive levels of substandard housing and conditions seemed to be growing worse. Public housing had been conceived at a time of urban dominance; by the 1960s New York was well into decline as its suburbs boomed and white, middle-class residents departed. During the 1960s the abandonment of buildings picked up speed, with an estimated two thousand to three thousand buildings being abandoned every year.

Abandonment resulted from the interplay of market and government programs. White flight, rent control, new state-funded housing, redlining, troublesome welfare tenants, milking of rental properties, and insurance fraud all played a role in this process. Loss of the city's housing stock, even accounting for population loss, led to a citywide vacancy rate of only 1.23 percent in 1968 and higher rental prices created by demand.[69] New York in 1963 still counted forty-three thousand old-law tenements. The poor citizens of other cities, such as Chicago and St. Louis, seemed to benefit more, at least temporarily, from filtering down of better housing during the postwar decades. Slowing demand combined with mismanagement to reduce demand for public housing in many American cities.[70]

Urban problems like these, as experienced in New York and elsewhere, may have moved to the fore of social policy in the Johnson administration, but this did not translate into a giant upswing in public housing because rhetoric during these years far exceeded action. New York City was no exception in expecting much but gaining little from the federal government. Johnson's housing programs introduced in 1965, for instance, delivered relatively little to New York. William Reid regretted that Johnson's plan for thirty-five thousand units a year actually meant just three thousand units per year for NYCHA. The Housing Act of 1965 actually authorized approximately twenty-eight thousand units total, over a four-year period, for New York. According to the general manager at the time, this allocation compared unfavorably with the twenty-five thousand units per year that the authority and its contractors were able to produce.[71]

The newly elected mayor, John Lindsay, not only hoped to build better quality public housing but also hoped to burnish his humanitarian resume with fifty-thousand new units in a five-year period. His actual accomplishments quickly put Wagner's achievements in perspective. By 1970, only approximately six thousand units had been built (of the twenty-eight thousand initially approved by the federal government for New York), and almost all of these completed units had actually been planned in the Wagner years. The rejection of the state housing amendment, neighborhood resistance, federal construction limits, higher interest costs on bond issues, and experiments in better designed, small "vest pocket" developments stymied the program. Lindsay did open the door to greater numbers of welfare tenants, which simply added another challenge to NCYHA management.[72]

Notwithstanding Lindsay's failings, many projects approved earlier reached fruition during his term. By the late 1960s the authority managed housing for approximately half a million people in 157 developments, or 6 percent of the city's population; New York City, at the time, accounted for approximately 20 percent of all public housing in the United States! To speak of public housing in America without discussing New York, as many have done, makes little sense when this proportion is comprehended.[73]

This massive system, contrary to popular belief, was not the result of New York being larger than other cities. The scale of the system resulted from the shared vision of Robert Moses, governors, mayors, and NYCHA administrators that New York should have more public housing, more slum clearance, and more towers in the park. These powerful figures also agreed, even before Moses' era of dominance, that city, state, and federal funds would all be necessary to build this vast program. Moses' occasional criticism of the leadership should not be confused with an antipathy to the organization as a valid municipal function. He did not love public housing, or most NYCHA chairmen, but he *never* put up serious roadblocks to construction or decent management. He also permitted the organization to grow in tandem with the volume of housing.

For all that Robert Moses helped NYCHA grow, Mayor Wagner saved the authority just in time. The reorganization in 1958 brought William Reid and Ira Robbins, talented administrators who restored management discipline and re-energized the notion of the authority as an essentially independent institution that would be led by qualified managers rather than by people appointed through patronage or personal connections. Reid and Robbins increased the transparency of the organization's affairs, initiated programs of renovation in affected projects, and reconfigured the slum clearance and design philosophies to better fit the zeitgeist of the age. NYCHA made it to the 1960s as a decently managed municipal service in spite of the fact that much of the city and country had soured on the whole notion of public housing.

Chapter 7

Designs for a New Metropolis

The *New York Times* predicted in 1946 that in East Harlem the combination of "large-scale public and private housing developments" with new parks, highways, and schools would "eradicate the slum areas and transform Harlem into one of the attractive neighborhoods of the city." Tower in the park public housing, an essential element of this renewed East Harlem as it took shape in the 1940s and 1950s, looked far less impressive when the dust had settled. Over 160 acres of the district had been cleared to make way for brick towers housing over sixty thousand tenants, but the atmospheric and social results seemed less than encouraging. The towers in New York and other large American cities were often so bleak that critics easily portrayed them as harbingers of a new, more menacing form of urban life.[1]

The blame for the lackluster, repetitive design of New York's public housing program has largely been placed on the shoulders of Robert Moses. The noted architectural historian Robert Stern, for instance, believes Moses "became the principle exponent of Modernist towers-in-the-park urbanism because it proved to be a relatively expedient way to rehouse large populations on cleared sites."[2] Moses' biographer Robert Caro also makes it sound as though Moses, because of his disdain for the poor, was responsible not only for the institutional towers in the park but even the lack of toilet bowl covers and closet doors. There is a natural desire to link all that is distasteful from the postwar period to Robert Moses.[3]

These characterizations of Moses' preferences have some justification, but they mistakenly fail to account for NYCHA's prewar experimentation. Much as in the political and economic shaping of the system, Moses' influence should be bracketed within the larger context of NYCHA as an institution. Moses should only be blamed for extending NYCHA's influence over more territory. As the previous chapters amply demonstrate, the minimalist, high-rise superblock had been generated from pragmatic sources before World War II. The lack of closet doors, for instance, was Alfred Rheinstein's innovation, not Robert Moses'. NYCHA by the 1940s was organized as a low-cost housing factory with the ability to build a standardized, mass-produced product. Moses merely put this well-oiled mechanism at his service.

Not only did Moses simply acquiesce to NYCHA design standards; he already shared the authority's growing preference for slum clearance. His controversial proposal on housing and recreation in 1938, for instance, had affirmed the growing preference for "genuine slum clearance." He envisioned high-density projects on the Lower East Side and in Harlem, Greenwich Village, the West Side of Manhattan, the Bronx, the Navy Yard, Brownsville, and South Jamaica.[4] This particular plan did not come to fruition, but it paralleled thinking at the housing authority.[5]

Moses exercised growing power over NYCHA in the 1940s through his position on the City Planning Commission's Committee on Housing; state legislation mandated the commission's approval of public housing projects. Moses had gained his power on the City Planning Commission by impressing Mayor La Guardia with the scale of his housing vision. In the fall of 1942 the mayor announced "the largest post-war program of any city" and credited Robert Moses rather than the housing authority. These plans would "clear the most slums for the dollar."[6]

NYCHA chairman, Gerard Swope, had, in fact, already announced a postwar program focusing on high-density slum neighborhoods,[7] but Moses dismissed Swope's suggestions as being of "no value in the selection of specific sites."[8] By 1943, however, the authority would report that its postwar program now met with the approval of the City Planning Commission and "these projects [would] go far towards clearing the worst of the remaining slums." NYCHA had likely shifted its sites to match Moses', but the record of changes is unclear. The final targeted areas proposed by NYCHA predictably included the same dense tenement districts such as the Lower East Side, Brownsville, and East Harlem. Moses and the authority may have cooked up their plans separately, but few meaningful differences ultimately distinguished their outlook. New York's high-density slums would be replaced with high-rise superblocks.[9]

The illustrations published in 1942 of the eleven- and twelve-story Elliott Houses (1947) in Chelsea correctly reflected the future. The nearly block-long towers, which were turned at an angle from the block lines, connoted hygienic living and utility. The population density actually achieved, 314 persons per acre, reflected the potential of true high-rise towers—even when the buildings covered only 22 percent of the site. The Elliott Houses, in fact, became the first "large-scale post-war rental development to open in the city."[10]

Perceptive outsiders detected potential side effects in this style of planning and wondered if the best motives really shaped the future housing projects. The Citizens Housing Council, in particular, scored NYCHA on its soaring densities in an analysis of envisioned postwar plans in 1942, viewing "with extreme alarm the Authority's trend toward ever-increasing densities, overcrowding of the land in an effort to justify fancy land costs." It believed that the authority was "bowing to racial prejudices, creating overcrowded projects in the face of declining population."[11]

Moses called this racial criticism "tripe," because "there is no racial prejudice involved in doing something for a neglected part of our population." He reminded his critics that while 'the densities are a little high . . . the tremendous cost of land must be considered if public subsidized housing involving expensive slum clearance is to proceed."[12] NYCHA chairman, Edmond Butler, made fun of those housing reformers who sought to build housing "on the periphery of the city . . . thus draining the congested areas." He thought that they overlooked the simple fact that "people do not want to live on the 'periphery.'"[13]

Slum clearance remained a top priority in the postwar years, but in the context of a postwar housing shortage, destruction of existing homes became questionable. Much to Moses' chagrin, vacant land projects re-entered the frame. Chairman Butler explained in 1946 that slums had been the focus, but the housing crisis meant that slum clearance might worsen the situation. It might be true that vacant sites would mean expensive new public services, but they would "eliminate the time consuming process of relocating families."[14]

Moses was at first outraged by the authority's shift in direction. He claimed that the authority's plan in 1946 "to locate any projects on the outskirts of the city instead of doing slum clearance" was an "asinine proposal."[15] As he would inform the mayor, "extension of rapid transit lines to build up the old suburbs . . . is no substitute for rebuilding the old slums" because "central decay destroys the vital parts, and . . . nothing is more destructive than decentralization." This was an odd comment coming from perhaps America's greatest highway builder, but Moses seemed to operate on a very different basis for New York City planning versus region-wide suburban policy.[16]

His nastiness appears self-serving because the authority was as committed to slum clearance as he was. His complaints concerning the authority's head nevertheless had the desired effect of weakening Butler's position. Thomas Farrell, who replaced Butler partly as a result of Moses' dissatisfaction, actually proved just as flexible on site location. Even though he believed "subsidized housing should be built largely in slum areas," large-scale slum clearance would await the point at which the "housing supply becomes adequate."[17] Moses just could not win on this issue in large measure because he did not understand the different pressures faced by NYCHA chairmen.

Moses found that he, too, had to relent on vacant land projects in

1947. Beginning in 1947, the state commissioner of housing, Herman Stichman, forced NYCHA to initiate vacant land projects to relieve the shortage. Mayor O'Dwyer also focused the higher-income city program on vacant sites in the outer boroughs. Because of this external pressure, the scale of his own redevelopment and highway plans, and the volume of public housing projects underway,[18] Moses reported that new federal projects and most state-sponsored projects would expand "genuine slum clearance projects," but part of the state program would be focused on "vacant land projects to aid in solving the problem of moving tenants."[19] Moses, however, always drifted back to centralization and slum clearance. Federal housing approved under the 1949 Housing Act, for instance, he designated for "slum sites" not only because of federal rules emphasizing slum clearance, but because of his deep commitment to clearing out the old city.[20]

NYCHA rarely restricted itself to tokenism when a new area of enterprise revealed itself. By 1955, NYCHA had built public housing projects evenly on 500 acres of slum land and 500 acres of vacant land. By 1961, the authority would claim to have "wiped out 831 acres of slums, and cleared 1,009 acres of wasteland." That year, NYCHA counted 52 vacant land projects out of approximately 150 projects in total. While administrators had concentrated the majority of public housing units in slum areas, and some vacant land projects rose adjacent to slum districts, the volume of public housing outside traditional slum zones was substantial. Because of this dispersion, even in 2006 "one out of five developments [was] integrated into census tracts containing a majority white population." Indeed, properly managed projects have become an unplanned tool of racial integration in many neighborhoods across the city.[21]

Postwar vacant land sites, alas, would be just as unimaginatively designed as their slum clearance relatives, but they were sturdy. An external review of the city program in 1958 indicated that "the projects . . . inspected are neat, appear to be well built, but are definitely not competitive with private housing. . . ."[22] These developments covered only between 15 and 18 percent of their sites; featured very low population densities, ranging between 85 and 124 persons per acre; and stood mostly between six and eight stories tall. The vacant land came cheap and NYCHA used it profligately. The groundsmen, for instance, at Throgg's Neck (1953) have to keep forty-nine acres of grass cut during the summer months. Although the developments lacked the subtlety of Stein's Hillside Homes (1935), they did represent a partial return to the garden apartment style. Even today their lower height and generous open spaces help them blend into neighborhoods.[23]

These vacant land projects, in retrospect, appear as merely a distraction from the main stage in urban transformation: slum clearance.

Clearance reached its apogee as a result not only of NYCHA's and Moses' longstanding emphasis on tenement clearance, but also on federal and state policies in the postwar era that favored clearance over vacant land projects. More than a billion dollars had been spent by 1965 on "the planning or construction of 88,445 new housing units in the lower East Side, the upper West Side, east and central Harlem . . . Bedford Stuyvesant, Brownsville and Coney Island . . . and in the lower Bronx." Projects in these districts, long targeted by Robert Moses and the NYCHA, replaced areas defined as slums.[24]

Cyril Grossman, a longtime administrator at NYCHA, admitted that in this period the authority "destroyed the neighborhood, flattened out the neighborhood for a couple of years before they could built it up. By that time nobody wanted to live in a deserted area with all this construction. . . . They did blocks at a time, zipped it all down, every tree, every whatever it was there."[25] The scale of condemnation reached staggering levels; in one request, in 1951, for instance, the authority asked to condemn "159 acres of slum property to advance nine low-rent housing projects."[26]

A NYCHA official, looking back on his work on the Fredrick Douglass Houses in the 1950s, remembered that while the majority of properties "were in terrible condition . . . on the verge of collapsing . . . some of the buildings on the site were really in excellent shape . . . I sort of regret that we weren't able to save . . . many brownstones."[27] Some black middle-class residents of better quality brownstones in Harlem, for instance, had no choice to move when their properties were condemned; even though they could "point to glistening hardwood floors" and "had spent thousands of dollars renovating." Slum clearance likely accelerated racial change in areas such as the South Bronx, as vast numbers of displaced blacks and Puerto Ricans from Manhattan crowded into already substandard tenements and other housing.[28]

A few observers began to worry about these clearance policies, but it would take years for criticism to be translated into revised policies. Charles Abrams in 1953 called for more vacant land projects because "the slum program . . . displaces too many persons and serves only to aggravate housing problems."[29] Moses considered this type of criticism "simply the climax of a series of attacks . . . from the phoneys, stooges and fake uplifters among the so-called civic organizations." He reminded Chairman Philip Cruise that "these people for several generations were howling for slum clearance."[30]

For a long time, the outrage over slum clearance and the loss of so many wonderful if substandard buildings conditioned the view of public housing both in New York and across the country. Public housing in most cities had created a "second ghetto" that was unmanageable and in many respects worse than the first. New York's story actually reveals that site location is an important factor but not a deciding one in the long-term success of public housing communities. There are, for instance, some results of the slum clearance program that, when linked to good management and a thriving central business district, have yielded long-term benefits.

In a study conducted in 2001, tenants in centrally located South Manhattan and West Brooklyn projects (most the result of slum clearance) had "the lowest probability of exit"; North Manhattan projects were not far behind. Tenants stay in such large numbers because "the relative attractiveness of these districts, coupled with the tightness of these sub-market areas, may provide strong inducements for tenants to remain in place." Staten Island, in contrast, where developments are decentralized and lack good transit access, had the shortest waiting lists. These decentralized projects, however, are not without redeeming features. They are lower density and are often located in middle-class neighborhoods. As the authority's tenancy has shifted to mostly minority, the decentralized projects have helped to integrate white neighborhoods. When management disaster is not the immediate outcome, as in New York, these subtle results of site selection can be considered.[31]

Paired for Mixture

Robert Moses and the authority not only mixed up the locations of public housing, but unlike cities across the country they paired middle-income projects with public housing in many low-income neighborhoods. This mixture put middle-income people on the edge or directly in the heart of many low-income neighborhoods such as Harlem. As this class mixture is now seen as essential to good planning, NYCHA and Moses certainly deserve credit for paying attention to this issue. It must be admitted, however, that external pressure again played a role in their plans.

The intimacy of Stuyvesant Town and adjacent public housing is an example of early attempts to blend low- and middle-income tenants. Moses may have created little public housing in center city slum clearance areas, but he did believe that "slum clearance areas will logically adjoin public housing areas." When public housing did seem too concentrated, as on the Lower East Side, he blamed it on inaction by private interests who refused to take up sites offered to them.[32]

Political pressure forced Moses and the authority to extend further their attention to pairing public housing with private housing. In 1945, Moses could report that "Governor [Dewey] and his advisors are very insistent on having redevelopment projects in the same neighborhoods in which public housing projects are located."[33] Herman Stichman, the state commissioner of housing, made a splash in the 1940s by criticizing the concentration of subsidized housing in areas such as the Lower East Side because it led to "'ghettos' of low income families [and] prevents those of different income levels from meeting in neighborhood activities and fosters class feeling." Butler, Moses, and O'Dwyer agreed to Stichman's demand that more private housing be mixed with public housing.[34]

Moses could proudly announce in 1953 that on the Lower East Side, "We are building here not only for the poor but for people of many income groups. This is not socialism. We see here progressive government working with progressive private capital."[35] By 1955, NYCHA also followed a balanced program that in some instances placed "a low-income and middle-income project . . . on one 'combined' site." If it was not as ambitious as some might have wanted, and hardly relieved the concentration of public housing, it was more than just tokenism.[36]

Title I redevelopment, according to the historian Joel Schwartz, became the key to linking middle-class projects to public housing. Title I of the Housing Act of 1949 not only expanded Moses' redevelopment schemes, but also provided the resources to build middle-income housing beyond the commercial core. Neighboring redevelopment/public projects (approximately twelve in total) include the cooperative Morningside Gardens and Grant Houses (1957) and Webb and Knapp's Park West Village and Frederick Douglass Houses (1958). Harlem might have had the largest concentration of public housing in New York (by 1962 there were twenty-six developments either built or underway with 27,717 units), but the area also had four middle-income and two luxury developments with a total of 7,518 units. These middle-income units remain in place today.[37]

Tower-block Designs

NYCHA has survived to the present in spite of the fact that most of its postwar projects were merely exaggerated versions of the tower in the park invented before the war. In light of how many similar towers NYCHA built and has kept in decent condition until the present, the tendency to portray high rises as inherently unworkable needs further justification. As in the prewar era, NYCHA used economies of scale to build *basic but not shoddy buildings*. These durable towers are hard on the eyes, but they can be maintained, unlike many in Chicago and St. Louis, with appropriate staffing. For all these factors, they have withstood decades of abuse.[38]

Moses' insistence that new construction match units cleared accentuated the authority's predisposition to the high-rise superblock. An associate of Moses remembered that Moses also desired projects "that would not be swamped, that could have an impact in the area." He favored "large complexes of more than a thousand units and . . . towers seven or more stories high."[39] NYCHA chairmen such as Thomas Farrell, during the authority's time of explosive growth, also favored the large "superblocks with wide open spaces" and low ground coverage.[40]

These superblocks filled with unremarkable red brick towers. Richard Rosenthal, a longtime director of design at the authority, explained that "two factors largely shaped the buildings of this period . . . efficient use of elevators and economical fireproof construction." The high concrete and brick buildings that resulted from these concerns, when combined with the designers' aim to provide every apartment with equal air and light, resulted in "the typical 'alphabet shaped' towers, X's, T's, Y's, that were repeated." Rosenthal had his reservations from an aesthetic point of view: "With complete standardization of exterior detail—red brick with standard window types, and little or no elaboration such as balconies or articulation of wall surfaces—these buildings lost the warmth and character of the best early housing."[41]

The average projects during this time ranged between fifteen hundred and three thousand units for reason of efficiency and were as large as many of the biggest projects in other American cities. Many of New York's projects adjoined others to form vast modernist neighborhoods. Concentrations of these high rises, only nominally in separate projects, in Manhattan, Brooklyn, and the South Bronx often had more than ten thousand units.[42]

Occasional mixture of these high rises with six-story buildings did little to relieve the visual or psychological impact. Internally, high rises often had long hallways (double-loaded corridors) with many units per floor, thus creating more anonymity. Managers today believe that these high towers are more difficult, although not impossible, to maintain. Most developments composed of six or seven story buildings rose in the outer boroughs where land costs were lower. These lower-rise buildings (at least in the New York context) are considered to be easier to manage and usually have only approximately five apartments per landing, naturally lighted stairwells, and small elevators.[43]

Designers, many from prestigious firms such as Skidmore, Owens, and Merrill and Emery Roth and Sons, won design contracts in the postwar era, but NYCHA resisted innovation. Compared to housing experimentation in Europe during this time, with elaborate balcony systems and new materials, NYCHA held closely to its redbrick anti-architecture. Uniformity, however, proved best for long-term maintenance. Standardization is essential to NYCHA maintenance and renovation efficiency today, even if the developments are not aesthetically uplifting.[44]

NYCHA achieved its record growth in the face of rising costs through both true economizing and financial legerdemain. By 1948, Farrell estimated that "the $5,000 apartment of 1940 costs $11,000 today."[45] NYCHA only achieved its record numbers by dipping further into state funds and seeking renewed levels of economy. In 1949 costs temporarily dropped to $7,000 per apartment through wider accessibility of materials and higher building trade productivity. NYCHA continued its policies of minimal interior furnishings as towers rose higher and identical plans were reproduced at different sites.[46]

During the 1950s NYCHA technically met the federal statutory room cost limits, but the actual total development costs per apartment during this period (including the costs of site acquisition, infrastructure, and non-dwelling construction) might run as much as twice as high if the land was expensive. For instance, La Guardia Houses (1957) on the Lower East Side cost $1,745 per room. At that level it easily beat the statutory limit of $2,500 per room. Slum clearance and other development costs, however, actually added another $1,609 per room to the total development costs. This financial sleight of hand was possible because the Housing Act of 1949 did not clearly limit total development costs. One researcher found that the actual total development cost *per unit* was $15,680 for La Guardia Houses, a comparable cost to a nice single-family home during this time. Federal officials, realizing the political liability of building expensive low-cost housing, finally created a cap in 1955 of $16,000 per unit nationally.[47]

NYCHA administrators constantly demanded that renovation was more expensive than new buildings, but there is room for doubt. Renovations would not likely last for fifty years, as public housing was designed to do, but much more might have been accomplished in this line had NYCHA aggressively pursued this path. High costs did not, alas, lead to luxury housing. City-sponsored higher-income developments, many on vacant land sites and exempted from federal or state limits, did proudly boast closet doors, toilet seat covers, showers, and faster elevators.[48] The federal and state projects built before 1958, however, included eighty thousand apartments lacking showers (tubs were provided) and closet doors. According to NYCHA's own later analysis, "the failure to provide any covering for the concrete hall floors, [and] the use of rather unattractive grade C asphalt tile in apartments" gave NYCHA's state and federal projects the designation of "dwellings for the poor." Strict room costs, as opposed to higher development costs, meant that apartments had to be built to minimal standards.[49]

By the 1950s, the Lower East Side reflected the general pattern of projects from the 1940s and 1950s (Figures 15–17). The Lillian Wald Houses (1949), for instance, featured sixteen towers often to thirteen

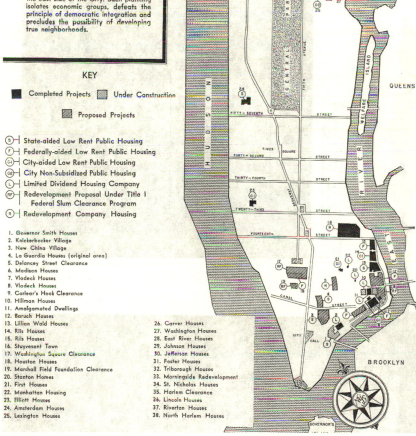

THE "EAST WALL"
OF PUBLIC
HOUSING ON
MANHATTAN
ISLAND

This map of the current status of projected and completed government-aided
housing shows extreme concentration on
the east side of the City. Such planning
isolates economic groups, defeats the
principle of democratic integration and
precludes the possibility of developing
true neighborhoods.

KEY

Completed Projects   Under Construction

Proposed Projects

(S) State-aided Low Rent Public Housing
(F) Federally-aided Low Rent Public Housing
(C4) City-aided Low Rent Public Housing
(G2) City Non-Subsidized Public Housing
(L) Limited Dividend Housing Company
(RF) Redevelopment Proposal Under Title I
     Federal Slum Clearance Program
(R) Redevelopment Company Housing

1. Governor Smith Houses
2. Knickerbocker Village
3. New China Village
4. La Guardia Houses (original area)
5. Delancey Street Clearance
6. Madison Houses
7. Vladeck Houses
8. Vladeck Houses
9. Corlear's Hook Clearance
10. Hillman Houses
11. Amalgamated Dwellings
12. Baruch Houses
13. Lillian Wald Houses
14. Riis Houses
15. Riis Houses
16. Stuyvesant Town
17. Washington Square Clearance
18. Houston Houses
19. Marshall Field Foundation Clearance
20. Stanton Homes
21. First Houses
22. Manhattan Housing
23. Elliott Houses
24. Amsterdam Houses
25. Lexington Houses

26. Carver Houses
27. Washington Houses
28. East River Houses
29. Johnson Houses
30. Jefferson Houses
31. Foster Houses
32. Triborough Houses
33. Morningside Redevelopment
34. St. Nicholas Houses
35. Harlem Clearance
36. Lincoln Houses
37. Riverton Houses
38. North Harlem Houses

Figure 15. The concentration of public housing in an area such as the Lower East Side became common in the postwar period. New York State Annual Report, 1951, Box 61C6, Folder 6, NYCHAR.

Figure 16. Lillian Wald Houses (1949) was typical of minimalist postwar public housing in New York. La Guardia Wagner Archive/NYCHA Photograph Collection.

stories. All had skip-stop elevators. Even with only 18.6 percent site coverage, it achieved densities of 238 persons per acre. Nearby, the Jacob Riis Houses (1949) continued the same pattern and scale, covering only 20 percent of its site but still fitting 240 persons per acre into a mix of six-, thirteen-, and fourteen-story buildings rotated off the traditional grid. By the time NYCHA stopped building on the Lower East Side it had constructed approximately eleven thousand public housing units there. The pattern set at First Houses (basic brick), Williamsburg (angled placement, the superblock), and East River (high-rise development) had created this shocking new urban vision.[50]

NYCHA leaders and Robert Moses believed that by replacing tenement slums with modern superblocks they were not only providing a better life for tenants, but also giving the city as a whole a valuable public service. NYCHA was replacing the most notorious slum districts with modern, regulated, low-income complexes with abundant open space—and spending a lot of money both to clear land and to build new hous-

Figure 17. The Jacob Riis Houses (1949) as seen in the 1950s. Projects like this and the Lillian Wald Houses collectively brought forth an unfamiliar landscape on the Lower East Side. La Guardia Wagner Archive/NYCHA Photograph Collection.

ing. Public housing districts such as the Lower East Side are today impressive showpieces of NYCHA's vast collection, but the authority took an enormous risk by concentrating so many housing projects in former slum zones. Only management skill in New York saved what could have been another American tragedy. Similar concentrations of public housing in other cities experienced significantly worse outcomes.

Selective Hearing: The Critics Speak

What had once been NYCHA's successes—economical construction and the superblock—quickly became one of its perceived failings. The authority had nobly aimed to create the basis for a renewed urban democracy where all had the chance for air, light, and sanitation. Such a mission gave it enormous social power, but NYCHA's insulated and hierarchical bureaucracy also made it tone-deaf.

Criticism came from many quarters. As early as 1938, Louis Pink, then the chairman of the State Housing Board and an advocate of European-style public housing, found fault that at Queensbridge "all the buildings are the same height and style and there is no variety in the development."[51] In 1945 the Citizens Housing Council worried that NYCHA failed to show a "constructive approach toward the problem of excessive land costs in slum areas, but had, instead, resorted . . . to thirteen and fourteen story skyscrapers on expensive land, resulting in greater population densities."[52]

Lewis Mumford, a legendary foe of high-density urbanism, became even more outspoken in his criticism as the years went by. In 1950 he remarked that the Manhattan projects, for the poor and middle class, "look as if they had all been designed by one mind, carried out by one organization, intended for one class of people, bred like bees to fit into these honeycombs." Mumford still liked the superblocks for their quiet and safety, but he now believed that "to correct a pathological condition, it [NYHCA] employed a pathological remedy" that might ultimately exchange "slums for super-slums."[53] Nationally, Catherine Bauer shocked her colleagues in 1954 with her article "The Dreary Deadlock of Public Housing" in which she distinguished her own housing ideals from the reality of ugly, isolated, institutional public housing found in most American cities.[54]

Robert Moses, in 1951, even sent Chairman Philip Cruise his concerns: "A number of people have talked to me about the monotonous sameness and institutional character of [public housing.] There seems to me to be a good deal to these criticisms. I know, however, that it is not easy to produce a more pleasing variety without additional expense; nevertheless, we ought to try. More and more we have tall identical buildings constructed out of the same brick and presenting a deadening appearance." He wondered, "Can't we have bricks of different colors?"[55] Cruise admitted to Moses that "the institutional character of the public housing projects" made them into an "eyesore." He documented the fact that "at the present time there are 43 permanent projects in the city, all with the same color brick." He estimated that another 35 were on their way in the very same brick. Cruise looked over the files and found, however, that "the matter was always discarded because of money."[56]

The authority had a working formula for mass clearance and construction and substantive changes to the authority's housing methods would have slowed Moses' other redevelopment projects. NYCHA did, however, make much of a "new" look in the mid-1950s. A number of architects proposed, and NYCHA applied, cosmetic changes including more exotic footprints for buildings, additional variations in building height, colorful sections of glazed brick, and decorative color panels. The authority's architects also boasted of public balconies on some buildings and better window standards. At Grant Houses (1957), for instance, "bricks of mixed pink and buff" were added, with limited success, to break up the monotony of identical red brick towers. The designers poorly integrated the colored bricks and they appear as an odd afterthought. Similar experiments now seem more dated than the average red brick tower.[57]

NYCHA officials and Robert Moses, moreover, stood by the high-rise superblock philosophy while they tweaked the design details. The authority maintained in 1952 that "high land costs dictate high buildings on any slum site in New York City." The Development Department "had found that buildings of approximately 14 stories were at least 10% cheaper to construct than low buildings."[58] The authority defensively claimed in 1955 that these "tall buildings are a mark of public housing in New York City just as they are a mark of private apartment housing, and for the same reasons: high land costs and lack of room."[59]

These administrators knew their business, but they overlooked a central issue. Hundreds of minimal brick high rises built privately for the middle and upper classes did sprout across New York, but the addition of balconies, more plentiful windows, and glazed brick broke up the monotony of most private sector towers. Most Manhattan private housing also blended in better by following the existing lot lines. NYCHA was not as hamstrung by economics as it let on. An ideological preference for the tower in the park that offered both high densities and abundant light and air strongly influenced its choices. New York would not be doomed by its high-rise style, but it was not necessarily helped either.

The Unstoppable Superblock

> *New York has more to be preserved than it has to be eliminated. There is much in neighborhood tradition, loyalty, commerce, capital investment and social activities which would be destroyed by the majestic sweep of a royal wand.*
>
> —*Alfred Rheinstein, 1939*[60]

Alfred Rheinstein might have worried occasionally during his brief tenure about clear-cutting New York's neighborhoods, but NYCHA chairman Thomas Farrell offered an idyllic description of superblocks under construction or already in existence by 1950: "Viewed from a distance," NYCHA's housing projects "will attract attention by their reddish brick coloring and their planned openness—great superblock developments that will have been freed from the lot and street pattern of a horse and buggy age. Close up, you will be less conscious of the buildings than of the broad open spaces that surround and separate them; of the shaded walks and benches; and of children playing in protected playgrounds in fresh air and sunshine."[61]

The superblock remained one of the authority's pillars of faith and administrators long viewed it as the principle design benefit that could survive even the most draconian cost cutting and high-rise alienation. By the 1950s, the superblock had lost the careful composition of the early years and had become a technocratic solution to slum clearance. Ever greater percentages of open space made possible by high buildings overwhelmed a deeper appreciation for the potential role of open space in the lives of tenants. At Baruch Houses (1959) the buildings covered just 12 percent of the twenty-seven-acre tract, the remaining land was taken up by lawns, paths, benches, and playgrounds. Fourteen densely packed city blocks had been boiled down to two massive, mostly open, superblocks.[62]

The authority's program of large-scale construction began to lose its support, even among housing advocates, when the scale of projects reached a tipping point in slum neighborhoods. Large areas of the Lower East Side and East Harlem, for instance, had become nearly perfect versions of the tower in the park philosophy. While NYCHA landscaping outshone that of other authorities, no one had known how distressing these urban environments—as a whole—would be once they leaped off the page. The fireproof construction, sanitary services, light, air, and green spaces may have represented distinct improvements over the tenement districts that had preceded and often surrounded them, but the commercial, social, and cultural liveliness of New York neighborhoods, however squalid, had evaporated. One of the best places to consider the effect of the massed superblock, and the processes that contributed to its formulation, is East Harlem.[63]

In the 1930s and 1940s, civic leaders in Harlem had demanded that the city take action to build public housing in Harlem. In 1942, Justice Steven Jackson, for instance, demanded that Robert Moses and other civic leaders address substandard housing, which was a "public disgrace and constitutes a breeding ground for disease and crime."[64] The concentration of public housing in East Harlem, in particular, resulted from the many efforts of the liberal councilman Vito Marcantonio, who represented the area; not only did he believe in the benefits of clearing tenements, but his support for public housing helped win him new allies as the district shifted from Italian Americans to mostly minority. Robert Moses indeed did what he could, as did a number of authority chairmen, to send public housing to Harlem. In 1955, Philip Cruise refused to stop construction in Harlem and plans in "other concentrated Negro areas" because to do otherwise would "leave untouched some of the worst of the festering slums that blight the city," but Harlem had also become a path of least resistance in an increasingly segregated city.[65]

By 1957, the authority had cleared 137 acres in East Harlem alone. The *New York Times* discovered that "in a mass attack on one of the worst slum areas in the metropolitan area . . . blocks of old, dark buildings have been ripped out, letting in sunlight and air." New superblocks, combinations of six to seven older blocks, made "planning, construction and management more economical and efficient. In addition, the buildings can be widely spaced, exposing them to sunshine and air on all sides" with parks, playgrounds, and parking interspersed. Between the East River and Thomas Jefferson Park a linked series of superblocks created one of the largest concentrations of public housing in the country.[66]

Why had NYCHA superblocks in East Harlem, and other public housing concentrations across the city, become so dull? NYCHA's early developments had, in fact, taught NYCHA administrators lessons that encouraged single-use environments. At Williamsburg Houses the authority had built stores but found that tenants did not necessarily frequent them. Tenant families avoided the fancier shops and took their trade to cheaper stores nearby. Shop owners claimed that their rents were excessive. Of fifty-one stores, only twenty-seven had been rented in 1938. The authority had to drop rental rates by 50 percent in order to attract more tenants. These early difficulties helped steer NYCHA away from providing stores in its projects, a factor in the lack of liveliness and social cohesiveness in the later superblocks.[67]

Experience would be affirmed by ideology. Officials of NYCHA walked a narrow tightrope when they were building any public housing and they certainly did not want to invite charges of socialism. In 1938 Chairman Alfred Rheinstein opposed stores in public housing, except in remote locations, because "unfair competition with going private enterprises should be avoided." Queensbridge Houses, for instance, did benefit from a small, well-planned, central shopping district, but only because Queensbridge met Rheinstein's standard of isolation (Figure 18). East River Houses in Harlem, for instance, had no stores at all.[68]

By 1944 NYCHA policy stated that the authority "would depend entirely upon private enterprise to supply the necessary shopping facilities" in thirteen planned postwar projects because of past problems, unwillingness to compete with private interests, and a belief that existing shops could meet the new demand. In 1944 the authority ran only 160 stores (compared to 17,000 apartments) in all its developments. It was noted at that time that many stores in Williamsburg Houses had remained empty from day one. It was projected, however, that the authority would also destroy 599 stores as part of its postwar program—a figure that turned out to be conservative.[69]

After the war state officials sternly reprimanded NYCHA when it actually tried to create more stores. In 1947, the deputy state commissioner of housing reminded the authority that not only had the Williamsburg stores been an "indifferent success," but "there is, as you know, a great deal of opposition from certain real estate, building and banking interests." The authority's proposal at Governor Smith Houses for a neighborhood shopping center of six stores might unfairly compete with stores nearby. The state allowed only a supermarket and perhaps one or two other stores. By the 1950s the federal government also forbid the building of stores. The authority eventually tried planning projects near existing shopping, negotiating with business owners to modernize their stores, and even sold excess land to those who would build stores, but this had little obvious impact on the atmosphere as a whole.[70]

As projects in vacant areas increased after World War II, calls for shops re-emerged. Robert Moses, who was perhaps ignorant of this longer history, wrote to Thomas Farrell in 1948, inquiring "if you have considered with sufficient care providing stores in some of the new housing projects" because many were in remote locations.[71] Farrell responded, "We include stores in the plans only where adequate shopping facilities are not available . . . and where it is concluded that private enterprise will not provide such facilities."[72]

Some of the reluctance to build stores originated from management difficulties during this time. Renting the stores had become easier after the war, but the authority suffered, in stores rented on a percentage basis, from retail tenants who would "chisel" the authority and thus avoid pay-

Figure 18. NYCHA's early projects, such as Queensbridge (1940), showed evidence of concern for community planning and neighborhood shopping. Photo taken January 15, 1940. La Guardia Wagner Archive/NYCHA Photograph Collection.

ing the percentage of gross sales due to it. As one report made clear: "Store tenants show every indication of affluence" and "people of this type could not be expected to dabble with a non-paying store." A storeowner at Fort Greene Houses, for instance, in 1948 only reported to NYCHA an annual net profit of $12 yet "requested permission to sell a half interest in this going concern for the sum of $40,000." The authority realized that managing commercial tenants represented a distinct challenge from the already difficult task of regulating residential projects.[73]

NYCHA had its own distressing reasons for attacking existing stores. Internal memos, like the following one from 1950, indicate that neighborhood loyalty, generated through stores and other local institutions, could be an impediment to slum clearance: "This common bond makes for strong family ties, friendships, and . . . strong identification on the part of the slum dweller with the neighborhood in which he lives. . . . Each area has its own shops, stores, markets, theatres, places of worship" that made neighborhoods almost self-sufficient. Administrators overcame tenant resistance by "demolition of commercial buildings on the site" to emphasize "the inevitable fate of the neighborhood." This artificially generated inconvenience, they bragged, "tends to also accelerate the relocation of residential tenants."[74]

By the mid-1950s as the full scale of the NYCHA superblocks began to transform large districts into single-use residential neighborhoods, the effects of policies restricting or destroying stores came into focus (Figure 19). Harlem leaders, for instance, in 1955 expressed concern that in East Harlem only two of nine planned projects included stores. The director of Union Settlement explained that in low-income neighborhoods "a store is not only a place where articles are vended, but a social center. . . . None of this is taken into account in the new housing projects."[75] The East Harlem Merchants Association, which was hard hit by demolition, made a number of acute observations in 1957 about the value of retail districts: "Stores stimulate friendliness among tenants of projects (shopping chores bring tenants into same stores) . . . stores provide more light and animate the tempo of outside life . . . stores provide a linking process of unity between tenants and organized authority . . . stores help supervision and policing of project sites due to stores' long hours of business." Stores, in other words, made a neighborhood a neighborhood.[76]

By 1957 the association counted two thousand stores directly lost due to NYCHA project development in East Harlem, declines of between 20 and 60 percent for remaining businesses, and great hardship for dislocated shop owners. Even worse, it blamed NYCHA clearance for a general loss in the attractiveness of its area for shopping: "Now the entire area has a 'dead' quality at dusk. With radically reduced lighting there is

Figure 19. Like the Lower East Side, East Harlem became a concentrated zone of public housing projects. NYCHA Map, 25 June 1952, Box 59D3, Folder 2, NYCHAR.

a corresponding decline in the number of people circulating through the shopping area." Another unintended side effect of the superblock design undermined commerce; the loss of cross streets in new superblocks meant less parking for shoppers in the area.[77]

The authority seemed to give way under pressure. In 1955 it now claimed that it encouraged stores because so much public housing had started "to take a far higher toll of neighborhood shopping facilities than could originally have been anticipated. In East Harlem, for example, the Authority estimated that the ten projects built or planned . . . would result in the cumulative displacement of some eighteen hundred stores." The authority added a few more stores at two planned projects (eighteen at Taft Houses [1962], for instance), but hardly made up for the nearly two thousand businesses eliminated in East Harlem alone (Figure 20).[78]

Older merchants had been driven out of many areas by the long construction time, and the new rent structure of the few new stores discouraged many small businesspeople. The limited number of stores also discouraged the mixture of uses—including clubs, services, and churches—in ordinary neighborhoods that prospered from marginal commercial space. The few shopping districts added by NYCHA are generally unattractive, single-story retail strips usually on one side of a superblock only. They hardly add up to a genuine shopping district and even today many of the stores are empty or converted to nonprofit use.

White flight, crime, and urban unrest would take its own toll on neighborhood retail in New York City, and the increasingly impoverished tenancy of public housing would have difficulty keeping alive many more stores than built, but NYCHA policies in slum clearance and superblock development certainly did nothing to help neighborhood commerce and much to harm it. In this respect NYCHA developments did not fulfill a positive service to the community.[79]

The numbers speak for themselves. By 1957, *of 82 projects, only 9 had built-in stores.* The authority admitted to demolishing 500 stores in 1961 alone. By 1965, the authority counted only *170 stores in all of its 150 projects* and 18 of the stores remained vacant. The slowdown in construction during the 1960s gave neighborhood retail a break in New York, but the end of major construction would also mean that NYCHA would be left with enormous housing projects and little retail.[80]

Shoddy versus Economical Development

The authority's developments provided light, air, fireproof construction, full services of heat, sewage, electricity, and water, and plenty of high-quality open space for play and relaxation. That is no small matter. As

Figure 20. The Taft Houses (1962) included a small shopping strip (visible in the center of the image) as a result of pressure for a more normal streetscape. NYCHA had already destroyed thousands of stores. La Guardia Wagner Archive/NYCHA Photograph Collection.

Ira Robbins defensively noted, "How can any unprejudiced informed observer compare these well-designed, well-constructed and well-maintained buildings with the damp, dark, rat-infested cold water, fire-trap tenements in the slums of New York?"[81] In spite of the obvious design defects, New York possessed two advantages that enabled Robbins to make this claim: 1) high construction standards, and 2) the fact that its housing was much more than a physical environment; it was a new type of carefully managed public space (as described in other chapters). In other cities officials thought that the buildings, often physically worse to begin with than those in New York, should suffice.

The urban historian Alexander von Hoffman has shown that St. Louis embarked on high-rise public housing because Mayor Joseph Darst was so impressed by New York's skyscrapers and NYCHA's towers that in 1949 he returned "to St. Louis with visions of New York skyscrapers dancing in his head." St. Louis would be a "Manhattan on the Mississippi."[82] As the plans for the combined public housing project known as Pruitt-Igoe developed, the architect Minoru Yamasaki chose in 1950 a "slab design instead of a cross-shaped layout" more common in New York. He did, however, adopt New York's skip-stop system for reasons of economy at a time when New York had largely abandoned the system because tenants disliked it. He also created glass-enclosed communal galleries on each floor that were supposed to generate community life. By the time of Pruitt-Igoe's completion in 1956, the combined superblock included 2,870 units in thirty-three identical eleven-story buildings.[83] Compared to New York this was not that big a project.

The St. Louis Housing Authority (SLHA) failed to garner cost savings from its high-rise developments, including Pruitt-Igoe, because construction costs were "40 percent above that of public housing construction in New York City." Contractors so inflated their bids that high-rise buildings failed to save money. Because the Federal Public Housing Authority would "not budge in its maximum limits, the authority raised the densities, the architects reduced room sizes and removed amenities, and the contractors cut corners" to make big profits. [84] *Architectural Forum* in 1965 revealed that the tenants paid the price for this corruption: "The landscaping was reduced to virtually nothing, and such 'luxuries' as paint on the concrete block walls of the galleries and stairwells, [and] insulation on exposed steam pipes" revealed callous disregard for tenants. The towers "loom[ed] formidably over broad expanses of scrubby grass, broken glass and litter." In addition, Pruitt-Igoe's tiny skip-stop elevators moved painfully slowly.[85]

Such deficiencies could be found in varying degrees at other housing authorities by the 1950s and 1960s. Chicago's high-rise towers, for instance, which were based loosely on the New York model, proved exces-

sively expensive from the beginning because of uncompetitive contracting. When Chicago finally cut costs under federal pressure, absurd
economies made the developments taller, badly built, shockingly ugly,
and minimally landscaped. A massive highway alongside the length of
the Robert Taylor homes certainly did nothing to attract tenants. The
city failed to provide necessary community services such as schools, and
the Chicago Housing Authority's playgrounds and recreation programs
remained spotty at best compared to those of NYCHA.[86]

Cities such as St. Louis, Chicago, and Newark failed to design, build
and maintain housing that could be competitive with even the low end
of the private sector. Elected officials had turned to public housing out
of convenience and failed to realize that public housing, just to pay the
bills, had to be better than conventional slum housing. Disorderly tenants played a role in public housing decline, but to a great extent tenants became victims of administrators who did not understand the
straightforward difference between economical and shoddy public housing. New York's housing was no paradise, but it was already far superior
to tower-block housing in other cities.

Chapter 8

The Price of Design Reform

By the 1950s, the New York City Housing Authority had become a housing factory that specialized in a limited range of low-cost housing products. This industrialized housing organization could clear slums, move site tenants, build towers, and find new tenants at an awesome speed because it repeated rather than innovated. To tinker with this system, as with any high-speed assembly line, would prove exceedingly dangerous. Yet even NYCHA eventually had to answer its critics, particularly as it lost the patronage of Robert Moses after 1958.

Administrators quietly pursued slum clearance as long as they could after 1958, but the painful, lurching shift to less destructive and monotonous design systems absorbed NYCHA in the 1960s. Unfortunately, declining subsidies fatally combined with more diversified and expensive housing products to stall the production line by the end of that decade. Substantive reform had actually been made in the 1960s, but the end result was that the authority ceased to be an engine of housing production. Innovations never made the leap from demonstrations to mass housing. New critics now wondered why NYCHA no longer produced large quantities of low-cost housing for New York's poor.

Pressure from local critics, federal officials, and housing experts had its first notable impact in 1956 when the authority promised to scatter its new federal projects. Instead of bulldozing vast areas it now promised to disperse future projects. In a number of new developments underway in 1956, NYCHA promised and did leave in place a few of the better quality apartment buildings, some churches, school buildings, and even some stores. Alas, these represented a fraction of the original site structures and remaining buildings often floated uncomfortably in the open superblocks. State housing developments, moreover, continued in the old pattern of "large clusters of buildings."[1]

Changes in practices accelerated with the reorganization of the authority in 1958. Ira Robbins, the new executive director, admitted that in the old days NYCHA had been able to find "very large areas which were all slums with no hope of rehabilitating individual buildings." By the early 1960s, however, with "relocation getting more difficult, we have seen the necessity of building smaller developments" that reduced the "monotonous design."[2] By 1962, the authority was claiming that 32 percent of its projects either planned or in construction were of the "vest pocket" variety. Out of the eleven standard projects underway that year, and fourteen more that had been approved, only one would comprise over one thousand apartments. Senior high-rise housing accounted for 20 percent of new apartments; in many ways this population was better suited to the high rise.[3]

NYCHA was generally pleased with this new method, but it began to identify serious deficiencies with it: "Construction costs are consistently higher for single buildings or small developments than for the larger (in excess of 500 D.U.'s [dwelling units])." Small-scale projects threatened the authority's ability to provide large numbers of units to meet demand on its waiting list, please politicians, and expand its empire.[4] By 1968 the authority had fifty-four vest project developments underway that were slated to create three thousand apartments. In other words, *it now took fifty-four individual projects to build the same number of units as had been formerly squeezed into only one or two large superblock-style projects.* By the late 1960s, the state housing commissioner was most concerned that "it takes as much work by planners to clear the way for 100 units as for 1,000, and what New York needs is a large quantity of housing in a hurry."[5]

The loss of productivity was in no way compensated for by critical accolades. As *Architectural Forum's* Richard Miller remarked, "vest pocket" housing usually "turned out to be merely a junior version of the dreary giants of the past."[6] The Citizens Housing and Planning Council also dismissed increasing densities at the vest pocket developments, including "791 persons per acre at West 60th Street, Manhattan, 808 persons per acre at 155th Street and Amsterdam Avenue and 934 per acre in Chelsea." The CHPC called the new housing "vertical sardine cans."[7]

This criticism seems unfair. Smaller superblocks and high buildings meant that density would increase without necessarily negatively influencing tenant or neighborhood life. These developments, after all, were far less alienating. Stephen Wise Houses, on the Upper West Side, for instance, housed 327 persons per acre at 35 percent ground coverage in high-rise brick towers; then again, it featured only two towers, a nicely landscaped plaza oriented to the neighborhood, and entrances that faced the street (Figure 21). NYCHA also devoted much of its budget to subtle interior changes—such as tile and glazed brick for easier cleaning, faster elevators, and more closet doors—but most of these changes went unappreciated by architectural critics (see Chapter 10). By this time, NYCHA could do no right in the eyes of its many adversaries.[8]

The planning critics missed the bigger and perhaps more troubling story during these years. It turned out that the scatter-site program complemented, rather than replaced, slum clearance. The planning methods for some large superblocks seemed remarkably similar to the old days. Claremont Village, announced in 1962, was a $76 million slum clearance project in the Bronx that grouped four different projects with four thousand total apartments for seventeen thousand people. The many towers of Claremont Village were in theory "architecturally diverse," with a mix of square, T, rectangular, and bar-shaped structures. But what kind of village was this? It was the tower in the park superblock in a new package.[9]

Harlem civic leaders also remained unimpressed with massive new public housing towers—thirty stories high—on the Polo Grounds site designed to house 7,440 people (Figure 22). The New York State Committee on Discrimination pointed out that Polo Grounds "is immediately adjacent to another public housing project (Colonial Park) with 1,000 units. Thus, 2,600 units of public housing would be concentrated in a small, self-contained area." Finally, "Thirty-story-high public housing buildings, with the large number of children involved, is just too high." When completed in 1968 the Polo Grounds did include four thirty-story towers at only 12 percent land coverage. The criticism had little altered the outcome.[10]

NYCHA had quietly discovered a way to maintain high-volume construction by only partially adapting its techniques—such a compromise had obvious costs and benefits. Positively, NYCHA continued to build in the early 1960s even with escalating costs. By 1961 NYCHA had already built 110,000 apartments and had another 38,520 in the pipeline. Volume could only be met with high-rise, large-scale construction of a fairly institutional quality in a limited number of neighborhoods. Even many vest pocket projects were surprisingly large. Most NYCHA projects of the early 1960s were smaller than 1,000 units, but many still contained more than 500 units.[11]

That the authority still uprooted tens of thousands every year during the early 1960s further undermined claims of a new path. Those within the authority had never fully abandoned the bulldozer or tower in the park concept even after years of criticism. Joseph Christian (then the director of program planning and later a respected chairman) in 1964 boasted that twenty-four vest pocket developments were underway, but he opined, "We cannot fall prey to the error of believing that this type of development is the panacea or cure-all for the housing ills that beset the city. . . . Slum areas cannot be contained. . . . Radical action means employment of the bulldozer technique."[12] Slum clearance, according to administrators, pretty well demanded large high rises, too: "Where land costs permit, we still build six-story developments today. However, when the price of land runs from $13 (Gompers Houses, 1964) to $21

STEPHEN WISE HOUSES
MANHATTAN, NEW YORK

NEW YORK STATE DIVISION OF HOUSING
AND COMMUNITY RENEWAL
NEW YORK CITY HOUSING AUTHORITY
KNAPPE & JOHNSON, ARCHITECTS

Figure 21. Even the vest pocket public housing projects look big compared to projects in other cities. This is the Stephen Wise Houses (1965) from the Upper West Side. La Guardia Wagner Archive/NYCHA Photograph Collection.

Figure 22. Even after Robert Moses left, NYCHA did not abandon the high rise. This is Polo Grounds Houses (1968), featuring thirty-story buildings. La Guardia Wagner Archive/NYCHA Photograph Collection.

per square foot (Straus Houses, 1965), both in lower Manhattan, we are compelled to go up 19 or 20 stories."[13]

A Fresh Design Vision

There seemed to be little hope for enhanced architectural quality during the 1960s. A bitter architect who had designed a NYCHA project complained anonymously in the *New York Times* in 1961 that with the overlapping rules from the city, state, and federal governments good design was an impossibility. Any attempt by an architect to "create a more livable environment" would spark a battle with the "various unenlightened and unsympathetic strata of the hierarchy until his defeat is sounded."[14]

The authority claimed, in its internal rebuttal to this criticism, "Almost any designer can produce beautiful or functional designs if the factor of cost could be ignored. The trick is to produce such buildings within the statutory limitation of $2,750 per room, as fixed by the National Housing Act." The authority failed to mention that the room cost did not include slum clearance and other development costs. If the authority only chose to build in slum sites, as had increasingly become the only political path to more public housing, then in fact there was very little wiggle room.[15]

The architect Albert Mayer, in a series of tough radio conversations with NYCHA administrator Ira Robbins in 1962, asserted that the authority's obsession with low ground coverage inhibited the creation of better architecture. Robbins responded defensively, but he grudgingly agreed that he would be happy "to look at [Mayer's] estimates."[16] In a different public appearance in 1960, Robbins sounded like the old guard when he defended the use of "Hudson River red" brick because anything else "was very much more expensive."[17]

Robbins believed that design failings could actually be blamed on the Eisenhower administration, which had created cost limitations ruling out good design. Even when the Kennedy administration in 1961 gave more power over design choices to local authorities, however, New York initially showed little interest. In 1963 Chairman William Reid complained that new federal insistence on a $20,000 total development limit per apartment "permits no flexibility" and was "causing grave problems to the Authority" to build any buildings, much less beautiful ones. Leaders of NYCHA, still clearing slums, knew that they could only meet the $2,750 limit per room with the land and other development costs added separately. Reid's complaint also indicates that even the minimal towers of New York might be costing more than $20,000 per apartment by this time—a significant sum.[18]

Pressure from a new mayor, John Lindsay, finally brought a new era to New York public housing, but his approach quickly confirmed NYCHA's conservative style. Lindsay worried that "the city has settled for stereotyped design of the most depressing sort. Public housing should not be a reminder of how grim life is, but rather how rich. . . ." He set Ira Robbins and others on a search for original forms of public housing—some of which reached fruition. Unfortunately, by this time the declining subsidies, rising construction costs, and complex designs severely limited the number of innovative projects to approximately a dozen. The federal government had loosened the rules but had not dramatically increased the funding so that these new more expensive designs could not have as great an impact. As housing authorities became more creative, they inevitably became less productive.[19]

The few new projects with comparatively dazzling architecture brought fulsome praise. The senior apartment house, 2440 Boston Road (1972), in the Bronx by Davis, Brody, and Associates was twenty stories high and featured an unwieldy but eye-catching overhanging "top eight floors, which have larger apartments with picture windows." Large windows in the hallways were also said to brighten up the interior (Figure 23). The Amsterdam Addition (1974) of twenty-seven stories near Lincoln Center by Oppenheimer, Brady, and Associates "is more like the luxury housing to the east than the public housing to its south. Instead of sheer brick walls, there are triangular columns projecting from the structure's façade. They contain what are in effect bay windows."[20]

Model City housing projects represented a brief return to the older garden-apartment-style buildings last seen in the 1930s. By 1968, the authority had an estimated 64 sites selected with a projected 8,000 apartments. A development in Bedford Stuyvesant, for instance, featured a protective canopy, ceramic mosaics, and underground parking garages with play and sitting areas above; in other words, the landscape was humane. The authority also experimented with rehabilitation and low-scale housing during the 1960s but not on a large scale.[21]

The emphasis on better design, when coupled to declining subsidies, had meanwhile stalled the whole program. The housing authority actually built only approximately six thousand units between 1965 and 1970, the slowest pace since the end of World War II. The architects, according to NYCHA chairman Simeon Golar, "were designing for the ages . . . and no one could afford it." A few architects even "had to be discharged for non-production."[22] As an article lauding these projects indicated, "Only about a dozen of the developments reflect the new design trend, and in view of the Federal Government's moratorium on housing commitments, officials are reluctant to predict whether the trend will continue." These projects proved very expensive. The Amsterdam addition

2440 BOSTON ROAD BRONX, NEW YORK
NEW YORK CITY HOUSING AUTHORITY

DAVIS, BRODY & ASSOCIATES, ARCHITECTS
HOUSING ASSISTANCE ADMINISTRATION

Figure 23. 2440 Boston Road (1972) was part of a brief era of design reform at the Authority. Developments like this were different, but were they better? La Guardia Wagner Archive/NYCHA Photograph Collection.

apparently cost $47,484 per unit, including all development costs. Such high costs had only been made possible by changes in federal law designed to encourage better design, but they were indefensible as part of a low-rent housing program.[23]

Even traditional-style construction faltered. As Albert Walsh explained to a U.S. House of Representatives subcommittee in 1969, construction costs (even for standard buildings) imperiled new housing: "New York

City, where competitive low bids on public housing projects are currently averaging 30% above the statutory cost limits, is not unique."[24] The city, in many cases, would have to make up the difference in subsidies in order to continue building, but this yielded a decreasing number of projects. The Board of Estimate, at a time when the city's financial picture had worsened, began to balk at ever increasing costs and outer borough sites.[25]

When the pipeline did temporarily reopen in the early 1970s, the low quality of the developments built did not necessarily make a case for public housing. Simeon Golar, then the chairman, hoped to get NYCHA back in the construction business at any price. Much of the construction, which had to be very fast, was to be through "turnkey" projects. This development process used private developers to build projects that were then sold, as completed units, to the city. A longtime NYCHA administrator John Simon remembered in 1990, "We rushed like crazy to finish 10,000 units. The bad effect was that it was 10,000 units that were built on a shoestring, and secondly, not built well. The Authority suffers from that now." These developments remain a sore spot for NYCHA managers. Innovation in architecture and contracting luckily played a minor role in NYCHA's history.[26]

As ugly as many of the red brick towers were, they were built economically and with durability in mind. Mass housing for the poor in the United States is, quite simply, unlikely to be beautiful. A leading architectural analyst lamented, "In spite of well-meaning efforts . . . we have built not one internationally distinguished . . . housing example within many miles of City Hall."[27] In retrospect, this might have been for the best. Not only did innovation cost more—but as in St. Louis and Great Britain—experimentation often led to untested designs that proved unsustainable.[28]

Postwar Landscape Design: From Passive to Active Recreation

New York's administrators proved more talented in ensuring that their grounds served the tenants in meaningful ways. One might argue, in fact, that the willingness to change and maintain the superblock landscape helped save projects as the population became younger and more destructive. Unlike housing authorities across the country, NYCHA's grounds softened the appearance of the towers. Managers added useful passive and active recreation spaces for tenants of all ages even though more elaborate landscape renovations, just like the high-cost architectural experiments, failed to be widely applied.

The expansion in NYCHA superblocks in the postwar era did not at first promise a verdant future. The towers, now often ten stories or higher, overwhelmed the landscapes, but the authority publicly boasted of "park-like settings with benches, playgrounds, winding paths, large open lawn areas and dense tree plantings." The authority had also donated many acres of open space to the Parks Department because sufficient park and playground space would aid the transformation of slums into good neighborhoods.[29]

NYCHA invested millions in its landscapes during the postwar boom. At large centrally located projects such as the Jacob Riis Houses (1949) and the Alfred Smith Houses (1953), for instance, tenants benefited from a large central mall, wide pathways with curbs, rows of trees, and densely planted bushes and trees around the buildings (see Figure 17 on p. 139). By the 1950s the mature trees and lawns partly humanized the massive towers. Outer-borough projects such as Woodside Houses (1949) and Eastchester Houses (1950) in the city program were probably the most attractive of this era because lower-rise buildings could be comfortably surrounded with trees, grassy central malls, and walkways lined with trees and benches (see Figure 14 on p. 115).

Less impressive landscapes from this time featured hard surfaces with randomly placed lines of trees and benches at projects such as Brownsville Houses (1948). The hard surfaces for the children in the project likely reflected the neighborhood's tough reputation. Truly massive towers, usually floating in space, could be only slightly softened by landscaping; such developments include Dyckman Houses (1951), Bushwick Gardens (1960), and Claremont Village (1964). Vandalism problems associated with these projects made these landscapes even harder to maintain in the long term (Figure 24).[30]

NYCHA's staff did not shy away from occasional self-criticism. In 1962, Luciano Miceli, an assistant landscape architect, decried "the monotone or rigidness of the atmosphere created." As he saw it, "In our projects we are often dwarfed by buildings one hundred or more feet high." In his opinion, "Our efforts have too often resulted in a stereotyped, monotonous atmosphere. High-rise buildings are even, symmetrically placed on a leveled off site. Trees are then placed at 40' intervals along walks, playgrounds . . . and sitting areas are inserted. This is not design." Aside from these momentary twinges of regret, rarefied aesthetics factored very little into NYCHA calculations.[31]

The relationship between buildings and plantings had become predictable, but NYCHA had mastered the basics of large-scale horticulture. Landscapers now looked after grounds that were far superior to those of their peers in other cities. A member of the landscaping staff enumerated a decade's activity in 1960: "In the past ten years the Authority has planted over 26,000 shade trees, 22,000 minor trees, nearly 300,000 miscellaneous hedge plants, over 300,000 Regels privet, 28,000 evergreen

Figure 24. Landscaping could hardly make up for high-rise alienation at Dyckman Houses (1951) in Manhattan. La Guardia Wagner Archive/NYCHA Photograph Collection.

shrubs and over 200,000 miscellaneous shrubs." It added to these plants "annually about 57,000 pounds of grass seed; 700,000 pounds of commercial fertilizer; 1,800 cubic yards of humus, and 1,000 cubic yards of manure." Most remarkably, in an average year such as 1959, it replaced 35,000 shrubs and 624 of 41,000 trees.[32]

Replacement had a cumulative effect. In 1964, Chairman William Reid boasted of 55,000 trees in place and annual replacement of 100,000 shrubs. This landscape was by no means a no-frills operation: "Landscaping costs for 16 new developments under construction in 1961 totaled slightly more than $5,000,000. Maintenance costs, including payroll for a work force of 1,100 permanent and seasonal employees, approximated $3,600,00 in 1961." By 1961 NYCHA buildings sat on only 300 of the 1,540 acres in its possession.[33]

The numbers, however impressive, failed to account for functionality. Growing numbers of children in the authority's projects in the late 1950s had created pressure for active recreation. Some of the lawns eroded under "illegal" tenant use, and the fines for children who dared to play on them would have had to have been issued, as they often were not, to have an effect. Keeping children off the plants and malls had, for instance, become a growing part of the authority's job. By 1959, the authority was reporting that it "contracted for over 50,000 lineal feet of chain link fence" in just that year.[34]

The newly appointed chairman William Reid notified the public in 1958 that changes would have to be made, largely because the average public housing project with "approximately one thousand families, has a population of more than two thousand youngsters under twenty-one." Fort Greene Houses, for instance, had seventy-nine hundred tenants under the age of twenty-one and Smith Houses had forty-two hundred. Across NYCHA, 55 percent of project residents were now under twenty-one, a rate double the city-wide average. It is a percentage, in certain respects, that illustrates NYCHA's similarity to other housing authorities facing growing numbers of unsupervised children and teenagers.[35]

Reid now promised, "Instead of building large lawns that nobody can walk on, we'll build more and bigger playgrounds." He estimated that while this new emphasis would be initially expensive, it would "save in repair costs by giving youngsters places to use up their energy in play rather than in mischief in the buildings and on the grounds."[36] Thus, the authority "decided to dig up grass and uproot shrubbery at some of its projects and pave the space for hopscotch, lotsie, roller skating, top spinning and other traditional games." At Stephen Foster Houses, for instance, "an acre of lawn and benches will be pared to one-fifth its present size and the freed area converted into play space."[37]

The management staff, facing thousands of children on their

grounds, still thought in the early 1960s that insufficient attention was being paid to "usefulness" as had been promised in 1958. Sam Becker, the deputy director of design, nevertheless refused to accept that open green space lacked utility: lawns were "dust-free and sound absorbing" and increased "usefulness of a project in making a project quieter, cleaner, cooler and more livable." He thought most tenants passively enjoyed these places. A way was found, temporarily, to bridge these different points of view.[38]

NYCHA embarked on a memorable era of design experimentation in order to pioneer a better blend of aesthetics and utility. Innovative landscaping of the 1960s became the hallmark of NYCHA publicity, even though it affected only a few developments. Some additions were modest; for instance, the artist Constantino Nivola added animal sculptures as ornaments at Alexander Hamilton Houses and Stephen Wise Houses in 1963. With outside grants other developments could add murals, canopies, and "colored asphalt walks, tubular steel fencing, solid hedges . . . and new paving patterns to provide texture and variety."[39]

A number of high-profile renovations more dramatically revolutionized a few public housing grounds. Chairman William Reid in 1965 reported that "with outside funds, a number of (sterile) lawns have been converted to active use, designed as plazas for social interaction or outdoor amphitheatres for music, dance, drama and other forms of cultural expression." These renovations, by prominent designers and funded by the Astor Foundation, earned NYCHA awards from the American Society of Landscape Architects and the New York State AIA.[40]

One of those called upon to redesign grounds, the landscape architect Pedro Friedberg, dismissed what passed for renovation at most public housing sites, including "concrete tables, shielded by striped umbrellas made of metal, thus achieving a grim proletarian parody of the country-club terrace."[41] Friedberg created the first of his innovative play areas at Carver Houses in East Harlem. "All fences and grass were eliminated; trees were saved. Huge mounds of earth were moved in order to change the previously flat three-block expanse into one with varied levels. The multi-leveled amphitheater . . . placed in the middle thus seemed to be carved out of the ground."[42]

At Jacob Riis Houses (Figure 25), the *New York Times* critic Ada Louise Huxtable raved about Friedberg's "four 'outdoor rooms' . . . that run between the brick apartment towers for two full blocks formerly filled with off-limits grass." She was captivated by "a quiet, raised sitting area with fountain and flowers, a sunken amphitheater surrounded by a pergola and promenade, a social plaza with benches and planters, and chil-

Figure 25. NYCHA entered into a brief but well-publicized era of landscape innovation in the 1960s. The amphitheater at the Jacob Riis Houses (seen here as a model) garnered much praise. La Guardia Wagner Archive/NYCHA Photograph Collection.

dren's playground, all executed to an exceptionally high standard."
Friedberg also designed innovative grounds at Sutter Houses and Seth
Low Houses. As attractive as they were, these landscapes were expensive
and the application of a similar landscape program to many more
NYCHA developments was inconceivable. These experimental landscapes also suffered from vandalism in the long term, some of which
may been related to impractical design concepts.[43]

More successful in the long term, and innovative in a quiet way, would
be NYCHA's constructive subsidy of tenant gardens (Figure 26). The
Tenant Garden Contest, initiated in 1962, reflects NYCHA's willingness
to commit resources that grease participation. After assigning plots to
groups of tenants, the authority provided "assistance in the form of manpower to dig up the bed, gardening instruction, and a small stipend to
each garden group for the purchase of plants and other materials." The
authority gave the push, but as was its custom, it left the planting choices
and cultivation to the residents. The contests ultimately involved thousands of tenants. Over time a number of observers have found that many
of the tenant gardens were better preserved than the common spaces
because the tenants felt a sense of ownership. Even today, tenants maintain approximately six hundred gardens. [44]

The decade of the 1960s proved to be one of the authority's most creative eras. Bold architectural designs came off the drawing boards and
landscape designs won awards. Yet creativity had limits. These designs, as
lovely as they seemed, were not mass designs; in the context of tightening budgets they proved prohibitively expensive. Innovation touched
very few superblocks.

That New York was not innovative has proved to be a godsend in long-
term management. Similar, durable buildings have led to economical
management, maintenance, and renovation today. NYCHA actually devoted much of its innovative spirit to quietly retrofitting its project interiors, grounds, and apartments to survive a more troubled population
(Chapter 10). It is sad to say that one of the keys of good public housing
is a numbing standardization, but as the following chapters indicate, the
authority was lucky to have resisted architectural innovation.

Figure 26. NYCHA's tenant garden program, as seen here in Lafayette Gardens Houses (1962), proved an enduring element of NYCHA landscapes. La Guardia Wagner Archive/NYCHA Photograph Collection.

Chapter 9
The Benefits of Social Engineering

Does high-rise public housing inevitably become unmanageable? The process of decline happened so fast in other American cities that the conventional wisdom now holds that disorder was the predestined result of building any high-rise public housing. Yet New York avoided this fate for decades, delaying the onset of serious problems until the late 1960s. The New York City Housing Authority demonstrated that well-managed tower-block housing could remain a long-term option for the working class. The authority accomplished this feat by engineering its towers to an extent that other cities did not think possible or desirable.

New York abandoned its most paternalistic management practices in the 1940s, but just beneath the surface managers continued their quest for social control. NYCHA's most ambitious exercise in postwar social engineering—aggressively engineering racial balance in its projects—represented enlightened social policy in its day, but in the long term it failed to stop racial concentration. This effort did serve, however, an important short-term political function by showing many politicians that the authority remained committed to the notion of a city-wide housing system serving both whites and minorities.

Far more effective policies in the 1950s and 1960s to restrict the number of "problem" and welfare tenants, in spite of racial change, helped preserve the notion of model housing as a legitimate public service rather than a new form of welfare. NYCHA found minority tenants that in everything but skin color were identical to the carefully chosen, primarily white tenancy that was heading to the door. New York, as part of Robert Moses' redevelopment machine, had initially accepted many more welfare and problem families than before, but Moses did not stop what became a successful internal administrative effort to enhance screening.

The combination of liberal racial policies with traditional social mores proved essential to NYCHA's continuing success and contrasts sharply with the policies of many other housing authorities during the 1950s. By opening public housing to all comers as early as the 1930s, administrators in many other cities undermined their reputation and management effectiveness. Most administrators discovered too late the dangers of open admissions in public housing and either did not take effective steps to address these issues—from political or practical perspectives—or faced projects too far gone for reform.

Discrimination in the private housing market made public housing in New York an important source of housing for the city's minorities in the postwar years. One estimate found in 1956 that "less than 1 percent of the private housing built since World War II" in New York State was available on a nondiscriminatory basis.[1] In light of the fact that between 1940 and 1950 the city's black population grew by 63 percent and its Puerto Rican population by 200 percent, discrimination meant crowded and overpriced rentals. Minority families had lower incomes and public housing represented an important and viable option. Whites, after the initial postwar shortage, had plenty of options both in the city and the growing suburbs.[2]

NYCHA in the immediate postwar decade developed a remarkably progressive integration program, but it did so in a very quiet way. In light of the fact that NYCHA hit record levels of growth, the degree of integration detailed below is particularly heartening. Compared to a city such as Chicago, where even token integration set off rioting and political turbidity that destabilized the whole program, New York City's initial acceptance of the principle of integration reflects wise leadership, which chose not to make grand statements about integration, as well as a general open-mindedness of New York's population. Whites ultimately abandoned public housing and eventually fought its expansion in their neighborhoods, but NYCHA's ability to put integrated public housing, particularly the higher-income city-aided projects, in primarily white neighborhoods made a major difference in keeping public housing in the mainstream of the city's life.

NYCHA's record through the mid-1950s had been impressive. Federal projects in operation by 1954 had been *initially tenanted* (going back to the 1930s) on a cumulative average of 74.9 percent white and 21.1 percent black; state projects at 53.5 percent white and 38.7 percent black; city parts I and II at 73.6 percent white and 24.2 percent black; and city part III at 87 percent white and 12.2 percent black. (Puerto Ricans primarily made up the remainder in all of these different projects.) The black population was spread much more evenly among the growing number of postwar federal and state projects compared to the prewar pattern, in contrast not only to private housing in New York City but most public housing elsewhere. That the city projects, often in all white neighborhoods, had been tenanted with an appreciable black population is particularly impressive.[3]

Unfortunately, the speed of racial change muted integration in federal and state projects by 1954, when these statistics were compiled. By 1954, federal projects had slipped to 58.9 percent white, 34.7 percent black, and approximately 8 percent Puerto Rican; state projects were only 40.7 percent white, 47.7 percent black, and approximately 11 percent Puerto Rican. Only the higher-income city-funded programs, which were not subject to strict federal and state income rules, remained relatively static: city parts I and II were collectively 27.5 percent black, and city part III only 14.6 percent black. Whites still made up a majority (58.7 percent) in all NYCHA projects in 1954, but blacks (33.7 percent) and Puerto Ricans (7.4 percent) were rising fast as a proportion. New York was more integrated than Chicago, where by 1955 nonwhites made up 75 percent of tenants, but New York was headed in the same direction. Between 1954 and 1955, for instance, while blacks and whites continued to move into NYCHA projects in about even numbers, more than twice as many white families (5,740) moved out as black (2,197).[4]

Maintaining integration became NYCHA's new battle. The Housing Act of 1949, which encouraged eviction of high-income tenants, was a major factor in racial change, but state-project income levels rose slowly as well. Between 1946 and 1955, 4,464 mostly white families left "involuntarily" primarily because of excessive income. When NYCHA successfully built high-rise towers in predominantly white areas, as in the lower Bronx, protests and white flight often undercut temporary gains in neighborhood integration. Condemnation of land for Moses' redevelopment placed a heavy burden on fragilely housed minorities and tended to speed up racial change in NYCHA development because site tenants gained an edge in admissions. By 1956, for instance, at least 40 percent of slum clearance site tenants and 50 percent of public housing site clearance tenants were black or Puerto Rican. NYCHA's statistics indicate that between 1954 and 1955 the number one source of new tenants were site occupants with the largest number being Puerto Ricans.[5]

To informed outsiders it appeared that NYCHA was building a second ghetto that would replicate the social problems of the first. The noted urbanist Charles Abrams, then in charge of the State Commission Against Discrimination (SCAD), accused NYCHA in 1956 of "building racial 'ghettos' in Harlem."[6] He revealed to the public that "14 public housing projects are 85 percent or more minority occupied" in previously minority neighborhoods.[7] The New York Committee of Racial Equality also objected to yet another Harlem project in 1958: "Since New York City housing is predominantly segregated, merely placing people in projects in the neighborhoods in which they have been living perpetuates and seals segregation in official mortar and brick."[8]

The authority was on its way to becoming a minority-concentrated system in a still overwhelmingly white city, but NYCHA officials at first temporized. In 1956, Warren Moscow, the executive director, stood firmly against the use of a "quota" system to maintain racial integration, saying, "We would not have white apartments and black apartments."[9] Yet NYCHA also touted racially based integration programs it optimistically called a success. While 99 percent black tenancy had been common for even new projects in minority areas, officials would boast that a blend of civic promotion and NYCHA publicity generated "a 58% Negro and 42% Non-Negro tenancy" at Forest Houses (1956). On closer examination, however, the "Non-Negro" percentage looked less impressive, bolstered as it was by 132 Puerto Rican families. White families actually made up only 10 percent of the tenancy. NYCHA optimistically "stressed the achievement of a 10% White tenancy as proof of community endorsement of desegregation."[10]

A few so-called success stories obscured the real story. Projects on the whole still remained unevenly tenanted by race. For example, Marlboro Houses (1958) in Coney Island Houses in 1959 featured a 93.3 percent white tenancy, like many on the fringe of the city, while the percentage of minorities in projects in mostly black neighborhoods closer in skyrocketed.[11]

It was only when Mayor Wagner reorganized NYCHA in 1958 that the authority made a genuine attempt to deal with both all-white projects and segregated black projects. By 1959 blacks and Puerto Ricans accounted for 57 percent of public housing families. After reorganization, the new administrators aimed to rebalance projects on a path to segregation. William Reid welcomed a 1957 state law that gave priority to residents already living within one mile of a new project because it might attract more white tenants. At the same time, he was optimistic that "open land sites, away from minority and ethnic concentrations, offer the best possible opportunity for integration."[12] Reid bracketed the new policy by promising, as in the past, "We don't try to create too sharp or too sudden a difference between our projects and the neighborhoods around them. It is our aim to stimulate integration, not to force it."[13]

NYCHA created a new division, Intergroup Relations, to actively encourage integration. A NAACP veteran, Madison Jones, lead the unit and announced, "We're trying to kill the idea that public housing is minority housing" in order to "reverse the tendency towards segregation." In areas resistant to blacks, however, "as little as 10 per cent Negro or Puerto Rican tenancy would be regarded as satisfactory."[14] Intergroup Relations worked with area civic and religious groups to find diverse tenants and created brochures to promote particular projects to targeted groups. The authority, in partnership with this outreach, ranked its different developments by their relative need for integration. Administrators called these different levels "phases," "The phases [could] be summarized as: I—whites first; II—whites only; III—nonwhites first, half the time."[15]

At first it appeared that the unit was having great success. In 1960 NYCHA reported: "Fifty-five percent of all tenants who moved into projects during the past calendar quarter were White. For the entire year that the Authority has utilized the Phase program, White tenants have constituted 52% [compared to 40 percent the year before] of all new tenants admitted to projects." In Phase III, blacks and Puerto Ricans went from 7.5 percent to 20 percent of new tenants. NYCHA had to admit, however, "Although the Phase Program has succeeded in increasing the number of White tenants moving into projects, it has failed to reduce the number of such tenants who continue to move out of projects."[16] Not even all the new projects were integrated. The new tenants of St. Mary's Park Houses in the Bronx, for instance, wondered in 1959, "Why is the project segregated? We were promised that it would be integrated." The management responded only, "We tried."[17]

Bernard Roscho, a NYCHA whistleblower, argued in *The New Leader* that NYCHA's integration program was not only ineffective but also unfair: "The immediate result [of the phase system] for non-white applicants is a sharp reduction in the number of apartments available." Not only were many low-income minority tenants priced out of higher phases, but in some of the phase buildings, "Apartments have been held vacant, sometimes for months." In certain cases, too, smaller white families got larger apartments as an incentive for moving into a minority-dominated development.[18]

"The article is filled with misstatements, half truths, innuendoes and misleading assertions," was NYCHA's curt response. Authority officials did not, however, actually refute Roscho's description of the system. Instead, administrators took him to task on his larger analysis: "The article is based largely on the assumption that Negro and Puerto Rican families comprise the bulk of residents of this City who need public housing." They believed, however, "there are many more White families than minority families who are living under substandard or grossly overcrowded conditions" and that there were many more poor whites than blacks eligible for public housing in the city as a whole. Because "public housing is virtually the most important source of decent urban housing for White, as well as for non-White, families of low income" it should not be allowed to become racially exclusive. They could identify 230,000 white families in substandard housing versus 140,000 black and Puerto Rican families. NYCHA still pursued its vision of public housing as a municipal service that could potentially serve a wide range of New Yorkers.[19]

The authority eventually provided the public some clarity on the operation of the phase program. Initial selection of tenants remained, it claimed, an "objective system which measure[s] the housing needs of the applicant" along with factors such as neighborhood preferences, slum clearance priorities, and veteran status. Above all, the policy merely "encourages, but does not require, those who are entitled to apartments to live in certain projects" and it claimed that there had been no decrease in minority families since the integration program had been established (which was true).[20] William Reid downplayed intentional vacancy rates even though he admitted that "managers are authorized to hold apartments vacant when applicants whose occupancy would further integration appear to be interested in renting," yet "the number of apartments kept vacant for this purpose is very small. . . . Excluding projects in their initial stages of renting, only 65 apartments out of more than 105,000 were not rented" in 1960.[21]

The New York State Commission Against Discrimination called in NYCHA administrators to question them about the allegations in the article. Reid informed the commission that the process of application, now using an IBM machine, remained colorblind, and that "3.5 percent of the white population of the city and 13.6 of the Negro population are living in public housing."[22] Almost all of the city's leading civic organizations *endorsed* NYCHA's program, including the NAACP, the Urban League, unions, and the Community Service Society.[23] Elements of the black press, in contrast, accused NYCHA of trying to "discriminate against Negroes and Puerto Ricans."[24]

By September the State Commission Against Discrimination had launched an investigation of the program and by 1962 it disagreed that NYCHA's system was a "benign quota." Evidence of "a record system identifying all applicants and tenants according to their race" did not help NYCHA's case. Investigators considered the policy to be in violation of the state law against discrimination. The analysis ended by chastising NYCHA administrators: "The determination of the Authority that the quota system is meritorious does not justify its adoption in contravention of law."[25] NYCHA tweaked its system with an eye to legality. In 1963, NYCHA would report that while the phase system still operated after tenants had been accepted, "the Authority has no record system identifying applicants according to their race or color by colored tags, by special markings, or by any other designating method."[26]

Beyond the harsh words, SCAD's investigation established the legal basis for NYCHA's integration policies; Intergroup moved ahead with its outreach programs and the phase system. Intergroup worked doubly hard to sell projects to whites. Efforts in 1964 brought forth new success stories, including Williams Houses tenanted at 70 percent white, Chelsea at 68 percent white, Claremont at 33 percent white, and McKinley at 27 percent white. NYCHA explained away any discrepancies: "While some of the above might appear to have small proportions of white families, they are largely those located in areas in which our chances of achieving larger proportions were very small. . . ." The Bronx's Edenwald Houses, too, "improved" from 44.7 percent white in 1959 to 52.7 percent white in 1964.[27]

Even with this scattered progress, the figures for the authority as a whole remained sobering. In 1966, for instance, whites were leaving in far larger numbers from all the different phases than could be replaced. In 1967, Intergroup Relations listed twenty-four developments as "predominantly white"; twenty-three developments as "quite well balanced"; and the remaining developments (approximately one hundred) as "predominantly minority."[28] The white population, in spite of a decade of integration projects, in 1969 stood at only 27.9 percent (down from 42.7 percent in 1962, for instance), whereas the black population accounted for 46.2 percent and the Puerto Rican population for 25.9 percent. By 1970 the authority would frankly admit that, among many reasons for racial change, "the pressures generated by the Housing and Development Administration and the Urban Renewal areas make academic and ineffective much of the planning done by the Housing Authority toward integration."[29]

The authority had two different public housing systems: predominantly white, higher-income projects in the outer boroughs, and primarily black or Puerto Rican projects in the rebuilt slums. In 1970, Northeast Bronx projects remained "predominantly white with an average of 73.5%"; South and Central Bronx projects had experienced the departure of "a little less than half the white population," leaving projects "one-half white, one-third black, and one-sixth Puerto Rican." South Brooklyn and Williamsburg projects had become mostly minority whereas Coney Island and Sheepshead Bay projects retained "their original primary white tenancy." East New York remained well integrated, but whites were dropping fast. Harlem projects had become almost entirely minority and West Side projects were on their way to nonwhite status. On the Lower East Side "the trend is toward a population which is nearly one-half Puerto Rican." Queens projects appeared more balanced, but whites were headed for the door. Most Staten Island projects were 80 percent white with only a few exceptions. In most parts of the city the phase program was abandoned "because there were not enough whites to sustain it city-wide."[30]

That older white tenants had become easy marks for criminals did not help the attempts to maintain racial integration. In 1967, NYCHA officials reported that muggings and purse snatchings, which were growing system-wide, "are frequently committed by young Negro youth against older White senior citizens and therefore the whole problem has racial overtones."[31] By 1971 the white percentage had fallen to 29.1 percent of tenants and remained concentrated in city projects. NYCHA would also report that by 1973 over "88% of the applications filed were from non-whites." The white exodus proceeded at a blistering pace. By 1974, NYCHA was 14.1 percent white, 57.7 percent black, and 28.2 percent Puerto Rican. NYCHA had obviously reached and passed the racial tipping point. In 1995, whites had slipped to 8 percent of families, and in 2006 whites constituted only about 5 percent of families. Blacks accounted for 50 percent of all families and Hispanics another 40 percent. NYCHA had become and remains the racially segregated system its founders had feared. Yet the NYCHA system survives.[32]

Looking back at this integration policy reveals certain lessons. The effort as a whole was obviously a failure when seen in the long term. In the short term, however, it did preserve political support for housing by making it clear that NYCHA intended to create a system for all ill-housed New Yorkers rather than just poor minorities. The reality of racial change was less upbeat, and the program at best stalled overwhelming demographic pressures, but the effort counted in the maintenance of such a large program that stretched over many boroughs.

> *Sometimes I yearn for a new invention—something akin to a Geiger counter that would enable us to reject unerringly the potential troublemakers, when they apply for an apartment. How tranquil life might become!*
>
> —*NYCHA chairman William Reid, 1959*[33]

NYCHA board member Ira Robbins might have sounded heartless in 1965, but like other housing advocates he still dreamed of model housing: "If we had no screening, that would be the end of the movement for good housing. . . . These problem families would make a hash out of it. It's a welfare and social problem first. Treat them first and then we'll house them." Robbins's opinion reflects the dominant NYCHA opinion until 1968, when NYCHA lifted some of its restrictions on welfare tenants. And even then, public housing as welfare housing never sat right with NYCHA administrators.[34]

Racial change was worrisome, but the changing social situation of the increasingly minority population seemed far more threatening. Had NYCHA developments filled to the brim only with working, two-parent, black or Puerto Rican families all would have been well. Up until the 1950s it was obvious that white or black, NYCHA tenants were largely working families with two parents. By 1951, however, managers worried that "during the past year, the Authority has admitted to projects a large number of unmarried women with out of wedlock children. Most of these have been relief recipients" sent by the Welfare Department or the authority's own slum clearance operations. Most were "non-white" and concentrated in federal projects; collectively they absorbed "practically every vacancy which has occurred in the latter projects." Administrators found that "these women, as a rule, exercise very little control over their children" and inflicted "considerable damage to project property."[35]

Although it seemed "impossible to deny apartments to those living on sites which the Authority is clearing," NYCHA officials as early as 1951 believed they should. Commissioner Stichman of the State Housing Commission was already "adamant in his insistence that apartments in State-aided projects be made available solely to the normal family and that in no event shall an apartment be rented to an unmarried woman with children." NYCHA managers agreed: "The position taken by the State Division of Housing is, in our opinion, sound." They proposed, too, "that the Authority adopt as a policy for all projects that occupancy be limited to normal types of families and that unwed women with out of wedlock children be denied admission." NYCHA was not a social housing program: "Our experience definitely establishes the fact that admission to public housing projects does not change their manner of living."[36]

In 1953, NYCHA raised income levels to allow entry of higher income but still poor families, but this exercised at best a mild effect on changing social patterns in public housing. The more dramatic addition in 1953 of "desirability" to the authority's overall standards of admission and continued occupancy had a much more significant impact (Appendix B). A total of twenty-one factors now denoted non-desirability, including narcotic addiction, single parenthood, out-of-wedlock children, teen parenting, "highly irregular work history," "lack of parental control," mental illness, poor housekeeping, and even "lack of furniture." Factors such as these would be considered to determine if a tenant would endanger the health, safety, or morals of a project. A Tenant Review Board staffed by the director of management and other high-ranking officials would review admission and continued occupancy on the basis of non-desirability. By 1960 applicants culled under these factors had to be separately evaluated by NYCHA's Social Consultation Unit; essentially, their application process came to an end.[37]

NYCHA believed in keeping out and controlling problem families, but it did not want to appear elitist. The authority would claim in 1958, for instance, that "out-of-wedlock children are not necessarily a bar to admission to public housing."[38] Some years later, however, the authority frankly admitted that while "none of the 21 traits necessarily disqualified a family," now "the evaluation process took so long that if an applying family was referred to the social service division its chance of getting an apartment was remote." Problem families in many cases knew not to apply.[39] A longtime resident of Patterson Houses in the Bronx remembered what it was like in the 1950s: "I think the Housing Authority had a law that you had to be married in order to live there. And initially, most of the families in our buildings had two parents present." Another older tenant at Queensbridge Houses remembered, "When you moved in, you had to show a marriage license."[40]

Chairman Philip Cruise, the longtime protégé of Robert Moses, approved this policy in spite of the fact that it meant even fewer Title I site tenants would actually gain public housing apartments. The policy, in tandem with factors such as income limits and better options elsewhere, cancelled out the bold promises for public housing relocation in Moses' Title I planning materials. The policy also subtly defied the emphasis in the Housing Acts of 1949 (and later 1954) that public housing serve as a destination for those displaced for Title I or other redevelopment activities. The selectivity of public housing would, in fact, become a serious political liability to Robert Moses by the late 1950s. Moses and Cruise likely approved the policy at the time not only because at heart Moses cared little about relocation, but also because management concerns trumped all others.[41]

Such provisions would keep out a great many disorderly tenants, but low federal and state income limits, white departures, tenant divorce, and the pressure of both Title I and the authority's own slum clearance program meant that NYCHA had to house at least some welfare families (and some single mothers), a higher proportion of which were troubled. NYCHA, for instance, gave "Title I site tenants . . . top priority" in spite of the fact that Moses allowed the authority plenty of selectivity.[42] Managers believed that relocation officials often "refrain from asking questions that would reveal a negative history."[43] NYCHA estimated that 330,000 families would be relocated just between 1955 and 1957 for Title I, highways, and public housing clearance. To put this in perspective, in 1955 only 18,213 public housing units were completed. Site pressure meant, for instance, that of 2,009 Puerto Rican families accepted for public housing between 1954 and 1955 (about half of whom were site tenants), 475 were on welfare in spite of the twenty-one factors that should have kept them out.[44]

Even with the authority's rules, and a vacancy rate of only approximately 0.2 percent between 1946 and 1956, the welfare and lowest income tenancy inched upward. Vacancies available for site tenants increased in new buildings and as a result of the enforcement of income limits on white families. Between 1946 and 1955, 11,254 families moved out of NYCHA projects (6,790 voluntarily and 4,464 involuntarily). Welfare tenancy increased from 6.1 percent in all projects in 1944 to 13 percent in 1956, and in federal projects alone went from 6.2 percent to 16.8 percent. Annual turnover in a year such as 1954 was 9.13 percent for all projects. Other cities experienced more dramatic turnover, but New York's figures were more dangerous in light of NYCHA's high-rise structure. Nor did they augur well for NYCHA's financial future. In 1947, the annual federal contribution had been only 22 percent of the contractual costs, but by 1956 the subsidy had risen to 86 percent. Simply put, poorer tenants had to be subsidized at a higher level to keep NYCHA solvent.[45]

A highly publicized report by the housing expert Elizabeth Wood, who as executive director of the Chicago Housing Authority had opened that system to welfare families, warned that now New York was collecting "families who represent the consolidated failure of social agencies."[46] She warned that "the tendency of normal families to reject our projects is an indication of an illness that may well be fatal. . . . They don't sign petitions against the injustices . . . they just go elsewhere."[47]

Under pressure the authority thus initiated another "'get tough' policy" in 1957, this time to "oust 'unsalvageable' families unable to control their delinquent children." Management aimed to protect "decent families" and managers were now "required to report every incident of hoodlums or vandalism involving tenants" to speed eviction.[48] Activists from the Citizens Housing and Planning Council now could be found protesting two thousand eviction cases in process in 1958. In reality, critics had little reason to worry. Even a decision for eviction by the Tenant Review Board went to Municipal Court, and "if the Judge grants eviction, the Court still gives the tenant what it considers enough time to find another apartment. It takes nine months to a year to evict a tenant." As the authority openly admitted, "Very few tenants are evicted for undesirability. We now have more than 100,000 families living in public housing and last year only 227 families were evicted for undesirability."[49]

Well-intentioned social agencies had fallen far behind the realities of life in the developments. In 1960, NYCHA counted 3,402 families that "posed serious management problems during the first six months of this year."[50] Managers of NYCHA identified welfare tenants as a disproportionate source of trouble: "37.8 percent of the problem families receive assistance from the Department of Welfare. Their role as problem families is grossly disproportionate, since they constitute only 12 percent of the total tenant body." Certain behaviors had become ethnic specialties: assault, gang activity and unstable family situations were mostly black problems; narcotics involved mostly Puerto Ricans; and housekeeping problems related to senility and mental instability affected mostly whites.

Problem families by the mid-1960s had become concentrated in federal projects such as Brevort (6.6 percent problem families) and state projects such as Brownsville (9.5 percent problem families). Although a few higher-income city projects had growing disorder—Vladeck City had 5 percent problem families—most housed under 1 percent problem families. New York's system as a whole was still less troubled than other cities, but even a comparatively small number of problem families in high-rise public housing could make life unpleasant for their neighbors.[51]

The authority created a new policy in 1957 to prevent additional concentration of welfare tenants: "A new order prohibits the assignment of relief clients . . . to any project in which 20 per cent or more of the apartments are occupied" by families on welfare. The policy, really just a reversion to older methods, emerged because in some projects the welfare population had risen as high as 54 percent. The total NYCHA population might have been only 12 percent relief at this point, but this percentage includes the unsubsidized city-funded projects where relief was almost zero vs. 17.5 percent in state or federal projects. One in three Fort Greene families, for instance, subsisted on welfare.[52]

The policy at first did not necessarily have a salutary effect because many projects, formerly with low welfare figures, took on more: "As of June 1, 1958 there are 22 projects (including the original 14), whose welfare tenancy is over 20%. This is perhaps a natural consequence since under our present policy the eligible Welfare families channeled into other projects and gradually increased their percentages." NYCHA considered removing the 20 percent ban but ultimately took no action.[53] By 1962, however, the authority would claim the program was working. The authority's comparatively low level of welfare tenancy city-wide, 11.7 percent, resulted from a policy, it believed, that "endeavors to house public assistance families so that no one development will have an undue proportion."[54]

The combination of the twenty-one factors *with* the dispersion system, in the context of a relatively tight housing market, made the system work. Welfare administrators, for instance, knew firsthand that the use of the twenty-one factors, including a category marking "irregular work history," kept out a large number of welfare tenants. Indeed, NYCHA after 1957 managed to keep its welfare percentage below 15 percent into the mid-1960s, a figure approximately half the national average and significantly lower than rates in many of America's most troubled big-city housing systems.[55]

Social engineering aided management. In New York, the effort to maintain racial integration may have proved quixotic, but the integration effort had intangible public relations benefits. Many whites, and even many black civil rights leaders, could at least have confidence that NYCHA intended to keep public housing integrated. Most effective were the twenty-one factors and restrictions on welfare concentration that made sure the new minority tenancy would be a good match for the high standards of rent collection and maintenance that NYCHA had established. These policies would come under fire in the 1960s and were never absolute blocks to welfare clients and single mothers, but they played a critical role in bolstering management in the short term by slowing the shift to a more dependent population.

NYCHA had faced many of the same challenges that bedeviled housing authorities in other cities. Its projects tipped to mostly minority and the number of disorderly tenants rose. The authority had an advantage working in a tight housing market when it chose to retighten admissions, but from the 1930s onward it had always carefully considered and tweaked its policies. The Chicago Housing Authority, like many less successful housing authorities, had already built a system in the 1930s that was oriented to minorities and very low-income tenants. Steps after the war to attract higher-income tenants and whites had little chance of success especially as new projects were poorly designed and managed. Two-parent families deserted public housing in the 1960s while single-parent families, usually on welfare, skyrocketed to about 70 percent of the population by the mid-1970s.[56]

In St. Louis filtering of housing to working- and middle-class blacks in the 1950s and 1960s reduced demand. The Pruitt-Igoe complex, already falling apart in the 1960s, could in no way compete. In desperation, the St. Louis Housing Authority filled some of the Pruitt-Igoe vacancies with mostly single mothers on welfare who did little to control their children or pay their rent. The SLHA slashed essential services in maintenance and security as it books tilted into the red. A rent strike, the result of righteous anger against rising rents in no way justified by continuing weak management, bankrupted the authority. By 1970 the vacancy rate at Pruitt-Igoe hit 65 percent. Realizing that rehabilitation could not be justified, because even the poorest of the poor could not be coaxed to live there, the SLHA began demolishing Pruitt-Igoe in 1972.[57]

Chapter 10

Meeting the Management Challenge

The appalling conditions in public housing projects in most American cities by the 1960s created the impression that managing large public housing projects was simply impossible. Appearances could be deceiving. New York found a way to manage projects that while not as disordered as those in other cities already showed signs of strain. The New York City Housing Authority had slowed the growth of problem tenants, but even a small percentage of troubled tenants began to disrupt life in many housing projects by the 1950s.

The staff of NYCHA, faced with vandalism and other antisocial behavior, continued to clean and update the authority's buildings; initiated what became the largest public housing police force in the country; and expanded community programs. These efforts, in no way equally imitated at other housing authorities, helped preserve public housing's competitive advantages in New York's housing market. Cities such as Chicago and St. Louis borrowed only the most superficial aspects of New York's approach to public housing—the high-rise superblocks—rather than the more important methods of management. When buildings became hard to manage, they walked away and left the tenants to fend for themselves.

The first sign of NYCHA's problems actually came early, with an overhaul of New York's largest project, Fort Greene Houses (1944), which contained 3501 units. As early as 1945, Chairman Edmond Butler admitted that in one of the thirteen-story buildings, unsanitary conditions had been "created by the children's misuse of the elevators and public halls, showing an absence of parental guidance and supervision."[1] Problems persisted to the extent that in 1957, for instance, the development had "two gangs of men assigned solely to the task of replacing glass" because "one of the forms of amusement for the children in the area seems to be throwing stones at these large panes of glass."[2] Fort Greene by this time not only had broken glass, but also cracking walls, broken light fixtures, and unhinged doors. The authority had to replace all of the plumbing, repave the paths, substitute wood doors with stainless steel, renovate benches, and replace broken glass. The authority also split the mammoth project in two administratively, creating what are known today as Whitman and Ingersoll Houses.³

Fort Greene was the type of distressed project most attractive to journalists, and NYCHA spent much money to remediate the decline, yet other NYCHA projects contained telltale, if not as severe, signs of disorder by the 1950s. Robert Moses wrote to Chairman Philip Cruise in 1954 to warn him that he had heard "more and more caustic criticisms of conditions in City public housing projects, all pointing to the fact that tenants are not taking care of the property." He added that "these criticisms relate to only a few projects—about five of them."⁴ One longtime NYCHA administrator, Bernard Moses, remembered that by the mid-1950s, Farragut Houses (1952) was "beginning to have some problems in the high rise buildings in maintaining them. There was some degree of vandalism."⁵

The Preusse Report of 1957 confirmed anecdotal muttering and exposés in local newspapers. The report noted that "because of poor procedures of maintenance and repair, at least 5 projects have fallen into a state of disrepair, and in a few cases, real obsolescence is setting in." That approximately 80 projects were already in operation provides some perspective on NYCHA's relative problems, but Preusse also identified troubling trends: "20 percent of the housing projects were suffering from 'heavy vandalism and serious disorder'" and "29.5 per cent of the projects were experiencing 'constant vandalism of a petty nature.'" What defined New York best was that it responded constructively to this criticism on both project and management levels.⁶

After the authority was reorganized in 1958 the new leadership directly inspected all of the authority's projects. Some of the findings were heartening, including the fact that the few troubled projects much publicized in the press did not constitute the bulk of the program: "To our great satisfaction, we have found that the program as a whole consists of well built, well maintained, well managed, modern structures."⁷ The new leadership initiated a program of renovation for the most "run-down" projects and in general rejected the "'penny-wise, pound-foolish' policy of so-called economics in construction that result in high maintenance costs." Subtle improvements during the 1950s had been underway even before reorganization, but they now gained new impetus.⁸

New materials, for instance, meant easier maintenance by the staff and greater tenant satisfaction. Older projects had featured lobbies and hallways with cement floors and apartments often lacked "closets with doors, bathrooms with showers, [and] toilet bowls with seat covers." The newer projects, however, featured lobbies with "inviting entrances with floors of polished tile and multicolored walls of paint, tile, or wallpaper." Hallways were wider and "have bright tile floors and a contrast of color

Figure 27. The typical NYCHA lobby is designed for hard use. Glazed brick, shatterproof glass, and stainless steel have become the materials of choice as NYCHA battles vandals. Photograph by Nicholas Dagen Bloom.

on doors and walls." Apartment interiors now had "light-colored, practical tile floors, modern kitchens and separate dinettes, larger windows, and the simple amenities of closet doors, showers, and toilet covers." Staff and tenants approved of the changes because cleaning became much easier (Figure 27).[9]

Elevators, another initial cost-cutting measure, had quickly proved a liability. Buildings lacked supervised lobbies and rowdy children began to play on the equipment. Managers had found by the 1950s that "while the use of slow speed small cab elevators was more economical . . . they tended to increase vandalism in the lobbies by reason of the congregation of the children at the noon school recess and at 3 o'clock. While waiting for the elevators they did considerable damage to the lobbies." Rather than throw up their hands, they responded constructively: "In our later projects we not only have increased the speed of the elevators but the size of cabs." The skip-stop system (disliked by most tenants) was also eliminated in new buildings.[10]

These different enhancements were not selectively applied but became standard in the late 1950s in *all* of NYCHA's projects then under construction. Many of the NYCHA's older projects were updated to meet the new standards. The quick turnaround on reform made a major difference by the 1960s. Upgrades in design seem to have registered with tenants. A study by the Community Service Society in 1966 of tenant satisfaction in the newly built Claremont Village (1962) found that 70 percent of tenants rated their apartments highly. Tenants may have disliked inconvenient shopping and noisy neighbors, but when asked if "'On the whole would you say Claremont Village is a better or worse place to live than where you lived before?' . . . 78.7 per cent [said] 'better,' 13.9 per cent [said] 'about the same,' and 7.4 per cent [said] 'worse.'"[11]

NYCHA resisted shifting large-scale design theory, but administrators showed a genuine talent for the day-to-day reengineering of high-rise housing. Can the authority's long waiting lists really be attributed simply to New York's housing market, as many would have it, or did a reputation for high-quality interiors play a role? Few apartments for this class of renter, and at such a low price, featured equal amenities or service.

The NYCHA System

New York's housing operations system grew in step with the new superblocks and complemented updates. New York was never afraid to staff its projects at what it considered to be an appropriate level, one borrowed not from tenements but from better apartment houses. Robert Moses, who exercised so much control over the authority's chairmen, permitted the rapid growth in NYCHA staff. As in his parks, he believed that heavy, militaristic-type staffing was an essential element of order in public enterprises. Other housing authorities either tried to cut corners on staffing or allowed patronage and various forms of corruption to undermine the effectiveness of often expensive staff members. It is not simply that NYCHA had a lot of staff members, either; it also organized them to support the housing mission.

High levels of staffing appear to have been the norm at NYCHA projects in the postwar years. As part of an AIA tour in 1952, for instance, officials explained that on average they maintained a ratio of staff to residents of 1 employee to 20 families (80 residents). At Johnson Houses (1948), an average size project with 1,300 apartments in 10 14-story buildings, they maintained a "staff of 56, of which approximately 10 are office employees, the rest being firemen, porters, maintenance men, a gardener, laborers, etc." Officials believed that projects of between 1,200 to 1,600 units could be most efficiently managed. Administrators defended clearance of neighborhoods partly on this basis of labor economies achieved at large developments.[12]

On the grounds heavy staffing translated into constant maintenance. The authority described its maintenance system in 1957: "Our basic method of staffing is one Housing Caretaker (porter) for each high-rise building (14 stories or over), and one Housing Caretaker for three-six story buildings." The porter, on a daily basis, swept all the stairways and mopped the elevators; weekly, he or she mopped the stairwells. A foreman of porters ensured quality control. Every apartment was also painted every three years. These operation standards reflect, if on a more economical basis, methods of operation in privately run apartment buildings in New York City.[13]

Cyril Grossman, a longtime NYCHA manager, recounted the regimented management of the 1950s "Most of the men that subsequently became superintendents and managers were army people. He [a particular superintendent he remembered] would line up all the caretakers in the morning . . . and he would march them down the project and they would drop off at their buildings." He averred that "we did maintain a good, tight running ship, and a good project" under the strict management of the time.[14]

During these years NYCHA continued to demand high expectations from tenants and officials continued apartment inspections. Grossman bragged, "I used to go to every single room . . . and we threw people out for poor housekeeping." He explained, "If you didn't answer promptly, I'd take the key and walk right into the apartment."[15] In 1967 annual visiting still included only one visit by a maintenance man and a more traditional visit by "a housing assistant who comes in to discuss the housing situation in each apartment."[16]

The head of maintenance in 1950, Charles Rutter, took offense at faddish calls for more tenant maintenance. "If you live in an area like New York" he said, "you have been living most of your life in an apartment house of one kind or another . . . you may not be prepared either mentally or physically to accept such responsibility." He had found in his experience at NYCHA's low-rise developments of Clason Point and Edwin Markham that tenant participation "was a gross failure." Tenants lacked the skills, physical ability, or interest in maintenance.[17]

One longtime manager of NYHCA housing remembered the continuing strength of maintenance organization of the 1960s but like others acknowledged the problems at Johnson Houses:

The field staff was excellent. The caretakers who are sort of the forgotten soldiers of this fight . . . would go from week to week. They'd start out on a Monday and start cleaning up the place, straightening out the place, and by Thursday or Friday, the project looked good and really nice. Then of course we got bombed on the weekends, even though we had a crew coming in, but a limited number, on Saturday and Sunday . . . so that Monday morning the work had to begin again almost from scratch.[18]

A weekly regime like this succeeded in holding the line, even though it was obviously frustrating to fall back on weekends. The authority, as a result of management pressure, had increased its weekend janitorial coverage, but it would have been too expensive then (or now) to keep a full staff on duty for weekends.[19]

Contributing to NYCHA maintenance success is the fact that many staff lived in the projects. Such a system was comparable to the "super" in most New York apartment buildings. The authority aimed by 1961 to increase residential staff, particularly on the ground floor of buildings. Such staff would thus become the eyes of the street. The policy evidently worked because by 1978, 26 percent of NYCHA's twelve thousand staff members resided in the projects. Can there be much doubt that the presence of staff in buildings made a difference in maintenance and security? I have no figures for other cities, but the record indicates little interest in such a simple security measure.[20]

Staff members, from all indications, had a very strong sense of their abilities and roles in managing housing. According to a number of longtime officials, NYCHA benefited at the highest levels from what it called "Depression babies" who had come to work for the authority in the 1930s and stayed for decades. Roy Metcalf, the deputy director of public information, believed that "these people were the cadre of executives that kept this place going."[21] An external review of the management and purchasing departments in 1952 by an engineering firm "found that the Management Department and the Purchasing Division have, in general, competent staffs with well-formulated organization plans, operating procedure, and reports." Tellingly, "*It was also found that many of the operating practices were the same as those used by large, private housing operators and considered to be sound, economical, operating procedures.*"[22]

An emphasis on NYCHA achievements should not be taken as a testament to perfection. The Preusse Report of 1957 documented many staff failings, but primarily at the top of the organization rather than in the field. In such a large housing program some projects were inevitably better organized and run than others. The authority also overlooked contracting fraud in its painting division during the late 1950s and mid-1960s. Private contractors executed shoddy paint and plaster jobs, including a fake "test sample" can used to dupe inspectors when inferior paint was used. The authority subsequently reorganized its contract system and more than tripled the number of painters on its own staff. The authority's major contracting scandal of the 1960s, then, seems minor compared to other cities.[23]

NYCHA thus faced the 1960s as a comparatively well-run organization that still offered a housing product superior to that of the tenement slums. NYCHA may not have been free of corruption, but the forces of disorder by no means dominated its administrative structure. Running a housing authority was a difficult enterprise, with a troublesome blend of political and economic factors, but NYCHA success in this era—in federal as well as state and city projects—makes it clear that nothing in federal law, funding, or administrative direction ruled out local competence.

A Necessary Evil: Police Power in Public Housing Communities

> We felt that no project is Utopia and that we have to have a very hard-headed point of view that there are some tenants who do need correction and . . . will have to be under Management control.
>
> —*Edgemere Tenant's Association, 1961*[24]

As long as public housing's tenancy remained carefully selected, faith in the transformative power of public housing could be sustained. As the Edgemere Tenant's Association was quickly learning, good housing did not necessarily turn swines into swans. Some housing reformers of the 1930s honestly believed that regulated housing environments could, of themselves, transform the antisocial behavior of even the most difficult tenants. A notable drop, for instance, in Liverpool's arrests in the early twentieth century after clearance and rehousing seemed clear evidence of the impressive results that could be expected from housing reform in the United States.[25]

The belief in the power of the built environment to transform behavior sustained NYCHA only into its first decade and then only in combination with sharp-eyed tenant selection and nosy "friendly visitors." By the 1950s administrators as well as many tenants came to a stark realization. Not only did antisocial tenant behavior increase, but also NYCHA administrators found that the tower-in-the-park superblock environments, with grounds open to the public, often interfered with social control. In a nightmarish reversal of conventional reform belief, administrators found that the environment did indeed affect behavior—often for the worse.

The naiveté of the early hopes seems laughable now that most Americans view public housing as a major source of social disorder in American society. In cities such as Chicago and St. Louis social problems began so rapidly in high-rise, superblock public housing that it became impossible to separate the various effects of environment and tenancy on social order. New York was different because selectivity of tenants lasted longer and social disorder took decades to set in. As tenants became more troubled, crime did grow. Yet New York's aggressive response to criminality demonstrated that it was possible to maintain order in tower-block environments.

Low delinquency figures had been the rule in housing projects during the 1930s and early 1940s. Minor crime emerged at Queensbridge Houses and Red Hook Houses during this period, but it did not threaten the order of the projects as a whole. Nationally, too, the planner Albert Mayer could claim that the juvenile delinquency rate in the USHA program "was virtually zero in 1939 among the 40,000 children of 25,0000 low-income families." A carefully selected population and the novelty of new and better housing heralded the dawn of a new age.[26]

During the 1930s and the 1940s, NYCHA developed a small guard patrol. By all accounts, this service matched the comparably peaceful and orderly projects of those decades, but by the end of the 1940s officials felt the "need for a better organized and more professional system."[27] NYCHA, like developers of superblock private housing developments such as Stuyvesant Town, felt it had to initiate a security force because the New York Police Department (NYPD) officers "refused to enter non-dedicated streets, or buildings whose entrances were not parallel to dedicated streets.'"[28] Vandalism of great variety (landscape damage, littering, public urination, and so forth) had also become serious at developments such as Red Hook Houses, Williamsburg Houses, and Fort Greene Houses.[29] NYCHA in 1949 could count 179 watchmen spread across its 41 developments.[30]

The first indication that the authority intended to take a tough stand on crime came in 1952 when the authority established its police patrol. Funding came from the operating budgets of the projects during this time, but eventually the city would contribute financial support. Administrators drew names for housing police candidates from civil service lists and the requirements were the same as regular police. Housing officers, for instance, began their careers with special training at the Police Academy. Special patrolmen (upgraded to peace officers by 1956) made the rounds and conducted vertical patrols of troubled developments plagued by delinquency and vandalism. During this time, and for some time after, authority figures claimed that crime primarily originated from surrounding neighborhoods. The development grounds, after all, were officially open to the public and most of the buildings were unsecured.[31]

By 1954, housing officers directly covered forty-eight out of sixty-eight projects and they made "periodic visits" to the remaining projects. The authority even claimed a partial, and premature, victory in its war on disorder: "The reduction in vandalism and crime at projects having Housing Officers assigned has proven the value of the work done by this Division." As proof of success NYCHA noted, "While there has been an increase in crime throughout the city, records indicate that there has been a decrease in those projects policed by Housing Officers." Crime fighting, as contrasted with safety patrols, had already started as indicated by the fact that the "number of arrests has doubled, and the number of juveniles brought to the attention of the proper authorities has tripled." The total incidents and activity of the housing officers from 1953 to 1954 jumped from 3,754 to 9,924.[32]

NYCHA administrators always aimed to put the best spin on conditions, but sensational articles in the *New York Daily News* turned the spotlight on project crime in 1957. Reporters described serious attacks by teenage gangs, gang fights, shootings, serious vandalism, and rape. They reported ominously that "decent tenants live in terror." At the time, sensational problems in a relatively calm sea provoked action.[33]

In 1957, the city investigation commissioner Charles Tenney recommended that the authority expand its 233-man force in order to deal with mounting disorder. The authority already housed hundreds of thousands of tenants so it is reasonable to think that such a small number of police exercised at best a mild cumulative effect. The NYPD retained primary responsibility for public safety, but Tenney still thought the Housing Police was "far too small to cope with the upsurge in vandalism, juvenile delinquency and crimes"; in particular, the lack of coverage between midnight and the morning rendered them of very limited value.[34]

In his NYCHA evaluation of 1957, Charles Preusse found that crime in projects might be lower than surrounding poor neighborhoods but still warranted an increase in officers. Vandalism by teenagers appeared to be the biggest problem and it came in many forms: "smashing of windows, breakage and theft of light bulbs; defacing of corridor walls . . . slashing of fire hose; the ripping-off of copper roof flashings; trampling of grass and shrubbery; sabotaging of elevators."[35]

An even more scathing report than Preusse's came from NYCHA managers in 1958, but they took a social point of view that echoes the "broken windows" philosophy so important today. The NYPD might not be "concerned with the fact that children play in our halls; write on walls in crayon; ride bicycles on our sidewalks and pick leaves from the shrubbery," but housing police should be "concentrated on this type of control as well as the more serious vandalism involving window breakage; gambling in stairhalls; loitering in lobbies; and peace disturbances."[36] They reminded the leadership that "the Authority is primarily a landlord and its policing operations are subsidiary functions."[37]

Tenants at Williamsburg Houses concurred the same year that the shift from watchmen to housing police altered their role in the project: "Apparently enraptured with their new status, the constables are concentrating solely on the chore of policing major crimes." They "inspect the insides of the housing only infrequently and more often than not turn their heads on petty vandalism committed by the youths." William Reid seemed to hear these complaints and in 1959 would report that another expansion of the police force had recently reduced destruction of windows, trees, and benches.[38]

Disorder by teenagers emerged as the leading threat to project tranquility during these years. At Fort Greene, for instance, a "teenage rumble in the process of starting was broken up on one occasion" by the use of a patrol car siren. Juvenile record cards, complaint cards, and arrest cards increased 477 percent from 1957 to 1958. Better enforcement was likely part of the story, but so was disorder.[39] John Mitchell of the Housing Police in 1959 documented an emerging drug problem in many projects that threatened order: "narcotic users frequenting the roof and landings to administer a 'shot' or to smoke marijuana."[40]

Vandalism remained a top priority at the dawn of a new decade. Irving Wise, then the director of management, reported in 1960, "In spite of the excellent work done by our Housing Officers force, vandalism remains the number one problem. . . . Unless we can reduce vandalism in our projects, we will continue to pour money down a bottomless well." He reported that a "crash program" to clean up Jacob Riis Houses "was made useless by acts of vandalism."[41] By 1962 approximately 66 percent of NYCHA projects reported "that vandalism control is a prime management problem."[42] Nor could this vandalism be blamed more on outsiders as it had been in the past. The authority may have claimed that only 2.5 percent of all tenants could be classified as "problem families" but "almost half of these problem families are either poor housekeepers or have children whose behavior has resulted in damage to property." Growing vandalism by tenants made NYCHA's job that much more difficult.[43]

In light of growing problems, in 1962 the city government made its first major contribution of $2.5 million to NYCHA's police force. By 1966, the city government had agreed to pay the salaries of 180 officers and half the remaining cost of policing. NYCHA nevertheless tried to put the best spin possible on growing problems. Ira Robbins, a member of the board, made the dubious assertion in 1965 "that project tenants are less criminally prone than residents of nonpublic urban housing." Statistics cited indicated that the "citywide crime rate of 2,258 per 100,000 during the period contrasted with a rate of 595 per 100,000 among project tenants." In this period NYCHA lumped together property crimes and more serious index crimes, giving an absurdly low appearance to NYCHA criminal statistics. Because NYCHA had studiously avoided building stores (which were widely acknowledged as important criminal targets), it would be able for many years to make this dubious claim.[44]

The authority made inflated claims about safety but always hedged its bets. The ratio of patrolmen to tenants had improved by 1965, with 1 officer to every 520 tenants. A separate Detective Bureau operated by the 1960s and the Housing Police had established its own training academy. By this period the vertical patrol of the authority was well established and internal patrolling took up 75 percent of officers' time. These vertical patrols began by clearing loiterers from entryways then riding the elevator to the top floor. Random stops at certain floors were followed by a visit to the roof to look for "runaway children, teenagers 'petting' or smoking marijuana, vagrants sleeping, or addicts administering narcotics." Only then "the officer descends the stairs, stopping at each floor, checking halls for suspicious persons." Officers looked for drugs stashed in fire hoses and navigated darkened stairhalls because electric "bulbs are frequently stripped from entire buildings by addicts or vagrants for sale to theaters . . . children also strip bulbs from buildings to use as 'bombs' to be thrown in mock wars." Officers likely hated the vertical patrol, but without it NYCHA's projects would have been more like those in other cities.[45]

The total number of police officers engaged in these patrol tactics seemed impressive (1,070 in 1966), but because they were spread over a vast system they were stretched to the limit. Tenants might, as at Elliott-Chelsea Houses, request locks and guards for overnight coverage, but the best the authority could provide was new locks and continuing spotty coverage. At this project six officers had to cover a full week of policing, thus leaving large blocks of time unguarded. The authority explained why it could not expand coverage: "The agency controls 1,500 buildings throughout the city [and] to provide guards for all of them would mean a tremendous increase in expenditures."[46] Doormen and larger permanent police forces seemed out of the question, but the authority in 1966 began an experiment in "deep intensive saturation of security forces" at Van Dyke Houses. Thirty plainclothes men made numerous arrests over an eight-week period. Conditions at the project seemed to improve and tenants did not have an "adverse reaction" to this show of force. This heavy-handed policing would become more common as crime and vandalism skyrocketed.[47]

The late 1960s accelerated crime and disorderly conduct that much more. In 1968, one officer reported, "Every time we make an arrest in Queensbridge alone or with a fellow officer, we have to run for the office due to the crowds that gather and try to take the prisoner away. One officer was hit over the head with a chair."[48] The tenants had become restive. Total arrests for index crimes (including murder, rape, robbery, assault, burglary, and larceny) in public housing totaled 918 in 1967 and 1,098 in 1968, a 19.6 percent increase. Of these crimes, tenants had committed 52 percent. These figures probably do not include all crime in public housing because NYCHA did not seem to be combining both NYPD and Housing Police statistics.[49]

For housing developments putatively safer than the average, it is remarkable that by 1966 the Housing Police had become "the fourth largest police organization in the state of New York and the *twenty-fourth largest in the nation.*" New York was evidently trending in the same direction as other housing authorities by the late 1960s. Yet NYCHA had a tighter grip on its housing projects.[50]

Policing that extended into the projects likely had the effect of bringing more crime to the attention of officers. The vertical and foot patrols, if one accepts contemporary philosophies of policing, represented conservatism in the best sense. Other housing authorities during this time did not create professional patrol forces and when they did hire security guards their powers were weak and their coverage was even spottier than NYCHA's. The job of a NYCHA housing patrol officer was unpleasant, but the combination of crime fighting and quality of life issues played an important role in keeping order.

Building Community in the Postwar Era

Managing daily life in these communities focused on maintenance and policing, but some thought that NYCHA should use community programs as a way to defuse teenage violence and to build healthier new communities. The authority at first resisted this movement, but as in the prewar days it quietly did much to expand community programs. City agencies and nonprofits helped NYCHA create an impressive web of social programs in new developments. Community center recreation programs, in contrast, still suffered from a lack of sponsors and thus had a limited impact.

Ira Robbins, a longtime authority administrator and later vice chairman at the authority, recalled that settlement houses created pressure for "some of the most beautiful, modern and spacious centers." There certainly seemed to be no immediate crisis in the late 1940s. NYCHA's Department of Social and Community Services eventually coordinated the expansion of preschool, after school, senior, and health programs. The authority boasted of "winning the support and confidence of so many social agencies" by avoiding "the bugaboo of 'Government Control.'"[51] Administrators believed, too, that their community programs served the entire neighborhood rather than just a particular development. A United Neighborhood Houses Report complemented the authority as early as 1945: "Where health centers, nursery schools, or child care centers exist in city public housing projects they are well used, adequately equipped, and have excellent supervision."[52]

Participating agencies included not only public agencies such as the Boards of Education, Health, and Welfare, but also settlement houses, the YWCA, the YMCA, the Ethical Culture Society, and the Community Service Society. By the mid-1950s, the authority's developments housed fifty-three nursery and school-age centers, twenty-five health centers, twelve libraries, and six mental health clinics. The different facilities clocked 1,250,000 individual visits in 1949 alone.[53] Because NYCHA essentially paid for the construction of these facilities, which served more than just authority residents, the NYCHA administrator Ira Robbins wondered, "Would it not seem appropriate for the city to provide operating costs in those areas [such as community centers] which the Authority cannot finance?"[54]

Indeed, the community centers, as opposed to the city- and private-sponsored social programs, still stumbled along.[55] State and federal limits on staffing for community centers continued to prevent effective programs, even in beautiful new spaces. In the mid-1950s the fifty completed centers, with skeleton staffs, regularly served at most twenty-five thousand adults and children out of a population of over a quarter million. Major civic and social organizations in 1954 could still identify twenty-five projects without sponsors and eleven more with limited sponsorship. They estimated that with all the new construction, a total of seventy-four recreation sponsors would have to be found. These organizations recommended an enhanced role for the Bureau of Community Education of the Board of Education in the running of centers (already in seven centers and "doing an excellent job").[56]

Mayor Robert F. Wagner Jr. heard the call and responded constructively. The city government announced in 1954 that it planned "to increase recreational facilities at twenty-five public housing developments as part of the city's campaign to prevent juvenile delinquency." The city would help pay for staff

to supplement the work of private social agencies at six developments; the Board of Education will have full responsibility for operation of community centers at housing projects where there are no recreational programs; the housing authority will operate community centers at two new projects, and Board of Education workers will be added to the recreational staffs at projects where limited programs are in effect.[57]

The mayor directly addressed the reason for the novel interference of the city in housing recreation: "While we have always believed that it is the function of the private social agencies to operate the Housing Authority's community centers, as it is now the case in sixteen subsidized projects where excellent programs are in existence, there is at present insufficient private philanthropy to finance further activities."[58] Wagner also directed NYCHA to continue building community spaces even when a sponsor could not be immediately found.[59]

Fear of juvenile delinquency pushed NYCHA ever closer to a direct role in recreation. By the 1950s it appeared to many that children in the projects possibly behaved worse than children in the slums (or at least their exploits were better publicized). A *New York Times* reporter in 1958 reported ominously, "The first thing that strikes a visitor is the number of children, many unattended by mothers, roaming about inside and outside of the project. Swarms of children are the rule at all projects."[60] Ira Robbins claimed, "In one of our projects we have over 13,000 people, 7,600 of whom are children."[61]

Fears of bureaucratized community life evaporated before the far more frightening reality of juvenile misbehavior. The reorganization of the authority in 1958 produced a more dramatic ideological shift. Chairman William Reid added one hundred members to NYCHA's community center staff in 1961 specifically for adolescent summer programs.[62] By 1962, NYCHA had a summer recreation staff of almost two thousand people. A former resident of Patterson Houses remembered growing up in the 1950s and 1960s: "We had a lot of fun. We had a vacation day camp, every summer, for the children in the projects. We went to museums on a daily basis . . . to baseball games, to the planetarium. . . . I don't think there was one spot in the city that we didn't cover."[63]

The reform spirit carried over into the question of tenant involvement. Tenant organization had faced far greater challenges than recreation because NYCHA, into the 1950s, showed no hesitation in limiting organizing and speech: "Social workers point out that the public rooms may not be used for political meetings, birth-control clinics, gatherings at which liquor is served, or denominational religious meetings." Neighborhood civic fabric had been flattened with the tenements and NYCHA blithely pretended that this comprehensive destruction did not mandate a more liberal approach.[64]

Politics scared the authority because of challenges to its power and the red scare. The Inter-Project Tenants Council, a descendant of earlier city-wide tenant efforts, tried during the 1940s to become the voice of collective tenant power in public housing. The organization's growing militancy in the postwar period, including evidence of left-wing organizing, led to restrictions on the activities of the council, including "use of community rooms, particularly for [Henry] Wallace presidential rallies in 1948."[65] Chairman Thomas Farrell worried that large-scale public housing might become a "'fertile field' for organized pressure or political groups" and affirmed that "no one group should be allowed to represent all or a large percentage of tenants."[66] Only local tenant groups survived. By the late 1950s NYCHA could count at most thirty tenant organizations in its eighty-five projects. However, it noted, "Some of them show so little signs of life that we cannot definitely say whether they are active or not." With such limited powers, it is hardly surprising that they were weakly supported.[67]

According to John Simon (a former general manager), the situation changed in 1958 with the reorganization. After that point, "there was encouragement of tenant organization. . . . Good tenant relations became one of the criteria on which a manager was judged. . . ." Simon conducted "an average of 80 tenant meetings a year." He noted the difficulty, "As we had more tenant input, more tenant demands, greater expectations, costs went up."[68] Preston David, the head of Social and Community Services, in 1965 testified that NYCHA tenant "programs build various organizations, provide roles for association officers, newspaper editors, committee chairmen and similar assignments so familiar to middle-class culture."[69]

Tenant participation in community meetings remained low in the late 1960s and primarily concerned quality of life emergencies. One study from 1970 found that in the three projects under study, only 39 percent of the tenants attended meetings. A small group of committed, sometimes self-interested, leaders engaged management. Many projects published newsletters, but communication primarily flowed from above in the form of sanitized NYCHA newsletters (which were apparently read carefully by all tenants surveyed).[70] Mamie Jackson, a major housing activist, still faulted NYCHA in 1962 because although "the Authority encourages project tenant associations, it refuses to acknowledge the federation of those tenant associations into a body of the whole."[71]

It was fairly obvious to outside observers by the mid-1960s that in spite of many continuing deficiencies, NYCHA had not ignored community affairs. One of the few positive articles ever on public housing appeared in 1964 in the *New York Times*:

A visitor spot-touring . . . projects in the five boroughs on any day might have seen an elderly man bending over an easel in the arts and crafts room of an old age center; a row of mothers clutching bright-eyed babies, waiting for a physical check-up in a well baby clinic; people with time-worn faces waiting to be treated at a health maintenance center for the elderly; preschool children scampering over a jungle gym or munching cookies at a polished table in a day-care center; older children from the surrounding neighborhood sitting shyly on a bench, waiting to be taken on a tour of a day-care center in a new project . . . a young woman with a small child tugging at her arm, borrowing a book from the project library, and teen-agers grouped around a table in [a] community center planning a newsletter or a dance.[72]

This portrait is a little too rosy, but it is as representative of life in New York public housing as the sensational crime stories that dominate the public mind even today.

Failing the Management Challenge

This overwhelming evidence of NYCHA's attention to management detail provides compelling corroboration that it was not luck or context that left the authority in better shape in the 1960s. Not only did the authority use tenant selection methods to slow the change to a more disordered population, but managers organized a solid and consistent defense against signs of growing disorder. Cleaning and policing the halls, repairing damage, searching out new and better materials, and pioneering large-scale recreation programs are not glamorous activities, but simple acts like these ensured that the massive system was not left to rot. If the experience of other cities is any indication, it is deceptively difficult to carry out these fairly obvious and basic management activities. Lacking a tradition of apartment house management, or unwilling to shift these systems to low-income housing, other cities quickly ran into major problems.

The bureaucrats who ran the Chicago Housing Authority in the 1950s, according to the urban historian Bradford Hunt, overlooked the fact that "maintenance hires undoubtedly involved some element of patronage." The unions who benefited from this patronage killed

reform efforts and by the 1970s "outright fraud hobbled maintenance." Chicago's maintenance costs by this time, in spite of mediocre
performance, were almost twice (proportionately) those of New York!
Otis Elevator repairmen, in particular, cheated the CHA "while providing substandard service"; some even "deliberately failed to perform repairs or sabotaged their work to ensure that return calls would be
made." By 1982, "half of the elevators" in the system were "inopera-
tive." Nor did the CHA get a grip on growing vandalism and crime. In
1967 there were still only 115 special officers and limited vertical patrols only began in 1970—almost two decades after NYCHA had
started its police force.[73]

The carefully screened population in the early years of St. Louis's program also disguised deep-seated management incompetence. The local
craft unions, according to the analyst Eugene Meehan, stymied maintenance by the St. Louis Housing Authority:

The principal operational problem, which plagued the Authority for decades
and contributed significantly to its ultimate collapse, was the failure to provide
adequate maintenance and repairs. . . . As early as 1943, the auditors complained of the absence of sufficient controls over maintenance. . . . Year after
year, the same shortcomings were noted in the audits: daily activities tended to
be ad hoc and unsystematic . . . response time was slow; performance was poor.
Labor gangs dominated by union representatives were sufficiently powerful to
force uncontrolled and inefficient use of very expensive labor.[74]

When design shifted to high-rise projects, as it did during the 1950s with
projects such as Pruitt-Igoe, these management deficiencies hobbled the
program. St. Louis and Chicago are representative of the problems that
bedeviled most high-rise public housing projects.

The problems experienced in Boston can stand in for those experienced at low-rise public housing across this country. The failure of these
projects, described in great detail by the planning historian Lawrence
Vale, again highlights the centrality of good management. Administrators in Boston built low-rise, decentralized housing projects on mostly
vacant land, but administrative incompetence accelerated the shift to
anarchy:

Throughout the 1960s and 1970s, the financial and managerial difficulties of
the Authority mounted, and project maintenance declined. The result was both
physical degeneration of projects and social incapacity to stop either depreda-
tions of "problem families" within the projects or the destructive incursions of
outsiders. . . . By the end of the 1970s, the BHA and its tenants suffered from
the highest vacancy rate of any major housing authority in the country; many
family developments were between one-third and one-half empty, and their vacant apartments were quickly vandalized. In many developments, major building systems collapsed and residents felt fearful, angry, and abandoned.[75]

The placement and scale of public housing could not apparently compensate for "egregious management problems at the Authority," which ultimately led to dramatic reorganization of the agency in 1980. Boston's failure to adequately manage low-rise projects was similar to administrative breakdowns in cities such as Cleveland and New Orleans.[76]

Lackluster management is by no means restricted to the United States. Great Britain has had more than its share of public housing horror stories. It is difficult to generalize about a national program that in postwar Britain generated four million units (about four times the American total). In general, however, local housing councils, the equivalent of American housing authorities, seemed most interested in getting housing built rather than keeping it healthy. The shift to cheaply constructed, prefabricated tower-block housing projects demanded an even more sophisticated system of maintenance, but most estates had "no caretaking or custodial services and no front-line base at all." Many towers have had to be destroyed and others entirely rebuilt. Even social housing managers in France and Germany, who for many years had maintained better management practices, lost sight of the demands of housing management and are now engaged in significant rebuilding programs in order to "rescue" or redevelop many housing estates.[77]

The failure of these cities, when set beside New York's comparative success, raises interesting questions about arguments that rest on design, density, or location as leading factors in public housing management. Interest in building public housing both here and abroad has too often surpassed interest in management—with dire consequences in almost every instance.

Part III
Welfare-State Public Housing

Chapter 11
Surviving the Welfare State

In most American cities public housing and the welfare state became synonymous. The success of New York in the late 1960s could in large measure be attributed to its stubborn refusal to change its old-fashioned ideology in spite of the rise of New York's massive welfare system. The New York City Housing Authority in this era was conservative in the best sense. It paid its bills, collected its rents, chose its tenants and employees carefully, and adhered to daily schedules of maintenance. The authority maintained this record of success in spite of the fact that its tenancy had become mostly minority and that the number of welfare and problem families had slowly expanded. There was room for pride.

NYCHA successfully housed nearly half a million tenants by the 1960s, but the criticism of NYCHA's methods grew louder and better organized. Being conservative in the context of urban municipal services came to be considered a failure of social justice. Running a housing system as a decent, partly self-supporting municipal function would no longer be enough. After 1968, NYCHA would try to use housing to integrate neighborhoods, would welcome significantly more welfare tenants, and become more lenient to existing tenants—much like other housing authorities.

What saved New York in the 1970s and 1980s was a quiet return to the principles that had made it strong in the first place. Administrators realized that the desire to do right had to be tempered by a realistic attitude of what made NYCHA successful as an institution. New methods of tenant selection, enhanced maintenance, and tougher security kept all hell from breaking loose. NYCHA lost ground, but unlike other authorities it did not lose its footing.

Reckoning with Neighborhood Integration

An inflammatory editorial in the *New York Amsterdam News* in 1968 accused NYCHA of being a "city within a city" composed of a majority of nonwhite citizens who were ruled by a "'Mayor'" who was a "conservative white lawyer who lives in a nearby wealthy suburb." The livid author of the letter, Homer Smith, reported that the "commissioners and assistant commissioners of every department in this 'city' is [*sic*] white. As a matter of fact, all of the 100 or more policy making jobs in this city are held by whites." NYCHA finally faced the civil rights mentality.[1]

NYCHA had developed an innovative program of tenant integration in the 1950s, but it had made less headway in administrative integration. In light of the high percentage of minority tenants by this time (71.2 percent in 1969), lack of minority leadership appeared to many as racial paternalism. Smith's letter may have been inflammatory, but it was correct. Smith, a pseudonym perhaps, may have had personal familiarity with NYCHA's inner workings.[2]

The authority's internal statistics confirm the editorialist's charges of white dominance. Minorities, blacks, and Puerto Ricans were listed at 46 percent of employees in 1964, but they were more heavily weighted at the bottom of the authority. In the Construction Department, for instance, beyond the clerical level, almost all of the professionals were white. Even in 1976 blacks represented only 15 percent of management positions (and yet had become 41 percent of total employees). Blacks held significant numbers of management positions only in police and community services, not incidentally, the public faces of the institution. The most notable African American long-term member of NYCHA's management had been NYCHA board member and well-known socialist labor organizer Frank Crosswaith, who served from 1942 until 1957.[3]

NYCHA administrators frequently cited civil service requirements as the primary reason for the lack of minority leadership. As NYCHA primarily hired from civil service lists, there might be some validity to this defense. Obviously it would take years for the authority to recruit a large number of minority professionals from this source. Hiring black chairmen, however, was an obvious and rapid way to address racial inequality at the authority. The brief tenures of African American leaders preceded the long period of low-key white leadership under Joseph Christian (1973–85).

Walter Washington's (1966–67) and Simeon Golar's (1970–73) terms as chairmen reflected an important acknowledgment of the civil rights era in New York. Washington came with good recommendations from the National Capital Housing Authority and stayed for only one year before returning to Washington, D.C. as the commissioner-mayor of the District of Columbia. Walter Washington not only initiated the process of easing restrictions on welfare tenants but also presided over another push to disperse public housing.[4]

Mayor Lindsay had started pushing for a diffusion of public housing units under NYCHA's "scatter-site" program in 1966. Civil rights activists, including Lindsay, viewed public housing as a tool to aid school and

THE WALLS OF JERICHO

NEW PUBLIC HOUSING

BIGOTRY

DISCRIMINATION

INFLATION

BUREAUCRACY

RACISM   RED TAPE

COST LIMITATION

Figure 28. For a brief moment in the 1960s and 1970s NYCHA tried to scatter public housing in a very obvious manner, to no avail. *New York City Housing Authority Journal*, September/October 1970, Box 99D2, NYCHAR.

housing desegregation on a grander scale.[5] NYCHA had spread its developments more evenly than authorities in cities such as Chicago or St. Louis, but sections of neighborhoods in East Harlem and Brownsville could be considered second ghettos, albeit far better managed. By 1965 NYCHA had on the books a $2.2 billion program, of which better than half focused on eight poor neighborhoods. Even in 1972, "almost 90 percent of the Housing Authority's building program [continued] to be focused on ghetto areas."[6] What had been built in primarily white neighborhoods, the city-sponsored program for higher-income, primarily white tenants, had been carefully designed not to offend. These city projects, approximately one-quarter of NYCHA's developments, were tilting toward mostly minority in the early 1970s, but Mayor Lindsay refused to see the changing racial profile of these developments as an adequate substitute for new, racially integrated projects.[7]

Lindsay likely saw little to lose and everything to gain politically in standing up to the city's declining, increasingly defensive, white population. He miscalculated when he discounted the political capital at stake in openly challenging social divisions. The Board of Estimate, since the 1940s, had effectively defended white middle-income areas from subsidized housing while allowing city-aided, higher-income projects targeted at whites or higher-income minorities.[8] Charles Abrams in 1956, for instance, had disclosed "political pressure from the Borough presidents against the construction of low-rent housing on vacant land because of fear of an over-concentration of Negroes."[9] By the 1960s, outer-borough, middle-class neighborhood opposition to public housing of any kind became vocal. NYCHA now had an open integrationist policy that spelled the end of majority white projects. Between 1963 and 1965, for instance, the borough presidents of Queens, Richmond, and the Bronx all rejected numerous projects primarily because of middle-class, neighborhood resistance.[10]

Mayor Lindsay's "scatter-site" program did nothing to cool emotions. Lindsay even knew that "the fight to get low-income units approved in middle class neighborhoods was 'a real bloodbath'" but he pushed ahead anyway (Figure 28).[11] NYCHA administrator Joseph Christian naïvely wrote to a scatter-site enemy in 1968: "The construction of such housing in middle income areas provides a choice of housing location for the low-income family desiring to move out of the . . . ghetto area." He believed that "the immigration of low income families to the middle income communities tends to breach the barrier of economic stratification to the enrichment of the community generally." Christian and other NYCHA administrators counted on a high level of city-wide liberal sentiment in revealing their sociological aims. Had NYCHA administrators looked closely at other American cities, they would have realized that overt attempts to scatter projects had crippled public housing programs elsewhere in America in the 1950s and early 1960s.[12]

Opponents in New York, as in other cities, fought hard against what they considered to be an attack on their middle-class neighborhoods. The Scatter-site approach foundered. By 1971, NYCHA had already abandoned eight of thirteen sites designated for scattered projects by the City Planning Department in 1967; it had, according to the *New York Times*, "bowed to white community resistance" when it revoked these eight projects. It had, however, moved ahead with the remaining projects, some of which proved relatively uncontroversial. However, one of these would prove particularly vexing: the project planned for white, primarily Jewish Forest Hills.[13]

NYCHA chairman Simeon Golar presided over the Forest Hills debacle. Were it not for Forest Hills he would have likely continued his brilliant rise in New York politics. Golar spent part of his youth in Fort

Greene Houses, attended New York University law school, and held a number of important positions in the Lindsay administration. As chairman of NYCHA, Golar predictably set about promoting minorities in everything from administration to contracting. Golar publicly stated his belief that "public housing is being dismantled and destroyed" by President Nixon, but the federal government actually allowed one final spurt of public housing during Nixon's administration. Golar, in fact, launched an impressive ten thousand units. Many of these lacked the traditional oversight of the authority contracting system and were built to a low standard, but that number of units in a time of declining productivity should not be dismissed as a minor accomplishment.[14]

The Forest Hills project that proved his undoing had originated in the Italian-dominated Corona section of Queens, which fiercely fought the project. Through a complex and fairly secret series of negotiations and swaps the project ended up designated for the Forest Hills area by 1966. Opposition began almost immediately in Forest Hills even though city officials may have believed that "their plans would meet a kinder, or at least quieter, reception from the Jewish apartment dwellers," assumed to be more liberal. With few minority residents (3 percent), "it did not seem likely that a low-income project would 'tip' the neighborhood into ghettoism." A major obstacle to any building on the site, an underground stream, forced the authority to plan, after a number of revisions, three over-scaled twenty-four-story buildings by 1969. Ground was not broken, however, until 1971.[15]

Forest Hills opposition coalesced around Jerry Birbach, an outspoken real estate man. The outraged residents used every means at their disposal to try and stop or radically revise the project. Opponents such as Birbach thought that the city was not living up to its promise of local control and community participation even though it now trumpeted such values for poor communities. He had had enough of the city's "social engineering" that might bring more crime and minorities. As the *New York Times* astutely observed, "Golar's announcement that 'less than half of the crimes committed in public housing are committed by public housing tenants' may not seem reassuring to people who have never known a fellow tenant to be arrested for anything worse than speeding."[16]

The Forest Hills project, when finally passed by a reluctant Board of Estimate in 1971, set aside 40 percent of the units for the elderly. The authority even promised to select a tenant population in line with other Queens communities, which at that time were 60 percent white. These promises were not enough for Forest Hills opponents, who, rather than openly opposing the project on racial grounds, claimed that it would "alter the middle-income community and overtax its facilities." The claim that the project would overtax the neighborhood was a false claim about a project with only 840 apartments, of which 40 percent were for seniors, but such language provided a cover for race and class opposition.[17]

Opponents, sometimes numbering over one thousand individuals picketed the proposed site on a daily basis. Local opposition catalyzed political resistance. Donald Manes, the Queens borough president, who had initially signed off on the project, still sought buildings half as large as the three twenty-four-story towers planned.[18] The Nixon administration, Golar believed, made the situation even worse by agreeing to review the project. He thought that this interference fit closely with the administration's "conscious policy . . . that deliberately pits white against black, middle-class against poor."[19] Roy Metcalf, the authority's deputy director of public information, described the Forest Hills period thus: "The most harrowing times I think we spent here. That was when the tide began to turn. I think that marks the juncture as far as public housing goes." He also recalled spending six months on the phone just trying to counter the opposition.[20]

In time, opponents catalyzed a state supreme court ruling halting the project until further public review. New state laws expressly designed to slow the project, including county referenda for any public housing and mandatory resubmission of long-delayed projects, seemed on their way to passage. On appeal the authority actually won the right to move ahead because the justices thought that only minor changes had been made since 1966. Governor Rockefeller vetoed the special state legislation that had been created to slow public housing. Lindsay sensed that his career was on the line (he had, after all, been heavily supported by liberal Jews) and decided to compromise. Mario Cuomo, then a Queens lawyer, brokered a compromise on behalf of the mayor. The project was cut in half, with only 432 apartments in three twelve-story buildings. The mayor approved the project in 1972, but Golar himself was "disappointed in the Mayor's choice."[21]

By 1978, the Forest Hills development, which was organized along cooperative lines, was 63 percent white and had only 2 percent welfare tenants. The careers of Simeon Golar and John Lindsay never recovered. Golar stepped down in 1973 and Lindsay faded into obscurity after a failed run for the presidency. The Forest Hills debacle blurred New York's comparatively better record on dispersion of public housing. As city-sponsored projects shifted to minority tenancy in the ensuing decades, they actually became more effective tools of neighborhood integration. The quiet foresight of an earlier generation of NYCHA leaders, who placed the central emphasis on housing rather than race, becomes more admirable when viewed through the filter of Forest Hills.[22]

The Forest Hills debacle, HUD's ill-fated national scatter-site policy, and the growing disrepute of so many public projects in cities such as St. Louis and Chicago infuriated President Richard Nixon. Handily re-elected by his suburban and southern supporters in 1972, he had decided that the urban crisis had been addressed to his satisfaction. On 5 January 1973 he declared a moratorium on new public housing. Public housing, described by Nixon as "monstrous, depressing places—run-down, overcrowded, crime-ridden," would be halted along with other controversial housing subsidies for private developers. The worst fears of 1930s public housing advocates had now been realized.[23]

New York's city government estimated that because of Nixon's moratorium it lost twenty-nine projects worth $500 million. Particularly hard hit was NYCHA's role in the Model Cities Program. For the rest of the 1970s the authority's production slowed to a trickle. Nixon aided New York City in one manner by creating the groundwork for Section 8, which quickly became another NYCHA specialty. Nixon described this program as "direct cash assistance" that would enable poor families to "seek out 'safe and sanitary housing' in the private market" in cities or suburbs.[24] There were many progressive dimensions to this program because in theory it allowed for a decentralization of poverty. NYCHA did not hesitate. The number of units overseen by NYCHA jumped from approximately one thousand in the first year (1975) to thirteen thousand in 1977.[25]

The political cost of using public housing as a tool of overt racial integration had proved costly. Far more effective had been the authority's earlier focus on building so much housing that it could not help but serve as a tool of neighborhood social integration. The truth of the matter is that figures such as Robert Moses and Chairman Thomas Farrell—ham-handed as they were—likely did more to integrate New York than genteel, high-minded idealists such as Mayor John Lindsay.

Opening the Welfare Gates

By the 1960s NYCHA's tenancy had shifted to mostly minority, but now the majority of that minority came into question. Was not public housing for the truly impoverished rather than the working-class black, Puerto Rican, or white family? If so, why were so many minority working-class people living in NYCHA apartments? America's "two-tier" welfare system envisioned only generous middle-class benefits and limited aid for the indigent. NYCHA's focus on the working poor proved to be a mismatch for the wider contours of the American welfare state. NYCHA was forced, at least for a while, to adapt its system to America's dominant, and arguably dysfunctional, approach to social welfare.

Public housing, even in New York, would now be for the poorest of the poor.[26]

In 1965, Welfare commissioner James R. Dimpson was absolutely "convinced that . . . problem families must first have new housing before they can be helped." He estimated that there were "300,000 'ineligibles' among the 1.5 million people forced to live in this city's slums and rat-infested tenements." Dimpson showed his ignorance of New York's history when he lumped NYCHA's history with that of other authorities: "an enabling concept that public housing is to take care of the city's impoverished people vs. 30 hurdles which exclude most of the people who are the most impoverished." NYCHA chairman William Reid, in contrast, responded as authority administrators always had: "'It's a welfare and social problem,' . . . 'They have to learn to live in public housing before they move into the projects.'" Such an attitude might have silenced critics earlier, but by the 1960s it had lost its power. Government was now supposed to help the poorest, not cherry pick.[27]

The political temperature rose with the years. According to the *New York Times* in 1965, "A high official at the city's Bureau of Child Health charged that the Housing Authority condemned unwed mothers to a 'vicious cycle' of squalor and depravity by barring them from public housing." A spokesman at NYCHA claimed that unwed motherhood did not categorically lead to rejection, but an official at the bureau claimed that "'with a few exceptions, there's an unwritten policy' that unwed mothers 'are excluded from public housing.'" The welfare department made some extreme claims, including an argument that mothers "may turn to prostitution as a result" of rejection from public housing. Not surprisingly, 60 percent of 321 unwed mothers they identified wanted public housing; yet only 7 percent successfully entered public housing in the first eighteen months of motherhood.[28]

The state supreme court upheld the right of the authority to "screen out undesirables" in 1966 "to prevent the development of unsafe conditions," but NYCHA was under tremendous pressure to alter its policies to conform better to the *zeitgeist*. Officials at NYCHA worried that turning unwed motherhood from a negative to either a neutral or positive factor for public housing admission could in fact bring in more disordered families. Such a policy might even encourage women to have children in order to gain access to public housing; after all, overcrowded housing was a positive factor in admission. The tail could all too easily wag the dog in social policy.[29]

The welfare department returned to its favorite themes in 1966 but now received a warmer welcome from NYCHA leadership. Mitchell Ginsberg, the commissioner of the Department of Welfare, reminded Chairman Walter Washington about "the progress of the special project in which we are jointly engaged with the objective of increasing the number of relief recipients in public housing projects." His department had "grave concern . . . that the present occupancy rate by welfare clients is an estimated 10–15% in contrast to the nation-wide average of 30%." Ginsberg made it sound as though a higher welfare percentage was necessarily better.[30]

Ginsberg even testified to the federal government that in New York "welfare recipients are not getting their fair share. . . . Of the 600,000 welfare clients in the City, only 8 percent live in public housing." The "21 social criteria" eliminated many welfare families because many of these factors "are endemic to many of our welfare families," including irregular work history, single parenthood, and poor housekeeping. Ginsberg reported hopefully that NYCHA "is now revising these criteria."[31] He later wrote to Washington, "We would like to see the more subjective criteria eliminated"; he wished to see each potential tenant treated on an individual basis.[32]

The welfare department had its own public relations problems that NYCHA could solve. Not only had welfare recipients become more militant in their demands, but the department had become a de facto housing authority for welfare tenants living in state-subsidized slum dwellings. The welfare department routinely paid four times the normal rent for their emergency cases. By the 1960s, New York State was dispersing separate rent supports for welfare tenants, an estimated half billion dollars annually. These programs, in spite of their costs, rarely purchased quality housing; "newspapers repeatedly publish[ed] stories about the inadequacies of the housing facilities that are secured."[33]

Welfare was booming in New York. The historian Fred Siegel has identified the growth of a "welfare state society" in the 1960s that, through militant action, led to rising benefits even though "New York's unemployment rate at 4 percent" should have prevented the doubling of welfare rates between 1965 and 1970. Siegel explains that "Lindsay's effort to recruit new people onto the welfare rolls baffled many. . . . The goal was a welfare-state society." While deindustrialization and an influx of unskilled workers played a role in growing unemployment and welfare, the skyrocketing numbers seemed to rise with logic of their own.[34]

Under enormous pressure, Chairman Albert Walsh in 1968 finally revised the authority's standards for admission. Tenant selection, according to Walsh, would no longer "deal with the morals of the applicants. Thus, for example, no family may be declared ineligible solely because the applicant has an out-of-wedlock child." The standards remained for criminal activity, violent behavior, drug addition, sexual crimes, poor housekeeping, and related social defects, but "before such determination is made, consideration will be given to favorable changes in the family's pattern of behavior, a lapse of years since an offense and to other extenuating circumstances."[35] Many of the old standards remained, but NYCHA staff now had more "latitude" when judging a potential tenant. A strain of cultural relativism may have conditioned this change. Some years later, Chairman Simeon Golar noted that single parent households had finally been admitted because "many black and Spanish-speaking families have a tradition of stability through 'extension' that embrace[s] grandparents, uncles and aunts in a household."[36]

By this point NYCHA had its own reason for loosening standards. Welfare tenants may have been more trouble, but at least temporarily they brought in higher rents. The urban expert Roger Starr discovered this hidden subsidy: "Because the city has to pay only 27 percent of the rent bill for welfare eligible—the remainder coming from federal and state governments—the city DSS has been willing to pay higher rents in public housing for welfare families. . . . The surcharge paid by the city to the Housing Authority runs as high as 60 per cent." Starr understood NYCHA's dilemma: "At a time when the Authority is running badly in the red, welfare tenants provide it with some financial relief."[37]

The effect of the loosened admissions was evident in no time: "Welfare tenants in all projects continued to rise to a new all time high figure totaling . . . 15.4 percent of all tenants at the end of June" in 1968.[38] Managers were not pleased. "Over the past few years the practice in the NYCHA has been the relaxing of its policy which formerly provided Managers with the means by which they attempted to control unacceptable behavior." Their analysis lacked subtlety but would be confirmed in practice: "The social implications of filling up a community with families who are undisciplined, selfish, petty criminals, narcotic addicts, and parasites are obvious." NYCHA, however, was temporarily leaving behind *model housing as a municipal service* for what became a problematic role as *welfare-state public housing*.[39]

At the same time, NYCHA lost much of its power to evict tenants for poor behavior. Roger Starr explained that under the old system a problem tenant would meet with the manager, and if that meeting failed to heal the breach, "the tenant would be given notice of the intention of the Authority to terminate his tenancy." The tenant could appeal the decision before the Tenant Review Board, which still had to send the case to the civil court to evict the tenant. Eviction was possible, but not as easy as many critics of NYCHA's system claimed.[40]

Lawyers for the Office of Economic Opportunity, funded by the Great Society, had failed in their legal challenge to this system on "due process" grounds in 1968. In an entirely separate case the U.S. Supreme Court ruled in favor of welfare tenants, which resulted in the NYCHA cases being overturned in 1970. Now the tenant had to "be granted an evidentiary hearing at which he would have an opportunity to confront the opposing witnesses." Starr understood the absurdity of this new rule even if the courts did not: "The witnesses are, in fact neighbors" and might fear "retaliation" for testifying against neighbors. He believed the ruling would "speed the departure from the projects of the working poor."[41] NYCHA would restart its eviction processes in 1971, but it would not be until the 1990s that NYCHA would again develop a more effective eviction system. Problem families could now act with far greater impunity.[42]

As Elizabeth Wood had warned, the working poor would abandon public housing projects as they became concentrated with more troubled and now empowered welfare tenants. At Ingersoll Houses, for instance, "of the 67 apartments vacated since April 1, 1969 . . . 62 have been rented to Welfare families. Over 40% of the tenant body now receives public assistance" and many were socially troubled. Now, "the older, more stable tenants are 'up in arms', insisting that the Authority stop admitting so many undesirable families" and many cited problem families as a reason for moving.[43] At Woodside Houses, "a number of families with lower living standards were admitted during 1969. This is resulting in an increase in—rent delinquency, family disturbances, complaints of loud and noisy parties," and misbehaving teenagers. These types of complaints became common rather than extraordinary.[44]

External factors accelerated the shift to lower-income tenants. The federal government's Brooke Amendment raised rents for the working poor and reduced rents for welfare tenants. Not only did this cut into revenues, but also it made public housing less attractive to working families. By 1971, NYCHA, in partnership with the city government, started to accept large numbers of tenants directly from welfare hotels. In 1971, for instance, one thousand families were accepted under this program.[45]

For these reasons, and the declining reputation of public housing in general, NYCHA's long waiting lists started to change. In 1972, NYCHA actually made 50 percent of rentals to welfare families and the welfare population, including partial welfare cases and Social Security, had leaped to 27 percent. In 1973, NYCHA hit its highest welfare figure of 34 percent of tenants. The state program, *with 40 percent welfare families*, was particularly worrisome, but even 35.8 percent of federal tenant families were on the dole. Only the city remained stable at 7.5 percent. Because New York publicized its combined figures for all programs, it became standard to believe that NYCHA did not have a welfare concentration problem. NYCHA was better off than the troubled Chicago Housing Authority, 49 percent of whose tenants were on welfare by 1973, but the future in New York looked equally perilous if one looked at the state and federal programs separately.[46]

A man who grew up in the James Monroe Houses in the Bronx remembered that while the "60's were good" (welfare families accounted for only 3.9 percent of Monroe families in 1961), by the mid-1970s the comfort level had shifted (the welfare population reached 38.6 percent in 1975). He thought that the "the culture had changed. The welfare population brought a defeatist attitude," antisocial behavior increased, and many working families departed for Co-op City (a new middle-income development in the Bronx).[47]

The ideal way to restrict problem tenants, and mute these policy changes, would be to attract and keep higher-income tenants. NYCHA had discovered that in general its tenants' incomes did not rise in tandem with society at large. The authority constantly raised income limits for admission in the 1950s and 1960s, but these increases had relatively little success in large measure because lower-income applicants had priorities through site clearance or overcrowding. The federal government, which had formerly discouraged higher-income tenants, had by now revised its policies to encourage income diversity.

As early as 1962 Ira Robbins informed the public that the federal government permitted families to "stay in no matter how much their incomes increase, provided that they pay a slight increase in their rents."[48] NYCHA could boast in 1967 of a "policy of rent review, whereby tenants are permitted to earn more than maximum in order to ensure stability to the development and the community."[49] In 1973, NYCHA raised income limits for admittance by 20 percent, with an impressive $11,000 maximum in city projects. Throughout the 1970s NYCHA raised its income limits further. In 1977, for instance, it raised limits to attract "more 'upwardly mobile' families." A new top rate of $17,500 for large families seeking large apartments would have been more effective if the average income of current NYCHA families at that time had not been $7,000 a year (a figure itself skewed higher by the city projects). All things being equal, the very poor in emergency situations still moved off the waiting list faster than working families.[50]

Administrators tried more radical means in the 1970s to mix up the population and seemed to have some success. Because NYCHA still wanted the "wage earner and two-parent families" it developed what came to be known as the Tier system. In 1973 the new chairman, Joseph Christian, in a departure from the policies established by his predecessors, had floated to HUD "a proposal to set up a two-tier admission program. This involves dividing our applicants into two groups: those with incomes below $5,500 and those with incomes above that amount. Each group would be permitted a fixed percentage of the total number of vacancies."[51]

The Department of Housing and Urban Development (HUD) approved the Tier system and by 1979 NYCHA defined "3 income levels, into which applicants are divided. Of those interviewed [the first step to moving from the waiting list to an apartment rental], 20 percent are from the lowest level, and 40 percent each from the 2 higher ones. The system was established with the goal that an equal number of applicants from each level would accept housing offered."[52] Higher-income tenants were clearly favored under such a scheme. By 1980, Tier I incomes ranged from $3,300 (for one person) to $10,600 (for nine or more people); Tier II from $3,301 to $13,000; and Tier III from $7,201 to $13,000 (all levels were within federal limits at the time). The Tier system openly sought "to address income imbalances in each project by channeling higher or lower income families as the situation demands." At the same time the Tier system did not mean the end of other preferences for emergency situations (homeless or welfare hotels), overcrowding, and so forth, which tended to favor the very poor.[53]

Tier programs had the most success in Staten Island because, according to NYCHA officials, "these projects are in good physical condition with neighborhood strengths such as excellent recreational, educational, cultural and medical facilities."[54] Central city projects had mixed results. At Claremont Village in the Bronx, for instance, not only were 40 percent of tenant families single-parent and on welfare, but in "the 16 years that the complex has been in operation there has been a nearly 100% turnover at all three projects." The managers there had difficulty getting a mix of tenants through the Tier program. Higher-income Tier II and III families "are turning down apartments . . . at each project in greater numbers than we hoped."[55]

In 1985, NYCHA nevertheless presented data to HUD that "reinforced, over the years, the Authority's income tier percentage break-out policy."[56] The authority would claim that its comparative success could be linked to assigning "people to projects so that a mix of very low, low and moderate income is maintained."[57] Although it is impossible to directly link these policies with lower welfare statistics, after 1974 NYCHA's welfare population actually dropped to about 25 percent and stayed there until the mid-1980s. This consistency is remarkable in light of the fact that racial change continued in every type of NYCHA development, including the city-sponsored projects. Even a new rent structure from Congress in 1981 that required an increase from 25 to 30 percent on the limit on annual income, which NYCHA had initially fought, did not create a wholesale exodus of working families. The welfare percentage remained relatively stable at approximately 25 percent until 1985 and slowly inched back up to 30 percent of all families in the 1990s. This proportion was significantly lower than that of most other housing authorities (for example, 73 percent of Chicago's families were on AFDC by 1984).[58]

NYCHA's relatively low welfare level, of course, obscured some depressing trends. Certain projects had consistently higher levels of welfare concentration and tenant income had stagnated. Further evidence of social immobility could be found in the average length of tenancy. At the Alfred E. Smith Houses, for instance, average tenancy increased from 7.9 years in 1963 to 18.6 in 1990. Such low-income families in long-term residence made it difficult for NYCHA to raise rents.[59] By the mid-1980s NYCHA was also offering two thousand out of six thousand apartments that opened *every year* to the emergency cases on the edge of homelessness or in overpriced welfare hotels. Administrators of NYCHA thought that "the homeless need a whole range of social and medical services that the public housing program is simply not prepared to provide," but the city administration forced their hand. Becoming homeless now became a faster way to move up the list.[60] Public housing tenant leaders protested, "We've already taken in enough garbage in our public housing," but there was no choice. Today, a full 16.6 percent of NYCHA households were formerly homeless, or 77,229 persons.[61]

NYCHA's housing was becoming housing of the last resort in the 1980s. NYCHA had never entirely lost sight of the working poor and continued to recruit them as best it could, but the external pressure from federal and city officials had seriously undermined its ability to attract paying tenants and thus pay its bills. This section clearly demonstrates that NYCHA was not bypassed by many of the social issues that flattened public housing elsewhere; it just held the line better than most. Come the 1990s, the working poor would again become the authority's target population.

The Aftermath

Albert Walsh, the chairman of NYCHA from 1967 to 1970, was one of the first chairmen to link a growing financial crisis to the changing profile of NYCHA tenancy. "Let there be no doubt about it," he told a conference in 1968, "public housing is not heading for a fiscal crisis; it is already in a fiscal crisis." The federal subsidy formula had failed to take into account the drag weight of an impoverished tenancy: "The average income of New York City public housing tenants, largely the unskilled and semi-skilled, rose at a much slower rate than those of our lowest level of Housing Authority employees." NYCHA's thousands of employees, an essential element in project order, garnered stiff wage increases through collective bargaining. This mismatch between costs and revenues tilted NYCHA into the red. The authority had a comparatively miniscule reserve by this time because it had turned over extra income in the good years to the federal government to reduce subsidies. The federal government introduced some extra subsidies in the late 1960s, and NYCHA raised rents, but future years looked even more disastrous.[62]

NYCHA had plenty of company as its finances bled. By the early 1970s, the City of New York was suffering from stagnant economic growth, inflation, the energy crisis, skyrocketing payrolls, and costly debt. La Guardia's and Wagner's visionary big government city now seemed unsupportable in a time of inflation and declining federal and state subsidies. The urban expert Roger Starr had seen the handwriting on the wall back in 1971: "The 1970 expense budget of the City of New York allocated approximately $1,000 per capita to provide education, health, police, hospital, social welfare." In practice this meant that an "imaginary four-person family was costing the city approximately $4,000—about 80 percent as much as it earned, gross. In the same year—1970—Jackson, Miss. was spending $680 on municipal services for the same, mythical four-person family."[63] City activists particularly disliked Starr's call in 1976 for "planned shrinkage" of city commitments to urban redevelopment in areas such as the South Bronx, but budget cuts were made to balance the books. For NYCHA, less money in the city's coffers meant reduced annual subsidies (at state and city projects) in areas such as policing, community programs, and maintenance.[64]

NYCHA's rental incomes from a downwardly mobile tenancy failed to cover increasing labor, maintenance, and energy costs. Energy alone tripled in price from 1973 to 1974 because of the worldwide oil shortage. NYCHA would eventually cut its fuel use during the 1970s, but for years it suffered. Had NYCHA maintained its upwardly mobile tenancy over the years its rents could have been raised more rapidly to cover the growing fuel and labor costs, which is what happened in the private sector. As NYCHA had temporarily accepted its role in *welfare-state public housing*, however, the authority felt political pressure to keep rents low. Thus rents failed to keep pace with increasing costs in society at large. The logjam on rents in New York had been broken with a much needed rent hike in 1972 of 8 percent, but it had a limited effect in light of more dramatic federal actions that stymied rent collection.[65]

Not only did federal subsidies fail to keep pace, but well-meaning liberals at the federal level had passed the Brooke Amendment in 1969; it capped tenant rents at 25 percent of income. Rent reductions for very low-income tenants, triggered by the new law, cost NYCHA millions and threatened to push the authority into bankruptcy. The authority's shortfall by the end of 1974 was projected at $75 million in the federal program alone. Even though the federal government provided a $45 million extra subsidy (made possible by the Brooke and Sparkman

Amendments for operating deficits), budget woes still left a projected $30 million gap that could not even be covered by using all of the $16.5 million in authority reserves. The Brooke Amendment became the nickel fare of all American authorities, a sop to the people that bankrupted a valuable public service.[66]

The growing financial crisis finally provided the political justification for rent increases. The deficit in 1974 was met by another 8 percent rent increase and an additional $11 million federal donation to cover rising fuel costs. The authority also froze hiring, cut positions (including police), deferred maintenance, trimmed community programs, turned down the heat, and made cuts wherever possible. The authority obviously could not long continue on this path without either losing its low-income character, enduring a rent strike, or seriously compromising its management abilities. Rent increases of the early 1970s sound high and pinched many, but because of the Brooke Amendment restrictions they still did not yield as much revenue as the authority needed.[67]

The conservative shift in Washington, with a new emphasis on accountability, turned out to be a godsend for NYCHA in one sense. Washington implemented a new system of funding in 1975 that rewarded the better housing authorities. Known as the Performance-Oriented Prototype Funding Formula, it ultimately helped NYCHA pay its bills. By 1977, authority administrators could report, "The Federal government has poured over 150 million dollars into programs of physical upgrading and tenant education in recent years. . . . There is simply no question that the public housing in NYC is by far the best in the nation, so we make out very well when the yearly subsidy is computed." This money made a major difference in the most distressed of NYCHA's housing projects, generally pulling them back from the brink.[68]

A shift to a Democratic administration in Washington gave NYCHA another monetary breathing space. The movement away from public housing nationally cloaked New York's special relationship to the federal government. Patricia Harris, the secretary of HUD, had set a stern tone before her appointment by President Carter: "I would rather have people in the marketplace purchasing their own shelter . . . than have the government put up the kind of public housing monstrosities. . . . We should make it clear that we are abandoning the whole notion of public housing." Her bark proved worse than her bite.[69] Harris limited new construction but approved a program that quietly funneled hundreds of millions of dollars for renovation to NYCHA's faltering state and city projects. The financial crisis of the city government had cut back on its operating subsidy to the nonfederal projects. By this time, tenants in federal projects seemed better off than their state and city counterparts because of comparatively generous federal modernization funds.[70]

NYCHA thus began a process of "transferring" city and state projects to the federal government and would nearly complete this process for all its nonfederal developments during the Carter Administration. The federal government thus gained housing units (in a time when it built few others). The city and state governments achieved cost savings by having the federal government assume the debts and yearly subsidy for these projects (up to $1.1 billion of city money saved by 1990 alone). This transfer, even more to the point, freed up money for renovation.[71]

By 1990, the transfer program had generated $400 million for renovation—a bonus New York desperately needed but was also lucky to receive. One NYCHA official called the program "a hidden subsidy for New York City." This money proved essential in the 1980s as NYCHA could now replace windows, lobbies, heating systems, and elevators, and update the grounds. Today, only fifteen developments remain in the state program and six in the city program. They are still a drag on the authority's finances.[72]

New York also proved to be a winner in the race for other federal funds. The annual federal subsidy increased from $18,985,900 in 1971 to $275,057,555 in 1982 (even with a stagnant building program), primarily as a result of inflation driven by increasing energy and labor costs. Even so, these subsidies barely kept pace with mounting costs. To put the energy issue in perspective, an article from 1983 pointed out that over the previous eighteen years NYCHA's "utility costs have increased by over 1,000 percent on a per-apartment basis, but rents have increased by only 120 percent."[73] Better news were federal modernization funds granted between 1975 and 1982 that totaled $331,267,737; these hundreds of millions of dollars helped the authority cut energy costs through new windows and additional insulation. Unlike most of its peer authorities, NYCHA actually used that money for renovation.[74]

NYCHA did not maximize its rents in these difficult times, but it did not forget them either. By the early 1980s NYCHA had greatly exceeded its peer authorities in labor and contract costs, but it also "demonstrated a superior performance in exceeding the national, regional and large authority averages for Total Operating Receipts" by a significant margin.[75] Rents had been raised in both 1976 and 1980; even better, the Carter administration allowed the authority to keep the extra revenues from the increases. During this era NYCHA proved particularly adept at raising welfare rents (without forcing welfare tenants to pay more rent) from its increasingly impoverished tenancy. Welfare department costs rose because of this program, but it seemed like a fair trade as welfare officials had long encouraged NYCHA to accept more of its tenants, who often demanded more services.

According to Raymond Henson, a major figure in this financial reorganization, the new Performance Funding System and Federal Transfer Program, in combination with federal permission to retain funds from rent increases and welfare rents again ended the worst fiscal crisis by 1980. The general manager during this time, John Simon, admitted to running "the Authority as a business, albeit with a social conscious. . . . I was a little . . . stingy."[76] New York also benefited not only from quiet and steady leadership from Joseph Christian (1973–85), but also from consistently strong mayoral support. The general manager, John Simon, found that "as distinguished from many mayors in the country, the city administration [and] the city council generally [were] supportive of public housing, more so than most other big cities in the United States." Spreading the public housing across the city had yielded political dividends; the authority's decent reputation for management also likely aided political support.[77] One administrator explained, "If we had 10 patronage jobs in the Authority it was a lot."[78] This study had already made clear the strong backing for public housing from Mayors LaGuardia to Wagner, but Mayors Lindsay, Beame, Koch, and Dinkins all became strong NYCHA advocates.[79]

This support did not, however, translate into funds for NYCHA to build new housing. During the 1980s the renovation of private and city-owned in rem property became the major source of new, city-subsidized housing. Mayor Edward Koch's $5.1 billion program launched in 1987 yielded an estimated 250,000 apartments through public/private partnerships. The New York City Housing Development Corporation and the Department of Housing Preservation and Development, rather than NYCHA, became the major forces in this program. The billions in city funds, combined with low-income housing tax credits, fostered a dynamic program of housing rehabilitation and construction. The combined efforts of these city agencies, community development corporations, the Enterprise Foundation, and LISC have as of 2006 eliminated almost all of New York's derelict, tax delinquent properties. In the private market, immigrants in all the boroughs have also purchased and renovated properties in what seemed like marginal neighborhoods.[80]

NYCHA did not participate in these exciting movements during the 1980s and 1990s because it had primarily become a housing maintenance program under fire from both the federal government and an impoverished, often disorderly, tenant base. During the Reagan years, a rent delinquency rate increase hurt revenues, capital costs skyrocketed, and subsidies withered. Even when the authority raised rents again, these increases failed to affect large numbers of poor tenants already paying maximum rents. The Reagan administration not only slashed national housing funds (from 1981 to 1987 housing funding was cut 70

percent), but it also implemented a new 30 percent income requirement that in no way helped the retention of working families who could
pay decent rents.[81]

NYCHA looked better than its fellow housing authorities in the 1980s
and early 1990s, but it showed signs of trending in the same direction.
NYCHA's years as a *welfare-state public housing* authority nearly destroyed
it. Clever financing and attempts to roll back admission standards to the
old days could only do so much when so much of the population was already impoverished. These were dark days and the authority's reputation suffered. What kept NYCHA projects viable was the ongoing focus
on the basics in housing management.

Chapter 12

The Value of Consistency

The pressure of a more troubled tenancy tested, but did not break, the New York City Housing Authority's design and management practices. The contrast with half-hearted reforms in Chicago and St. Louis cannot be understated. Most other authorities had never mastered daily management and growing disorder threw their systems into deeper chaos. NYCHA, in contrast, staved off disaster through consistency. These techniques became delaying tactics that made it possible in the 1990s to market the authority's housing, once again, to the working class. Decades of seemingly futile effort had reaped dividends in the long term.

Elevator management is the most instructive example of a technical system imperiled by a more troubled tenancy. For most working- and middle-class families, the elevator was an object of respect. NYCHA, however, confronted intentional vandalism as its tenancy grew younger and more disordered. A report from 1971 found that "aside from normal wear and tear, much of the mechanical difficulties with elevators has been due to misuse and vandalism by children." Elevator roof "joy riding" occasionally resulted in fatalities; bored kids had found that "riding on top provides a great deal of excitement." Vandalism of hatch doors was often so complete that the entire door had to be replaced.[1]

NYCHA had 350 mechanics solely devoted to the maintenance of its approximately 3,000 elevators by the 1970s. The effectiveness of the elevator team was demonstrated in 1973 when repairmen refused to work overtime (as had become customary) as part of a labor dispute. In just a few days, at least 12,000 tenants found themselves without elevator service because 400 out of 3,000 elevators had stalled. The dispute was settled within ten days but the fragility of the system had been revealed. Keeping the staff in line could occasionally be as difficult as the elevators. NYCHA disciplined 85 elevator repairmen for overtime fraud in 1977; many lost their jobs, were suspended, or were forced to pay restitution.[2]

The authority, in spite of these challenges, constantly replaced its damaged equipment. Even a critical report from 1975, which described "weaknesses" in the elevator maintenance system, conceded, "It must be said that the Authority has made a continuous and conscientious effort to provide good elevator service for its tenants."[3] At Stapleton Houses, for instance, "although there are frequent outages, repairs are more rapid. Nine-tenths of the outages are attributed to vandalism."[4] Alan Rudolph in his 1970s study of NYCHA projects acknowledged the large NYCHA manpower commitment and the use of fast high-capacity elevators. The authority's performance made its elevator service "theoretically as good or better than that provided in most private residential or commercial buildings." By this time NYCHA had a ratio of mechanics to elevator cars that was better than that of most buildings in the city. As had other researchers, Rudolph found that "groups of youngsters of all ages loiter in the lobbies and ride the cars. They are playthings."[5]

In 1980, NYCHA had 390 members of its elevator maintenance staff and it spent $17 million annually on elevator maintenance. Children continued to play on the elevators in the 1980s, causing the occasional loss of life and many injuries. Between 1985 and 1990, for instance, ten children lost their lives in connection to elevator pranks. The authority became so desperate it made a serious film with a funny title, *Children Are Too Young to Die*, which gruesomely and realistically reenacts the severing of a young boy's arm at Polo Grounds Houses and includes shocking images of actual elevator fatalities. When renovating elevators today NYCHA repairmen now replace the swing doors, which could be circumvented by kids with a shoelace or other improvised contraption, in order to prevent kids from gaining access to elevator roofs.[6]

Soldiering On

Elevator problems had become just the tip of the growing disorder faced by NYCHA staff in the late 1960s and the 1970s. The number of tenants under twenty-one grew, the welfare tenancy increased, the homeless filed in, and doubled-up, crowded apartments sometimes overwhelmed site staff. The manager of the Samuel Tilden Houses (1961), Mildred O'Loughlin, described the heartbreaking challenges there in 1971. Returning from a three-week vacation, she "was disheartened to find that the rate of vandalism . . . appears out of control. Every day another building is literally 'bombed' and we find that we are helpless in maintaining the project, even at minimum standards. . . . Staff morale is very low, and understandably so, because regardless of how much work is done, it appears that it is for naught." As bleak as things became, the authority's employees soldiered on. Crews still did their best to clean projects even though tenants treated the grounds and towers in a disrespectful manner.[7]

Variation among the projects remained a hallmark of the authority's program. An extensive project survey conducted by the authority in 1967 found 4 projects with unsatisfactory grounds, 7 with mechanical maintenance problems, and 10 with structural problems. The vast majority of 123 projects were found to be satisfactory in terms of maintenance and only a few excellent in certain maintenance categories. One might dismiss this internal report as exceedingly generous, but it praised only one project, Baisley Park (1961), as "excellent in overall maintenance."[8]

One of the developments singled out as unsatisfactory because of vandalism and crime, Van Dyke Houses (1955) in Brownsville, is representative of the lengths NYCHA took to keep its housing in passable condition. Van Dyke was saved in the 1970s, but as in other housing developments such rescue demanded human and physical resources. As Van Dyke was Oscar Newman's prime example of high-rise pathology in his book *Defensible Space*, and very well could have become uninhabitable in the same manner as Pruitt-Igoe, NYCHA's ability to master its problems is particularly notable.[9]

NYCHA at first committed supplemental funds to Van Dyke (and a number of other troubled projects), on a temporary basis, but this did not seem to have a positive long-term impact: "Janitorial standards have deteriorated since removal of supplementary Task Force Program which ended November 30, 1970. Buildings suffer from abnormally high tenant abuse, no tenant cooperation. Janitorial time cards reflect a high absenteeism rate." Even "the use of a carpenter full time does not keep pace with the damaged doors and hardware. . . . Glass breakage averages 450 lites [a lite or light is equivalent to a window pane] per month, and standpipe valves are constantly turned on, flooding halls and apartments." Tenants claimed, too, that "simple services such as hot water, heat, decent lighting in halls . . . seem very hard to come by."[10]

The authority responded by adding permanent staff at Van Dyke in the early 1970s. A quick clean-up campaign would not do. Administrators hired nineteen additional caretakers and one additional foreman of caretakers. According to the authority, "The added staff is concentrating on washing and waxing of the buildings . . . and cleaning up the grounds. In addition, a painter has been assigned full time" and "two glaziers have been added to the staff to handle the heavy replacement of glass lights." The authority even hired a full-time elevator mechanic and helper in the Brownsville projects and extra teams of repairmen.[11]

In 1975 Van Dyke finally received a satisfactory mark, as "the alarming trend towards an irreversible decline has been halted." Morale was up and the grounds cleaner. *This turnaround happened at the very time that public housing projects around the country reached their nadir.* One starts realizing why staffing increased over the decades (reaching a high of fifteen thousand employees) even as construction slowed: NYCHA hired more staff to deal with the growing problems. This increase, while expensive, does appear to have been the only way to maintain renovation progress.[12]

The determination to maintain projects in spite of damage remained constant. The "Target Projects Program" of renovation in 1976 focused on seven projects that, like Van Dyke, had suffered from crime, vandalism, and extremely poor janitorial conditions. To counter decline, teams worked their way through each building. Janitorial service, in particular, was reorganized to be more effective. According to the authority, "There have been dramatic improvements in the appearance of building corridors, floors and lobbies through the use of improved materials, better techniques and modern equipment as well as the utilization of plain old elbow grease."[13]

In order to reduce future vandalism costs, the authority now installed system wide what it considered to be "Vandal Resistant Fixtures": "We have substituted sturdy plastic light fixtures for the exposed, naked bulb fixtures in public halls and stairway[s]." It eventually shifted to metal cages in a desperate effort to protect lights. Management also began "using more Plexiglas as well as tempered glass in high breakage areas" and simply reduced the amount of glass in entrances, lobbies, and stairwells.[14]

The scale of NYCHA maintenance is best reflected in a series of figures. In 1972, NYCHA reported that system wide "more than 188,000 panes" of glass were replaced at a cost of more than $1.2 million. The staff at Wagner Houses (1958), for instance, replaced 2,280 lights of glass, and staff at Albany Houses (1950) repaired 1,498 lights of glass. By 1974, the authority, on an annual basis, was spending $3 million just to remove graffiti, primarily in stairwells.[15]

New York's public housing endured in this period because of this constant repair and maintenance. The tenants themselves understood the role of the workers in maintaining order. During a union action by NYCHA maintenance workers in 1967, tenants sent telegrams and letters demanding a quick end to the action. As one tenant wrote, "We feel as most others do that the maintenance men being around the buildings doing their work had helped in safeguarding our homes and children, especially in regards to elevators, lights in the hall, etc."[16] Managers primarily viewed tenants as the source of problems, however: "The increase in number of tenants in the lowest income groups seems to have had an adverse impact upon janitorial conditions of some buildings and grounds."[17]

The implementation of Oscar Newman's concept of defensible space in the 1970s introduced new ideas in maintenance, but in the long term the application of his ideas proved unsuccessful. Newman boasted of success at one of NYCHA's only low-rise developments, Clason Point, but he published *Defensible Space* before his landscape designs had been fully implemented at the high-rise Bronxdale (1955), a project more characteristic of the NYCHA system. At Bronxdale, as at Clason Point, Newman redesigned grounds "to provide, among other things, a grouping of buildings into clusters containing play areas for young children, and sitting areas to offer a natural setting for tenant observation of strangers." Not only would Bronxdale be divided into discrete areas, but "strategically located iron fencing was installed, as well as new exterior lighting, to strengthen the security of each cluster." Newman made plans and drawings for other NYCHA projects.[18]

According to NYCHA landscape architect Len Hopper, of NYCHA's Site Improvements Department, in the long term the tall fences at these projects destroyed sight lines and made entering and leaving projects inconvenient and scary. All tenants, for instance, had to venture on the same path into the center of superblocks in order to get to their individual entrances. The tall iron pickets when viewed from an angle created opaque surfaces that turned out to be ideal for criminals. Fences could rarely be maintained against vandalism and when fences failed so did the concept of defensible space. Above all, keeping out crime only made sense when tenants were never a threat to each other, as was increasingly not the case in the 1970s; "locking" them in could make tenants more easily victimized. The metal picket fences do, however, seem to have been widely introduced to NYCHA by Newman; much lower versions of these fences are now in place at almost all developments. Newman's experimental sites have all been redesigned in recent years.

More distressing than the failure of the defensible space model was the general financial crisis of the city and the authority that set in by 1974. The authority had always faced high costs maintaining the grounds and the job was not getting easier. After 1974 "fences could not be maintained," "planting areas [were] worn," unprotected planted areas were destroyed, and in an attempt at economy a "sea of asphalt from building to building" sometimes covered "virtually every planted area."[19] Steel benches and sodium vapor lighting gave the grounds of public housing in New York an institutional appearance. Mature trees survived these changes, but many project grounds began to look more like large parking areas than green spaces. With some green spaces converted to asphalt areas in the 1970s, car owners consciously failed to distinguish between parking areas and play areas. Now, criminals could commit drive-through muggings, creating an "urban recreation of the wild west." Visitors to NYCHA grounds today, filled with trees, lawns, and play equipment, will have little sense of the temporary decline experienced during these difficult years.[20]

Financial resources proved to be one of the determining factors in NYCHA's ability to add staff and modernize developments beginning in the late 1970s. As with all housing, New York's towers had been built for a lifespan of about fifty years. The hard use they endured accelerated the need for renovation. The bedrock of operations was the authority's insistence on rent collection, even with a growing proportion of welfare tenants. New York, based on the success of its rent collection rates and management style, then became a winner in the race for hundreds of millions of federal modernization dollars. New York was able to use this modernization money for genuine updates.

Financial sleights of hand pumped resources into the projects at critical moments. NYCHA's successful "transfer" of projects from state and city control to federal control in the late 1970s revitalized maintenance. NYCHA began the transfer program by begging the state for support of its state-sponsored projects. This appeal provides a frank portrait of conditions for about half of the NYCHA population. According to Chairman Joseph Christian, the fifty-three state projects built by the state since 1944 (housing 186,000 tenants) "were designed to minimum standards when building materials were in short supply." In the poorest parts of the city (Harlem, East Harlem, and Brownsville), the state projects housed a slightly higher level of welfare tenants than federal projects (35 percent versus 25 percent) and faced the daunting challenge of a population 53.1 percent under the age of twenty-one.[21]

The state subsidy formula and increased rents failed to cover the maintenance and fuel costs in the state projects by the mid-1960s, thus "an inexorable process of physical deterioration . . . set in." Christian reminded officials that some of these buildings still had apartments that lacked closet doors, hallway floor tile, and vandal-proof fixtures. According to Christian, the general "physical deterioration . . . is even more serious. We need new heating systems in many locations. We need adequate roofing. We need improved elevators in 60% of the projects. We need new fuel oil tanks, plumbing, weatherproofing, and massive window repairs." Whereas federal projects had recently benefited from $150 million in rehabilitation money, the state projects had not. Nor was extra state aid likely in an era of straightened government budgets.[22]

In 1977, the authority transferred eleven state developments to the federal program. Essentially, the federal government assumed the projects' debts and annual debt service, freeing up the existing state funds that formerly serviced the debt for "a broad program of physical and social revitalization" on the scale of $70 million. The authority, with these funds, updated lobbies, elevators, lighting, fencing, and outdoor

furniture. In order to maintain competitiveness, the authority modernized apartments, including installing new kitchens, closet doors, windows, and plumbing.[23] By 1990 transfers of most state and city projects
had generated an impressive $400 million for renovation. The Reagan
administration had halted the program only after approximately 80
percent of the transfers had been formalized.[24]

Modernization made possible by federal intervention had a multiplier
effect in areas such as energy conservation. New windows, for instance,
"saved millions of dollars" in a time of accelerating fuel costs. General
Manager John Simon remembered, "We made a major effort in replacing windows. That's where the biggest heat loss was."[25] The authority was
able through these means to cut fuel costs dramatically. (The authority
had to acknowledge, however, that "short of maintaining a temperature
of 85–90 [Fahrenheit] in the projects, nothing except individual meter-
ing will prevent tenants from using the gas stove to raise the inside apartment temperatures from 68–72 [Fahrenheit] to 85–90 [Fahrenheit].")[26]
Projects also looked better with new windows and helped further distinguish public housing in New York from that elsewhere.

These modernization programs could barely keep pace with continued vandalism in the 1980s. The tenants of Bushwick Houses (1960), for
instance, claimed that the authority had neglected them, but the authority "cited vandalism as the cause of many of the conditions." Project
managers, even with a thirty-man staff for 1,220 units, could barely keep
pace with destruction. In one month, for instance, they had to replace
seventy windows in the complex (at a rate of six windows per day per
man). The manager recounted confronting a "teenage tenant who
smashed several windows. 'He was just going from floor to floor whack-
ing out windows, and when I asked him why, he told me he didn't know.
How do you deal with that?"[27]

A top administrator, Cyril Grossman, revealed the Sisyphean challenge in the 1980s: "I remember I was director of Manhattan South, and
they were painting the stair halls. This painter was painting from the top
down. This was . . . a 14 story building, and he was up to about the 10th
floor. . . . I went up to see how the 14th floor looked, because he had finished painting. He was just on the 10th floor, [but] the 14th floor was already marked up with graffiti." Grossman discovered that the quality of
much of his staff had slipped as the workload became more difficult:
"Now the same caretaker has more garbage to handle, he has more filthy
halls, has more garbage on the lawns. . . . The filthier he finds the building in the morning, the less he's going to work." Rent delinquency increased from 3 to 7 percent between 1977 and 1986 as the welfare
caseload grew (and remained about that high in 2006).[28]

The managers who maintained the NYCHA system during these difficult decades had a right to be frustrated. Even heroic renovation barely kept pace with depredation. A historical perspective illustrates that timely insertion of money, effort, and innovation would prove essential to eventually reframing public housing as a worthwhile government activity. New York did not survive these years just because it managed to limit its welfare tenancy to below 50 percent of its population. It also held the line against an antisocial element.

Trial by Fire: Housing Police Face the Enemy Within

Chairman Albert Walsh admitted in 1968 that public housing design had not worked out as planned: "The site planning of super-block developments . . . was the subject of great admiration by planners twenty, and even ten years ago—because of the open space, light and air that were provided." Times had changed, however. He now believed that "the super-block designs of the past" *conjoined* with growing crime, demanded housing policing. New York administrators never believed that design made their work impossible; other cities seemed at best halfhearted when it came to security. According to Walsh, New York still had "the only housing authority police department in the country."[29]

This force had become more sophisticated over the years. Walsh highlighted call boxes, two way radios, and motor scooters. Mayor Lindsay had agreed by this point to expand the authority's force, proposing and ultimately agreeing to add four hundred men from 1968 to 1969. Half of this expansion came out of city funds and the authority reached the fifteen hundred men target by 1969. The force had doubled in only six years.[30]

Drugs had been noted in the developments as early as the 1950s, but the magnitude of the problem reached new heights in the 1960s and 1970s. "Despite the constant thorough and determined screening by the Authority," wrote housing detectives, "a small number of undesirables are using Authority apartments for the sale and/or use of narcotics. This condition, unless checked, attracts addicts to the location who are certainly not adverse to committing crimes. . . ."[31] At the project level, problems in drugs gained notice from managers, too. One housing manager remembered that at his project at Johnson Houses in the 1960s, "You had a lot of drugs" and that the drug of choice at that time was "heroin. Sad stories were told over and over again of children overdosing."[32] A longtime resident of Patterson Houses remembered that heroin use began to destabilize the development in the 1960s: "All of a sudden, everyone in the projects is talking about break-ins. . . . Then I started hearing about folk that I grew up with getting thrown off rooftops because they were dealing."[33]

In desperation NYCHA tried to restore the informal social control it had destroyed in its rush to slum clearance. Most urban neighborhoods failed to maintain strong self-policing during this time, but the human-scaled physical environment and diversity of uses in traditional neighborhoods at least left open the potential for reorganization. NYCHA had to invest in tenant patrols as an artificial substitute for Jane Jacobs's naturally occurring "eyes on the street."

Cyril Grossman in 1968 described the tenant patrol system to an interested official from San Francisco. The patrol comprised volunteer tenants in the lobby equipped with a phone and armbands. These tenants directly challenged those trying "to gain entrance without a key." According to Grossman, in one of the projects where the program had been initiated, "We have had no incidents of vandalism such as we experience in other buildings—i.e., broken bulbs, walls marked with ink and playing in the halls." Grossman found, however, that because "all antisocial behavior has practically been eliminated . . . the patrol worker [has] nothing to do." He found that interest in the patrols, after initial success, was difficult to sustain because boredom often set in. He encouraged payment to participating tenants to sustain interest.[34]

NYCHA never dallied. By late 1968 lobby and elevator patrol groups were operating in twenty-four projects. The authority now paid thirty patrol supervisors for their services. NYCHA officials such as Grossman had identified pure voluntarism as a limiting factor in the earlier experience, so they added a financial element. The cost of this program quickly rose that year, with NYCHA spending $500,000 on a city-wide basis. Participants received walkie-talkies, telephones, and special "identification gear." The *Sunday News* touted significant improvements in the state of affairs at Linden Houses, where patrols had restored order: "Nothing has been reported in the three buildings being patrolled by tenants."[35]

Always proud of its numbers, in 1976 NYCHA counted 11,906 volunteers covering 733 buildings in 129 developments. Tenant patrols also began, in 1974, to distribute free lunches daily to project children in order to build relationships between patrols and the young. The number of lunches reached 45,635 by 1976. "The sites maintained by various tenant patrol volunteers," NYCHA reported, "received excellent or superior rating when they were inspected by State Inspectors."[36]

As much as these patrols tended to help good projects and involved thousands of residents, they had little noticeable effect on the general trend toward greater lawlessness brought on by a growing impoverished, drug-addled population. Simeon Golar, NYCHA chairman, could still make the familiar arguments about lower proportional crime in public housing in 1970: "Crime in the projects was about one-third of that in surrounding areas," but these figures had little relevance.[37] Index crime arrests increased to 1,520 in 1970 and reached 2,188 by 1975. Even more disturbing was that tenants represented 65 percent of arrests in 1975 (as compared to 52 percent in 1968). The quantity change was just as impressive, shifting from only 572 tenants arrested in 1968 to 1,193 in 1975. This represented an important shift in the nature of criminality in the projects and rarely received mention by housing officials. Crime had come inside, but NYCHA dodged a full public accounting.[38]

Even more frightening than raw numbers during this period was the fact that crime in public housing grew at a faster rate than that in the city as a whole, jumping 26 percent from 1970 to 1971 versus a city-wide increase of 2.3 percent. Homicide was far worse, with a 428.5 percent increase for NYCHA and only a 31.3 percent increase in the city as a whole. Manpower had jumped by 44 percent between 1966 and 1971, and arrests had increased 111 percent, but criminal complaints alone had increased 170 percent. This frightening upswing came in spite of the fact that NYCHA almost entirely lacked stores, which were often criminal targets.[39]

Residents criticized NYCHA's reporting style that failed to acknowledge the acceleration of crime. In 1971 they noted that NYCHA "neglected to state that six years ago, the rate of serious crime per 1,000 population was 6 times greater outside of public housing, than inside."[40] The majority of tenants in Alan Rudolph's 1970 study gave the authority only fair grades for security. Whites, often on their way out, generally gave the lowest ratings. More ominous was Rudolph's finding that NYCHA "seems much less able to protect its tenants from each other. Racial tensions, the exuberance of youth, cultural and educational deficiencies and other factors, manifest themselves as anti-social acts which affect property and people."[41]

The authority in this period would have liked to establish order by weeding out the bad tenants, but in fact it evicted very few tenants for disorderly behavior. The Resident Advisory Council of tenants in 1976 demanded that "any tenant that violates the rules and regulations . . . must be dealt with promptly."[42] The longtime administrator Cyril Grossman also remembered that tenant organizations became outspoken in their frustration that NYCHA had backed off from strict rule enforcement: "Almost invariably we'd go to a meeting in the seventies [of] a tenant organization meeting. . . . You would have them come up at you with: when I moved into the project you did this, that and the other thing. Why aren't you doing that now? Why aren't you as strict as you were when we moved in?"[43]

NYCHA had, in fact, lost much of its ability to evict tenants who had committed crimes or were accused of crimes. Of one thousand evictions in 1975, for instance, nondesirability accounted for only one-third of these cases. The 1971 consent decree had granted due process rights that made eviction so time consuming and arduous that evictions now took from one to two years.[44] Officials could report in 1973 of over one hundred hearings monthly, but the authority had much less clout.[45] Cyril Grossman remembered that "a good number of managers . . . felt that they could no longer be part of this . . . more liberalized public housing, and they left long before their time to retire."[46]

Tenant concerns would not be helped by the fiscal woes of the city as a whole during the mid-1970s that undercut the policing force. In 1970, for instance, the city annually provided 30 percent of the police funding.[47] But budget cuts had dire effects. Stapleton Houses, for instance, in 1975 had experienced a loss of two of its five officers. This reduction came in spite of the fact that "the number of reported crimes at Stapleton Houses per thousand has jumped from 11.3 in 1973 to 23.8 in 1974."[48]

Officials in 1978 stood by their figures and still claimed that "crime in public housing stays consistently at a level from 3 to 4 times lower than the rate of crime outside public housing," but it is likely that few people believed them.[49] As visual proof of public housing's comparative peacefulness, and NYCHA's selective vision, Chairman Christian boasted that "when President Carter came to the South Bronx about a year ago, he looked around a devastated landscape and remarked that public housing was the only decent housing that he could see."[50] One of the happiest moments for the authority had come in 1977 when public relations splashed across the internal *Housing Authority Journal* the headline "How We Beat the Blackout! Authority Projects Were 'Islands of Calm.'" Managers gave extra time, as did officers, and tenant patrols worked through the crisis. The lack of stores, however, again likely played a role in comparative calm.[51]

Authority figures were not being frank about the growing problems. The first *six months* of 1978, for instance, yielded 1,123 felony and 1,839 misdemeanor arrests, numbers worrisome enough to inspire the City Council Hearings on Security in Public Housing that year. Chairman Joseph Christian defended NYCHA's record by pointing out that the authority was spending "more money on security in total dollars ($55 million), as a percentage of budget (11.0%), and in cost per dwelling unit than any another Housing Authority in the United States." Christian put the best spin possible on these costs: "Most other public housing authorities have quasi-police forces at much less cost" whereas New York paid the high cost of fringe benefits. He believed, however, "It has been our decision that a professional force, although expensive, does provide the best security for our residents, rather than a simple guard service."[52]

Leading members of the patrolmens' union and officer corps offered a much tougher assessment of the security situation in 1978. One called the projects "a haven for criminals and a jungle nightmare and a living hell for tenants." Officers were "afraid to go out on post by their self [*sic*]." Because of the city's general financial crisis and low morale, the force had slipped to 1,361 officers (from 1,800 in 1975). In 1977, the force also suffered a shockingly high 7 percent injury rate.[53] The chief of the NYPD "testified that regular police in a normal tour of duty would not go into the confines of a large project that is 'self-contained.'"[54] To give NYCHA its due, in most American cities policing of high-rise housing projects by regular police became almost nonexistent. In New York, however, the Housing Police had to patrol housing projects that NYPD officers avoided. Vertical patrolling was doubtless unpleasant, but that did not make it any less necessary.

The authority responded as best it could to these disturbing trends in terms of physical redesign. Administrators invested in updates they thought would aid security. They introduced armored mailboxes, security plates for apartment door locks, and better door chains, and on the grounds they added more "sodium vapor lighting to significantly brighten outdoor space." In building entrances administrators installed stainless steel and high-impact vandal resistant glass.[55]

NYCHA's police administrators modernized their policing to include a pinpointed crime identification system utilizing "a daily mimeographed report of all crimes taking place in public housing." Officers used the report to focus staff on troubled areas. A police task force of seventy men backed up this work. The housing force, however, was still "principally a neighborhood residential police force with emphasis on the 'vertical' patrol of building interiors." In spite of the crime fighting, the housing police still retained a social function, as it devoted "a large part of its patrol time reconciling family and personal disputes, providing escorts for the elderly and vulnerable and in generally relieving tension throughout the projects." Numerous Housing Authority police officers even called NYCHA projects home.[56]

These new techniques went far in helping to fight crime, but housing police morale had slipped in the late 1970s according to Benjamin Ward, who took over and turned the force around (and later became the city's police commissioner). When Ward arrived he found "poor organization, inadequate deployment, lack of training, a gross lack of leadership, political interference and low level corruption." He entirely reorganized the staff and redeployed many desk officers to direct policing. He increased coverage of projects to a twenty-four-hour basis by reorganizing the officers and notably decreasing sick leave.[57] The NYCHA police force had almost returned to 1975 levels by 1983, with 1,628 staff members. *The city's contribution by 1984 on a yearly basis was*

$50 million. John Simon, the general manager, believed, "[Other] cities that have problems didn't have the support that we had in New York City for security."[58]

The increase in force and reorganization could barely keep pace with harrowing drug problems. The rate of crime in NYCHA projects roughly doubled from the mid-1970s to the mid-1980s while the city's crime rate increased by only 50 percent. The eighty-three murders in the projects in 1982 represented a rate of 17.2 per 1,000 population compared to 20.4 for the city as a whole. Aggravated assault was almost exactly at the city's rate of 6 per 1,000. Only in property crime was NYCHA significantly lower, achieving a rate of 17.8 per 1,000 as opposed to 77 per 1,000 in the city as a whole. These figures give credence to the criticism of NYCHA reporting over the years. NYCHA's crime index figure for 1982, the blended figure of crimes against property and persons, was 34.9 per 1,000 at NYCHA compared to 97.4 per 1,000 in the city as a whole: it was the comforting statistic that administrators favored.[59]

More distressing is the fact that violent crime constituted 48.8 percent of total crime in NYCHA projects and only 20.9 percent in the city as a whole in 1982. NYCHA's projects had become more mean places to live where crime in sheer numbers may have been lower, but severity of crime was a real factor. The most likely place to be robbed in a NYCHA project was the elevator (34.8 percent of crimes), followed by apartments (18.5 percent), hallways (15 percent), and finally lobbies (14.1 percent). The danger posed by elevators lends some weight to criticism of the high-rise form of housing. The most likely time of day was between noon and 8 PM and the most popular day for robbery were paycheck Fridays. The most dangerous projects were in Brooklyn and the South Bronx, with total crime rates comparable to those in the city as a whole.[60] Nor had the authority become more effective in evicting tenants for anything other than nonpayment of rent.[61]

A 1983 report gives a good sense of what public housing security was and was not. The high-rise Claremont Village project in the Bronx was surrounded by "abandoned, vandalized buildings, rubble-strewn lots and general anarchy," but its sixteen thousand residents in thirty high-rise buildings were not living on an "island many people would wish to visit." The report noted that "although the crime rate within the complex is lower than that for the 46th and 48th Precincts for which it is located, residents live in a permanent sense of fear—fear of burglary, fear of robbery, fear of violence, fear of vandalism and muggings." Claremont Village was particularly notorious, as its crime rate in 1984 exceeded the average of the other housing projects by an astounding 80 percent.[62]

Drug crime, in particular, fueled these massive increases in public housing crime. According to Roy Metcalf, the deputy director of public information, "crack came in . . . the summer [of] 1986," and unlike the heroin addict, who just "nods off somewhere . . . a crack guy gets violent, psychotic."[63] Emanuel Popolozio, then NYCHA chairman, might have boasted to congressman Charles Rangel that "the rate of crime in public housing . . . in 1988 is still one half that of the city as a whole," but this figure represented a far worse comparative rate than the old days; the lower property crimes no longer watered down the more serious crimes. By 1988, index crimes were 46 per 1,000 in public housing compared to a city-wide average of 99.26. Popolozio admitted that "in one category alone, murder, the increase in the actual number of murders (from 122 in '87 to 201 in '88) actually caught up with the city." He presented the astonishing change that "public housing houses about 9% of the people of New York City. We also now have 9% of the murders." *Arrests on NYCHA grounds reached 28,860 in 1989.* These high annual arrest rates had been achieved by the mid-1980s and have remained similarly high until the present. Rikers Island and Sing Sing had become de facto annexes of NYCHA developments.[64]

A tougher approach to drug crime accounted for the mounting arrest rates. In projects that seemed fine by day, drug dealers ruled at night. The *New York Times* found that "at Smith Houses, as at many of the other 316 projects . . . the problem is crack, the cheap, smokable cocaine derivative whose ravaging effects on whole neighborhoods were officially recognized about two years ago."[65] It could become so bad at the Edenwald Houses in the Bronx that a "drug-dealing ring . . . held the project's 6,000 residents 'under siege.'" Bodies were found on a regular basis around the project. The community had gone from being "a quiet, relatively safe community into a hellish place where gunfire often rings out in hallways or on playgrounds, where drug dealers recruit teenagers to sell crack." This was more than journalistic overstatement; in Edenwald alone in 1988 there were 149 assaults, 99 robberies, and 4 murders.[66]

These descriptions of drug operations are often sobering. In the Jacob Riis Houses, for instance, one drug dealer had "installed a steel door to section off the bedroom from which she sold an ounce to an undercover police officer" and "she had a closed circuit television system by which she could monitor what her customers did in the hall."[67] Cyril Grossman recounted the shocking fact that he had managed projects where crack "was sold so openly that each floor in the building had its own crack dealer." Housing officials at many projects "barricaded" themselves behind locked doors and one could find, throughout the city, beginning in the 1970s, "bookkeeping office[s] behind bullet proof glass. Then [the authority] went to the receptionist with the bullet proof glass." The authority did not sit still at Riis, Edenwald, or the rest of the city.[68]

Because the authority was being walloped by the crack epidemic, Popolozio established a narcotics task force that conducted sweeps through the projects (with the NYPD and the DEA), created a communication blitz against drugs, and invented new ways to attack drug use. Rudolph Giuliani, then the U.S. attorney for the Southern District of New York, collaborated with Police Commissioner Benjamin Ward, Chairman Popolizio, and Mayor Ed Koch to begin seizing apartments of those arrested for drug dealing in public housing under a federal law created in 1984. Giuliani claimed that although the law had generally been used for commercial and private property, it had "never been used before to go after a lease in public housing." Now, "the suspects can regain the apartments only if they win subsequent criminal and civil cases in court."[69]

A series of posters (Figure 29) that warned drug dealers to "stay the hell out of public housing or we'll nail you" featured a beefy Popolizio grimacing in a suitably menacing way; others featured groups of concerned tenants with stern looks on their faces. Results could be counted: "Drug arrests in public housing increased from 760 in 1986 . . . to 9,763 in 1988" (accounting for the record arrest rates established at this time) Over one thousand tenants filled out forms to report on drug dealing in their neighborhoods.[70] At Edenwald, for instance, the drug epidemic led to 380 drug arrests in just half of 1989. The police secured the first floor of a building and "like soldiers establishing a beachhead, pushed the drug dealers out. Officers now use its roof to spy on dealers in other parts of the complex." The officers in time grabbed cars, guns, and tenants from adjacent buildings. This was war.[71]

Drugs, part of an undesirability category, still do not seem to have been the primary reason for eviction even at this time. The number of evictions strictly for "undesirability" remained low. According to Cyril Grossman, in 1988, "I think they evicted 17 families the whole year for undesirability," because of the extensive footwork required, "it's just not worth the effort of the manager."[72] One set of figures from 1988 counted 4,550 eviction cases pursued with only 101 evictions actually accomplished. The secretary of HUD, Jack Kemp, finally eased rules to allow for evictions of the families of drug dealers in 1989.[73]

Popolizio responded defensively to the growing criticism of eviction procedures against families of those charged with drug crimes. He argued that, in spite of soft-hearted sentiment to the contrary, "the authority's experience with the administrative grievance procedures . . . amounts to a grisly farce. A Housing Authority study shows that excluded family members rarely stay excluded." He noted too that crack

A MESSAGE FOR DRUG DEALERS:

"Stay the hell <u>out</u> of public housing or we'll <u>nail</u> you."

Figure 29. New York got tough on crime in the 1980s and 1990s. *New York City Housing Authority Journal*, February/March 1989, Box 99D3, NYCHAR.

presented certain special problems: "Worse, the drug crack is a cottage industry, manufactured and sold from the home, creating the infamous crack house." He squarely faced the accusations of class injustice: "Why does this agreement translate into hostility to 'poor people of color'? . . . The pressure to evict comes not from us, but from tenants."[74]

In 1993, for instance, there were *11,092 arrests in public housing for drug crimes alone,* but it still took approximately twenty months to evict a tenant. The Legal Aid Society's Judith Goldiner believed that a further acceleration in eviction, proposed by the authority (by sending cases to the Special Narcotics Unit of Housing Court), "would violate constitutional rights and would be unfair to innocent family members." Diane Jackson, a tenant resident and leader, did not accept the notion of family innocence, "when your kids are walking around in $100 sneakers and they don't have jobs, something is going on. People have to be held accountable."[75]

NYCHA, in partnership with the NYPD, certainly seemed to take the notion of accountability seriously, but with a population of over four hundred thousand tenants, even such a tough program had limits. The popularity of drugs appears to be a symptom of economic marginality rather than a characteristic of public housing. Are trailer parks and small towns to blame for the crystal meth epidemic? The only obvious way to reduce crime was to continue to repair the damage in the short-term and in the long term find tenants whose better economic position would help reduce the attractiveness of drugs. The final chapter of the book details these innovations, which when combined with a continuation of large-scale policing (and an aging population) has finally led to a recent decline in NYCHA crime.

Community Programs

The unswerving idealists among NYCHA staff thought that enhanced community programs might turn around the lives of problem tenants. In retrospect, it does seem that community programs—which grew in scale during this time—improved the quality of life of many families, but there is no evidence that they helped the more troubled tenants. It appears, in fact, that the less troubled families were more likely to benefit from community affairs.

Fear of riots and juvenile delinquency had led in the 1960s to a new tenant affairs division: "Outside events—the hot tense days of the early and middle Sixties—prompted a major change. . . . The Authority applied for and received Federal funds in the amount of $740,000 for . . . summer activities."[76] By 1965 NYCHA was participating in Operation Head Start, Neighborhood Youth Corps, Job Corps, Vista, and new expanded summer programs. The authority bused kids to state parks in those hot summers and initiated a summer camp program. The summer programs had to be cut back in the 1970s, but participation in sheer numbers (if not depth of activity) actually increased.[77]

Community programs during the 1960s and after shifted to traditional forms of American community activities that would demand less NYCHA oversight and funding. By 1976, with just three staff members and about $350,000 dollars, the division could count 53,500 tenants in sports leagues; 2,300 tenants in a talent search program; 15,000 tenants maintaining 1,000 flower and vegetable gardens. The NYCHA Symphony, by then in operation six years, continued to give concerts, although it was dominated by professional players, and new tenant newsletters were launched. These are just some of many programs.[78]

Tenant participation numbers improved, but community centers still limped along into the 1970s. A careful study of community centers by Ira Robbins in 1973 identified familiar weaknesses. He found eight centers run by the Youth Services Administration to be "low grade" and noted that fifteen run by the "Board of Education Centers present the same picture that has been of concern to the Authority for many years. . . . They may possibly be described as custodial or baby sitting operations." He found that, remarkably, "the centers are closed on every day that the public schools are closed" because they were staffed by teachers working on a school calendar. Gang warfare had reduced the use of these centers for dances and many lacked evening hours. The most edifying use of the centers was for tenant meetings, weddings, and other parties that filled "a very important need of the tenants" because they could not afford other venues.[79]

The blend of NYCHA community activities, while uneven, did provide a satisfactory base for socially cohesive tenant families. A longtime tenant remembered that for her daughter "growing up in NYCHA meant you were NYCHA children, and most NYCHA children attended NYCHA sponsored programs and events, day care centers, community center programs such as Partners in Reading, after school programs, summer programs."[80] A 1970 study of tenant life found a more complicated mix of success and failure. Tenants in the three projects that planner Alan Rudolph studied could "get health, psychiatric, welfare, recreational, cultural, job and educational services within the project or nearby." This was no small matter. In his opinion, however, "few of these services are sufficiently well funded, or well administered to make a real impact." Among the tenants he observed a "social thrust . . . towards middle class, indeed bourgeois values," thus residents tended to deemphasize community participation and "only a minute fraction used the [community] center."[81]

Nor had the community center situation noticeably improved a decade later. By 1980, the authority was trying "to operate some 86 of the centers [out of 150] with its own resources." Only about 64 sponsoring agencies operated in the centers because of financial problems; in frustration, the Board of Education had also pulled out in 1976. The authority admitted that its own efforts in this area were only minimal: "Since these resources are limited, we find that we have been unable to properly maintain and expand the delivery of community center services." Youth programs and Head Start were crammed together as were other externally funded activities. The modest funding for the centers came from the Federal Performance Funding system.[82]

These programs struggled for primarily financial reasons. A report noted that "although the US. Housing Acts for over 25 years have made provision for specific monies for Social Services, no specifically designated funds have ever been appropriated for this purpose. In order to maintain its extensive social service program, the Authority has been forced to rely on the outside sponsorship of many centers, private foundation grants and budget gimmicks."[83] Chairman Joseph Christian, in apparent financial desperation, asked the mayor's office for help in 1980, but the deputy mayor for operations replied, [I am] "not sure how I can be helpful to you in your efforts to forestall additional closures."[84] NYCHA apparently found a way to supplement its staff, but this then displeased HUD, which in a 1983 review wondered why, in light of declining use, "the number of employees to support this mission shows a budgeted increase of 43 employees." NYCHA was in a catch-22; skeleton staffing meant fewer organized programs that could boost participation.[85]

Unlike other housing authorities, most of which left tenants with no social or community resources, community programs survived at NYCHA even during these difficult years. The city and externally funded social services continued to offer their quality services in areas such as health care and senior services; tenant participation in certain programs remained high; and the community centers did not evaporate. I would not underestimate the influence of these programs on the attitude of law-abiding families. The survival, and augmentation, of this combination of institutions became an important factor in boosting morale in the 1990s as NYCHA recommitted to community programming.

NYCHA under the Microscope

During these difficult years outsiders examined NYCHA and the reflected image proved flattering. Planner Alan Rudolph's detailed survey from 1970 of tenant life found both flaws and evidence of NYCHA management finesse. Rudolph studied the newer projects of moderate size, including Seth Low (mostly black), Stanley Isaacs (mostly white), and Andrew Jackson (integrated). Respondents to his surveys gave high marks to the physical aspects of their apartments, with 55 percent of all respondents giving the "good" or highest rating and another 34.8 percent giving a moderate response. A majority, both black and white, "would recommend this project to friends." One reason for the high marks is that, according to the author, "There is no doubt that to many if not most of the tenants, these apartments represent a vast improvement." NYCHA's long-term investments in apartment improvement had the desired effect. In terms of management service, too, "almost all tenants agreed verbally that maintenance of all equipment was good to excellent." The majority said that the management responded "quickly" to complaints.[86]

Oscar Newman's influential *Defensible Space* (1973) inadvertently attested to NYCHA's maintenance ability. His book primarily examined security problems in NYCHA's high-rise and low-rise projects as justification for a new theory of urban security, but even Newman had to acknowledge that maintenance of these buildings was superior to their initial design. Newman called NYCHA's "record of enlightened policies and management . . . second to none." The pictures of poorly maintained high-rise housing projects came not from NYCHA but from other authorities. The interior grounds of Breukelen Houses (1952), for instance, are displayed because residents saw them as the most dangerous areas of the projects, but the grounds and planting pictured are immaculate. The worst examples of project decline actually came from St. Louis and Philadelphia. That NYCHA worked with Newman in redesigning grounds also speaks to NYCHA's responsive administration.[87]

NYCHA officials, who had worked closely with Newman, were nevertheless displeased both with the findings (they disagreed that his research indicated a direct relationship between building height and criminality) and with the association of certain NYCHA projects, such as Van Dyke Houses (1955), with complete disasters like Pruitt-Igoe.[88] As NYCHA statistician Harry Fialkin remarked in a memo, "The deplorable conditions in public housing which he observed in St. Louis and other cities, are presented in various sections of the book in a manner that suggests they are characteristic of the program in New York City." What had been a pleasant relationship turned sour, but Newman's book can now be read as a testament to NYCHA's management skills. The authority had done everything wrong in design, so to speak, and yet its projects worked better than most others around the country.[89]

Camilo José Vergara, known for his work as a photographer of urban decline, in an otherwise chilling description of life in some New York projects, still found much to admire in NYCHA management in the 1980s: "Entering a project during the day . . . gives one a view of public housing at its best. I usually saw the buildings' public spaces soon after the caretaker had done the morning cleaning and at a time when school was in session and few children were around. My first impression was one of clean floors and quiet buildings." That the buildings began every day clean—and he visited a large number of them—testifies directly to NYCHA's management proficiency. After that point, Vergara's tone is decidedly negative, finding busted locks in entrance

doors, drug-related graffiti, cracked windows. As a caretaker emphasized, most of these problems came from hard use: "Every time we put
a new lock in, they break it." Perhaps the most moving section of the
article follows: "Despite their pessimistic outlook . . . workers and officials made lists of things that needed to be done, picked up garbage
left behind by careless residents, and addressed tenants politely. Not
one expressed the desire to look for other work." Stuck looking after a
large antisocial population, and relatively well paid to do so, the employees did their best.[90]

Terry Williams and William Kornblum's long-term community study,
The Uptown Kids (1994), found that tenants suffered from drug crime,
but these sociologists still believed that "the Harlem projects we studied
are better environments in which to raise children than the tenement
neighborhoods surrounding them. Severe urban blight . . . continues to
ravage other parts of Harlem." They had found, too, that public housing
is "better maintained and more secure than most market rentals." A tenant activist acknowledged NYCHA maintenance policies by reporting on
her trip to Cleveland, where she had found that the housing authority
failed to replace broken windows: "If somebody broke a pane the housing authority wouldn't replace it with glass, they'd replace it with
wood. . . . There was wood up all over the place. There were some apartments completely boarded up, because when all the glass was broken
out and the stove was broken . . . the person found somewhere else to
live."[91]Cleveland was not alone in failing to remedy defects quickly.

Federal officials comprise an even tougher group of critics. Yet even
they have been upbeat, in spite of growing frustration with public housing nationally. The Department of Housing and Urban Development
has subjected NYCHA, and all other American authorities, to extensive
review over the decades. Generally, NYCHA shines. In 1971, HUD found
"the Authority to be well run and administered by a highly professional
staff with first rate leadership at its highest level."[92] In 1977, after a near
fiscal meltdown, HUD still considered NYCHA a "national model of successful management of limited income housing."[93] The sociologists Kornblum and Williams reported in 1994 that at HUD "New York City
public housing has the reputation of being better designed and constructed and in general better managed than that of most other U.S.
cities." During this decade, HUD designated NYCHA a high-performing
housing authority.[94] In 1997, it gave NYCHA a rating of 99.25 percent
(on a 0–100 percent scale) on a mix of management factors including
vacancy rate, annual inspections, and financial management. In 2004,
the last year it was analyzed, NYCHA remained a high-performing authority.[95]

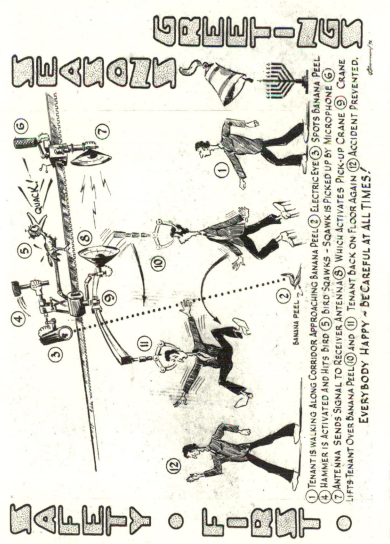

Figure 30. This cartoon is a metaphor for NYCHA management in the period of the welfare state. Rather than abandoning their posts, administrators continued to pursue a high level of tenant control. *NYCHA Journal*, December/January 1973, Box 92D2, NYCHAR.

The staff of NYCHA cleaned lobbies and hallways, constantly repaired elevators, collected trash, repaired windows, and collected rents in spite of the fact that tenants showed diminishing respect for the housing projects. The housing police arrested tens of thousands of lawbreakers every year. Functioning families found a web of social and community programs that provided compensations for life in increasingly difficult environments (Figure 30).

This chapter presents some horrifying descriptions, putting to rest the common notion that NYCHA did not face challenges similar to those in other cities. Decent public administration in New York, at least, allowed for the survival of socially troubled housing projects. The constant repair work and tough policing frequently seemed to many of the authority's administrators as expensive and unpromising, but it made a difference when combined with tenant selection methods such as the Tier programs. The adherence to the details of management preserved a massive housing system that could be fine-tuned when the notion of *welfare-state public housing* had run its course. Other housing authorities by the 1990s, in contrast, faced emptying projects, many of which appeared far beyond salvation.

Part IV
Affordable Housing

Chapter 13

Model Housing Revisited

America's dominant political parties had by the 1990s abandoned the entire notion of a welfare state. Public housing appeared as a key, troubled element in this fading paradigm. However, the New York City Housing Authority did not fit comfortably into this more skeptical milieu. Unlike housing authorities across the country it had weathered two decades of higher welfare concentration and disorder. Maintenance had become strained, and the future seemed bleak, but public housing in New York was too large and successful to be dismantled as it was in cities such as Chicago and Baltimore. Savvy tenants and their advocates quickly scotched any hint of demolition or privatization of apartments.

NYCHA then and now has had to manage a large and subsidy-needing system of housing that the federal government dislikes supporting. In 2006, for instance, NYCHA still had 345 full developments with 420,000 official residents. The authority also housed, in a more distant fashion, 270,000 city residents in 90,000 apartments funded by Section 8. The salaries of approximately 13,000 total employees remained its responsibility. Dismantling this vast system, one of the last bastions of cheap housing in New York, and one of the city's largest employers, was out of the question. Reforming it was not.[1]

Since the 1990s NYCHA has been carefully charting a course away from *welfare-state public housing*. In so doing, the organization has looked to its past when working-class people constituted most of the tenancy. NYCHA now aims to remake its system, using management techniques, into *affordable housing*. The term affordable housing denotes a programmatic shift in American housing policy toward lower-cost housing that serves the working poor rather than the poorest or welfare tenants. Not only are these working-poor tenants able to cover a more reasonable proportion of the cost, but also their behavior is, with some justification, considered to be superior to the welfare underclass.

Most affordable housing has been built by nonprofits operating with government subsidies, but NYCHA is also openly reconfiguring its existing public housing system along this model. The tight housing market in New York has played a role in NYCHA's ability to change tracks by creating a large pool of potential tenants who are employed, but without its management practices there is little chance that working families would ever select to live in NYCHA developments. New York's towers—both physically and socially—remain competitive with the low end of the private sector.

NYCHA has been able to reshape itself as *affordable housing* because almost all of its interest groups stand to benefit. The local and federal governments understandably support any changes that will in the long term reduce subsidies and improve performance. NYCHA's recent investments in building and grounds renovation accompanying the new model have aided acceptance by existing tenants because they benefit from an appreciable upgrade in their environments. Many of the authority's current and most vocal tenants, some of whom depend on government support themselves, would also prefer fewer additional welfare tenants. Because admissions have become the tool to social integration, existing tenants face little danger of losing their apartments. The only group expressing reservation is the city's loose confederation of poverty activists. Even most of them would concede, however, that the *welfare-state public housing* model has serious defects and should be reformed.

New York City had by the 1990s made enviable progress in housing renovation compared to cities such as Philadelphia and Baltimore. The city in 1999 still had a higher percentage of housing with serious physical problems than most cities nationwide (7.6 percent in New York versus 2 percent nationally), but compared to the old days such a figure for New York should be viewed as a sign of progress. Not only had large areas been bulldozed in the Moses era, but also nonprofit housing development and market renovation made the problems of tenement districts a distant memory. The city government's substantial commitment to housing renovation positioned many blighted neighborhoods on the road to recovery.[2]

This success in renovation, and the renewed attractiveness of New York as a global destination for capital and immigrants, created a new crisis. Cumulatively the city had lost hundreds of thousands of low-cost apartments to rent increases, conversions, and dilapidation. A population in the hundreds of thousands was thought to live in illegal and/or unhealthy apartments, doubled up, or in severely overcrowded conditions. New York's private developers built only 85,000 new units in the 1990s for an additional 456,000 city residents, and many of those units were designed for higher-income New Yorkers. In 2004, for instance, "One out of three New York households [paid] more than 30% of its income for rent . . . one out of four [paid] more than 50%." Of the latter group, approximately 500,000 households, 9 of 10 were low income.[3]

The failure of salaries, particularly for the poorest workers, to keep pace with skyrocketing prices was a major factor in the affordability predicament. Hundreds of thousands of New Yorkers left welfare (between 1996 and 2005 welfare recipients in New York City dropped from 1 million to approximately 400,000), but these workers were stuck in low-wage labor settings where "salaries . . . adjusted for inflation— [were] lower than in the late 1980s." A flood of immigrants, while reenergizing neighborhoods, likely played some role in keeping wages low, but New York's service economy in general created a more polarized economy of winners and losers. Total household salaries of this lowest group stretched between $10,000 and $20,000. In New York these low wages presented a survival challenge. As has always been the case, NYCHA did not have to serve exclusively the poorest residents in the city to make an impact. The working poor were just as hungry for quality affordable housing as welfare recipients.[4]

In spite of a tight housing market, and contrary to the notion that market forces determined the fate of public housing in New York, NYCHA faced a perilous situation in the 1990s. New York's rebirth did not automatically improve the tenant selection situation. The NYCHA waiting list had hit 240,000 families in 1992, a record, but it was by no means filled with ideal tenants. Administrators at NYCHA worried that "the percentage of families on welfare has jumped from nearly 35 percent to nearly 50 percent of" of those on the waiting list. By 1995, too, "77 percent of new admissions were people in the lowest income category, while only 8 percent of new applicants were working families." Certain projects had, in spite of the Tier program, become "known as virtual dumping grounds for the very poorest." Approximately half the population of the six projects in the Rockaways, for instance, was on welfare by the mid-1990s.[5] NYCHA tenant *family* incomes had only reached $12,476 in 1995 and welfare families made up 30.2 percent of all families. The length of tenancy had increased from 13.2 years in 1985 to 16.7 years in 1995.[6]

Administrators in 1995 were particularly concerned about the lack of working families, whom they believed provided stability to developments and could also pay higher rents. As the *New York Times* discovered: "In the last decade, the agency has seen the number of working families drop from 46 percent to 32 percent." An aging population contributed to this decline, but the waiting lists tipped the system even more toward welfare. Ceiling rents, the rents higher-income tenants pay, had not been raised since the 1980s in part to keep working families in public housing, but the looser rental market of the 1980s and early 1990s proved irresistible to many working families. Above all, admission priorities still favored the very poor who came from shelters or experienced other housing emergencies.[7]

NYCHA aggressively used shifting political winds to its advantage. In 1992, HUD gave local housing authorities the power to set standards for up to 50 percent of new tenants. NYCHA jumped on board. In 1996, NYCHA gave top priority, with HUD's approval, to working families whose incomes ranged between $24,000 and $49,000 a year. NYCHA aimed "to bring to public housing one working family for every two vacancies."[8] The initial plan failed in a court challenge, but NYCHA created a revised version, exempting whiter Staten Island and Queens developments, that the courts approved in 1997.[9]

NYCHA put in place its working family preference because administrators thought that working families did not even bother to apply because of well-known priorities in the admission process for the homeless, overcrowded, and emergency cases. In the new system the higher-income Tiers II and III of the old system became the working family designation. Working families, however, now benefited from a special track to admission. That working families in 2005, for instance, had a 70 percent success rate renting an apartment as opposed to 57 percent for applicants and transfers overall, is exactly what the designers of the program had in mind.[10]

By 1999, working families had returned to 35 percent of the tenant population as a result of both the working family preference and welfare reform that sent many welfare families back to work. In 1999, for instance, NYCHA announced it had "placed 2,833 additional working families, 38.1% of our total admissions, into our developments."[11] By this time these working families were also being steered with some success to the forty-one lowest income developments. These policies have become even more successful with time. In both 2004 and 2005 working families filled approximately *half* of all new vacancies. If NYCHA's housing turned over faster, this program would have had an even more extraordinary effect. Welfare tenants in 2006 accounted for less than 20 percent of families. Social Security, disability, and other forms of income support accounted for about another 40 percent of the population. Working families, in an impressive shift, comprise over 40 percent of the public housing population—a statistic that would come as a surprise to many New Yorkers who believe public housing is only for welfare recipients.[12]

These statistics must be read with some care. The working families statistic is not divided between new families and old (that is, existing tenants who leave welfare). With NYCHA's low turnover rate (about 1 percent per year) it must be assumed that the shift to working families has been in part a result of improving employment conditions, or at least the end of welfare support, for NYCHA's existing tenants. A certain number of tenants have also likely transitioned from welfare to Social Security, either old age or disability (Supplemental Security Insurance,

SSI). The housing authority provides only one Social Security figure, but I suspect that disability support is a growing category at NYCHA, as it is in many other poor communities.

These statistical caveats aside, a number of factors likely contribute to the authority's clear success in attracting and keeping new working families. NYCHA has significantly renovated its buildings over the last decade, added new community centers, redesigned its grounds, and taken a hard line on crime. NYCHA's maintenance crews generally keep grounds and buildings clean and managers are comparatively responsive landlords. NYCHA's developments are well located along transit lines and are close to community resources. NYCHA also has more large apartments than many complexes in the city. Finally, these apartments are cheap. Maximum rental prices in 2005, for instance, in NYCHA developments ranged from $347 for a studio to $901 for 6 or more bedrooms, but actual rents fluctuated based upon the percentage of income. Even rent increases in 2006 did not change the fact that NYCHA's top rents were *lower* than those for public housing in cities such as Chicago and San Francisco.[13]

How successful NYCHA has been keeping higher-income families in its housing is reflected in the fact that in 2006 the top 27 percent of families earned an average of $41,480. The average income in the other 73 percent of families was only $11,587. NYCHA's desire to hold onto its high-income tenants is reflected in continued occupancy limits that range from $52,750 for an individual to $81,400 for a five-person family. In spite of having upper limits on the books, excess income tenants, according to administrators, are actually never evicted. While approximately 60 percent of NYCHA families still receive some type of government support, the retention of higher-income families at all is notable.[14]

The working and even dependent poor who are being selected for traditional developments are again likely to make public housing look good. A Columbia University study in 2003 found that "NYCHA disqualifies applicants who fail to meet a series of criteria that include rent payment history, the stability of a family's composition and previous criminal convictions or drug use." The results, according to NYCHA, spoke for themselves: "72 percent, or nearly four out of five applicants, are found ineligible for public housing." In order to find desirable tenants, according to Legal Aid, "the Authority [granted] three interviews for every one vacancy in anticipation of rejecting a high percentage of applicants."[15]

This high ineligible rate was, and remains, more complicated than poverty advocates realize. The potential tenants are equally responsible for the high failure rate. In 2005, for instance, 27 percent failed to show up for their interviews; about 20 percent failed to pass criminal checks, and about 8 percent failed landlord checks. Of those offered apartments, almost 40 percent ultimately declined one. Officials of NYCHA estimated that from the start of the application process to the finish, only about 17 percent of tenants scheduled for interviews would either rent or be able to rent an apartment.[16]

Those who are most welcome in NYCHA housing, as in the old days, are those who need housing yet are likely to impress others with the wisdom of the program: working families who will care for their apartments, create community life, and pay a rent that helps cover the cost of the housing enterprise as a whole. These are model tenants for a model of urban transformation. When this selection system temporarily broke down, New York suffered. Public housing elsewhere was too far gone, and other options more abundant, for public housing to rebound without drastic reinvention under Hope VI. NYCHA appears to be on the route to what Jane Jacobs famously called "unslumming": incremental improvements in the socioeconomic and physical condition of an urban neighborhood without dramatic displacement of the current occupants.

NYCHA's recent history reflects what New Yorkers and Europeans knew in the 1930s, but the rest of America denied. Those who would build subsidized housing are far more likely to have success building for the working poor rather than the poorest of the poor. The working poor can partly pay their way and, by mimicking middle-class standards of behavior, are less likely to give subsidized housing a bad name. The modern community development movement has internalized these lessons by carefully screening tenants. One of the leading forces in South Bronx community development, Genevieve Brooks, explained that her rehabilitated housing "only works because I interview each and every family who moves in." The *welfare-state public housing* paradigm, both in New York and more dramatically on a national basis, inadequately addressed the notions of aspiration and social decorum while underestimating the liabilities of concentrating the long-term unemployed.[17]

Matching a New Mood

The shift away from *welfare-state public housing to affordable housing* has been a logical response to declining federal support since the 1980s. During the last two decades, NYCHA chairmen have been more representative of the racial hue of the authority's tenancy, but they have all guided NYCHA away from the welfare-state model. The chairmen, and most leading administrators, refused to see NYCHA as a charity organization.[18] The fiscally conservative political shift, realized under Mayors Edward Koch, Rudolph Giuliani, and Michael Bloomberg has led chairmen to position NYCHA as an efficient municipal service that delivers a decent product to its tenants.[19]

NYCHA must turn to its tenants, employees, and the city and state governments to make up for declining federal support. The conservative Congress of the 1990s continued to slash housing funds and undermined President Bill Clinton's efforts to maintain subsidies. From 1994 to 1997, for instance, subsidies failed to keep pace with inflation, leading to cuts in staffing and proposals for more outsourcing and privatization. Subsidies from HUD at that time and today counted for approximately half of NYCHA's "rent" from its apartments, so these cuts made a major difference in operations. Under the administration of George W. Bush HUD has even more dramatically cut subsidy levels to NYCHA—threatening the organization's very solvency.[20]

For some years NYCHA drew on its reserves ($414 million was spent between 2001 and 2006) to cover operating deficits, but such a strategy is unsustainable. Declining federal subsidies have been compounded by twenty thousand remaining nonfederalized apartments that receive no subsidy at all yet must be maintained to a decent standard. The rest of NYCHA's deficit can be linked to the steady increase in administrative, energy, and maintenance expenditures. Pension costs have increased 752 percent between 2001 and 2005 because of unfunded state mandates and now account for 17 percent of the agency's annual budget. Health insurance, fuel, wages, and worker's compensation have also skyrocketed. Strict budgeting has cut hundreds of millions in spending over the last few years (and staff has shrunk from 14,658 in 2003 to 13,215 in 2006), but annual deficits remain. Mayor Michael Bloomberg provided $100 million as part of an agreement in 2006 to raise rents on the top 27 percent of tenants, levy new fees, and further tighten administrative spending, but NYCHA will for the foreseeable future face serious financial challenges.[21]

The federal government may be dramatically cutting annual subsidies, but it has not overlooked NYCHA in capital spending that is essential to attracting the working poor. Since the 1990s renovation funding has come from both federal funds, the Public Housing Capital Fund, and locally financed bond initiatives. By 2005, the authority could boast of a cumulative $4.7 billion in capital improvements over the previous twelve years. Renovation financing and the solidity of NYCHA's bonds have been bolstered by a vacancy rate of 0.47 percent. Mayor Michael Bloomberg and Chairman Tino Hernandez inaugurated an additional $2 billion renovation plan in 2005, even in the face of growing operating deficits. Capital renovation has been funded primarily out of federal funds and bond issues, with only about 10 percent provided through state and city funding.[22]

This money is sorely needed. Decades of hard use and deferred maintenance during the hard years have taken their toll (Figure 31). Many of NYCHA's buildings had neared the end of their projected lifespans. The state comptroller found in 1999 that 120,000 units (of approximately 180,000) could be found in buildings "riddled with lousy plumbing, bad boilers and leaking roofs." Declining conditions were not the result of malfeasance, although tenant destructiveness had taken a toll, but of insufficient capital for repairs. The few remaining city and state projects, however, were in far worse shape than their federal counterparts because they lacked federal modernization funds. NYCHA at that time estimated it would need $5.3 billion to renovate its projects to a decent standard.[23]

As indicated above, NYCHA will, by the time it has completed its recent cycle of renovations, have spent over $6 billion. Renovation still in process at many developments across the city includes new windows, facade renovation (replacing and repointing brickwork), elevator replacement, new stainless steel front entrances, and extensive landscaping. This is not touch-up work but complete overhaul of buildings by private contractors working for NYCHA. The results are dramatic to say the least. Billions of dollars set aside for renovation sounds like a great deal of money, but it is important to remember that this large amount is spread across a system housing over four hundred thousand people.[24]

NYCHA is spending billions on renovation and maintenance, but it must maintain high standards with a smaller staff. The private sector, operating with lower labor costs, is directly engaged in major contract renovation, grounds maintenance, elevator services, and apartment painting. Day-to-day management by NYCHA staff has also shifted to a customer service model influenced by the private sector. The authority, for instance, manages a centralized call center for all five boroughs that fields approximately two thousand tenant maintenance complaints daily. Operators send work tickets to the local development staff or special technical teams in more specialized areas such as elevators. The centralized call center has cut costs by setting specific times and dates for apartment repairs. It used to be that 40 percent of tenants would not be at home for repairs whereas now only 10 percent miss their repair appointment. The center even makes quality assurance calls to verify that work has been completed.[25]

NYCHA's projects, in spite of cutbacks, continue to be well staffed. The authority in 2006 still had 13,687 employees, of which 9,640 were directly engaged in operations, mostly at the development level. Current NYCHA staff ratios call for one housing assistant for every 500 units; one

Figure 31. A solid steel metal fence was somehow damaged and metal flashing was ripped from a roof. NYCHA has faced a level of vandalism common to housing projects across this country. The difference is that the authority repairs the damage. Photographs by Nicholas Dagen Bloom.

maintenance worker for every 250–300 units; three to four clerical workers per development; and many more caretakers depending upon development size. Most developments also have a manager and a superintendent while those over 1,000 (of which NYCHA has many) will have an assistant manager and an assistant superintendent. My impression on visits, both formal and informal, is that NYCHA maintains a hierarchical, quasi-military type of organization that is partly responsible for the higher standards maintained as compared to other cities.[26]

This massive staff is both unionized and promoted through civil service standards. This is an expensive system, but in the long term it has encouraged professionalism by making NYCHA jobs well paid and by ensuring that those hired are actually in some ways qualified for the position. In order to monitor employee performance administrators have employed what they call APTS (Authority Productivity Tracking System): open style management meetings in which productivity and project conditions are analyzed. The meetings, including candid photographs and statistics projected onto screens, are a combination of the New York Police Department's COMPSTAT reporting meetings and modern management analysis. Administrators ask tough questions and demand changes during these open sessions. Almost all NYCHA developments have been reviewed under this system since 2001.[27]

In spite of the fact that APTS reviews primarily take place in open forums at NYCHA headquarters, much of the power at the authority has actually been decentralized to the borough and project levels. Project managers can now appeal high up on the administrative ladder to get what they need, but they are also held to account for deficiencies. Decentralization has smoothed the way to "Asset Management," a HUD-mandated program for decentralized property management modeled on the private sector. Under these new HUD rules individual developments are expected to be self-supporting (with the annual subsidy figured in). With the exception of the remaining city and state projects, most developments are able to meet these standards.[28]

Of note, as well, is that 29 percent, or approximately four thousand NYCHA employees, were also NYCHA residents in 2004, many of whom have worked their way up from teenage summer jobs. Approximately one-third of employees, then, have a personal stake in the well being of NYCHA as a whole. Employees are generally not assigned to work in buildings in which they live, but their presence likely makes a difference. Young people, for instance, have role models whose relative success indicates the value of participating in the summer work programs. In Brooklyn, for example, five hundred teenagers in an average summer help maintain the grounds.[29]

Tenants have not been overlooked in the emerging emphasis on decentralization and responsibility. The apartment inspection system had weakened in the 1970s, but NYCHA chairman Popolozio, in a bid to control growing disorder, initiated a 100 percent apartment inspection policy in the 1980s. By 1989, 67 percent of apartments had been inspected. All apartments today are in theory inspected on an annual basis and referrals are made if tenant apartments represent a danger to the health and welfare of other tenants. Those who repeatedly miss their inspection times can face eviction.[30]

The end result of all this effort is evident to the naked eye. In spite of the fact that crime and vandalism remain endemic to New York's housing system, the average NYCHA project today has limited or no exterior graffiti, neatly kept grounds (at least until kids return from school), shading trees, modern windows, glazed brick lobbies and hallways, slow but satisfactory elevators, and mostly tidy interiors. NYCHA has succeeded by pursuing a modified philosophy of environmental determinism. Damaging cutbacks to the annual subsidy in the coming years may ruin these decades of work, but such failure will be the fault of shortsighted federal officials.

Rewards for Renovation

Distinct areas of renovation deserve special attention because they are so crucial to the operation of high-rise public housing. Elevator repair, for instance, remains a costly challenge for NYCHA but one that must be met. In 1999, the state comptroller found that while 49 percent of elevators were in excellent or good condition, 16 percent were in fair condition and 37 percent were in poor condition. Without working elevators NYCHA could not keep or attract families to its high rises. Other cities fell down badly in this difficult area of high-rise management.[31]

During the last five years, over one thousand elevators, approximately one-third of the total number, have been replaced as part of comprehensive capital improvements. New elevators, featuring stainless steel interiors and sliding doors, are regularly coated with lemon oil to resist the graffiti that has marred older elevators. All of the new elevators include computerized systems with the potential for remote monitoring from NYCHA's central maintenance facility in Long Island City. Such monitoring cuts down on frivolous and expensive service calls; traditionally, about half of all calls had been false alarms. The staff remains at four hundred full-time repairmen, who in an average *month* respond to thirty-five hundred elevator outages. NYCHA also runs its own elevator school to train staff on the different eras of equipment.[32]

The fact that NYCHA elevators last fifteen to twenty years—as opposed to about twenty-five years in the private sector—is a continuing source of frustration. One longtime administrator in 1990 estimated humorously that "what they spend on maintaining those elevators probably could balance the city budget." What began as part of a cheap solution to housing the poor has revealed serious shortcomings, but NYCHA's record of elevator maintenance is far superior to that of other cities and helps account for the continuing desirability of its housing. Other cities, including Chicago and St. Louis, ignored the centrality of elevator repair in tower buildings and their tenants suffered mightily or left.[33]

Funding from the federal transfer program and federal modernization funds also reinvigorated NYCHA's landscaping (Figure 32). A visitor to public housing today will have almost no idea to what extent the grounds declined during the 1970s. Leonard Hopper, a NYCHA landscape designer who pioneered the system, realized that high-rise buildings needed functional open space for a sense of community. In the 1980s he identified impediments to public safety, and thus community life, by touring projects. He discovered that criminals had "numerous entries and escape routes from development grounds." Hopper also believed that lack of upkeep sent a signal that crime would be easy.[34]

Over the years Hopper has developed what he calls CPTED (Crime Prevention through Environmental Design), a more pragmatic version of the defensible space philosophy. CPTED, he believes, consistently reduces crime by 20 percent because the redesign reduces crimes of opportunity. Essentially the system gives tenants control of their spaces *and* fills project grounds with as much positive activity as possible. In 2005, he estimated that 275 NYCHA developments had been transformed through this process.[35] One does not have to accept all of Hopper's claims of crime reduction to admire the reconfiguring of formerly chaotic grounds into pleasant landscapes, or to believe that renovation positively influences tenant life.[36]

The CPTED process represents a confluence of influences. Hopper credits Jane Jacobs, whose emphasis on neighborhood activity and "the eyes of the street" as guarantors of public safety guided him to a new path. Jacobs actually singled out NYCHA grounds as poor substitutes for vibrant neighborhoods, but Hopper believes that even superblocks can provide the type of informal social control she valued. He and his staff have focused "on site activities and amenities" that bring people out into public space. During renovations they locate "play areas with seating for parents" and "gathering places for teenagers" to enhance building security. Wide pathways are designed so that tenants "walk through the development to take their children to school . . . rather than avoiding these routes."[37]

The process of redesign engages resident participation in design charettes. Hopper claims that he and the staff from the site improve-

Figure 32. A remarkable system of landscape redesign has made NYCHA open spaces more appealing and useful. Thick plantings, mature trees, spray fountains, play equipment, wide paths, and strong fences give most developments an attractive appearance. Photographs by Nicholas Dagen Bloom.

ments department bring "a blank sheet of paper when [they] start": "We listen to what their problems are." Staff members of the NYCHA do, however, offer a Power Point presentation of "before and after" landscapes from earlier NYCHA renovations that likely steers tenants to the authority's preferred approach. The standard design features, from which tenants can pick, is quite consistent across NYCHA landscapes—but it is of a very high quality.

Fences, for instance, are always solid steel and nearly indestructible. Because tenants still want high fences the authority's designers have developed new designs that have a bold visual impact but are much lower than earlier fences; variety in fencing is sometimes introduced to distinguish one development from another. Brightly colored vertical elements are often inserted to balance the ground plane with high rises—including pergolas and steel sculptures keyed to a neighborhood theme. After renovation the pathways are wider, newly paved, curbed, and lined with low steel fencing. Multicolored pavers create different zones and attractive patterns throughout the developments.[38]

Designers have also cut off vehicular traffic, replanted formerly paved areas, and transformed many parking lots into play areas. Sunken basketball courts often include low amphitheater-type seating that turn basketball courts into social spaces. Sinking basketball courts a few feet and adding seats also means a lower fence and less noise in the surrounding buildings. The ball courts themselves are colorful. Across the developments spray fountains and bright play furniture for small children are ubiquitous and of the highest quality. Run-down grounds have become the exception at NYCHA.[39]

The success of NYCHA landscaping is the result of good intentions properly understood and realized. The authority was lucky to get both modernization money and talented staff, but landscape success reflects the constant revision that is a hallmark of NYCHA policies. NYCHA did not succeed because it did everything right from the beginning; rather, constant revision and updating to meet new challenges appears to be an essential component of good public administration.

New and completely renovated community centers complement the new landscaping and have created beacons of light and activity in many drab super blocks (figure 33). Chairman Ruben Franco (1994–99) decided, based upon advice from community program administrators, to launch a program to build and renovate community centers. Working with residents, architects, and staff, NYCHA devoted approximately 5 percent of capital spending annually. Over more than a decade more than $100 million has been spent on sixty-two new or renovated facilities (with twelve more underway); almost 70 percent of NYCHA's centers have experienced some renovation.[40]

Figure 33. A new community center at Williamsburg Houses reflects the invest-ment NYCHA is making in community facilities across the city. Photograph by Nicholas Dagen Bloom.

Building new community centers was hardly radical, but staffing them and existing centers at realistic levels was. The current head of Community Operations convinced the NYCHA board in 1996 that the new centers demanded enhanced staffing because the Health Department intended to enforce mandated staff-to-child ratios of one staff member to ten children. NYCHA has paid for the staff increases in creative ways. General revenues have provided the bulk of funds. Other sources included the federally funded Drug Elimination Program and HUD funds designated for tenant participation activities. Summer camps and after school programs are fee-based services; community center rental for parties provides additional revenue.[41]

In 2006, NYCHA directly ran 111 of 163 community centers and 42 of 138 senior centers. Outside sponsors ran 52 community centers, 96 senior centers, 102 day care centers, and 35 health clinics.[42] In the context of New York's rebounding nonprofit environment, many community centers are actually finding new sponsors. City-wide programs such as Partners in Reading and a variety of police-sponsored recreation programs also help keep the centers busy.[43]

One of the many sleek new centers is that at Williamsburg Houses. With 31,000 square feet of space—including a gym, a dance studio, art studios, computer facilities, stages, a recording studio, and a commercial kitchen—it is a world away from the two rooms that preceded it. Its openness is designed both to attract children and facilitate supervision. The center's gym converts to an auditorium and is used for NYCHA city-wide events such as fashion shows and spelling bees. At the comprehensively renovated Bronx River Community Center over 200 teenagers use the center every night; they can mix their own music, play in a very nice game room, or exercise in an excellent gym and weight room. Bronx River's glass walls look out on the project's grounds and serve as a welcoming beacon for the area.[44]

These new and renovated centers are impressive, but they still comprise tiny parts of superblocks and serve a relatively small proportion of tenant populations. At many centers up to 50 percent of community center participants come from outside the developments. These centers are finally becoming a valuable service to the city as a whole, but it remains debatable if NYCHA should foot the bill for neighborhood community resources. Should current federal subsidies continue to decline, NYCHA may be forced to withdraw its support entirely for the community programs. The loss of these programs from a morale point of view for neighborhoods, rather than just housing projects, may have a more serious impact than is commonly realized.

In recent decades NYCHA has enhanced not only its community programs but also its once controversial commitment to social intervention.

NYCHA has reduced the contentious aspects of early paternalism by focusing on the problem families.[45] *Threat of eviction* for unacceptable behavior remains NYCHA's preferred tool for initiating social work. Over the decades the authority has annually placed hundreds of tenants into eviction proceedings on behavioral grounds even though it ultimately evicted few families. NYCHA's Social Services Division was instructed in the 1960s, for instance, to view eviction as a social tool: "The potential loss of the apartment mobilizes whatever strengths may exist in the family. . . . Casework intervention thus often means that the family is able to remain within public housing." Little has changed. A current member of the legal department explained that of 1,788 non-desirability cases brought in 2005, for instance, only 149 ended in termination—the actual loss of the apartment—because the process primarily focuses on behavioral modification.[46]

As of 2006, NYCHA's Social Services Department was comparatively well staffed (246 full-time staff) and focused on families with serious problems. This large staff, actually reduced from a few years ago, is a relatively new phenomenon at NYCHA. Social work staff members now undertake comprehensive case management, seek out financial help, and develop long-term service plans for families in trouble. Staff members make thousands of home visits every month to their casework families. Housing assistants at each development (staffed at approximately one housing assistant per five hundred units) also still knock on the doors of those who miss their rent payments. In just one section of Red Hook Houses today, for instance, two hundred families may be tardy every month; a significant amount of visiting thus follows.[47]

NYCHA's changing relationship to tenants includes enhanced responsibility for cultivating tenant participation and advisement. Federal rules now mandate that the authority stimulate tenant participation. The Resident Advisory Board (RAB), a city-wide tenant organization composed partly of resident association presidents, provides input on NYCHA's annual plan. A similar resident board composes the other city-wide organization, known as CCOP, which is most concerned with bread and butter issues relating to services for individual projects. According to the Community Service Society's Victor Bach, who serves as a self-appointed tenant advocate, the CCOP and the RAB generally support NYCHA positions and are dependent on NYCHA administration for leadership. Community affairs administrators I talked with view tenants groups as a means for communication but stress that NYCHA alone is responsible for final decisions. Nor do they view tenant activists necessarily as accurate barometers of tenant opinions.[48]

The emergence of a powerful and semi-independent voice for tenant activism has pushed back on NYCHA paternalism. While seeded and still advised by outside organizers such as Victor Bach, the New York City Public Housing Resident Alliance formed in 1996 to raise tenant awareness of congressional legislation that would affect NYCHA residents. Since the 1990s, the alliance has opposed NYCHA on issues such as increasing income levels for new residents, privatization schemes, public accountability, and community service requirements.[49]

The total budget for all of NYCHA's community and social programs in 2006 was an impressive $62 million, including both community and social service programs. Recent federal cuts reduced full-time staff from 1,500 in 2001 to approximately 1,200 in 2006, but this number was still far larger than in the past. Declining staff levels have probably contributed to a decline in community center utilization from 101 percent in 2004 to 72 percent in 2006. Senior centers, for instance, which remained well staffed from other city funds, had a 135 percent utilization rate in 2006. Tension remains between the ideals of community staff and NYCHA's general budget crisis. Understandably, NYCHA's "core real estate mission" will have to take priority over community programs in the coming years.[50]

The New (Electronic) Eyes on the Street

One of the key pieces in renewed public housing is crime control. NYCHA endeavors through its community and social programs to encourage socially acceptable forms of activity, but if NYCHA cannot control criminality on its grounds it will never attract or keep decent tenants. Crime is, in fact, finally declining in New York's public housing, but only through tremendous effort. Since the 1990s NYCHA has developed new tools for dealing with criminals, thus reversing some of the limitations imposed in the era of the welfare state. Unlike other housing authorities, NYCHA is demonstrating that crime control in public housing, while expensive and complicated, can be accomplished.

In 1996, "a federal judge made it far easier for authorities to evict drug dealers" in public housing. Administrators hoped that the time for termination (final eviction) would drop from two years to a few months. Tenant leaders welcomed the decision, but the Legal Aid Society thought that it would lead to unfair treatment of innocent family members. The decision eliminated the burden of both administrative hearings and a separate hearing in Housing Court, which was established in the early 1970s. NYCHA could now begin wider application of the Bawdy House law, which stated that "leases can be broken if a vice . . . was being practiced behind closed doors." The authority was, after the federal decision, able to take drug dealers right to Housing Court.[51]

This policy's effectiveness has been frequently overstated by advocates for the poor: "Since 1996, the Housing Authority . . . has more strictly enforced its severe evictions policy: one strike and you're out. As a tenant, you are vulnerable to eviction if your grandson gets caught smoking a joint on public housing grounds."[52] NYCHA managers I talked with, however, said that for an expedited drug eviction there must be a felony conviction, which is rare because plea bargains are so common. Most cases end up with exclusion of the offender from the family's home with provisions for spot checking by the police.[53]

In 1990, NYCHA still claimed that its tenant patrols, while unable to do much in the most troubled projects, played an important role in tenant safety elsewhere. Supervisors received payment and training by NYCHA staff and the total numbers of participants seemed impressive. Victor Bach explained in 2005 that the tenant activists he knows dismiss the tenant patrols because they "all have arthritis"; the tenant patrol is often seen as a senior citizen activity. Surviving patrols usually restrict their activity to the early evening hours, and substitutes for tough policing they are not. Luckily, NYCHA never tried to exchange tenant management for real policing.[54]

Both Mayors Ed Koch and David Dinkins had sought the merger of the Housing Police with the NYPD but failed. The unions (and tenants) successfully opposed this idea, but Mayor Rudolph Giuliani finally pulled off the merger. The *New York Times* noted that crime was dropping faster in the city than in the projects. It attributed this lag to the fact that in 1967, 90 percent of housing police "were on foot patrol, walking through the projects. In 1994, less than 12 percent were on foot." There were other reasons why public housing crime remained stubbornly high, but ineffective policing was not helping.[55] Mayor Rudolph Giuliani succeeded in 1995 in merging the forces only by playing hardball. He threatened to fire all of the housing police and rehire them through the NYPD in order to circumvent civil service laws and union opposition.[56] A 2004 report by the City Council judged the merger a success in spite of force reductions: "Reducing the duplication of services . . . redeploying some of the NYCHA uniformed officers to other divisions . . . translated to a reduction in the number of uniformed officers" from approximately 2,700 in 1995 to 1,810 in 2004. Even with this decline in the force, "violent crimes have fallen 44 percent in NYCHA developments and 48 percent citywide since the merger." These statistics are reviewed in more detail below, but it does appear that the loss of the NYCHA housing police has not resulted in a loss of police coverage.[57]

The NYPD Housing Bureau, at 1,700 officers, continues its core mission of vertical patrols. Saturation by extra police (60 to 70 officers), known as impact zones, has also scored major crime reduction in public housing complexes. The NYPD uses a special "crime reduction strategy deploying 1,000 police officers to targeted high-crime locations," including nine troubled NYCHA projects. Since the 1990s the NYPD, both the housing bureau and regular forces, have used controversial methods—including profiled frisking to check for drugs and firearms and so-called quality of life enforcement—to control the atmosphere of both poor neighborhoods and housing projects. The merger has not led to a loss of effectiveness by any reasonable standard because the NYPD has not abandoned public housing.[58]

The crime rate in NYCHA's developments has been falling, but developments cumulatively registered, for example, 287 shootings and 64 murders in 2003. Annual figures like these were a significant improvement over the 1980s, but by this point, with city-wide crime plummeting, such reductions meant a great deal less. New York as a whole has become America's safest big city, with crime statistics last seen back in the 1950s. Remaining crime in public housing has started to stand out that much more and now far exceeds its approximate 5 percent share of city-wide population. In 2003 NYCHA thus accounted for 11 percent of the city's murders, 11 percent of the city's rapes, and 16 percent of the city's shootings. More than half of all project shootings could be linked to drugs, as opposed to about one-third city-wide. The total arrest rate in 2003 on public housing grounds and buildings was 21,000—a typical annual figure for NYCHA since the 1980s. In addition, officers issued over 60,000 summonses for quality-of-life offenses. Since 2003 felony crimes have declined another 10 percent, but these reductions are not fast enough to reduce NYCHA's share of city wide crime.[59]

The persistence of crime is impressive in light of the fact that NYCHA has relatively few stores, strict enforcement, more working families, and a rapidly aging population. A certain percentage of those who stay in residence, and NYCHA no longer breaks down tenant versus non-tenant crime, obviously engage in fast living and they often chase out orderly families. Convicted felons are theoretically banned from NYCHA grounds and apartments, but enforcement of such a broad rule is difficult to enforce. The open grounds of most developments and buildings also remain ideal for clandestine drug dealing by tenants and outsiders.[60]

A detailed City Council report in 2004 found failings in NYCHA security related to tenant sabotage of security hardware. The investigators discovered, after looking at 479 buildings in 25 developments, "that a trespasser trying to gain access to a NYCHA building by the front door succeeded nearly half the time—without a key or entry card." The report openly linked tenant irresponsibility to security problems. NYCHA had devoted millions of dollars to security improvements, including intercoms, but "residents may nevertheless be jeopardizing their own safety by propping open doors and giving strangers access to their homes." In one Brooklyn development, for instance, 92 percent of all doors were propped open all of the time. Sabotage has not led to an abandonment of security measures in New York's public housing, but until the general tenant population improves its behavior there will be levels of disorder that many tenants themselves find distasteful.[61]

A growing video surveillance security program, which ends the essentially open nature of development grounds and interiors, promises major crime control in the future. NYCHA is finally creating a virtual doorman for its buildings. The first version of this system, the Video Interactive Patrol Enhancement Response (VIPER), has been installed in fifteen developments since 1997. This system as a whole now includes a total of 3,160 cameras in public spaces. Officers in special rooms monitors activity and will call in back up if trouble is spotted. The authority in the early years of implementation logged a 20 percent drop in crime at Grant Houses.

CCTV (closed circuit television), an unstaffed, more affordable, and smaller-scale surveillance system now installed at fourteen other developments, also features saturation videotaping. At Queensbridge Houses, for instance, the newly installed system includes 254 cameras that record all areas of the development night and day. Managers when I visited were already impressed with the reduction in crime. Authority figures estimate that since CCTV has been installed 2,800 arrests city wide have been linked to its use. Developments experience the biggest drop in the first year of installation (approximately 25 percent), but a modest downward trend continues even in subsequent years. Vandalism is also thought to drop 50 percent after CCTV installation.[62]

High-rise public housing is not, in retrospect, an ideal form of housing for a socially disordered population undergoing a serious drug crisis. What constitutes an ideal environment for such a population is unclear. NYCHA has full towers not because its tenancy is so much better than that in other cities. The authority from the 1950s onward has taken a hard line on criminality, even against its own tenants. A system that arrests over twenty thousand people a year and constantly monitors its grounds is engaged in a serious battle. Crime control is not only the result of long-term policing, but also of NYCHA's pursuit of decent maintenance standards (for example, working elevators, lighting replacement, and so forth) and improving standards of tenant selection. That crime is declining, if not as fast as that in the city as a whole, means that NYCHA has survived a war comparable to many civil wars around the world.

NYCHA's emphasis on control is a sufficient, if regrettable, substitute for the multiple sources of authority one finds in a typical urban

neighborhood. The price of this order is high, can cause further alienation of many tenants because of police error, and can lead to loss of
aspects of personal freedom that accompanies surveillance and crack-
downs. In my opinion it is preferable to unregulated "Wild West" housing projects left to gangs and drug dealers. Most cities have lacked the
will to enforce order. Sporadic policing sweeps, in projects already disordered and poorly maintained, rarely yielded a long-term restoration
in order in cities such as Chicago or Baltimore. Disorder even in low-
rise public housing, as in New Orleans, becomes far more suspicious in
light of NYCHA's relative success with difficult to manage tower blocks.[63]

Hope VI Deferred

Public housing projects in big cities have provided a focused example of
underclass life that was easier to conceptualize than the vast private
slums where equal disorder prevailed, but it would be foolish to deny
that much of American public housing has been abysmally designed,
built, and managed. Lacking an ideology of housing as a legitimate public service, or a tradition of multi-family management transferable to
projects, many city officials outside New York allowed public housing to
become a welfare program, a racial program, a slum clearance program,
a dumping ground for urban renewal, and only secondarily a long-term
housing program. They rarely got it right.

The authors of the *Final Report of the National Commission on Severely Distressed Public Housing* (1992), which laid the groundwork for Hope VI,
came away "rightly alarmed by the broader pattern of inadequate management and deepening resident poverty" at most public housing authorities. An "underclass culture" related to drugs and gangs seemed to
render all efforts at revitalization null. Most cities welcomed Hope VI's
opportunity to initiate project demolition with new funds for renovation
and reconstruction, but New York did not. The high vacancy rates and
decades of vandalism made destruction of towers much easier and less
controversial in cities such as Chicago and Baltimore.[64]

Chicago, for instance, had squandered generous HUD subsidies. By
the 1970s, according to Bradford Hunt, the Chicago Housing Authority
inventory was "clogged with trash, infested with vermin, and overrun by
gangs. Heat, water, light, elevator, and trash systems worked erratically."
By 1996, "over 17,800 of the Chicago Housing Authority's 30,000 family
housing units failed a . . . 'viability' test."[65] In spite of the fact that the
rest of Chicago has rebounded from decades of white flight, public
housing remained mired in crime and dilapidation. Most of the CHA's
high-rise inventory has either been demolished or is scheduled for clear-

ance and will be turned into low-rise, mixed-income communities. Low-rise public housing, as in Boston, can also be economically renovated into something that the planner Lawrence Vale believes approximates "the privacy, security, and sense of community expected of more desirable private residential neighborhoods." The long-term success of Hope VI redevelopment projects in other cities is still unknown, but beyond reducing poor people to a minority of the redeveloped site (one of the primary activities of Hope VI) these new projects will only prosper to the extent that new management practices emerge.[66]

New York's full towers, in contrast, are far more difficult to reorganize from both social and design perspectives, even when some problems do exist. New York's comparative success is best reflected in its nominal participation in the federal Hope VI program. Edgemere/Arverne Houses (1951/1961), now called Ocean Bay in Rockaway, are some of the few developments that have been targeted for Hope VI renovation. Their isolated location, high concentrations of welfare and single-parent families, crime, and other social problems made them better for Hope VI redevelopment, even though they were full and comparatively well maintained.[67]

The plan looks nothing like a conventional Hope VI project. According to NYCHA, the Rockaway plan is "unique among HOPE VI sites because it does not incorporate demolition of existing structures into its revitalization plan."[68] Only about 100 apartments were lost for community space, while significant resources were devoted to revitalizing nearby retail services, the renovation of 1,800 apartments, and community center enhancement. Other improvements included the elimination of balconies, renovated lobbies, and the addition of new marble lintels and other details that reduce the "project" look. The renovated apartments are now indistinguishable from private market rentals in every way except cost. Hope VI has become a community revitalization strategy rather than a dramatic redevelopment project in New York.[69]

NYCHA's vitality can also be appreciated in its return to what once was its most controversial activity: middle-income housing. Widespread concerns about affordability and the expiration of state-funded affordable housing programs have renewed calls for municipal leadership in middle-income housing. As one 1999 employer study found, "fully 86 percent of respondents cited housing costs as a serious deterrent to doing business in New York" and "45 percent of New Yorkers 'seriously considered moving out of the city' because of high housing costs." In order to compete as a global city, New York's government believes that it must offer relatively affordable housing to a range of the city's inhabitants.[70]

Mayor Michael Bloomberg has launched a multi-billion dollar, 165,000-unit program targeted at both lower- and *middle-income* New

Yorkers. He aims to create new housing with participation from NYCHA, the city's Housing Development Corporation, and the Department of Housing Preservation and Development. Land for new affordable housing is now at a premium, but NYCHA has comparatively vast reserves of open space. NYCHA controls land it has never developed and even its vast superblocks are approximately 85 percent open space. NYCHA may have extensively renovated its grounds, but plenty of underutilized parking lots and other spaces are ripe for development. Already, for instance, open spaces surrounding existing developments have been targeted for new middle-income buildings in Chelsea. The insertion of middle-income housing within high-rise public housing superblocks is doubtless one of NYCHA's more interesting social experiments. Given the authority's previous success rate, there is room for hope.[71]

A Century of Public Housing?

The housing authority will turn seventy-five in 2009. There should be every reason to celebrate such an impressive management record and to believe that NYHCA will make it to its centennial birthday. Yet skyrocketing fuel and pension costs, stingy federal administrators, and tenant resistance to modest rent increases threaten to undermine NYCHA's long-term management success. It seems likely that the authority will continue to make the right choices even with fewer resources, as it has in past hard times, but its continued survival is not guaranteed. Well-managed public housing will become a memory if NYCHA staffing is cut more deeply.

New Yorkers, many of whom conceive of public housing as largely a liability, easily discarded or privatized, fail to understand how embedded public housing is in New York's physical and urban fabric. NYCHA, as an institution, represents a legacy of good government and affordable housing every bit as valuable to the city as mass transportation and public water. Nor could these towers realistically be sold without a political uproar. Public housing tenants, and the politicians who represent them, must consider reasonable rent increases in order to maintain good services, but New Yorkers not living in public housing would be wise to prevent the decline of such a valuable system by encouraging local and state subsidy to replace federal support. Declining management, as in other cities, could have a dramatic impact on property values and neighborhood peace across the city. The effect that thousands of disordered towers would have in New York is almost beyond imagination.

Appendix A: Guide to Housing Developments

Appendix A reveals important elements of the New York public housing system in place by 1965. The first notable feature is the diversity of funding sources illustrated in the chart ("C" denotes city-funded projects, "S" denotes state funded, and "F" denotes federally funded). The scale of the individual projects is indicated, with many of these projects (almost all six stories or higher) containing over one thousand units. The diminishing size of the projects is also evident by the 1960s, as funding declined and pressure grew for neighborhood preservation. The diversity of sites is indicated in the range of addresses and boroughs indicated for the many projects. The numbering system follows NYCHA's conception of project sequence in the original document.

Adapted from "Guide to Housing Developments," Box 100A3, Folder 7, NYCHA Reports, 1965, NYCHAR. A complete list of NYCHA housing developments is available at http://www.nyc.gov/html/nycha/downloads/pdf/dev_data_book.pdf.

Projects Completed	Date Occupancy Completed	Program	Number of Apartments	Location
1 First Houses	5/31/36	(C-1)	123	E. 3rd St. & Ave. A, Manhattan
2 Williamsburg	4/10/38	(F)	1,630	Maujer & Leonard Sts., Brooklyn
3 Harlem River	10/1/37	(F)	577	W. 153rd St. & 7th Ave., Manhattan
4 Red Hook	11/20/39	(F)	2,545	Lorraine & Columbia Sts., Brooklyn
5 Queensbridge	3/15/40	(F)	3,149	41st Ave. & Vernon Blvd., Queens
6 Vladeck	11/25/40	(F)	1,531	Madison & Gouverneur Sts., Manhattan
7 Vladeck City	10/25/40	(C-I)	240	Madison & Jackson Sts., Manhattan
8 South Jamaica	8/1/40	(F)	448	159th St. & 107th Ave., Queens
9 East River	5/20/41	(F)	1,170	E. 102nd St. & 1st Ave., Manhattan
10 Kingsborough	10/31/41	(F)	1,166	Pacific St. & Rochester Ave., Brooklyn
11 Clason Point	12/20/41	(F)	400	Story & Metcalf Aves., Bronx
12 Lavanburg (absorbed by NYCHA)	12/28/27	(C-I)	113	Baruch Pl. & E. Houston St., Manhattan
13 Edwin Markham	6/30/43	(F)	360	Broadway & Richmond Terrace, Staten Island
14 Whitman-Ingersoll	2/24/44	(S)	3,503	Myrtle & Carlton Aves., Brooklyn
15 Elliott	7/15/47	(C-I)	608)	W. 26th St. & 10th Ave., Manhattan
16 Brownsville	4/16/48	(S)	1,338	Sutter & Rockaway Aves., Brooklyn
17 J. W. Johnson	12/27/48	(S)	1,310	E. 112th St. & Park Ave., Manhattan
18 Jacob Riis	1/17/49	(F)	1,190	E. 10th St. & F. D. Roosevelt Dr., Manhattan
19 Jacob Riis City	1/31/49	(C-I)	578	E. 6th St. & F. D. Roosevelt Dr., Manhattan
20 Abraham Lincoln	12/29/48	(S)	1,286	E. 132nd St. & 5th Ave., Manhattan
21 Marcy	1/19/49	(S)	1,717	Park & Nostrand Aves., Brooklyn
22 Amsterdam	12/17/48	(S)	1,084	W. 2nd & Amsterdam Ave., Manhattan

Projects Completed	Date Occupancy Completed	Program	Number of Apartments	Location
23 Lillian Wald	10/14/49	(S)	1,861	E. Houston St. & F. D. Roosevelt Dr., Manhattan
24 Patterson	12/31/50	(S)	1,791	Morris & 3rd Aves., Bronx
25 Gowanus	6/24/49	(S)	1,139	Wyckoff & Hoyt Sts., Brooklyn
26 Astoria	11/9/51	(S)	1,104	Astoria Blvd. & 1st St., Queens
27 Governor Smith	4/27/53	(S)	1,935	Catherine & South Sts., Manhattan
28 Melrose	6/20/52	(S)	1,023	E. 153rd St. & Morris Ave., Bronx
29 Farragut	5/7/52	(S)	1,390	York & Navy Sts., Brooklyn
30 Stephen Foster	11/1/54	(S)	1,379	W. 112th St. & 5th Ave., Manhattan
31 Albany	10/14/50	(S)	829	Albany & St. Marks Aves., Brooklyn
32 Bronx River	2/28/51	(S)	1,246	E. 174th St. & Bronx River Ave., Bronx
33 Woodside	12/30/49	(C-II)	1,357	Broadway & 51st Sts., Queens
34 Eastchester	6/1/50	(C-II)	874	Yates & Burke Aves., Bronx
35 South Beach	3/20/50	(C-II)	422	McClean Ave. & Lamport Blvd., Staten Island
36 Sheepshead Bay	8/8/50	(C-II)	1,056	Nostrand Ave. & Ave. V, Brooklyn
37 Colonial Park	10/8/51	(C-II)	984	W. 159th St. & 8th Ave., Manhattan
38 St. Nicholas	9/30/54	(F)	1,526	W. 127th St. & 7th Ave., Manhattan
39 Pelham Parkway	6/30/50	(C-III)	1,266	Pelham Pkwy. N. & Wallace Ave., Bronx
40 Gun Hill	11/30/50	(C-III)	733	Gun Hill Rd. & Holland Ave., Bronx
41 Dyckman	4/25/51	(C-III)	1,167	Dyckman St. & 10th Ave., Manhattan
42 Todt Hill	6/1/50	(C-III)	502	Manor Rd. & Schmidt's Lane, Staten Island
43 Nostrand	12/14/50	(C-III)	1,148	Batchelder St. & Ave. X, Brooklyn
44 Glenwood	7/14/50	(C-III)	1,188	E. 56th St. & Ave. H, Brooklyn

Projects Completed	Date Occupancy Completed	Program	Number of Apartments	Location
45 Sedgwick	3/23/51	(C-III)	786	W. 174th St. & University Ave., Bronx
46 Boulevard	3/22/51	(C-III)	1,441	Linden Blvd. & Ashford St., Brooklyn
47 Parkside	6/12/51	(C-III)	879	Bronx park E. & Arnow Ave., Bronx
78 Ravenswood	7/19/51	(C-III)	2,166	12th St. & 34th Ave., Queens
49 Marble Hill	3/6/52	(C-III)	1,682	W. 228th St. & Broadway, Manhattan
50 Lexington	3/16/51	(C-III)	448	E. 98th St. & 3rd Ave., Manhattan
51 Averne	2/28/51	(C-III)	418	Arverne Blvd. & Beach 56th St., Queens
52 General Berry	10/27/50	(C-III)	506	Dongan Hills Ave. & Richmond Rd., Staten Island
53 Pomonok	6/30/52	(C-III)	2,071	Kissena Blvd. & 71st Ave., Queens
54 James A. Bland	5/8/52	(S)	400	Lawrence St. & Roosevelt Ave., Queens
55 Redfern	8/28/59	(S)	604	Redfern Ave. & Hassock St., Queens
56 Breukelen	11/6/52	(F)	1,595	Farragut Rd. & E. 108th St., Brooklyn
57 Edenwald	10/30/53	(F)	2,039	Grenada Pl. & Baychester Ave., Bronx
58 Carver	2/14/58	(S)	1,246	E. 102nd St. & Madison Ave., Manhattan
59 Forest	12/12/56	(S)	1,350	E. 163rd St. & Tinton Ave., Bronx
60 Baruch	8/6/59	(F)	2,194	Columbia & Rivington Sts., Manhattan
61 Van Dyke	5/27/55	(F)	1,603	Stone & Livona Aves., Brooklyn
62 George Washington	9/20/57	(F)	1,515	E. 97th St. & 3rd Ave., Manhattan
63 Throggs Neck	11/27/53	(F)	1,185	E. 177th St. & Calhoun Ave., Bronx
64 Jefferson	8/28/59	(F)	1,493	E. 112th St. & 1st Ave., Manhattan
65 Brevoort	8/10/55	(F)	896	Fulton St. & Ralph Ave., Brooklyn
66 South Jamaica II	10/25/54	(F)	600	160th St. & South Rd., Queens

Projects Completed	Date Occupancy Completed	Program	Number of Apartments	Location
67 Bronxdale	2/28/55	(F)	1,497	Bruckner Blvd. & Soundview Ave., Bronx
68 Gravesend	6/28/54	(F)	634	Bayview & Neptune Aves., Brooklyn
69 Cooper Park	6/25/53	(F)	700	Frost St. & Morgan Ave., Brooklyn
70 Cypress Hills	5/25/55	(S)	1,444	Fountain & Sutter Aves., Brooklyn
71 Sound View	10/29/54	(S)	1,259	Seward & Rosedale Aves., Bronx
72 Howard	12/30/55	(S)	815	East New York & Stone Aves., Brooklyn
73 Sumner	5/14/58	(S)	1,099	Park & Throop Aves., Brooklyn
74 Sen. Robert F. Wagner	6/12/58	(F)	2,162	E. 124th St. & 2nd Ave., Manhattan
75 Hammel	4/20/55	(F)	712	Beach 81st St. & Hammels Blvd., Queens
76 La Guardia	8/8/57	(F)	1,094	Madison & Rutgers St.s., Manhattan
77 Mariners Harbor	9/3/54	(F)	607	Continental Pl. .& Lockman Ave., Staten Island
78 Highbridge	6/18/54	(F)	700	W. 167th St. & University Ave., Bronx
79 Red Hook II	5/27/55	(F)	346	King & Richard Sts., Brooklyn
80 Castle Hill	12/15/60	(S)	2,025	Randall & Castle Hill Aves., Bronx
81 Manhattanville	6/30/61	(S)	1,272	W. 133rd St. & Amsterdam Ave., Manhattan
82 Frederick Douglass	9/25/58	(S)	2,057	W. 102nd St. & Columbus Ave., Manhattan
83 Marlboro	2/27/58	(S)	1,765	Ave. V & Stillwell Ave., Brooklyn
84 Mill Brook	5/26/59	(S)	1,255	E. 137th St. & St. Ann's Ave., Bronx
85 Albany II	2/7/57	(S)	400	Bergen St. & Albany Ave., Brooklyn
86 Bushwick	4/1/60	(S)	1,220	Varet & Humbolt Sts., Brooklyn
87 General Grant	10/31/57	(F)	1,940	W. 125th St. & Amsterdam Ave., Manhattan
88 James Monroe	11/2/61	(F)	1,102	Lafayette & Beach Aves., Bronx
89 Louis Heaton Pink	9/30/59	(F)	1,500	Crescent St. & Stanley Ave., Brooklyn

Projects Completed	Date Occupancy Completed	Program	Number of Apartments	Location
90 Franklin Plaza	3/8/65	(C-IV)	1,635	E. 108th St. & 2nd Ave., Manhattan
91 Bailsey Park	4/30/61	(F)	386	Foch & New York Blvds., Queens
92 Bay View	6/7/56	(C-IV)	1,610	Rockaway Pkwy. & Seaview Ave., Brooklyn
93 St. Mary's park	4/30/59	(C-IV)	1,007	E. 149th St. & Cauldwell Ave., Bronx
94 Coney Island	2/25/57	(C-IV)	534	W. 29th & Surf Ave., Brooklyn
95 Linden	7/17/58	(C-IV)	1,586	Van Siclen & Stanley Aves., Brooklyn
96 Samuel J. Tilden	6/30/61	(F)	998	Rockaway & Livonia Aves., Brooklyn
97 Sen. Robert A. Taft	12/31/62	(F)	1,470	E. 112th St. & Park Ave., Manhattan
98 Edgemere	9/25/61	(S)	1,395	Beach 54th St. & Beach Channel Dr., Queens
99 Rutgers	3/31/65	(S)	721	Madison & Rutgers Sts., Manhattan
100 Gompers	4/30/64	(F)	474	Delancey & Pitt Sts., Manhattan
101 Lehman Village	11/30/63	(F)	622	E. 108th St. & Madison Ave., Manhattan
102 Gouverneur Morris	8/31/65	(F)	1,887	E. 169th St. & 3rd Ave., Bronx
103 McKinley	7/31/62	(F)	619	E. 161st St. & Trinton Ave., Bronx
106 Woodstock Terrace	6/2/65	(C-IV)	320	E. 161st St. & Trinity Ave., Bronx
107 Rosedale Gardens	1/21/64	(C-IV)	408	Bruckner Blvd. & Taylor Ave., Bronx
108 Cedar Manor	12/20/62	(C-IV)	216	157th St. & Foch Blvd., Queens
109 John F. Hylan	6/30/60	(C-IV)	209	Moore St. & Bushwick Ave., Brooklyn
110 Luna Park Village	10-10/62	(C-IV)	1,576	W. 8th St. & Neptune Ave., Brooklyn
111 Drew-Hamilton	9/30/65	(S)	1,217	W. 141st St. & 8th Ave., Manhattan
112 Woodrow Wilson	6/30/61	(S)	398	E. 106th St. & 1st Ave., Manhattan
113 Borgia Butler	12/31/64	(S)	1,492	E. 170th St. & Webster Ave., Bronx

Projects Completed	Date Occupancy Completed	Program	Number of Apartments	Location
114 Stapleton	5/31/62	(S)	693	Warren & Hill Sts., Staten Island
116 West Brighton Plaza I	12/31/62	(F)	490	Henderson Ave. & Broadway, Staten Island
117 Richmond Terrace	4/30/64	(F)	489	Cleveland & Jersey Sts., Staten Island
118 John Adams	8/31/64	(F)	925	E. 152nd St. & Westchester Ave., Bronx
119 Village View	5/28/65	(C-IV)	1,236	E. 6th St. & 1st Ave., Manhattan
120 Andrew Jackson	7/31/63	(F)	868	E. 156th St. & Park Ave., Bronx
121 Mott Haven	3/31/65	(F)	993	E. 144th St. & Willis Ave., Bronx
122 Lafayette Gardens	7/31/62	(F)	882	Classon & Lafayette Ave., Bronx
123 DeWitt Clinton	10/31/65	(F)	749	E. 110th St. & Park Ave., Manhattan
124 Gaylord White	9/30/64	(S)	248	E. 104th St. & 2nd Ave., Manhattan
125 Audubon Apartments	4/30/62	(S)	168	W. 155th St. & Amsterdam Ave., Manhattan
126 Baychester	10/31/63	(S)	441	E. 225th St. & Schieffelin Ave., Bronx
127 Wise Towers	1/31/65	(S)	399	W. 90th St. near Columbus Ave., Manhattan
128 Jonathan Williams	4/30/64	(S)	577	Roebling St. & Division Ave., Brooklyn
129 E. Roberts Moore	3/31/64	(F)	463	E. 149th St. & Jackson Ave., Bronx
130 Morrisania	5/31/63	(F)	206	E. 169th St. & Park Ave., Bronx
131 Tompkins	7/31/64	(F)	1,046	Park & Tompkins Aves., Brooklyn
132 Mill Brook Extension	1/31/62	(S)	125	E. 135th St. & Cypress Ave., Bronx
133 Arthur H. Murphy	3/31/64	(S)	281	E. 175th St. & Crotona Ave., Bronx
134 Chelsea	5/31/64	(S)	425	W. 25th St. & 9th Ave., Manhattan
135 Eleanor Roosevelt I	9/30/64	(F)	763	Dekalb & Lewis Aves., Brooklyn
136 Robert Fulton	3/31/65	(F)	944	W. 18th St. & 9th Ave., Manhattan

Projects Completed	Date Occupancy Completed	Program	Number of Apartments	Location
139 Stanley M. Isaacs	7/31/65	(F)	636	E. 93rd & 1st Ave., Manhattan
140 Independence	10/31/65	(S)	744	Wilson St. & Bedford Ave., Brooklyn
141 Daniel Webster	9/30/65	(F)	606	E. 168th St. & Webster ve., Bronx
142 Bernard Haber	6/30/65	(S)	380	W. 24th St. & Surf Ave., Brooklyn
143 Rehabilitation Program	1/31/64	(F)	336	Various Sites: W. 94th, 101st, 103rd, 104th, 112th, 117th, 119th Sts., Manhattan; 22nd Ave., Queens; and E. 141st St., Bronx
146 Van Dyke II	4/30/64	(F)	112	Powell St. & Dumont Ave., Brooklyn
147 Harlem River II	10/31/65	(F)	116	W. 151st St. & 8th Ave., Manhattan
148 Douglass Addition	6/30/65	(S)	135	W. 102nd St. & Amsterdam Ave., Manhattan
150 830 Amsterdam Ave.	8/31/65	(F)	159	W. 100th St. & Amsterdam Ave., Manhattan
151 120 W. 94th Street	9/30/65	(F)	70	W. 94th St. near Amsterdam Ave., Manhattan
152 La Guardia Addition	8/31/65	(F)	150	Cherry & Jefferson Sts., Manhattan
153 Nathan Straus	1/31/65	(F)	267	E. 27th St. & Second Ave., Manhattan
154 131 St. Nicholas Ave.	3/31/65	(F)	100	W. 117th St. & St. Nicholas Ave., Manhattan

Appendix B: Tenant Selection Policies and Procedures

Appendix B is a list of the twenty-one factors used in tenant screening by the New York City Housing Authority between 1953 and 1968. Unlike housing authorities in other cities, NYCHA used tenant screening as a powerful tool of social control well into the 1960s.

"Proposed Revision of Tenant Selection Policies and Procedures," 14 December 1961, Box 65C8, Folder 12, NYCHAR.

Other Conditions Indicating Potential Non-Desirability

The following conditions when detected during the course of processing an application shall be considered as indicative of potential non-desirability and shall require evaluation by the Social Consultation Unit:

1. Alcoholism resulting in behavior disturbing to others, neglected children, etc.
2. Record of past use of narcotics when there is no evidence of confirmed addiction.
3. A record of anti-social behavior as evidenced by a court contact within the last five years.
4. Record of poor rent payment or eviction for non-payment.
5. Highly irregular work history for any member of the family; unexplained gaps in work history.
6. Frequent separations of husband and wife.
7. One or both parents under 19 years of age.
8. Placement of children with relatives or foster parents without assistance from a social agency and for reasons other than illness, death, or other emergencies.
9. Birth of out-of-wedlock child or children to a member of the family, unless the person has since married and has lived continuously with his or her spouse as a family unit for the last two years.

10. Unmarried couple with or without children who have not lived together continuously as a family unit for the last two years.
11. Couple or single person with one or more children who are not their off-spring.
12. Family with minor children which does not include both parents, unless the absent parent is hospitalized, in an institution, or is deceased.
13. Evidence of lack of parental control over children.
14. Mental illness which required hospitalization.
15. Unusually frequent changes in place of residence.
16. Poor housekeeping, other than as defined under "clear and present danger."
17. Elderly persons whose ability adequately to care for themselves or the premises is questionable.
18. Lack of furniture.
19. Apparent mental retardation of parent or child.
20. Obnoxious conduct or behavior in connection with the processing of the application or the renting of the apartment.
21. Discharge from service with other than honorable discharge.

Notes

Abbreviations

CHPC Archive	Citizens Housing and Planning Council Archive
MA	Municipal Archive
NYCHAR	NYCHA Records, La Guardia Wagner Archive
NYPL	New York Public Library
NYT	*New York Times*

Introduction

1. In the text NYCHA is referred to without "the" as is customary in the New York region.

2. On design and public housing, see Catherine Bauer Wurster, "The Dreary Deadlock of Public Housing," *Architectural Forum* (May 1957) 140–42; Jane Jacobs, *The Death and Life of Great American Cities* (New York: Random House, 1961); Oscar Newman, *Defensible Space: Crime Prevention Through Urban Design* (New York: Macmillan, 1972); Clare Cooper, *Easter Hill Village: Some Social Implications of Design* (New York: Free Press, 1975); Peter Blake, *Form Follows Fiasco: Why Modern Architecture Hasn't Worked* (Boston: Little Brown, 1977); Peter Rowe, *Modernity and Housing* (Cambridge, Mass.: MIT, 1993); Christine Hunter, *Ranches, Roughhouses and Railroad Flats* (New York: Norton, 1999); Alexander Garvin, *The American City: What Works, What Doesn't* (New York: McGraw Hill, 1996); Eric Mumford, *The CIAM Discourse on Urbanism, 1928–1960* (Cambridge, Mass.: MIT, 2000). The sociological perspective includes Sudhir Alladi Venkatesh, *American Project: The Rise and Fall of a Modern Ghetto* (Cambridge, Mass.: Harvard, 2000); Rhonda Williams, *The Politics of Public Housing: Black Women's Struggles Against Urban Inequality* (New York: Oxford University Press, 2004); William Moore, *The Vertical Ghetto: Everyday Life in an Urban Project* (New York: Random House, 1969); Lee Rainwater, *Behind Ghetto Walls: Black Families in a Federal Slum* (Chicago: Aldine, 1970); Jay McLeod, *Ain't No Making It: Leveled Aspirations in a Low-Income Neighborhood* (Boulder, Colo.: Westview, 1987); Alex Kotlowitz, *There Are No Children Here* (New York: Doubleday, 1991); Daniel Coyle, *Hardball: A Season in the Projects* (New York: Putnam, 1993); Susan Popkin and Victoria Gwiasda, eds., *The Hidden War: Crime and the Tragedy of Public Housing in Chicago* (New Brunswick, N.J.: Rutgers, 2000).

3. Important public housing histories include Arnold Hirsch, *Making the Second Ghetto: Race and Housing in Chicago, 1940–1960* (New York: Cambridge, 1983); Roger Biles and John Bauman, et al., *From Tenements to the Taylor Homes* (University Park: Penn State, 2000); John Bauman, *Public Housing, Race, and Renewal: Urban Planning in Philadelphia, 1920–1974* (Philadelphia: Temple, 1987); Don Parson, *Making a Better World: Public Housing, the Red Scare, and the Direction of Modern Los Angeles* (Minneapolis: Minnesota, 2005); Dana Cuff, *The Provisional*

City: Los Angeles Stories of Architecture and Urbanism (Cambridge, Mass.: MIT, 2000); Joseph Heathcott, "The City Remade: Public Housing and the Urban Landscape in St. Louis, 1900–1960" (Ph.D. diss., Indiana University, 2002); Eugene Meehan, *The Quality of Federal Policymaking* (Columbia: Missouri, 1979); Lawrence Vale, *From the Puritans to the Projects: Public Housing and Public Neighbors* (Cambridge, Mass.: Harvard, 2000), and *Reclaiming Public Housing: A Half Century of Struggle in Three Public Neighborhoods* (Cambridge, Mass.: Harvard, 2002); D. Bradford Hunt, "What Went Wrong with Public Housing in Chicago? A History of the Chicago Housing Authority, 1933–1982" (Ph.D. diss., University of California, Berkeley, 2000); J. S. Fuerst and Bradford Hunt, *When Public Housing Was Paradise: Building Community in Chicago* (Urbana: Illinois, 2005); Devereux Bowly, *The Poorhouse: Subsidized Housing in Chicago, 1895–1976* (Carbondale: Southern Illinois, 1981); Raymond Mohl, "Making the Second Ghetto in Metropolitan Miami," *Journal of Urban History* (March 1995): 395–427.

4. Interview of Robert Podmore, the NYCHA deputy general manager, by the author, 21 July 2006.

5. James Barron, "Tiger Owner Faced Eviction from Apartment," *NYT* 7 October 2003, B3.

6. NYCHA's founding years have been covered in a number of texts, many of which were of great help in the writing of this book. Joel Schwartz's *The New York Approach: Robert Moses, Urban Liberals, and Redevelopment of the Inner City* (Columbus: Ohio State, 1993) treats the early history of the NYCHA and the role of public housing in Robert Moses' redevelopment plans. A collection of fine essays in the *Journal of Urban History* 12, no. 4 (August 1986) is also strong on the early years of NYCHA history. Gail Radford's *Modern Housing for America: Policy Struggles in the New Deal Era* (Chicago: Chicago, 1996) explores policy debates and housing design of the early years. A. Scott Henderson, *Housing and the Democratic Ideal: The Life and Thought of Charles Abrams* (New York: Columbia, 2000) helps set the legal basis for NYCHA work and early policy debates as they relate to Charles Abrams. Peter Marcuse's unfinished manuscript, *Public Housing in New York City: History of a Program* (NYCHA collection, 1989) is strongest on the 1930s but does provide important analysis of the larger housing context in New York City. Richard Plunz's *A History of Housing in New York City* (New York: Columbia, 1990) provides a concise summary of the process of design innovation at NYCHA in the early years and is still essential reading. The creative resistance to public housing in postwar East Harlem is documented in Samuel Zipp, "Manhattan Projects: Cold War Urbanism in the Age of Urban Renewal" (Ph.D. diss., Yale University, 2006). Wendell Pritchett's excellent *Brownsville, Brooklyn: Blacks, Jews, and the Changing Face of the Ghetto* (Chicago: Chicago, 2002) treats the rise and subsequent history of public housing in Brownsville as well as the larger context of NYCHA's relationship to tenement neighborhoods; Robert Caro's *The Power Broker* (New York: Knopf, 1974) occasionally touches on public housing history as does Hilary Ballon and Kenneth T. Jackson, eds., *Robert Moses and the Modern City: The Transformation of New York* (New York: Norton, 2007). For the social history of housing in New York, see Elizabeth Blackmar, *Manhattan for Rent, 1785–1850* (Ithaca, N.Y.: Cornell, 1989); Jared Day, *Urban Castles: Tenement Housing and Landlord Activism in New York City, 1890–1943* (New York: Columbia, 1999); Craig Wilder, *A Covenant with Color: Race and Social Power in Brooklyn* (New York: Columbia, 2000); Jill Jonnes, *We're Still Here: The Rise, Fall, and Resurrection of the South Bronx* (Boston: Atlantic Monthly Press, 1986); Evelyn Gonzalez, *The Bronx* (New York: Columbia, 2004); Max Page, *The Creative Destruction of Manhat-*

tan, 1900–1940 (Chicago: Chicago, 1999); Elizabeth Cromley, *Alone Together: A History of New York's Early Apartments* (Ithaca, N.Y.: Cornell, 1990); Lawrence Kaplan and Carol Kaplan, *Between Ocean and City: The Transformation of Rockaway, New York* (New York: Columbia, 2003); Anthony Jackson, *A Place Called Home: A History of Low-Cost Housing in Manhattan* (Cambridge, Mass.: MIT, 1976); Janet Abu-Lughod, *New York, Chicago, Los Angeles: America's Global Cities* (Minneapolis: Minnesota, 1999).

7. The larger urban historical context for this book has been shaped by works such as Robert Beauregard, *Voices of Decline: The Postwar Fate of U.S. Cities* (Cambridge, Mass.: Blackwell, 1993); Alison Isenberg, *Downtown* (Chicago: Chicago, 2004); Thomas Sugrue, *The Origins of the Urban Crisis: Race and Inequality in Postwar Detroit* (Princeton: Princeton, 1998); Kenneth T. Jackson, *Crabgrass Frontier: The Suburbanization of the United States* (New York: Oxford, 1985); and Jon Teaford, *The Rough Road to Renaissance: Urban Revitalization in America, 1940–1985* (Baltimore: Johns Hopkins, 1990).

My personal interest in exploring public sector leadership came from the study of one of the great advocates of private sector leadership, James Rouse. See Nicholas Dagen Bloom, *Merchant of Illusion: James Rouse, America's Salesman of the Businessman's Utopia* (Columbus: Ohio State, 2004), and *Suburban Alchemy: 1960s New Towns and the Transformation of the American Dream* (Columbus: Ohio State, 2001).

Chapter 1. Defining a Housing Crisis

1. La Guardia is quoted in Nathan Glazer, "Letter from East Harlem," *City Journal,* autumn 1991, www.city-journal.org/article02.php?aid=1584.

2. Peter Marcuse, "The Beginnings of Public Housing in New York" *Journal of Urban History* 12, no. 4 (August 1986): 355.

3. Langdon Post, Speech, WABC, 26 August 1934, Box 53A1, Folder 13, NY-CHAR.

4. "City Ready to Start Huge Housing Plan," *NYT,* 3 March 1935, section 4, 10.

5. The New York City Housing Authority, *Toward the End to Be Achieved: The New York City Housing Authority, Its History in Outline* (New York: NYCHA, 1937), 7–8; "City Ready to Start Huge Housing Plan," *NYT,* 3 March 1935, section 4, 10.

6. Langdon Post, Speech, First Washington Conference on Public Housing, National Public Housing Conference, 1934, Box 66A5, Folder 9, NYCHAR, 8.

7. Albert Mayer, "Attacking the City's Slum Problem," *NYT,* 18 February 1934, section 20, 3. See also Day, *Urban Castles,* 169–90.

8. Roy Lubove, *The Progressives and the Slums: Tenement House Reform in New York City, 1890–1917* (Pittsburgh: Pittsburgh, 1962), 133, 215; Joel Schwartz, "Housing," in Kenneth T. Jackson, *The Encyclopedia of New York City* (New Haven, Conn.: Yale, 1995), 166–67.

9. Lubove, *The Progressives and the Slums,* 159–65, 129, 181; Thomas Kessner, *Fiorello H. La Guardia and the Making of Modern New York* (New York: McGraw-Hill, 1989), 322. See also Henderson, *Housing and the Democratic Ideal,* 48–49; Robert Fairbanks, "From Better Dwellings to Better Neighborhoods," in *From Tenements to the Taylor Homes,* ed. Roger Biles and John Bauman et al. (University Park: Penn State, 2000), 21–42. For Progressive resistance to the New Deal, see John Buenker, *Urban Liberalism and Progressive Reform* (New York: Scribner, 1973), 232–33.

10. Marcuse, "The Beginnings of Public Housing in New York," 358; Kessner, *Fiorello H. La Guardia*, 322.

11. Lubove, *The Progressives and the Slums*, 175; Charles Abrams, *The Future of Housing* (New York: Harper, 1946), 175.

12. Frank Marsh, *Forty Profitable Years of Low Rent Housing, 1896–1936*, Federal Housing Administration, 1937, CHPC Archive, ix–x.

13. "Reports Success in State Housing," *NYT*, 22 February 1931, section 11–12, 1; Louis Pink, *A New Day in Housing* (New York: John Day, 1928), 133; Lubove, *The Progressives and the Slums*, 237; Muller Brief, Supreme Court of the State of New York, Box 55D2, Folder 4, NYCHAR, 21–22. See also "Huge Housing Plan Urged for Revival," *NYT*, 14 April 1932, 23; "America Backward in Model Housing," *NYT*, 8 May 1932, section 11–12, 2. Daniel Rodgers notes Simkhovitch's role in the project. Daniel T. Rodgers, *Atlantic Crossings: Social Politics in a Progressive Age* (Cambridge, Mass.: Harvard, 1998), 463.

14. "5 Housing Projects to Cost $72,000,000," *NYT*, 23 September 1932, 1. See also "State Board to Ask $150,000,000 of RFC," *NYT*, 4 February 1933, 1; "R.F.C. Lends $3,957,000 for Bronx Housing," *NYT*, 2 November 1932, 1.

15. Rodgers, *Atlantic Crossings*, 188.

16. The editors of Fortune, *Housing America* (New York: Harcourt, 1932), 21.

17. Ira Robbins and Gus Tyler, *Reminiscences of a Housing Advocate* (New York: Citizens Housing and Planning Council, 1984), CHPC Archive, 14; Langdon Post, Speech, First Washington Conference on Public Housing, National Public Housing Conference, 1934, Box 66A5, Folder 9, NYCHAR.

18. See, for instance, Max Page, *The Creative Destruction of Manhattan, 1900–1940* (Chicago: Chicago, 1999).

19. Regulation in the form of commissions, new housing codes, and civil service provisions seemed to many reformers a way to enforce a new order on the city while minimizing "democratized corruption." American cities were also creatures of states with comparatively limited debt and administrative powers; conservative courts further undercut municipal excess condemnation and planning (although not health regulation or zoning) on constitutional grounds. Rodgers, *Atlantic Crossings*, 70, 124–25, 130, 133, 135, 138, 143, 153, 155, 201. See also Gail Radford, "From Municipal Socialism to Public Authorities: Institutional Factors in the Shaping of American Public Enterprise," *Journal of American History* (December 2003): 863–90 for details on the expansion of quasi-governmental organizations that circumvented legal and financial limits on municipal power. See also Martin Melosi, *The Sanitary City: Urban Infrastructure in America from Colonial Times to the Present* (Baltimore: Johns Hopkins, 2000); Erik Monkkonen, *America Becomes Urban: The Development of U.S. Cities and Towns, 1780–1980* (Berkeley: California, 1988); Jameson Doig, *Empire on the Hudson: Entrepreneurial Vision and Political Power at the Port of New York Authority* (New York: Columbia, 2002). For the influence of Europe on the development of American planning, see also Jon Peterson, *The Birth of City Planning in the United States, 1840–1917* (Baltimore: Johns Hopkins, 2003); William H. Wilson, *The City Beautiful Movement* (Baltimore: Johns Hopkins, 1994); Thomas Hines, *Burnham of Chicago: Architect and Planner* (Chicago: Chicago, 1979).

20. Rodgers, *Atlantic Crossings*, 383.

21. Eve Blau, *The Architecture of Red Vienna, 1919–1934* (Cambridge, Mass.: MIT, 1999); Sir Harold Bellman, "Housing by Private and Public Initiative," 16 May 1938, Box 66A5, Folder 8, NYCHAR.

22. Louis Pink, *A New Day in Housing* (New York: John Day, 1928), 22. Some of

those who traveled to Europe included Helen Alfred, secretary of the National Public Housing Conference, who organized a European study tour "with a group of American enthusiasts" in 1936. See Elizabeth Hines, "Women to Clarify Housing Problems," *NYT*, 10 October 1937, 98. Nathan Straus Jr. traveled to Europe in 1935 as the mayor's special housing commissioner and on his return "contrasted the extensive housing projects of Europe with the 'piecemeal' low-cost projects of the United States." See "Vast Housing Plan Urged by Straus as a City Project," *NYT*, 21 October 1935, 1. For a debate on the practicalities of adopting British models of housing, see "Straus on Housing," *NYT*, 21 October 1935, 18; "Housing Plan Defended," *NYT*, 24 October 1935, 6; "The Housing Situation," *NYT*, 26 October 1935, 14; "The Housing Situation," *NYT*, 29 October 1935, 20; "Straus Slum Plan Held Too Costly," *NYT*, 3 November 1935, sections 13–14, 4. See also his obituary, "Nathan Straus, 72, Civic Leader and Chairman of WMCA, Dies," *NYT*, 14 September 1961, 1. See also Anthony Quiney, *House and Home: A History of the Small English House* (London: BBC Press, 1986), 132–45.

23. Catherine Bauer, *Modern Housing* (New York: Houghton Mifflin, 1934), 122, 129, 146–50.

24. Sir Raymond Unwin addressed the National Housing Conference (including the mayor-elect, Fiorello La Guardia) in 1933: "La Guardia to Seek Slum Clearance," *NYT*, 26 November 1933, 1. In 1934, Dr. Werner Hegemann, a planning expert, talked to the Welfare Council meeting at the New School: "High Realty Costs Held Housing Bar," *NYT*, 10 March 1934, 2. In 1937 Richard Reiss of the London County Council spoke to a mass meeting of housing advocates that again included Mayor La Guardia: "Cathedral to Put a 'Slum' on Display," *NYT*, 22 February 1937, 24. Hugo Breitner, a pioneer of public housing in Vienna, gave five lectures in 1938 at the Architectural League: "Housing in Vienna," *NYT*, 11 September 1938, 207.

25. Edith Elmer Wood, "The Costs of Bad Housing," *The Annals of the American Academy of Political and Social Science*, March 1937, CHPC Archive, 130.

26. Langdon Post, "A Letter to a Banker," circa 1936, NYCHA Publication, Box 74E5, no folder, NYCHAR.

27. Helen Alfred, *Municipal Housing*, published by the National Public Housing Conference, 1935, NYPL, 14.

28. Robbins and Tyler, *Reminiscences of a Housing Advocate*, 15.

29. "First Houses' Open, Roosevelt Hails New Slum Policy," *NYT*, 4 December 1935, 1.

30. "10,000 Hear Mayor Say Unsafe Slums Will Be Wiped Out," *NYT*, 9 April 1934, 1.

31. "Vast City Housing Plan to Aid 500,000 families," *NYT*, 28 January 1938, 1.

32. Business interest in slum clearance and high-rise, center city public housing is documented in Rosalie Genevro, "Site Selection and the New York City Housing Authority, 1934–1939," *Journal of Urban History* 12, no. 4 (August 1986): 334–52.

33. "Subsidized Housing Called a Menace," *NYT*, 4 September 1932, sections 10–11, 1. Anti-housing sentiment can be found in these documents, among others: "Sees Realty Menace in Housing Plans," *NYT*, 3 October 1932, 19; "Model Flat Loans Opposed in Bronx," *NYT*, 23 October 1932, sections 10–11, 2; "Protest R.F.C. Loan for Bronx Housing," *NYT*, 3 November 1932, 1; "Urges Restrictions on Public Housing," *NYT*, 26 December 1933, 23; "Tax Loss Called Housing Problem," *NYT*, 9 September 1934, sections 10–11, 1; "Ickes Housing

Plan Defended as Sound," *NYT*, 27 November 1934, 4; "Housing by PWA Is Upheld by Post," *NYT*, 11 February 1935; "Reviews Factors for Good Housing," *NYT*, 14 February 1937, section 12, 4; "Tenements in Manhattan," *NYT*, 16 March 1937, 22; "State Republicans Fire Upon Wagner," *NYT*, 5 May 1938, 10.

34. "The High Cost of Housing," *NYT*, 27 March 1937, 14.

35. "Opposes Changes in Housing Rules," *NYT*, 4 March 1934, sections 10–11, 1; "Oppose Housing Plan," *NYT*, 5 August 1933, 23; "City Asked to Buy Old Tenements," *NYT*, 8 March 1938, 13; "Low Cost Housing by City Authority—Private Interests Cannot Provide $5 Room Rentals," *NYT*, 31 December 1933, sections 10–11, 2.

36. "Find Impediment to Slum Clearance," *NYT*, 17 October 1932, 30; Day, *Urban Castles*, 176–77.

37. Ira Robbins, Address on WMCA, 18 March 1934, Box 53A7, Folder 20. NYCHAR.

38. "Admits Competition in Public Housing," *NYT*, 20 June 1937, section 12, 18.

39. "City Housing Plans Urged to Add Jobs," *NYT*, 28 March 1930, 2; "Post Urges Public to Demand Housing," *NYT*, 29 June 1935, 6; "Calls City Remiss on Housing Relief," *NYT*, 22 April 1931, 46.

40. "Public Housing Asked by Workers," *NYT*, 29 June 1934, 19.

41. Pritchett, *Brownsville, Brooklyn*, 63.

42. "Asks City to Form Own Housing Board," *NYT*, 6 November 1932, sections 10–11, 2; "New Housing Plan Offered for City," *NYT*, 16 February 1933, 21; "Asks City to Build Non-Profit Homes," *NYT*, 30 April 1933, section 2, 1; "Housing Authority Asked," *NYT*, 25 June 1933, 3; "Clubs Set Forth Legislative Aims," *NYT*, 22 January 1939, section 2, 4.

43. Robbins and Tyler, *Reminiscences of a Housing Advocate*, 15.

44. "Open Drive to Build Low-Cost Homes," *NYT*, 23 March 1932, 15. Mary Simkhovitch provides a direct link to earlier Progressive reform individuals and reform movements. Simkhovitch founded the Cooperative Social Settlement Society of New York in 1902 (later Greenwich House), which became a nonsectarian settlement well known for "sponsoring neighborhood participation projects . . . street concerts, plays, dances," English instruction, and craft programs (still famous today) as part of a "cooperative community venture." See "Mrs. Simkhovitch to Retire Friday," *NYT*, 30 January 1946, 20; "Mary Simkhovitch Dead at Age of 84," *NYT*, 16 November 1951, 25.

45. "City Is Urged to Build Low-Rent Homes at Once with Federal Loan to Aid Jobless, End Slums," *NYT*, 3 October 1932, 19; "Asks City to Provide $25,000,000 Housing," *NYT*, 7 July 1932, 19.

46. "Walker Is Skeptical of Housing Loan Plan," *NYT*, 8 July 1932, 2; "Removal of Slums Is Urged on O'Brien," *NYT*, 12 November 1933, 19; "Board Is Urged for Model Houses," *NYT*, 3 July 1933, 13.

47. "La Guardia Scores M'Kee in Wall Street," *NYT*, 3 November 1933, 3.

48. "Municipal Board for Housing Urged," *NYT*, 31 October 1932, 17; "La Guardia Victory Seen," *NYT*, 20 October 1933, 1. La Guardia's public housing and city transit ownership appeared mild in comparison to more radical ideas pursued by a candidate such as Charles Solomon, the Socialist candidate for mayor. See "Social Insurance Urged by Socialist," *NYT*, 30 October 1933, 2.

49. "La Guardia to Seek Slum Clearance," *NYT*, 26 November 1933, 1.

50. "Public Housing Era Visioned by Mayor," *NYT*, 9 July 1936, 23.

51. Langdon Post, Speech, First Washington Conference on Public Housing,

National Public Housing Conference, 1934, Box 66A5, Folder 9, NYCHAR, 8. Langdon Post was a "reform Democrat," an assemblyman, and a "close adviser to Governor Franklin Roosevelt." Post had already led the charge on the Multiple Dwelling Law of 1929 and unsuccessfully introduced housing legislation in the early 1930s to give the city the power to build housing. Post served briefly in the Roosevelt administration as assistant administrator of the FERA "but had resigned to run on the Fusion ticket" in 1933, unsuccessfully as it turned out, for the office of Manhattan Borough president. David Dunlap, "Langdon W. Post, 82, Dead; Housing Aide to La Guardia," *NYT*, 5 September 1981, 44; "La Guardia Speeds Action on Housing, *NYT*, 30 December 1933, 15; Robbins and Tyler, *Reminiscences of a Housing Advocate*, 24; "Post Is Named Head of Tenement Board to Clean Up Slums," *NYT*, 18 December 1933, 1.

52. Buenker, *Urban Liberalism and Progressive Reform*, 230.

53. "City Housing Bill Ready for Albany," *NYT*, 11 January 1934, 23; Langdon Post, "First Steps in New York Housing," 1934, Box 53A5, Folder 24, NYCHAR; Robbins and Tyler, *Reminiscences of a Housing Advocate*, 16. Lehman signed the bill paving the way for municipal housing authorities on 1 February 1934. See "Lehman Hails Law to Clear Up Slums," *NYT*, 1 February 1934, 2. See also "New Era in Housing Urged by Lehman," *NYT*, 3 January 1934, 5; Henderson, *Housing and the Democratic Ideal*, 56.

54. Ira Robbins, Speech, First Washington Conference on Public Housing, National Public Housing Conference, 1934, Box 66A5, Folder 9, NYCHAR, 39; Alfred, *Municipal Housing*; Henderson, *Housing and the Democratic Ideal*, 56–58.

55. "First Houses' Open, Roosevelt Hails New Slum Policy," *NYT*, 4 December 1935, 1. See also "New York and Housing," *The Commonweal* (2 March 1934): 479; "Mayor Names Five to Housing Board," *NYT*, 14 February 1934, 21.

56. Bauman, *Public Housing, Race, and Renewal*, 44.

57. Langdon Post, *The Challenge of Housing* (New York: Farrar, 1938), xv.

58. Langdon Post, "First Steps in New York Housing," 1934, Box 53A5, Folder 24, NYCHAR, 2.

59. "Drive Begins January 1 to Abolish Slums," *NYT*, December 1935, 8.

60. "Need for Low-Cost Housing," *NYT*, 25 March 1937, 24.

61. "Housing Authority Ready to Build," *NYT*, 10 October 1937, section 4, 9; Kessner, *Fiorello H. La Guardia*, 323. See also J. Schwartz, *The New York Approach*, 46–47.

62. "Housing Shortage of Major Extent on War, Says Post," *NYT*, 22 November 1936, 1.

63. "East Side Tenants Spared Eviction," *NYT*, 1 January 1937, 21.

64. Harold Riegelman, "Our Housing Problems," *NYT*, 13 March 1937, 18. See also Report of the Mayor on Housing and Living Conditions, 1936, Box 78A4, Folder 5, NYCHAR; Day, *Urban Castles*.

65. Jeanne Lowe, "From Shelter to Community, the First Thirty Five Years of the New York City Housing Authority," Typescript, 26 August 1969, Box 64E4, Folder 1, NYCHAR, 12; "City Speeds Work on Old-Law Houses," *NYT*, 30 June 1935, sections 12–13, 1; Kessner, *Fiorello H. La Guardia*, 324. Peter Marcuse provides evidence that Astor was happy to shed these properties because "these buildings were not worth remodeling or altering in any way." Marcuse, "The Beginnings of Public Housing in New York," 357.

66. Langdon Post to Norbert Brown, 26 December 1935, Box 55D5, Folder 4, NYCHAR; Langdon Post to Harold Kellogg, 17 March 1936, Box 53C2, Folder 14, NYCHAR.

67. NYCHA Board to Charles Abrams, 23 November 1937, Box 53C8, Folder 2, NYCHA Papers (LWA); The New York City Housing Authority, *Toward the End to Be Achieved*, 13–16. See also Robbins and Tyler, *Reminiscences of a Housing Advocate*, 27–30.

68. Muller Brief, Supreme Court of the State of New York, Box 55D2, Folder 4, NYCHAR, 5.

69. Henderson, *Housing and the Democratic Ideal*, 73.

70. The New York City Housing Authority, *Toward the End to Be Achieved*, 13–16; Henderson, *Housing and the Democratic Ideal*, 75. See also Robbins and Tyler, *Reminiscences of a Housing Advocate*, 27–30.

71. The decision is in line with a national judicial shift allowing for greater municipal power in the 1920s and 1930s. See Radford, "From Municipal Socialism to Public Authorities," 863–90.

72. Robbins and Tyler, *Reminiscences of a Housing Advocate*, 17; Radford, *Modern Housing for America*, 88–91. Daniel T. Rodgers notes Simkhovitch's role in convincing Wagner to take this stand. See Rodgers, *Atlantic Crossings*, 464. For the debate on federal versus local control, see "$25,000,000 for City Is Held Up by PWA," *NYT*, 29 August 1934, 11; "Ickes and Mayor Agree on Housing," *NYT*, 11 September 1934, 1; "PWA Loan Terms Accepted by City," *NYT*, 19 September 1934, 21.

73. "Confidential Report of Washington Trip," circa 7 March 1934, Box 55D2, Folder 4, NYCHAR, 1. Frances Perkins was far more upbeat about public housing than Ickes and others at the PWA.

74. Langdon Post to George Cabot, 8 June 1934, Box 53A1, Folder 4, NYCHA Papers (LWA).

75. "Brooklyn Picked for Model Housing," *NYT*, 16 May 1934, 21. See also "Permanent Board on Housing Urged," *NYT*, 7 September 1934, 23; Langdon Post, "First Steps in New York Housing," 1934, Box 53A5, Folder 24, NYCHAR.

76. Evans Clark, Memo, 7 September 1937, Box 53D1, Folder 4, NYCHAR. See also Abrams, *The Future of Housing*, 251, 256.

77. Henderson, *Housing and the Democratic Ideal*, 67; Robbins and Tyler, *Reminiscences of a Housing Advocate*, 21.

78. "Commissioner Promises Aid," *New York Amsterdam News*, 24 January 1934, 3; Harlem population statistics are from Radford, *Modern Housing for America*, 150; density estimate from Henry Lee Moon, "Housing Problem Is Acute in Harlem," *NYT*, 20 June 1937, 62. See also "Housing Mass Action Urged," *New York Amsterdam News*, 26 May 1934, 3; "F.D.R. Promises Consideration of Housing Here," *New York Amsterdam News*, 18 May 1935, 1.

79. Marcuse, "The Beginnings of Public Housing in New York," 369; "Reports on Existing Conditions and Recommendations . . ." 20 April 1935, Box A-97, Folder 37, Simkhovitch Papers, Schlesinger Library, 8A; "City Housing to Get $13,000,000 More," *NYT*, 1 January 1935, 4; "Federal Funds Buy Housing Sites Here," *NYT*, 11 January 1935, 1; "City Speeds Plans for Harlem Homes," *NYT*, 4 July 1935, 17. The authority was forced to condemn the property when the Rockefeller interests in control of the site refused to agree to the NYCHA's price. See also "$4,7000,000 Housing Planned in Harlem," *NYT*, 3 July 1935, 1. For details of the financial arrangement for transfer, see "$4,219,000 Housing Goes to City Today," *NYT*, 16 June 1937, 25.

80. "Finds Weak Point in Housing," *NYT*, 7 February 1937, 186. See also "Expert Urges Study of British Ideas for Low-Rental Housing in America," *NYT*, 18 July 1937, RE2.

81. "La Guardia Backed on PWA Loan Stand," *NYT*, 21 January 1935, 1.

82. "Government and Housing," *NYT*, 10 December 1937, 24. When the newly created USHA took over the PWA's projects in 1937, the new administrator, Nathan Straus, realized that in order to keep the housing rented "to the lowest income groups" it would demand "in effect . . . 'writing off' of the treasury loans amounting to 55 percent of the total (national) expenditure of $134,000,000" (the other 45 percent had already been provided as a grant). See "Funds Earmarked for Housing Plans," *NYT*, 9 December 1937, 16.

83. Radford, *Modern Housing for America*, 107.

84. The New York City Housing Authority, *Toward the End to Be Achieved*, 7–8; "$150,000,000 Plan for Housing Urged," *NYT*, 22 March 1935, 25; and Roland Wood, "Vast Housing Plan Envisaged for City," *NYT*, 8 December 1935, E10. See also "Reports on Existing Conditions and Recommendations in Respect to the Use of the Sum of $150,000,000 as an Initial Step in a Large Scale Slum Clearance and Low Rental Housing Program," 20 April 1935, Box A-97, Folder 37, Simkhovitch Papers, Schlesinger Library, 8; J. Schwartz, *The New York Approach*, 40–41; "NYCHA Summary of Activities, 1934–1939," circa 1939, Box 54E6, Folder 11, NYCHAR.

85. "La Guardia to Ask $150,000,000 Loan for Housing Here," *NYT*, 7 February 1935, 1; "City Housing Plan before President," *NYT*, 2 May 1935, 7; "City Housing Plans Seen Aiding Labor," *NYT*, 2 April 1935, 40; "City Housing Plan before President," *NYT*, 2 May 1935, 7; "Clergy Is Urged to Aid in Housing," *NYT*, 15 October 1935, 23; Langdon Post to Harold Kellogg, 17 March 1936, Box 53C2, Folder 14, NYCHAR.

86. Franklin Roosevelt to Langdon Post, 24 August 1936, Box 53C7, Folder 3, NYCHAR.

Chapter 2. Three Programs Are Better Than One

1. J. Joseph Huthmacher, *Senator Robert F. Wagner and the Rise of Urban Liberalism* (New York: Atheneum, 1968), 209.

2. Rodgers, *Atlantic Crossings*, 466, 473.

3. Buenker, *Urban Liberalism and Progressive Reform*, 206.

4. "U.S. Housing Drive Begins in Red Hook," *NYT*, 19 July 1938, 23. See also "Debate Is Curbed on Housing Bill," *NYT*, 4 August 1937, 13; Abrams, *The Future of Housing*, 314. See also Hunt, "What Went Wrong with Public Housing in Chicago?" One of the most readable and compelling accounts of the fight for the act can be found in H. Peter Oberlander and Eva Newbrun, *Houser: The Life and Work of Catherine Bauer* (Vancouver: UBC, 1999), 125–56. See also Alexander von Hoffman, "The End of the Dream: The Political Struggle of America's Public Housers," *Journal of Planning History* 4, no. 3 (2005): 222.

5. Huthmacher, *Senator Robert F. Wagner and the Rise of Urban Liberalism*, 136, 209.

6. Robbins and Tyler, *Reminiscences of a Housing Advocate*, 31; Abrams, *The Future of Housing*, 257; "Cathedral to Put a 'Slum' on Display," *NYT*, 22 February 1937, 24; "Exhibit to Stress Housing Progress," *NYT*, 9 May 1937, RE1. On Post's fight for higher funding, see "Housing Aid Limit Is Set for States," *NYT*, 6 August 1937, 6; "Ickes Signs Lease on Williamsburg Housing," *NYT*, 8 August 1937, 6; "Housing Act Steps Sped to Get Loans," *NYT*, 24 September 1937, 23; "Housing Authority Is Ready to Build," *NYT*, 10 October 1937, section 4, 9.

7. Abrams, *The Future of Housing*, 259. See also Lee Cooper, "Housing Act Will

Open New Era in Slum Clearance," *NYT*, 5 September 1937, 137; Rodgers, *Atlantic Crossings*, 476–77. The USHA was located within the Department of Interior, but Ickes had limited control. See Hunt, "What Went Wrong with Public Housing in Chicago?" 50.

8. Nathan Straus, *The Seven Myths of Housing* (New York: Knopf, 1944), 23.

9. "Government and Housing," *NYT*, 10 December 1937, 24. See also Abrams, *The Future of Housing*, 256; Alfred Rheinstein, "Why Slum Clearance May Fail," Undated, Box 54A3, Folder 8, NYCHAR. D. Bradford Hunt, in "What Went Wrong with Public Housing in Chicago?," 40–41, clearly argues that the "annual contributions" system was developed by Warren Vinton to reduce the upfront costs of public housing, its main political liability, while generously subsidizing public housing. See also Oberlander and Newbrun, *Houser: The Life and Work of Catherine Bauer*, 158

10. J. Schwartz, *The New York Approach*, 48–49.

11. "The Housing Squabble," *NYT*, 4 December 1937, 16. For more on political intrigue of this type, see "Washington Notes," *The New Republic*, 15 December 1937, 168; and for Wagner's perspective on the fight (Wagner favored Straus), see Huthmacher, *Senator Robert F. Wagner and the Rise of Urban Liberalism*, 228–30.

12. "Housing Counsel Quits in Protest Over Mayor's Ban," *NYT*, 23 November 1937, 1; "City Housing Body and Mayor Clash," *NYT*, 24 November 1937, 5; Charles Abrams to NYCHA Board Members, 22 November 1937, Box 53C8, Folder 2, NYCHAR. See also NYCHA Board to Charles Abrams, 23 November 1937, Box 53C8, Folder 2, NYCHAR.

13. "The Housing Squabble," *NYT*, 4 December 1937, 16; "Mayor Threatens Row Over Housing," *NYT*, 1 December 1937, 1.

14. "Post Defies Mayor; Quits Housing Body," *NYT*, 2 December 1937, 1.

15. "Mayor Forces Post Off Housing Board, Stone Is Appointed," *NYT*, 3 December 1937, 1.

16. Langdon Post, *The Challenge of Housing* (New York: Farrar, 1938), 261.

17. "Funds Earmarked for Housing Plans," *NYT*, 9 December 1937, 1; "Mayor Surprised at Talk of Straus Rift," *NYT*, 10 December 1937, 1.

18. "Speed on Housing Pledged to Mayor in Call on Straus," *NYT*, 12 December 1937, 1.

19. "Straus Earmarks $18,000,000 Funds for Housing Here," *NYT*, 24 December 1937, 1; "Additional Federal Money Earmarked," *NYT*, 8 April 1938, 2.

20. "Housing Technique Is Rheinstein's Aim," *NYT*, 21 January 1938, 4; Alfred Rheinstein, 9 February 1939, Box 54A3, Folder 8, NYCHAR; Alfred Rheinstein and Henry Pringle, "Why Slum Clearance May Fail," Undated, Box 54A3, Folder 8, NYCHAR.

21. "Rheinstein Builds Low-Cost Housing at Low Cost," *New York Post*, 17 September 1938, Box 53E3, Folder 4, NYCHAR. For room and management costs, see also interview of Alfred Rheinstein, 9 February 1939, Box 54A3, Folder 8, NYCHAR.

Thomas Kessner believes that Rheinstein pursued a conservative view of public housing's potential that matched diminished expectations set by La Guardia after he sacked Post. Kessner writes that "La Guardia did not lose faith in the idea of public housing or in the people; he scaled it down to the level at which he felt it could be supported." La Guardia, however, would plan with Robert Moses a vast postwar housing scheme for the city. La Guardia was also instrumental in laying the groundwork for what became vast state- and city-funded projects after World War II. Kessner, *Fiorello H. La Guardia*, 431–32. See also Thomas Kessner, "Fiorello La Guardia and the Challenge of Democratic Planning," in *The Landscape of Modernity, New York City, 1900–1940*, ed. David Ward (Baltimore: Johns Hopkins, 1992), 315–29.

22. Chicago would develop a small state-financed veteran's housing program after the war, but it in no way compares to New York's massive state housing enterprise. See Hunt, "What Went Wrong with Public Housing in Chicago?" for details.

23. Robbins and Tyler, *Reminiscences of a Housing Advocate*, 50. See also Robert Moses, *Public Works: A Dangerous Trade* (New York: McGraw Hill, 1970), 430; Edwin Salmon to Edward Butler, 12 May 1942, Box 68A7, Folder 2, NYCHAR; Robert Moses, "Housing and Recreation," 1938, Robert Moses Papers, MN 22813, Roll 13, Parks Department; "Housing Programs to Fore at Albany," *NYT*, 19 April 1938, 3; "Wagner Demands Social Approach on Constitution," *NYT*, 19 April 1938, 1; "The Housing Amendment," *NYT*, 19 August 1938, 18; "Amendment No. 4," *NYT*, 29 October 1938, 18. Moses and Al Smith did try to limit the extent of the program; see "Victory for Housing," *NYT*, 29 July 1938, 16; Langdon Post to Henry Bruere, 23 October 1937, Box 55D5, Folder 4, NYCHAR. The defeat of California's postwar housing program, Proposition 14, provides an interesting contrast with the general liberality that brought forth New York's program; Parson, *Making a Better World*, 90–91.

24. Robbins and Tyler, *Reminiscences of a Housing Advocate*, 51.

25. "La Guardia Seeks Housing Powers," *NYT*, 1 May 1938, 1. See also "Single Albany Bill to Cover Housing," *NYT*, 12 June 1938, 13.

26. "Housing Article Opposed in Bronx," *NYT*, 2 November 1938, 5; "Victory for Housing," *NYT*, 3 November 1938, 22; "Attacking the Slums," *NYT*, 12 November 1938, 14; "Dailey Backs Slum Plan," *NYT*, 1 February 1938, 12. "Rebuilding Urged to Solve Housing," *NYT*, 31 January 1938, 33; "Republicans Urge Housing and Limit in State Program," *NYT*, 27 December 1938, 1; Warren Moscow, "Housing Program Pushed at Albany," *NYT*, 18 January 1939, 1; Warren Moscow, "Agreement Is Won Housing Bill at Albany Parley," *NYT*, 16 May 1939, 1. See also "Votes for Housing Urged by Leaders," *NYT*, 7 November 1938, 3; "Housing Aid Issues Urged by Lehman," *NYT*, 24 March 1937, 9; "Amendments Vote Closest on No. 1," *NYT*, 10 November 1938, 12.

27. "Vast City Housing Plan to Aid 500,000 families," *NYT*, 28 January 1938, 1; New York Chamber of Commerce, "Public Housing in New York," December 1953, Box 100A4, Folder 5, NYCHAR. The five are First Houses (reclassified as City), Vladeck City (1940), Lavanburg (a converted limited-dividend project), Elliott (1947), and Jacob Riis City (1949).

28. "Toward More Housing," *NYT*, 29 January 1938, 14.

29. See, for instance, "Housing and Slum Clearance," *NYT*, 18 October 1938, 24; "Victory for Housing," *NYT*, 3 November 1938, 22; Alfred Rheinstein to Mayor La Guardia, 3 October 1939, Box 54B3, Folder 13, NYCHAR; "Civic Groups Urge Rheinstein Be Kept," *NYT*, 10 October 1939, 1; "Rheinstein's Work Praised in House," *NYT*, 11 October 1939, 22.

30. Robert Moses quoted in J. Schwartz, *The New York Approach*, 51.

31. "Moses Urges City to Spend $245,000,000 on Housing," *NYT*, 23 November 1938, 1. Moses' use of "genuine slum clearance" comes from Caro, *The Power Broker*, 611.

32. "Mayor Is Critical of Moses Program," *NYT*, 24 November 1938, 29. See also Memo, Citizens Housing Council, 3 December 1938, Box 53E3, Folder 14, NYCHAR, 3; "City Station Cut Moses off the Air," *NYT*, 24 November 1938, 29; "Moses Plan Scored by Housing Council," *NYT*, 5 December 1938, 1; "Mr. Moses

Replies on Housing," *NYT*, 7 December 1938, 22; "Mr. Moses' Plan Criticized," *NYT*, 3 December 1938, 18.

33. Caro, *The Power Broker*, 613.

34. "Gerard Swope Head of Housing Board," *NYT*, 12 December 1939, 1.

35. "City Will Erect $22,000,000 Housing in Navy Yard Area," *NYT*, 22 November 1939, 1; "Low-Rent Projects Aid 10,233 Families," *NYT*, 4 March 1941, 10; "Governor Starts Fort Greene Housing," *NYT*, 7 May 1941, 27.

36. "City Spurs Housing of 15,000 Families," *NYT*, 31 August 1939, n.p.; "Housing Authority Reports Progress," *NYT*, 29 May 1940, 33; "City Builds Homes for 2,943 Families," *NYT*, 2 February 1942, 17; "Housing Program to Expand," *NYT*, 18 June 1939, section 4, 6. See also, "Further Rise Due in Building Work," *NYT*, 28 January 1940, 1.

37. Marcuse, *Public Housing in New York City*, 34–35.

38. Gerard Swope to Fiorello La Guardia, 15 January 1942, Box 54E6, Folder 9, NYCHAR, 2.

39. Lee Cooper, "Defense Program Jeopardizes Housing Plans," *NYT*, 1 June 1940, 30. See also Warren Moscow, "Two Housing Bills Signed by Lehman," *NYT*, 1 May 1941, 47; "Public Housing on a War Basis," *NYT*, 10 May 1942, RE1. All federal housing during the war was targeted to major production areas of which New York City had comparatively few; relatively high vacancy rates in many areas of the city also undercut calls for defense housing. Most frustrating to traditional housing advocates such as Nathan Straus was a growing sense that "the national defense emergency" was being used at the national level "as a smoke screen to scuttle all programs of social progress." See "Defense May Halt City Housing Plan," *NYT*, 30 September 1941, 11. Straus stepped down in 1942 largely in response to provisions in the Lanham Act that called for the selling off of defense housing (built on a large scale) at the termination of the war. In fact, the government did sell off six hundred thousand defense-housing units at the end of the war, much to the chagrin of housing advocates. Winifred Mallon, "Straus Quits Post as Head of USHA," *NYT*, 6 January 1942, 17; "Straus Says Foes Seek to Kill USHA," *NYT*, 18 February 1942, 20; "Vast War Housing to Be Put on Sale," *NYT*, 9 October 1945, 1. See also "Bleak Future Seen for Public Housing," *NYT*, 4 December 1943, 15.

The authority made Fort Greene available for war workers and offered defense housing at Wallabout Houses and Edwin Markham Houses, but as has been well documented, the American South and West benefited disproportionately from defense spending during the Second World War. Records indicate, however, that many housing tenants in a variety of projects did become defense workers during the course of the war; "City Housing Ends Limits on Incomes," *NYT*, 15 September 1944, 1. See, for instance, Roger Lotchin, *Fortress California* (Champaign: Illinois, 2002); David Goldfield, *Cotton Fields to Skyscrapers* (Baton Rouge: Louisiana, 1982).

40. "City Builds Homes for 2,943 Families," *NYT*, 2 February 1942, 17; Mayor La Guardia, Annual Message, reprinted in the *NYT*, 7 January 1943, 14; Mayor La Guardia, Annual Message, reprinted in the *NYT*, 6 January 1944, 14; NYCHA, Annual Report, Draft, March 1947, Box 66A1, Folder 17, NYCHAR, 7.

Chapter 3. High-Rise Public Housing Begins

1. "Construction and Cost Analysis, Large Scale Low Rent Housing," NYCHA Report by Voorhees, Walker, Foley and Smith, 26 November 1945, included with

Borgia Butler Correspondence, December 1945, Parks Commissioner Papers MA 107880, Roll 35.

2. John Taylor Bond, "Garden Apartments in Cities," reprinted from the *Architectural Record* by the City and Suburban Homes Company, New York, 1920, CHPC Archive, 28–45. Andrew Thomas, the architect, also designed garden apartments, to only a slightly higher standard, for the Queensboro Corporation in Jackson Heights. See also Frank Marsh, *Forty Profitable Years of Low Rent Housing, 1896–1936*, Federal Housing Administration, 1937, CHPC Archive.

3. "Huge Housing Plan Urged for Revival," *NYT*, 14 April 1932, 23.

4. Richard Plunz, *A History of Housing in New York City* (New York: Columbia, 1990), 167–69.

5. J. Schwartz, *The New York Approach*, 8, 34.

6. L. E. Cooper, "Plan Community Life in Bronx," *NYT*, 16 December 1934, RE1.

7. L. E. Cooper, "Plan Community Life in Bronx," *NYT*, 16 December 1934, RE1; "Housing Too Elaborate, *NYT*, 16 November 1934, 22. The estimate on costs is from J. Schwartz, *The New York Approach*, 8, 34.

8. James Ford, "New York Resurveys Her Vast Housing Needs," *NYT Magazine*, 24 January 1937, 8.

9. Richard Pommer, "The Architecture of Urban Housing in the United States during the Early 1930s," *The Journal of the Society of Architectural Historians* 37, no. 4 (December 1978): 249.

10. NYCHA Minutes, 27 February 1935, Box 78A2, Folder 8. NYCHAR. See, for example, "Brooklyn Urges Rehabilitation of Old Housing," *Herald Tribune*, 5 June 1938, 6.

11. "Some Facts about Harlem River House and First Houses," 30 September 1938, Box 53E2, Folder 11, NYCHAR; Rachel Swarns, "60 Years Later and Still a Success," *NYT*, 18 December 1995, B1.

12. "City Built Homes Will Open Dec. 3," *NYT*, 21 November 1935, 3. Modernists such as Walter Gropius shared the belief that aesthetics should be secondary to light, air, heat, and privacy. See Walter Gropius, "Minimum Dwellings and Tall Buildings," in the catalog for the Housing Exhibition, *America Can't Have Housing*, Museum of Modern Art (1934), CHPC Archive, 41.

13. "Real Slum Clearance," *NYT*, 19 January 1935, 12.

14. "WPA Men Stoned by Union Strikers," *NYT*, 14 September 1935, 1; "City Built Homes Will Open Dec. 3," *NYT*, 21 November 1935, 3.

15. "WPA Men Stoned by Union Strikers," *NYT*, 14 September 1935, 1.

16. H. I. Feldman, "Slum Rehabilitation," *NYT*, 28 September 1935, 14.

17. Richard Plunz, *A History of Housing in New York City*, 209–10. See also Langdon Post to Harold Kellogg, 17 March 1936, Box 53C2, Folder 14, NYCHAR; "Costly Public Housing," *NYT*, 26 September 1936, 14; "First Houses Cost Defended by Post," *NYT*, 26 September 1936, 5.

18. "The Faithful Debtor," *NYT*, 4 December 1935, 22; "Vast Housing Plan Envisaged for City," *NYT*, 8 December 1935, 10.

19. "F. L. Ackerman, 71, Long an Architect," *NYT*, 18 March 1950, 13; Langdon Post, "First Steps in New York Housing," article for *Housing Magazine*, 1934, Box 53A5, Folder 24, NYCHA Papers, (LWA), 2, 4. Ackerman favored comprehensively planned communities and had led the division of Housing and Town Planning Design of the United States Shipping Board (which built the first and perhaps best American government housing during World War I); worked with Henry Wright and Clarence Stein on both Sunnyside and Radburn; and was a longtime member of the Regional Planning Association. World War I housing is

explored in Erik Karolak, "No Idea of Doing Anything Wonderful," in *From Tenements to the Taylor Homes*, ed. Roger Biles and John Bauman et al. (University Park: Penn State, 2000), 60–80. For details on Ackerman, see Edward K. Spann, *Designing Modern America: The Regional Planning Association of America and Its Members* (Columbus: Ohio State, 1996).

20. Spann, *Designing Modern America, 176*; Langdon Post to H. A. Gray, FERA, 24 November 1936, Box 78A4, Folder 4, NYCHAR. For the complex relationship of the NYCHA, the federal government, and architects, see "Re: Architect's Agreement," 18 February 1935, Box 78A7, Folder 9, NYCHAR, and NYCHA Minutes, 27 February 1935, Box 78A7, Folder 9. NYCHA shifted to two-man architectural teams in the early 1940s. See William Vladeck to Robert Weinberg, 14 November 1941, Box 68A7, Folder 4, NYCHAR. See also New York City Housing Authority, *Toward the End to Be Achieved*, 10; "Model Housing in Harlem," *NYT*, 23 May 1935, 27.

21. Richard Pommer, "The Architecture of Urban Housing in the United States during the Early 1930s," 255; Richard Plunz, *A History of Housing in New York City*, 214–216

22. Radford, *Modern Housing for America*, 163–64, 170–71.

23. "New Standard in Harlem Housing Is Set by Clinic and Amphitheatre," *NYT*, 14 June 1936, section 2, 1.

24. Genevro, "Site Selection and the New York City Housing Authority, 1934–1939," 345; "Physical Features of the Harlem River Houses," Box 53E2, Folder 11, circa 1938, NYCHAR, 1; apartments per hallway quotation from Marcuse, "The Beginnings of Public Housing in New York," 372.

25. Management Division, "Income Study of 4,832 Applications for Apartments," circa 1936, Box 78A7, Folder 3, NYCHAR.

26. Henry Lee Moon, "Housing Problem Is Still Acute in Harlem," *NYT*, 20 June 1937, 10.

27. "East Harlem's Future," *NYT*, 16 June 1937, 22.

28. "City as Landlord Hailed in Harlem," *NYT*, 17 June 1937, 25. See also "Lease Is Approved on Harlem Housing," *NYT*, 19 May 1937, 25; "Low Rents Sought on Projects Here," *NYT*, 19 November 1936, 18; H. A. Gray to Langdon Post, 17 November 1936, Box 78A4, Folder 4, NYCHAR; NYCHA Minutes, 14 December 1936, Box 78A4, Folder 1, NYCHAR; NYCHA Board Minutes, 6 October 1936, Box 78A4, Folder 1, NYCHAR; "Memorandum on the Terms . . . ," 8 October 1936, Box 78A4, Folder 4, NYCHAR.

29. An exhibition by the WPA and NYCHA at Rockefeller Center in 1936, in a series of models and presentations, made the case that public housing like Williamsburg represented the answer to a long tradition of building innovation designed to improve access to air and light in the city. See "Realty Follies Shown in Exhibit," *NYT*, 10 October 1936, section 2, 10.

30. Pommer, "The Architecture of Urban Housing in the United States during the Early 1930s," 249; Christopher Gray, "A $35 Million Fix for a 1938 Complex," NYT, 9 May 1993, R7. Gray also notes that the complex was poorly constructed and thus has had serious water damage over the years.

31. Plunz, *A History of Housing in New York City*, 216–23. Catherine Bauer in *Modern Housing* provides a clear description of the development of superblock planning, 176–87; William Lescaze, "Public Housing Praised," *NYT*, 24 October 1958, 32; Pommer, "The Architecture of Urban Housing in the United States during the Early 1930s," 249.

32. Walter Gropius, "Minimum Dwellings and Tall Buildings," in the catalog

for the Housing Exhibition, *America Can't Have Housing*, Museum of Modern Art (1934), CHPC Archive, 42; Catherine Bauer, "Large Scale Housing," reprint from *Architectural Record*, 1941, CHPC Archive, 97.

33. "Brooklyn Picked for Model Housing," *NYT*, 16 May 1934, 21. Although not a dense slum, the Williamsburg site ended up costing "$4.20 per square foot—more than 15 percent over the average assessed valuation." Genevro, "Site Selection and the New York City Housing Authority, 1934–1939," 341–42, 344.

34. Evans Clark to Wilfred Lewis, 26 October 1936, Box 78A4, Folder 4, NYCHAR; "City Housing Costs Cut by New Design," *NYT*, 23 April 1938, 17; Editorial, "Government's Absurd Worship of a Low Density Fetish Defeats Public Housing," *News and Opinion*, published by the Building Trades Employers Association, 6 February 1939, Box 54A3, Folder 11, NYCHAR. The Harlem River figure is from Plunz, *A History of Housing in New York City*, 236.

35. "10 Year Program of Housing Urged," *NYT*, 21 October 1937, 19. See also "Ickes Signs Lease on Williamsburg Housing," NYT, 29 August 1937, 6; "Funds Earmarked for Housing Plans," *NYT*, 9 December 1937, 1. This article details the assumption of PWA housing by the USHA and the necessity of essentially the "writing off" of all the Treasury loans (55 percent of $134 million spent) in order to maintain low rents.

36. Richard Davis, Proceedings of the Committee on New Housing, Citizens' Housing Council of New York, 14 March 1938, 20; H. I. Feldman, "Housing Problem Complex," *NYT*, 3 March 1937, 22; Louis Pink, *A New Day in Housing* (New York: John Day, 1928), 62. See also Rodgers, *Atlantic Crossings*, 384–85. See Bauer, *Modern Housing* for detailed descriptions of the relationship between costs and rents in European public housing (195–209); and Ian Cole and Robert Furbey, *The Eclipse of Council Housing* (London: Routledge, 1994), 52–57.

37. Plunz, *A History of Housing in New York City*, 236; Address by Alfred Rheinstein, Hotel Astor, 27 October 1938, Box 53E7, Folder 7, NYCHAR.

38. "City Forced to Cut Housing Plan 66%," *NYT*, 13 February 1938, 31; "Additional Federal Money Earmarked," *NYT*, 8 April 1938, 2.

39. Mr. Luther Bell, NYCHA Publicity, 28 November 1938, Box 53E3, Folder 3. NYCHAR.

40. Land cost estimates are from "Mr. Moses' Plan Criticized," *NYT*, 3 December 1938, 18.

41. Frederick L. Ackerman, "Memorandum on 'Density,'" 28 January 1938, La Guardia Papers, Roll 93, MA.

42. CHC Report, "Functions and Analysis," October 1941, Box 54D5, Folder 8, NYCHAR, 29.

43. Pommer, "The Architecture of Urban Housing in the United States during the Early 1930s," 256; Plunz, *A History of Housing in New York City*, 237–39. On elevators, see also May Lumsden, "Speech for WVFW," 24 January 1939, Box 54A3, Folder 8, NYCHAR.

44. "Super-Block Plan Favored by City," *NYT*, 15 January 1939, 13.

45. Editorial, "Government's Absurd Worship of a Low Density Fetish Defeats Public Housing," *News and Opinion*, published by the Building Trades Employers Association, 6 February 1939, Box 54A3, Folder 11, NYCHAR.

46. Address by Alfred Rheinstein, Hotel Astor, 27 October 1938, Box 53E7, Folder 7, NYCHAR.

47. "Red Hook Houses to be of 6 Stories," *NYT*, 21 February 1938, 21. See also "New York Meets Housing Terms," *NYT*, 6 March 1938, 1; "Red Hook's Houses," *NYT*, 13 November 1938, 8; Charles Yale Harrison, Press Release,

NYCHA, circa 1939, Box 53E7, Folder 2, NYCHAR, 2; "Tenants View the NYCHA," City Wide Tenants Council, 3 December 1941, Box 57E2, Folder 4, NYCHAR, 14. See also Third Annual Convention, City Wide Tenants Council, 25 May 1941, Box 54D5, Folder 9. NYCHAR. Not including closet doors came to be seen as a particularly good way to cut costs because the total of ten thousand closets at Queensbridge and Red Hook left without doors would save $250,000 and allow for extra apartments to be built. See Lee Cooper, "Public Housing Projects," *NYT*, 14 May 1938, 28.

48. Land cost estimates are from "Mr. Moses' Plan Criticized," *NYT*, 3 December 1938, 18.

49. "City Housing Costs Cut by New Design," *NYT*, 23 April 1938, 17; Editorial, "Government's Absurd Worship of a Low Density Fetish Defeats Public Housing," *News and Opinion*, published by the Building Trades Employers Association, 6 February 1939, Box 54A3, Folder 11, NYCHAR.

50. Pommer, "The Architecture of Urban Housing in the United States during the Early 1930s," 256. See also Plunz, *A History of Housing in New York City*, 240. Philadelphia and other cities also cut their USHA projects to the bone. Unlike New York, they proved unequal to the task of maintaining their projects. See Bauman, *Public Housing, Race, and Renewal*, 50–52.

51. "Housing in Queens Opens Next Month," *NYT*, 26 September 1939, 25. See also "Mayor Announces New Slum Housing to Cost 19,500,000," *NYT*, 2 November 1938, 1; "Mayor Hails Work on Vladeck Homes," *NYT*, 23 November 1939, 25. Land cost estimates are from "Mr. Moses' Plan Criticized," *NYT*, 3 December 1938, 18. See also Ann Buttenweiser, "Shelter for What and for Whom? On the Route Toward Vladeck Houses, 1930 to 1940," *Journal of Urban History* 12, no. 4 (August 1986): 394–95, 402.

52. NYCHA Board Minutes, 18 April 1940, Box 78B4, Folder 5, NYCHAR, 974.

53. "A Report," NYCHA, 1946, Box 98D1, Folder 6, NYCHAR; Office of the Secretary, Minutes, Resolution 274, 29 February 1940, Box 78B4, Folder 3, NYCHAR, 779; Bauer, *Modern Housing*, 183. See also "Housing Project in 1st Ave Started," *NYT*, 3 March 1940, 14.

54. Pommer argues, convincingly, that Queensbridge's "pragmatic" designs based on cost savings were not directly influenced by modernist models but were nevertheless "analogous to towers developed by Le Corbusier in the 1930s, and the taller towers and lower site coverage began to fulfill his earlier visions." Pommer, "The Architecture of Urban Housing in the United States during the Early 1930s," 256. Sir Raymond Unwin praised the multi-block projects of the 1930s in the United States as well. See Lee Cooper, "Large-Scale Housing Projects Give Hope of Better Town-Planning in the Future," *NYT*, 14 July 1938, 37.

55. Bauer, *Modern Housing*, 193.

56. F. L. Ackerman to Alfred Rheinstein, 26 September 1939, Box 54A3, Folder 3, NYCHAR.

57. Plunz, *A History of Housing in New York City*, 245.

58. Robert Moses to Allan Harrison, 12 July 1940, NYC Parks, Robert Moses Papers, MN 22703, Roll 3, MA.

59. Stanley Isaacs to Gerard Swope, 7 March 1941, Box 54D7, Folder 5, NYCHAR.

60. The Navy Yard project (known first as Fort Greene, now Ingersoll and Walt Whitman) became the largest project in the city and was designated to replace "one of the 'worst blighted' slum districts in the city." It would cover only 23.7

percent of the land through a mix of six- and nine-story buildings in the initial plan. See "Vast Housing Unit Approved for City," *NYT*, 1 February 1940, 1.

61. Catherine Lansing, "Fort Greene Houses," 20 September 1943, 56E1, Folder 7, NYCHAR.

62. Interview of Robert Podmore, NYCHA deputy general manager, by the author, 19 July 2006.

63. "Cutting Housing Costs," *NYT*, 28 April 1938, 22.

64. Lee Cooper, "Public Housing Projects . . . ," *NYT*, 14 May 1938, 28.

65. Lubove, *The Progressives and the Slums*, 191. See also Elizabeth Blackmar and Roy Rosenzweig, *The Park and the People: A History of Central Park* (Ithaca, N.Y.: Cornell, 1998); Paul S. Boyer, *Urban Masses and Moral Order in America, 1820–1920* (Cambridge, Mass.: Harvard, 1978); and Thomas Bender, *Toward an Urban Vision: Ideas and Institutions in Nineteenth-Century America* (Baltimore: Johns Hopkins, 1982).

66. See Ballon and Jackson, eds., *Robert Moses and the Modern City*.

67. Catherine Lansing, Daily Report, 21 May 1935, Box 56E1, Folder 4, NYCHAR.

68. Meeting No. 1 Minutes, Advisory Committee on Architecture and Design, 27 November 1964, Box 71C7, Folder 8, NYCHAR.

69. Interview of Leonard Hopper by the author, 29 December 2005.

70. Alfred Rheinstein and Henry Pringle, "Why Slum Clearance May Fail," Undated, Box 54A3, Folder 8, NYCHAR, 5.

71. Alfred Rheinstein, Speech to the City Gardens Club, 6 December 1938, Box 53E7, Folder 7, NYCHAR.

72. "Landscaping in Public Housing," New York City Housing Authority News, 15 October 1942, no box provided, NYCHAR.

73. Mrs. Lumsden and Miss Lansing to Alfred Rheinstein, 5 December 1938, Box 53E3, Folder 14, NYCHAR.

74. Minutes, Board of Estimate, 19 June 1941, NYC Parks, Robert Moses Papers, MN 22814, Roll 14, MA.

75. Robert Moses to Gerard Swope, 18 June 1940, Box 54D2, Folder 18, NYCHAR. See also "Moses Asks Rise in Play Area Fund," *NYT*, 28 October 1938, 9; Mrs. Lumsden to Alfred Rheinstein, 5 December 1938, Box 53E3, Folder 14, NYCHAR for the authority's defense of its park provisions.

76. Robert Moses to George Sokolsky, 3 September 1948, Box 69E4, Folder 7, NYCHAR, 2.

77. Allan Harrison to Gerard Swope, 14 June 1940, Box 54D2, Folder 18, NYCHAR. Clarke and Rapuano also designed the landscapes at Eastchester Houses. See "Apartment Plans Ready," *NYT*, 8 February 1948, 5.

78. Spargo to Moses, 2 December 1941, NYC Parks, Robert Moses Papers, MN 22814, Roll 14, MA.

79. NYCHA, "Our Community Planning Process," 20 February 1945, Box 78C6, Folder 10, NYCHAR.

80. A. J. Moffat to Catherine Lansing, "Experimental Structure for Playgrounds at Red Hook Houses," Box 69D6, Folder 1, NYCHAR.

81. See Catherine Mackenzie, "Sewer Pipe Is the Latest in 'Playthings,'" *NYT*, 18 September 1944, 15; "The Red Hook Dodger," *Newsweek*, 9 October 1944, 80; J. J. Spoon to John Riley, 18 June 1945, Box 57D3, Folder 25, NYCHAR; John Riley to Catherine Lansing, 4 September 1945, Box 57D3, Folder 25, NYCHAR.

82. Report on Observation of Experimental Playground at Fort Greene Houses, 18 July 1944, Box 69D6, Folder 1, NYCHAR.

83. See, for instance, Arnold Hirsch, "Less than *Plessy*: The Inner City, Suburbs, and State Sanctioned Segregation in the Age of Brown," in *The New Suburban History*, ed. Kevin Kruse and Thomas Sugrue, 33–56 (Chicago: Chicago, 2006). See also Hirsch, *Making the Second Ghetto*; Hunt, "What Went Wrong with Public Housing in Chicago?"; Biles and Bauman et al., *From Tenements to the Taylor Homes*; Von Hoffman, "The End of the Dream," 222–53.

84. In the early 1930s, the influential New York City Slum Clearance Committee (SCC) aimed to substitute "Lower East Side tenements with high-quality housing that few tenement dwellers could afford." It hoped that slum clearance below 96th Street in Manhattan, primarily for park space, would jumpstart private redevelopment. The historian Joel Schwartz found that public housing advocates at the SCC "gravitated toward outerborough sites, such as Greenpoint and Red Hook in Brooklyn and the Queens waterfront. It eventually settled on the dilapidated, wood-framed dwellings of Williamsburg" even if this area was by no means considered the most in need of redevelopment. J. Schwartz, *The New York Approach*, 36–38, 59. See also Albert Mayer, "Attacking the City's Slum Problem: A New Approach," *NYT*, 18 February 1934, section 8, 3. Rosalie Genevro affirms business interest in redeveloping center-city slums, even if up-front costs would be higher, because such interests worried about loss of their own values and added municipal costs for the future. See Genevro, "Site Selection and the New York City Housing Authority, 1934–1939," 334–52.

85. Langdon Post, Radio Address, WHN, 25 April 1935, Box 53A7, Folder 32, NYCHAR; J. Schwartz, *The New York Approach*, 42. For Post's frustration on Manhattan slum clearance, see Langdon Post, Speech, First Washington Conference on Public Housing, National Public Housing Conference, 1934, Box 66A5, Folder 9, NYCHAR, 10.

86. "Housing Program Attacked by Post," *NYT*, 11 March 1935, 33. The scale of Post's plans can be seen in Roland Wood, "Vast Housing Plan Envisaged for City," *NYT*, 8 December 1935, E10. Post's ideals parallel those of Catherine Bauer, who also believed vast peripheral public housing projects could be used to reset the entire housing market. See Bauer, *Modern Housing*, 245. The explosiveness of Post's formulation could be revealed in subtle ways. By 1943, for instance, the Real Estate Board of New York could argue that high vacancy rates in Manhattan's tenement districts could partly be linked to "the presence of low-rent public housing facilities in this and other boroughs." See "Realty Board Reports Sharp Increase in Vacancies," *NYT*, 17 March 1943, 33.

87. Genevro, "Site Selection and the New York City Housing Authority, 1934–1939," 341–42, 344; Radford, *Modern Housing for America*, 99–103. Radford notes that the fifty-one PWA projects were about evenly split between slum clearance and vacant land projects. The 50/50 estimate is from Hunt, "What Went Wrong with Public Housing in Chicago?," 34. Kohn, together with Ackerman, had led the creation of garden-city-style, primarily single-family home communities as part of the United States Shipping Board defense housing program. The summary of Kohn's career can be found in Spann, *Designing Modern America*, 13–15.

88. NYCHA Board Minutes, 2 October 1934, Box 78A2, Folder 2, 94, NYCHAR.

89. "Housing Conditions in Relation to the Williamsburg Project," 13 May 1937, Box 56D3, Folder 3, NYCHAR; NYCHA Board Minutes, 2 October 1934, Box 78A2, Folder 2, 94, NYCHAR.

90. "City Speeds Plans for Harlem Homes," *NYT*, 4 July 1935, 17; "Harlem Housing Plan Decried as 'Unsound,'" *NYT*, 7 July 1935, section 2, 4.

91. J. Schwartz, *The New York Approach,* 46.

92. Lee Cooper, "Public Housing Projects . . . ," *NYT,* 14 May 1938, 28; Edith Evans to James Kieran, 8 December 1939, La Guardia Papers, Roll 92A, MA; population density figures are from Alfred Rheinstein to Warren Vinton, 24 December 1937, Box 54A3, Folder 16, NYCHAR.

93. Robert Moses, "The End of Santa Claus," *Saturday Evening Post,* 27 July 1936, Robert Moses File, CHPC Archive, 32.

94. Chelsea Association for Planning and Action, Charles Lane Jr., chairman of the Housing Committee, and Dr. John Lovejoy Elliott, circa 1938, Robert Moses Papers, MN 22813, Roll 13, Parks Department, MA.

95. "Vast Housing Plan Urged by Straus as a City Project," *NYT,* 21 October 1935, 1. See also Andrzej Olechnowicz, *Working Class Housing in England Between the Wars: The Becontree Estate* (Oxford: Clarendon, 1997) for controversies in England surrounding Becontree. By no means was it necessarily considered to be a great success because it concentrated the working class, provided few social amenities, and was uniform in appearance.

96. J. Schwartz, *The New York Approach,* 31. See also, for instance, Albert Mayer, "Slum Clearance—But How?" *The New Republic,* 14 February 1934, 7. Progressive-era reformers as part of the New York Congestion Commission had also hoped to decentralize population using tools such as zoning for lower densities, subsidized mass transportation, and even farm schools that would "deflect immigrants from the congested industrial cities." Lubove, *The Progressives and the Slums,* 233. The Regional Plan Association "advocated decentralization" and preferred low-rise public housing intermixed with market-rate housing in Radburn-style superblocks. Genevro, "Site Selection and the New York City Housing Authority, 1934–1939," 339. See also Spann, *Designing Modern America,* 136.

97. Bauer, *Modern Housing,* 168–69.

98. Rodgers, *Atlantic Crossings,* 185; Nathan Straus to Alfred Rheinstein, 20 July 1938, Roll 94, La Guardia Papers, MA; "Housing Curb Seen in Land Price Limit," *NYT,* 20 October 1938, 25. The reference to weak slum clearance requirements is from Hunt, "What Went Wrong with Public Housing in Chicago?," 43.

99. Alfred Rheinstein to Fiorello La Guardia, 24 June 1938, Box 54A3, Folder 16, NYCHAR.

100. "Housing Curb Seen in Land Price Limit," *NYT,* 20 October 1938, 25; "Housing in Queens Opens Next Month," *NYT,* 26 September 1939, 25. For Rheinstein's description of a refilling of the slums, see Alfred Rheinstein to Nathan Straus, 29 July 1938, La Guardia Papers, Roll 94, MA. For the growing acrimony between the NYCHA and the USHA, see Alfred Rheinstein to Fiorello La Guardia, 14 February 1938, Box 54A3, Folder 16, NYCHAR.

101. Alfred Rheinstein, Speech, 18 October 1938, Box 53E6, Folder 4, NYCHAR; "City Housing Need Placed at Billion," *NYT,* 26 April 1938, 14.

102. "Straus Is Assailed on Housing Plan," *NYT,* 6 January 1938, 2. See also "Land Prices and Housing," *NYT,* 17 February 1938, 20 for Clark Dailey's support of central sites.

103. Alfred Rheinstein to Louis Pink, 29 August 1938, La Guardia Papers, Roll 93, MA.

104. Charles Yale Harrison, Press Release, circa 1938, Box 53E7, Folder 2, NYCHAR, 2.

105. Press Release, City of New York, 21 November 1938, La Guardia Papers, Roll 93, MA.

106. "Victory for Housing," *NYT*, 3 November 1938, 22. See also "Mayor Announces New Slum Housing to Cost $19,500,000," *NYT*, 2 November 1938, 1; "Housing and Slum Clearance," *NYT*, 18 October 1938, 24.

107. "Mayor Announces New Slum Housing to Cost 19,500,000," *NYT*, 2 November 1938, 1; "Mayor Hails Work on Vladeck Homes," *NYT*, 23 November 1939, 25.

108. "Housing in Queens Opens Next Month," *NYT*, 26 September 1939, 25.

109. "Rheinstein Quits, Charging Straus Blocks Projects," *NYT*, 9 October 1939, 1. See also "Civic Groups Urge Rheinstein Be Kept," *NYT*, 10 October 1939, 1; "Straus Approves Disputed Project," *NYT*, 13 October 1939, 25; "Rheinstein Denies Row with Mayor," *NYT*, 12 October 1939, 23. Alfred Rheinstein and Henry Pringle, "Why Slum Clearance May Fail," *Harper's* (October 1939): 520–26; "8,390,000 Lent City for More Housing," *NYT*, 16 December 1938, 9.

110. "Housing Project in 1st Ave. Started," *NYT*, 3 March 1940, 14.

111. Nathan Straus, Dedication Address, Box 54D5, Folder 10, 1941, NYCHAR; Mayor's Housing Conference, 6 January 1964, Box 68C4, Folder 2, NYCHAR, 3.

112. F. M. Didisheim to Gerard Swope, 29 December 1939, Box 54D1, Folder 2, NYCHAR. The South Jamaica site could be considered a very low-density slum.

113. NYCHA Meeting with CHC, 20 November 1941, Box 54D5, Folder 8, NYCHAR.

114. "City Will Remove 15,000 Slum Units for Housing Sites," *NYT*, 8 April 1945, sections 8–9, 1; "Housing Authority to Pay Higher Tax," *NYT*, 29 May 1945, 17; "Popular Home Types," *NYT*, 22 September 1940, RE4. The two-story projects of Clason Point and Edwin Markham Houses are representative of a very brief period of low-scale decentralization. See "One Family Houses with Individual Yards Included in Clason Point Housing Project," *NYT*, 21 October 1940, 19. See also "Straus Forecasts New Housing Era," *NYT*, 3 February 1939, 17; "City Takes Land for Edwin Markham Houses," *NYT*, 4 March 1942, 35; Maxwell Tretter, "New York's Public Housing Not All Tenements," *American City* (August 1943): 61.

Chapter 4. Model Tenants for Model Housing

1. Catherine Mackenzie, "120 'First' Families Get New Homes," *NYT*, 1 December 1935, section 4, 1.

2. Quoted in Marcuse, *Public Housing in New York City*, 49.

3. Rodgers, *Atlantic Crossings*, 188, 191, 385, 475. In the interwar years, "Council Housing was not an instrument of social justice," according to Andrzej Olechnowicz, *Working Class Housing in England between the Wars: The Becontree Estate* (Oxford: Clarendon, 1997), 71. The ability to pay the rent mattered the most in determining who among the needy would be rehoused; in fact, "the neediest probably never applied in the first place, knowing that their cause was hopeless."

4. Carol Aronovici and Elizabeth McCalmont, *Catching Up with Housing* (Newark: Beneficial Management, 1936), CHPC Archive, 165.

5. "Renting Office Opens for Housing Project," *NYT*, 17 January 1935, 21; "3,000 Seek Model Flats; Requests to Be Halted," *NYT*, 8 March 1935, 40. See also "1,000 Families Seeking Remodeled Av. A Suites," *NYT*, 2 February 1935, 27.

6. May Lumsden to Langdon Post, "Management of Federal-Aid Projects," 14 March 1935, Box 53B6, Folder 2, NYCHAR; "The End to Be Achieved: An Outline History of NYCHA," 1937, Box 53D5, Folder 11, NYCHAR, 10.

7. May Lumsden to Langdon Post, "Selection of Tenants," 29 March 1935, Box 53B3, Folder 7, NYCHAR.

8. "Housing Specialist Hailed for Record," *NYT*, 24 October 1937, section 6, 6; "The End to Be Achieved: An Outline History of NYCHA," 1937, Box 53D5, Folder 11, NYCHAR, 10. See also Beatrice Rosahn and Abraham Goldfield, *Housing Management: Principles and Practices* (New York: Covici, 1937), 37.

9. Catherine Lansing and May Lumsden, Annual Report, 28 October 1935, Box 53B6, Folder 3, NYCHAR, 9–10. See, for instance, May Lumsden, "Reasons for Rejection of Application of Joseph Rand," 4 October 1935, Box 53B6, Folder 6, NYCHAR.

10. "Statistics on Tenants," NYCHA, 7 October 1935, Box 53B3, Folder 7, NYCHAR; Catherine Lansing, Daily Report, 19 August 1935, Box 56E1, Folder 4, NYCHAR.

11. "Report Shows Poor Families Not Desirable," *Amsterdam News*, 1 February 1936, Box 53C1, Folder 8, NYCHAR.

12. "Would Pick Tenants by Point System," *NYT*, 29 January 1935, 14.

13. "Report of the Committee on the Selection of Tenants to the Harlem Housing Committee," 20 November 1935, Box 55D5, Folder 2, NYCHAR. Joel Schwartz documents an important role of tenant unions and other radicals in attracting more applications and pacifying opposition to slum clearance at the local level. Some representatives of local tenant unions also served on local committees created by the authority. See Joel Schwartz, "Tenant Unions in New York City's Low-Rent Housing, 1933–1949," *Journal of Urban History* 12, no. 4 (August 1986): 422–23.

14. "11,500 Seek, 574 Get Model Apartments," *NYT*, 19 August 1937, 21.

15. "7,500 Seek Homes in Ten Eyck Center," *NYT*, 14 April 1936, 23.

16. May Lumsden to Gerard Swope, 9 December 1940, Box 54D2, Folder 7, NYCHAR; "First Homes' Rent Always Is on Time," *NYT*, 20 February 1936, section 2, 2; "Housing Specialist Hailed for Record," *NYT*, 24 October 1937, section 6, 6.

17. Harry Ellis to Alfred Rheinstein, 16 July 1938, Box 71B5, Folder 3, NYCHAR.

18. May Lumsden, "Housing Management and Family Life: Tenant Selection," circa 1937, Box 70D6, Folder 2, NYCHAR, 2.

19. May Lumsden, "Memorandum, Tenant Selection," 6 November 1937, Box 70D6, Folder 2, NYCHAR.

20. Alfred Rheinstein, Speech Typescript, 1938, Box 53E7, Folder 6, NYCHAR.

21. "Model Homes Face a Tenant Problem," *NYT*, 11 June 1938, 17.

22. May Lumsden, Press Release, 1 February 1939, Box 54A3, Folder 8, NYCHAR, 4.

23. "City Housing Aims Held Not Realized," *NYT*, 6 June 1938, 19.

24. NYCHA, Annual Report, 1938, Selections of Tenants for Housing Developments," 23 February 1939, Box 70D6, Folder 2, NYCHAR; "City Will Erect $22,000,000 Housing in Navy Yard Area," *NYT*, 22 November 1939, 1.

25. May Lumsden to Nathan Straus, 24 May 1939, Box 70D6, Folder 2, NYCHAR.

26. Radford, *Modern Housing in America*, 97–98, 108.

27. NYCHA, Secretary Minutes, 14 March 1940, Box 78B4, Folder 3, NYCHAR, 804; "F.D.R. Asked to Intervene in Housing Row," *Brooklyn Eagle*, 11 July 1939, Box 54B3, Folder 14; Nathan Straus to Alfred Rheinstein, RCA Radiogram, 23 June 1939, Box 54B3, Folder 13, NYCHAR; Alfred Rheinstein to Nathan Straus, 23 June 1939, Box 54B3, Folder 13, NYCHAR.

28. "Federal Housing Rule Bars 30 Families," *NYT*, 30 June 1939, 21. See also "Rheinstein Seeks Housing Change," *NYT*, 22 July 1939, 17.

29. Interview of Alfred Rheinstein, Radio WNYC, 11 August 1939, Box 54B4, Folder 14, NYCHAR.

30. NYCHA Comments on Straus Letter, 7 August 1939, Box 59C2, Folder 10, NYCHAR.

31. NYCHA Resolution, 1939, La Guardia Papers, Roll 93, Item 2648, MA.

32. "Huge Housing Unit in Red Hook Opened," *NYT*, 5 July 1939, 1.

33. "A Handicap for Housing," *NYT*, 6 July 1939, 22.

34. Nathan Straus to NYCHA Administration, 10 July 1939, Box 70D6, Folder 2, NYCHAR; "Rheinstein Seeks Housing Change," *NYT*, 22 July 1939, 17.

35. Malcolm Logan, "Shall Housing for the Poor Go Begging?," *New York Post*, 1 August 1939, Box 71E5, Folder 9, NYCHAR; "City Poor Rush in Droves to Ask Red Hook Homes," 4 August 1939, Box 71E5, Folder 9, NYCHAR; Alfred Rheinstein to Fiorello La Guardia, 20 August 1939, Box 71E5, Folder 9, NYCHAR; figures are from NYCHA, "Summary of Investigation," August 1939, Box 71E5, Folder 9, NYCHAR; Alfred Rheinstein to Fiorello La Guardia, 22 August 1939, Box 54B3, Folder 13, NYCHAR.

36. "F.D.R. Asked to Intervene in Housing Row," *Brooklyn Eagle*, 11 July 1939, Box 54B3, Folder 14, NYCHAR; "Income Rule Eased for Housing in City," *NYT*, 11 September 1939, 1.

37. "From Slums to Sun," *NYT Magazine*, 28 April 1940, section 7, 12.

38. F.M. Didisheim to Gerard Swope, 29 December 1939, Box 54D1, Folder 2, NYCHAR.

39. "Housing Projects Ease Restrictions," *NYT*, 12 April 1940, 42.

40. See also Minutes, 18 April 1940, Box 78B4, Folder 5, NYCHAR.

41. F. Didisheim to George Smith, 12 March 1941, Box 54D5, Folder 3, NYCHAR.

42. May Lumsden to Gerard Swope, 9 December 1940, Box 54D2, Folder 7, NYCHAR; Minutes, Pre-School Education Committee, 5 April 1940, Box 56E1, Folder 16, NYCHAR.

43. Dishonesty in tenant applications appeared to be an unintended byproduct of the Red Hook conflict. By early 1940, the authority may have received tens of thousands of additional applications, but of the 91,870 investigated it estimated that fully "64% of all investigated applicants may be expected to [be] found ineligible." Large numbers (22 percent) underreported income because of "extensive publicity" that encouraged applicants to report "incomes well below actual incomes." NYCHA, "Study of 91,870 Applications for Dwellings," 2 March 1940, Box 70E1, Folder 6, NYCHAR.

44. "14,000 Families Seek Low-Rent Housing," *NYT*, 22 January 1940, 27; NYCHA, Secretary Minutes, 14 March 1940, Box 78B4, Folder 3, NYCHAR, 804–09.

45. May Lumsden to Gerard Swope, 9 December 1940, Box 54D2, Folder 7, NYCHAR; "Housing Projects Ease Restrictions," *NYT*, 12 April 1940, 42; Albert Mayer, "So Far, So Good in Public Housing," *NYT*, 15 September 1940, 115.

46. "City Notes Rises in Its Tenants' Pay," *NYT*, 13 August 1941; Lee Cooper, "Higher Incomes Change Tenancy in City Housing," *NYT*, 1 November 1942, section 9, 1; "Housing Policy Draws Criticism," *NYT*, 20 September 1942, section 9, 8. See also Harold Buttenheim to Maxwell Tretter, 9 November 1943, Box 71E5, Folder 7, NYCHAR.

47. "Housing Authority Eases Rent Policy," *NYT*, 1 November 1942, 49; "Pre-

sent Housing of Former Project Tenants," 7 May 1943, Box 71E5, Folder 1, NY-CHAR; "Report of Income of Tenants in Permanent Housing," circa 1946, Box 63C6, Folder 8, NYCHAR.

48. "Report of Income of Tenants in Permanent Housing," circa 1946, Box 63C6, Folder 8, NYCHAR; Lee Cooper, "City Housing Ends Limit on Incomes," NYT, 15 September 1944, 1; "Service Men Get Priority," NYT, 2 November 1944, 31. Organized tenant pressure played an important role in this change. See J. Schwartz, "Tenant Unions in New York City's Low-Rent Housing, 1933–1949," 428–29. See also "City Housing Units Ease Income Curbs," NYT, 17 February 1944, 21.

49. "Report of Income of Tenants in Permanent Housing," circa 1946, Box 63C6, Folder 8, NYCHAR; Maxwell Tretter, Press Release, 15 January 1947, Box 59D4, Folder 1, NYCHAR; NYCHA, Report on Slum Clearance and Relocation, circa 1950, Box 68C2, Folder 1, NYCHAR, chapter 3, 2; NYCHA Annual Report, 1950, Box 98D1, Folder 11. See also Edmond Butler to Robert Moses, 18 December 1946, Box 69B2, Folder 3, NYCHAR. Large veteran families could even stay with incomes "seven or eight times the rent." James England, Press Release, 31 August 1947, Box 67C2, Folder 22, NYCHAR.

50. "Butler Explains Housing Evictions," NYT, 26 January 1947, 4.

51. "City Would Evict 600 Low-Renters," NYT, 1 March 1949, 28; "More Eviction Suits Planned by City Unit," NYT, 2 March 1949, 3.

52. "Better Housing, Better Living," NYCHA, 1960, Box 98D1, Folder 23, NY-CHAR. See also "Program of the Inter-Project Tenants Council of New York," 19 October 1949, O'Dwyer Papers, MN 47035, Roll 35, MA.

53. George Genung, acting director of management, to Robert Weaver, American Council on Race Relations, 1 May 1947, Box 71B5, Folder 3, NYCHAR.

54. Philip Cruise, "Interracial Housing Succeeds," Interracial Review, April 1955, Box 67E2, Folder 12, NYCHAR.

55. NYCHA, Secretary Minutes, 14 March 1940, Box 78B4, Folder 3, NYCHAR, 804–9.

56. "Mayor Denounces Gambling in State," NYT, 16 April 1940, 25. Gail Radford, in Modern Housing in America, 104–5, notes that the PWA, in order "to avoid white backlash" followed "pre-existing racial patterns of neighborhoods."

57. Walter White (NAACP) to Nathan Straus, 25 September 1939, Box 71B5, Folder 3, NYCHAR; Nathan Straus to Mr. E. R. Alexander, 20 October 1939, Box 71B5, Folder 3, NYCHAR; F. M. Didisheim to Mary Simkhovitch, 15 November 1939, Box 71B5, Folder 3, NYCHAR; John Egan to Allan Harrison, 21 November 1939, Box 71B5, Folder 3, NYCHAR; Mary Simkhovitch to James Hubert, 21 November 1939, Box 71B5, Folder 3, NYCHAR.

58. Grace Aviles to Gerard Swope, 23 September 1941, Box 54D5, Folder 9, NYCHAR; F. M. Didisheim to Gerard Swope, 29 December 1939, Box 54D1, Folder 2, NYCHAR.

59. Thomas Farrell, "Object Lesson in Race Relations," NYT, Schomburg Center Clipping File, 1925–1974, SC-Micro, F-1, FSN, Sc 002, 325–2, NYPL.

60. Harlem Advisory Committee Meeting with NYCHA Board, 6 November 1939, Box 56E1, Folder 11, NYCHAR. The population statistic is from Gonzalez, The Bronx, 99.

61. Vladeck to Swope, "Harlem Project," 9 October 1940, Box 54D2, Folder 8, NYCHAR; F. Didisheim to Mr. Swope, 25 September 1941, Box 54D8, Folder 11, NYCHAR. City-wide statistics are from Jackson, The Encyclopedia of New York City, 920.

62. "Negro Tenants in Housing Authority Projects," 23 March 1943, Box 71B5, Folder 3, NYCHAR; Naudin Oswell to May Lumsden, 12 April 1943, Box 71B5, Folder 3, NYCHAR.

63. Rose Robinson to Catherine Lansing, 17 September 1943, Box 70D6, Folder 2, NYCHAR.

64. Frank Dorman to May Lumsden, "Colored Applications and Tenancy," 24 September 1943, no box number, NYCHAR.

65. Mary Simkhovitch, Statement, 17 December 1945, Box A-97, Folder 62, Simkhovitch Papers, Schlesinger Library, 1.

66. Much has been written about public housing in Chicago, but Bradford Hunt's dissertation (and forthcoming book) "What Went Wrong with Public Housing in Chicago" provides the greatest number of points of contrast with the New York experience. Chicago, among American cities, most closely parallels New York in terms of the scale and style of public housing, yet its fate has been entirely different. Hunt downplays the CHA's institutional failings and stresses a more flexible housing market, the result of metropolitan decentralization, as the root cause of public housing's failure to keep working tenants. His dissertation provides such overwhelming evidence of incompetence, however, that it is hard to take a market argument seriously. Hunt, "What Went Wrong with Public Housing in Chicago?" Arnold R. Hirsch, in *Making the Second Ghetto*, primarily focuses on the political and social tensions that shaped the location and style of public housing in Chicago. J. S. Fuerst and Bradford Hunt have collected upbeat oral histories from the early years of the Chicago Housing Authority (1940–60) that they claim contrast with traditional portraits of public housing. In fact, almost all of the early projects were comparatively peaceful across the United States. J. S. Fuerst and Bradford Hunt, *When Public Housing Was Paradise: Building Community in Chicago* (Urbana: Illinois, 2005). Sudhir Alladi Venkatesh's *American Project: The Rise and Fall of a Modern Ghetto* (Cambridge, Mass.: Harvard, 2000) is primarily a bleak study of tenant life and activism in Chicago's projects after the breakdown in CHA management. Popkin and Gwiasda, *The Hidden War*, provide more grim descriptions of the breakdown in Chicago's public housing system. See also David Ranney and Patricia Wright, "Race, Class, and the Abuse of State Power: The Case of Public Housing in Chicago," *Sage Race Relations Abstracts* (Institute of Race Relations), no. 3 (2000): 3–32; Alex Kotlowitz, *There Are No Children Here* (New York: Anchor, 1992); Martin Meyerson and Edward Banfield, *Politics, Planning, and the Public Interest: The Case of Public Housing in Chicago* (Glencoe, Ill.: Free Press, 1955).

67. Hunt, "What Went Wrong with Public Housing in Chicago?" 175.

68. Ibid, 385, 383, 384, 386, 391.

69. Ibid, 14, 180, 132.

70. Mark Gelfand, *A Nation of Cities: The Federal Government and Urban America, 1933–1965* (New York: Oxford, 1975) cites Detroit and Los Angeles as having similar patterns of racial concentration by the 1950s that led to public housing being viewed as black housing.

Chapter 5. Tightly Managed Communities

1. Lubove, *The Progressives and the Slums*, 249.

2. NYCHA, Information on Kingsborough Houses, November 1941, La Guardia Papers, Roll 93, MA.

3. "End of Patronage in Housing Asked," *NYT,* 5 April 1938, 9; Interview of Betty Friedman by Marcia Robertson, 23 July 1990, NYCHA Oral History Project, NYCHAR, 4.

4. Gerard Swope to Fiorello La Guardia, 15 January 1942, Box 54E6, Folder 9, NYCHAR, 2.

5. See Memorandum, 14 February 1939, probably by Alfred Rheinstein, Box 54A5, Folder 1, NYCHAR; "Rheinstein Denies 'Spoils Era' Charge by City Commission," *New York World Telegram,* 24 May 1939, Box 54A4, Folder 1, NYCHAR; Paul Kern to Mayor La Guardia, 13 June 1939, Box 54A4, Folder 1, NYCHAR.

6. "Conditions of Tenancy, Project No. 1," 1935, Box 53B3, Folder 7, NYCHAR, 2.

7. Beatrice Rosahn and Abraham Goldfield, *Housing Management: Principles and Practices* (New York: Covici, 1937) provide detailed summaries of rent collection practices across the United States. Not one of the nine philanthropic or limited-dividend projects they chose to describe collected rent at the door.

8. Ibid., 3–11.

9. Ibid.

10. Carol Aronovici and Elizabeth McCalmont, *Catching Up with Housing* (Newark, N.J.: Beneficial Management, 1936), CHPC Archive, 140; Lubove, *The Progressives and the Slums,* 199, 201.

11. "Housing Specialist Hailed for Record," *NYT,* 24 October 1937, section 6, 6; May Lumsden, Memo, 3 September 1936, Box 57E2, Folder 3, NYCHAR, 3. Joel Schwartz documents that Lansing came from Christadora Settlement House and worked for the SCC in helping to identify the first sites for public housing; Lumsden was a "limited dividends veteran." See J. Schwartz, *The New York Approach,* 40. Betty Friedman also gives credit to a staff member named Gladys LaFetra, whom she says "to a large extent . . . brought in the Octavia Hill system." Interview of Betty Friedman by Marcia Robertson, 23 July 1990, NYCHA Oral History Project, Box 1, NYCHAR, 5.

12. May Lumsden, "Management of Public Housing," Address at the New School for Social Research, 15 December 1937, Box 53D4, Folder 11, NYCHAR, 4.

13. J. Schwartz, "Tenant Unions in New York City's Low-Rent Housing, 1933–1949," 420–21.

14. May Lumsden to Langdon Post, "Management of Federal-Aid Projects," 14 March 1935, Box 53B6, Folder 2, NYCHAR; Catherine Lansing, Weekly Reports, 5 April 1935, Box 56E1, Folder 4, NYCHAR, 1.

15. May Lumsden, "Management of Public Housing," Address at the New School for Social Research, 15 December 1937, Box 53D4, Folder 11, NYCHAR, 10; "New Leases for Living," *Better Times: The New York Social Work Review,* 9 December 1938, CHPC Archive, 7.

16. Interview of Henry Bresky by Marcia Roberston, 27 July 1990, NYCHA Oral History Project, Box 1, NYCHAR, 4; Interview of Betty Friedman by Marcia Robertson, 23 July 1990, NYCHA Oral History Project, NYCHAR, 5. However favored women may have been at this low level, they were discriminated against in higher managerial levels until at least the 1970s. See Interview of Betty Friedman by Marcia Robertson, 23 July 1990, NYCHA Oral History Project, Box 1, NYCHAR, for extensive details of problems with sex discrimination at the authority.

17. Interview of Henry Bresky by Marcia Roberston, 27 July 1990, NYCHA Oral History Project, Box 1, NYCHAR, 3–4. Bresky also calls this the Leeds Plan.

18. Catherine Lansing, Daily Report, 29 September 1942, Box 56E1, Folder 7,

NYCHAR; Catherine Lansing, Daily Report, 1 September 1942, Box 56E1, Folder 7, NYCHAR. See also Catherine Lansing, Daily Report, 8 October 1942, Box 56E1, Folder 7, NYCHAR.

19. May Lumsden, Press Release, 1 February 1939, Box 54A3, Folder 8, NYCHAR, 4.

20. Edward DesVerney to Alfred Rheinstein, 30 December 1937, Box 53D2, Folder 6, NYCHAR, 2; J. Schwartz, "Tenant Unions in New York City's Low-Rent Housing, 1933–1949," 427.

21. May Lumsden to Alfred Rheinstein, 8 April 1938, Box 56E2, Folder 10, NYCHAR. Phipps Garden Apartments, a philanthropic unit, also maintained a "very satisfactory" system of weekly door collection by women managers according to Lumsden. See May Lumsden, Daily Report, 15 April 1935, Box 56E1, Folder 4, NYCHAR. An acquaintance of May Lumsden, Harriet Shadd Butcher (of the Russell Sage Foundation), conducted a survey of European housing and brought back forms and so forth from Europe to share with authority staff, but the details are sketchy from the records. See, for instance, Catherine Lansing, Daily Report, 15 May 1935, Box 56E1, Folder 4, NYCHAR; Catherine Lansing, Daily Report, 16 August 1935, Box 56E1, Folder 4, NYCHAR.

22. NYCHA Board Minutes, 21 March 1940, Box 78B4, Folder 4, NYCHAR, 914; Catherine Lansing, Daily Report, 1 September 1942, Box 56E1, Folder 7, NYCHAR; May Lumsden to Gerard Swope, "Rent Collection," 26 November 1940, Box 54D2, Folder 7, NYCHAR, 1–8.

23. "Prologue to Public Housing," circa 1944, Information Division, Box 57D7, Folder 7, NYCHAR; Memo, NYCHA, 7 November 1946, Box 71B7, Folder 3, NYCHAR. A mention is made in 1943 that tenants only paid their rent at the office after the first year as late as 1943. See "Management and Operation," 1943, Box 57D3, Folder 10, NYCHAR.

24. Harold Buttenheim to Gerard Swope, 17 March 1941, Box 57E2, Folder 4, NYCHAR.

25. "Tenants View the NYCHA," City-Wide Tenants Council, 3 December 1941, Box 57E2, Folder 4, NYCHAR, 7.

26. Rodgers, *Atlantic Crossings*, 385. See also Bauer, *Modern Housing*, 162–66.

27. Frederick Ackerman to Langdon Post, 28 April 1937, Box 53C8, Folder 5, NYCHAR, 1.

28. "Housing 'Utopias' Called Needless," *NYT*, 5 May 1949, 20.

29. Alfred Rheinstein, Speech Typescript, 1938, Box 53E7, Folder 6, NYCHAR.

30. A comprehensive look at bars in idealized planning schemes needs to be undertaken. Public housing, new towns, university plans, and other reformed models of community life have been notable for seeking control of public drinking and replacing it with more wholesome activities. See, for instance, Nicholas Dagen Bloom, *Suburban Alchemy: 1960s New Towns and the Transformation of the American Dream* (Columbus: Ohio State, 2001). See also Lubove, *The Progressives and the Slums*, 191.

31. "The New York City Housing Authority Tenant Programs Come of Age," 1976, Box 90B3, Folder 7, NYCHAR, 2; Rosahn and Goldfield, *Housing Management*, 42–50. For further details of community planning in European social housing, see Rodgers, *Atlantic Crossings*, 190.

32. Community Service at Hillside Homes, 1935–1939, Hillside Housing Corporation, July 1939, NYC Parks, Robert Moses Papers, Roll 14, MN 22814, MA, 1–8.

33. "Wider Housing Aim Outlined by Post," *NYT*, 20 March 1934, section 1, 25.

34. Catherine Lansing, "Nursery Schools," 7 April 1936, Box 69D5, Folder 2, NYCHAR, 1.

35. Catherine Lansing, Daily Report, 21 May 1935, Box 56E1, Folder 4, NYCHAR.

36. "New Standard in Harlem Housing Is Set by Clinic and Amphitheatre," *NYT*, 14 June 1936, section 2, 1; Interview of Cyril Grossman by Marcia Robertson, 1 August 1990, NYCHA Oral History Project, Box 1, NYCHAR, 21. Internal NYCHA documents indicate that the inclusion of nurseries at Harlem River Houses emerged from analysis of black employment in which "the woman is almost invariably a wage earner. . . . A very high percentage of negro women have always been gainfully employed." Lansing explained that "in a society where the mothers of young children work long hours outside their homes, the community must accept responsibility for the physical and moral protection of the children and their recreation." Catherine Lansing to Langdon Post, 16 August 1935, Box 53B6, Folder 3, NYCHAR, 1–2.

37. Catherine Lansing, Weekly Reports, 4 April 1935, Box 56E1, Folder 4, NYCHAR, 2.

38. "Child Care Study Hailed by Mothers," *NYT*, 20 March 1938, section 2, 1.

39. Minutes, New York City Housing Authority Nursery School Advisory Committee, 24 June 1943, Box 56E1, Folder 16, NYCHAR; "New Child Care Centers," *NYT*, 1 November 1943, 20; Unsigned letter to Fred Dakin, State Board of Housing, 26 June 1941, Box 69D5, Folder 2, NYCHAR, 1.

40. Catherine Lansing and May Lumsden, "Annual Report," 28 October 1935, Box 53B6, Folder 3, NYCHAR, 10. See Lubove, *The Progressives and the Slums*, 191–92, for insights into the connection between municipal health care and the settlement movement.

41. May Lumsden, "Health and the New Housing," Proceedings of the National Conference of Social Work, Atlantic City, N.J., 1936, Box 53C4, Folder 7, NYCHAR, 566–67.

42. "Our Community Planning Progress," 20 February 1945, Box 78C6, Folder 10, NYCHAR, 22.

43. Ruth Lewis, "Report on Project Activities, Harlem River Houses," Box 54D6, Folder 11, 27 May 1939, NYCHAR; "Our Community Planning Progress," 20 February 1945, Box 78C6, Folder 10, NYCHAR, 15.

44. "Will Be First in City Housing," *Brooklyn Eagle*, 1 December 1938, Box 53E3, Folder 14, NYCHAR.

45. "Our Community Planning Progress," 20 February 1945, Box 78C6, Folder 10, NYCHAR, 21; "Will Be First in City Housing," *Brooklyn Eagle*, 1 December 1938, Box 53E3, Folder 14, NYCHAR.

46. USHA Design of Social Facilities, 15 December 1939, Robert Moses Papers, MN 22813, Roll 13, Parks Department, MA.

47. May Lumsden to Catherine Lansing, "Meeting of the National Recreation Council," 19 May 1941, Box 56E1, Folder 6, NYCHAR.

48. WPA Recreation Programs in New York Housing Projects, October 1937–November 1940, 13 December 1940, Robert Moses Papers, MN 22813, Roll 13, Parks Department, MA.

49. Daniel Saunders, President, Queensbridge Tenants League, "Report and Recommendations . . . ," October 1941, Box 54D8, Folder 4, NYCHAR.

50. "Our Community Planning Progress," 20 February 1945, Box 78C6, Folder

10, NYCHAR, 26; "Community Activities and Recreation in Public Housing Program," Joint Committee on Community Activities in NYCHA Projects, 24 October 1941, no box or folder listed, NYCHAR. See also F. Didisheim to Edna Geissler, 14 November 1941, Box 54D8, Folder 4, NYCHAR.

51. Robert Moses to Edward Weinfeld, 4 December 1940, Parks Commissioner Papers, MN 22703, Roll 3, Folder 26, MA.

52. George Spargo to Robert Moses, 23 July 1941, Robert Moses Papers, MN 22813, Roll 13, Parks Department, MA.

53. Becky LaMonte to Robert Moses, "Community Facilities in New York City Housing Projects," 25 May 1942, NYC Parks, Robert Moses Papers, MN 22814, Roll 14, MA.

54. James Mulholland to George Spargo, 7 July 1941, NYC Parks, Robert Moses Papers, MN 22814, Roll 14, MA. For Lansing's support, see Catherine Lansing, Daily Report, 22 September 1941, Box 56E1, Folder 6, NYCHAR.

55. Community Service at Hillside Homes, 1935–1939, Hillside Housing Corporation, July 1939, NYC Parks, Robert Moses Papers, MN 22814, Roll 14, MA, 1–8; Day, Urban Castles, 181–88.

56. "First Homes' Rent Always Is on Time," NYT, 20 February 1936, section 2, 2.

57. Helen Hall quoted in J. Schwartz, "Tenant Unions in New York City's Low-Rent Housing, 1933–1949," 424.

58. City-Wide Tenants Council, "Civil Liberties in Housing Projects," 17 June 1940, Box 54D5, Folder 9, NYCHAR, 7. See also "New Leases for Living," Better Times: The New York Social Work Review, 9 December 1938, CHPC Archive, 7; J. Schwartz, "Tenant Unions in New York City's Low-Rent Housing, 1933–1949," 419.

59. "Tenants View the NYCHA," City Wide Tenants Council, 3 December 1941, Box 57E2, Folder 4, NYCHAR; Letter to American Labor Party by Earl Kauffman Jr., director of Queensbridge Center, 23 April 1941, Box 54D5, Folder 9, NYCHAR.

60. Frank Didisheim to Gerard Swope, 25 April 1941, Box 54D5, Folder 9, NYCHAR.

Chapter 6. The Boom Years

1. The reinterpretation of the Moses legacy has been underway for some time but has yet to unseat the vision of Robert Caro's The Power Broker. See, for instance, Ballon and Jackson, Robert Moses and the Modern City; J. Schwartz, The New York Approach; Ray Bromley, "Not So Simple! Caro, Moses, and the Impact of the Cross Bronx Expressway," Bronx County Historical Society Journal 35, no. 1 (spring 1998): 4–29; Jameson Doig, "Regional Conflict in the New York Metropolis: The Legend of Robert Moses and the Power of the Port Authority," Urban Studies 27 (1990): 201–32; Leonard Wallock, "The Myth of the Master Builder: Robert Moses, New York, and the Dynamics of Metropolitan Development Since World War II," Journal of Urban History 17 (1991): 339–62; Joann Kreig, ed., Robert Moses: Single-Minded Genius (Hempstead, N.Y.: Hofstra, 1989).

2. "Post-War Project Revealed by Mayor," NYT, 9 September 1942, 15.

3. "Mayor Announces 3 Housing Projects," NYT, 14 June 1943, 1.

4. Fred Siegel, "The Social Democratic City," The Public Interest (spring 2000), findarticles.com/p/articles/mi_mo377/is_2000_Spring/9i_61600829. See also "British Set to Whip Housing Shortage," NYT, 25 September 1945, 20.

5. NYCHA, "Application for Allotment of Funds," 18 December 1944, Parks Commissioner Papers, MN 22817, Roll 17, MA; Don Parson, *Making a Better World.*

6. Joseph McGoldrick, "Blueprints for a Greater New York," *NYT,* 30 April 1944, section 6, 16; "City Will Remove 15,000 Slum Units for Housing Sites," *NYT,* 8 April 1945, sections 8–9, 1. See also "City Housing Plans Go to $260,000,000," *NYT,* 27 December 1944, 1.

7. One example of Moses's nastiness can stand for many. He wrote to Chairman Butler, who had been picked over Moses' recommendations, "If you don't know that your authority and its staff are weak, there is nothing I can do to prove it to you." Robert Moses to E. Butler, 6 November 1942, NYC Parks, Robert Moses Papers, MN 22814, Roll 14, MA. See also Robert Moses, *Public Works: A Dangerous Trade* (New York: McGraw Hill, 1970), 436; Robert Moses, "Slums and City Planning," *The Atlantic,* January 1945, 65, Robert Moses File, CHPC Archive; Robert Moses to Edwin Salmon (of the City Planning Commission), 19 March 1942, Parks Commissioner Papers, MN 22815, Roll 15, MA; Robert Moses to Edmond Butler, 15 March 1945, Parks Commissioner Papers, MN 22723, Roll 23, MA. See also Edmond Butler to Robert Moses, 13 March 1945, Parks Commissioner Papers, MN 22723, Roll 23, MA; Robert Moses to Edmond Butler, 9 February 1945, Parks Commissioner Papers, MN 107873, Roll 23, MA; Edmond Butler to Robert Moses, 8 February 1945, Parks Commissioner Papers, MN 22723, Roll 23, MA.

8. Robert Moses to James Stiles, 3 October 1945, Parks Commissioner Papers, MN 22816, Roll 16, MA. See also Robert Moses to Mayor La Guardia, 21 September 1945, Parks Commissioner Papers, MN 22816, Roll 16, MA.

9. "City Set to Begin Post-War Housing," *NYT,* 23 August 1945, 38; "Temporary Housing Units Demanded of City in Crisis," *NYT,* 17 September 1945, 1.

10. Siegel, "The Social Democratic City."

11. "Segregation Held Breeder of Evils," *NYT,* 19 February 1949, 12; Chris McNickle, *To Be Mayor of New York* (New York: Columbia, 1993), 66.

12. "O'Dwyer Names Housing Group to Outline Program by Dec. 17," *NYT,* 27 November 1945, 1; "Report to Mayor-Elect William O'Dwyer," Emergency Committee on Housing, 17 December 1945, Box 68C3, Folder 10, NYCHAR, 3–4. See also "Moses Group Opens Its Housing Survey," *NYT,* 5 December 1945, 27; "Housing Shortage Held Realty Plot," *NYT,* 8 December 1945, 23.

13. "Temporary Housing Units Demanded of City in Crisis," *NYT,* 17 September 1945, 1; "FPHA Gives Steps on Getting Housing," *NYT,* 29 December 1945, 15; "2,000 Houses Given to the City by U.S. for Emergency Use," *NYT,* 17 January 1946, 1; "City, State Scored for Lag in Housing," *NYT,* 20 February 1946, 27; "City Housing Head Explains Delays," *NYT,* 28 April 1946, 27; Louis Pink, "City Housing Authority," *NYT,* 3 July 1947, 20; "Governor Signs Measure to Close Emergency Housing for Veterans," *NYT,* 27 March 1953, 20.

14. Robert Moses to Edmond Butler, 4 May 1942, NYC Parks, Robert Moses Papers, MN 22814, Roll 14, MA; Robert Bendiner, "The Achievements of Robert Moses," *NYT,* 13 December 1953, SM12; J. Schwartz, *The New York Approach,* 123.

15. Caro, *The Power Broker,* 797.

16. "4 Year Project to House 1,268,400 Offered by Moses," *NYT,* 2 June 1946, 1.

17. "32,808 Apartments Planned by City," *NYT,* 1 February 1948, 15. See also "City to Spend $200,000,000 for Housing 17,000 Families," *NYT,* 13 March 1948, 1; "$48,256,000 Lent for City Housing," *NYT,* 19 October 1948, 39; "Program of the Inter-Project Tenants Council," circa 1947, Box 69D7, Folder 1, NYCHAR.

18. "City Housing Agency Seeks U.S.. Aid to Provide for 'Forgotten' Families," *NYT*, 24 October 1945, 23.

19. Robert Moses to William Charney Vladeck, 10 November 1948, Box 69E4, Folder 7, NYCHAR.

20. NYCHA, 13th Annual Report, 1947, Box 98D1, Folder 7, NYCHAR, 37; Maxwell Tretter, "Public Housing without Cash Subsidy," *CHC Housing News* 5, no. 8 (June 1947): 1; "City Housing Need Put at 861,100 Units," *NYT*, 6 June 1946, 20. A brief description helps explain this complicated form of public housing found nowhere else in the United States (but similar to much in Europe): "We speak of these as 'unsubsidized' projects. There is, however, a tax forgiveness on the buildings themselves; the city receives from the rents an amount equal to the taxes paid on the site before it was improved. The reasons why the Authority can build good housing at a cost permitting a $17 monthly rent per room are that there are no profits, the financing cost in interest is lower, there is longer time to repay the 'mortgage,' and there are no taxes on the improvement." "New York's Public Housing," *NYT*, 8 June 1949, 28. Labor strongly supported city housing. See Joshua Freeman, *Working Class New York: Life and Labor Since World War II* (New York: New Press, 2000), 108–10.

21. Robbins and Tyler, *Reminiscences of a Housing Advocate*, 78; "Guide to Housing Developments," NYCHA Reports, 1965, Box 100A3, Folder 7, NYCHAR. The last phase of the city-sponsored program was known as City Part IV and six of these projects were sold as cooperatives. See also "New York City Gets Action on Housing with Huge 'Unsubsidized' Program," *American City*, August 1949, 82; "Draft," NYCHA document, circa 1952, Box 68C2, Folder 2, NYCHAR.

22. "City, State Agree on Housing Plan," *NYT*, 6 June 1947, 25; "Housing to Precede Clearing of Slums," *NYT*, 8 August 1947, 1; Louis Pink, "City Housing Authority," *NYT*, 3 July 1947, 20.

23. Robert Moses, Personal Memorandum to the Mayor, 10 June 1946, Robert Moses Papers, Roll 35, MN 47035, MA.

24. "Council Supports Mayor on Housing," *NYT*, 1 March 1947, 17. See also William Conklin, "Mayor Acts to End Housing Board and Create New Unit of His Own," *NYT*, 26 February 1947, 1; "Lehman Asks Vote on Housing Funds," *NYT*, 27 February 1947, 38.

25. "Mayor's Measure Held 'Ripper' Plan," *NYT*, 4 March 1947, 50; "O'Dwyer Plan Seen Facing Rejection," *NYT*, 9 March 1947, 47; "Dewey Signs Bill to Let Mayor Name City Housing Chief," *NYT*, 6 April 1947, 1.

26. "A Good Housing Chairman," *NYT*, 7 May 1947, 26; "West-Pointer Led Atom-Bomb Staff," *NYT*, 7 August 1945, 6. Caro reports that Farrell was Moses' recommendation to O'Dwyer. See Caro, *The Power Broker*, 763, 775.

27. "City Housing Unit Due for Shake-Up," *NYT*, 12 May 1947, 16.

28. "Tretter Will Quit City Housing Post," *NYT*, 25 June 1947, 27; "Key Housing Jobs Filled by Farrell," *NYT*, 2 July 1947, 17; "J. H. England Dies; City Housing Aide," *NYT*, 21 March 1950, 32; Moscow quoted in Caro, *The Power Broker*, 803.

29. "Mayor Elects Shanahan," *NYT*, 18 February 1948, 29. Robert Caro uses the Tammany reference. See Caro, *The Power Broker*, 724. Caro also believes that Shanahan "ran the Housing Authority for Moses. The Housing Authority projects built were the projects Moses wanted built—on the sites where Moses wanted them built." Caro, *The Power Broker*, 727.

30. "Public Housing Costs Cut 18% in 10 Months," *NYT*, 27 September 1949, 24; Thomas Farrell to William O'Dwyer, "The Activities of the New York City Housing Authority," 3 December 1948, Box 68B6, Folder 6, NYCHAR.

31. "Housing Projects for 9,500 Families," *NYT*, 16 January 1949, 56; "New York's Public Housing," *NYT*, 8 June 1949, 28; "Mayors Tell Need of U.S. Housing Aid," *NYT*, 18 February 1949, 3; "80,000 Apartments in City Projected," *NYT*, 20 November 1949, 76; "Dewey to Propose a Large Bond Issue for War on Slums," *NYT*, 27 December 1953, 1.

32. "Housing Bill Plea Sent to Congress," *NYT*, 30 July 1946, 13; "O'Dwyer Calls on Congress to Pass Housing Measure," *NYT*, 13 November 1947, 1; "Truman's Aid Sought by Mayor on Housing," *NYT*, 9 December 1948, 27; "Mayor Visits Capital on Housing Mission," *NYT*, 10 December 1948, 29; "Mayors Tell Need of U.S. Housing Aid," *NYT*, 18 February 1949, 3; "City Housing Gets Record U.S. Help," *NYT*, 22 June 1950, 29; "City Plans Scores of Slum Projects," *NYT*, 15 July 1949, 33. Among the many treatments of this history are Gelfand, *A Nation of Cities*; Nicholas Bloom, *Merchant of Illusion* (Columbus: Ohio State, 2004); Zipp, "Manhattan Projects."

33. "Public Housing Cut Opposed by Mayor," *NYT*, 19 March 1952, 41; "Cruise Becomes Head of Housing Agency," *NYT*, 30 September 1950, 8; "Retires December 31 as Head of City Housing Board," *NYT*, 28 November 1951, 27. Caro documents that Wagner tried with only limited success to use Warren Moscow as a tool of reform at the authority. Not only was the NYCHA board dominated for years by Moses' men, but much of the talent in large-scale construction retained loyalties to Moses. See Caro, *The Power Broker*, 804–5. See also "Housing Is Sought for Middle Group," *NYT*, 12 May 1952, 31; "Housing Fund Cuts Assailed by Mayor," *NYT*, 21 April 1953, 29; "24,000 Apartments Seen Lost to City," *NYT*, 6 May 1953, 33.

34. "U.S. Housing Cuts Have Impact Here," *NYT*, 29 July 1950, 10; "Maintenance Men Out in City Housing," *NYT*, 19 February 1952, 10; "20 Years Marked for City Housing," *NYT*, 2 June 1955, 31. See also "Housing Authority Sets Records," *NYT*, 2 April 1951, 27; "Big Housing Plan Disclosed by City," *NYT*, 11 July 1951, 22.

35. "$225,000,000 Plan for Slum Razing in City Approved," *NYT*, 20 April 1955, 1. The story of the Housing Act of 1954 has been told many times. See Gelfand, *A Nation of Cities*.

36. "$20,000,000 U.S. Aid Slated for Slums," *NYT*, 22 December 1953, 33; Robert Moses to Arthur Hays Sulzberger, 27 July 1953, Box 91, Robert Moses Papers, NYPL.

37. Gerald Carey, "Remarks," National Association of Housing Officers, 17 October 1952, Box 59C6, Folder 10, NYCHAR; "Washington Square South," Slum Clearance Plan, Title I, Box 91, Robert Moses Papers, NYPL.

38. Charles Grutzner, "Council Fight Due on Housing Policy," *NYT*, 2 February 1956, 1; Paul Goldberger, "Robert Moses, Master Builder, Is Dead at 92," *NYT*, 30 July 1981, A1. See also "What Price Slum Clearance?," New York State Commission on Discrimination in Housing," circa 1953, Box 68C2, Folder 2, NYCHAR; "Title I Projects Total 13 in City," *NYT*, 13 April 1959, 33; "U.S. to Trust City Over Relocation," *NYT*, 1 May 1959, 31; Charles Grutzner, "Relocation Rule of U.S. Is Opposed," *NYT*, 2 May 1959, 11. Joel Schwartz's *The New York Approach* provides a fascinating portrait of the symbiotic relationship between Moses and leading civic institutions. Hilary Ballon also cites a 12 percent relocation figure for Title I by 1959 and documents Moses' growing frustration with NYCHA. See Ballon and Jackson, *Robert Moses and the Modern City*, 102.

39. Moses, *Public Works*, 454.

40. "City Lags in Help to Slum Tenants," *NYT*, 2 April 1954, 29; "20 Years

Marked for City Housing," *NYT*, 2 June 1955, 31; "20 Years of Public Housing," *NYT*, 3 June 1955, 22; "City Projects Add 40,000 Homes," *NYT*, 25 November 1955, 36. See George Genung to Philip Cruise, 4 February 1954, Box 63D4, Folder 11 for figures from 1950 to 1954; "Number of Site Occupants of Projects Completed Prior to 1/1/57," Box 63D4, Folder 10, NYCHAR, indicates that only 18 percent of tenants from sites prior to 1957 relocated to public housing. Robert Moses actually came to Cruise's defense in 1954 as growing opposition from "liberal groups who have differed with Mr. Moses and Mr. Cruise on arrangements for finding new quarters for tenants displaced by slum clearance programs" sought Cruise's ouster. "City Hall Divided on Housing Office," *NYT*, 9 January 1954, 28. See also Edith Asbury, "Slum Fight Boils in Washington Sq.," *NYT*, 29 January 1954, 23.

41. "23,000 Relocated for City Housing," *NYT*, 23 September 1962.

42. William C. Vladeck, "The Nature and Complexity of the Housing Problem," June 1957, CHPC Archive, Miscellaneous File, 6.

43. "Public Housing Opposed," *NYT*, 29 March 1954, 18.

44. "Sales Plan Urged for City Housing," *NYT*, 9 July 1956, 23; Marcuse, *Public Housing in New York City*, 224.

45. Interview of Warren Moscow by CBS Radio, 15 May 1956, Box 71B6, Folder 1 (LWA).

46. "City Housing Unit Scored in Albany," *NYT*, 15 January 1958, 34; "New Housing Unit Is Voted for City," *NYT*, 27 March 1958, 21; Thomas Ennis, "Aids to Housing—II," *NYT*, 16 November 1958, R1; "City Plans Co-Ops at 8 Housing Sites," *NYT*, 15 January 1960, 16. See also "4 Co-Op Sponsors Set to Take Over," *NYT*, 12 March 1961, R1; "City Votes to Sell Big Luna Housing," *NYT*, 13 May 1961, 19; "New Type of Co-op Called Pioneer," *NYT*, 17 September 1961, R13. The co-ops (7,282 apartments total) proved, after an initial delay, easy to sell and were sponsored as cooperatives by a great variety of cooperating educational, religious, and civic organizations. Thomas Ennis, "City Co-Op Venture Is Popular; Two-Thirds of Apartments Sold," *NYT*, 9 June 1963, 351.

47. Robbins and Tyler, *Reminiscences of a Housing Advocate*, 131–32. Back in 1952 NYCHA had, like all housing authorities, complied with the Gwinn Amendment, which required loyalty oaths for public housing tenants. See "'Subversives' Face Housing Eviction," *NYT*, 18 December 1952, 24. See also Box 65C8 and 71C5 in the NYCHAR for further details of red hunting, mostly fruitless, directed at the NYCHA staff after the Security Risk Law of 1953. Wagner's attempts to reign in the authority are detailed in Caro, *The Power Broker*, 726–27.

48. Interview of Henry Bresky by Marcia Robertson, 27 July 1990, NYCHA Oral History Project, NYCHAR, 17.

49. "City Dropped 3 in Red Inquiry," *NYT*, 20 March 1957, 22; "Mayor Backs State on Housing Inquiry," *NYT*, 8 March 1957, 27; "No Red Cells Found in Housing Agency," *NYT*, 12 November 1957, 1; Paul Crowell, "City Will Survey Its Housing Body," *NYT*, 18 March 1957, 1. Charles Tenney, the investigation commissioner charged with finding communists in housing, did admit that a "substantial number of employees in the higher echelon of NYCHA management have prior records of Communist affiliation." He counted at least 136 about whom he had his doubts but no evidence. He had been stymied in his efforts to find "corroboration" because of the unwillingness of their associates to testify against them. Tenants were also required to take loyalty oaths. Management employees of the NYCHA also left their union, United Public Workers, because of its association with communists. For details see, "No Red Cells Found in Hous-

ing Agency," *NYT*, 12 November 1957, 1; Interview of Cyril Grossman by Marcia Robertson, 1 August 1990, NYCHA Oral History Project, NYCHAR, 24.

50. E. W. Kenworthy, "City Housing Unit Faces U.S. Inquiry," *NYT*, 22 August 1957, 31; Paul Crowell, "City Study Urges Drastic Changes in Housing Board," *NYT*, 23 September 1957, 1.

51. "City Told to Hire Housing Experts," *NYT*, 26 September 1957, 16; "Housing Changes Backed by Mayor," *NYT*, 24 September 1957, 38; "City Housing Unit Scored in Albany," *NYT*, 15 January 1958, 34; "Mayor Gives Bill for Housing Body," *NYT*, 20 January 1958, 25; "New Housing Unit Is Voted for City," *NYT*, 27 March 1958, 21; "Governor Signs City Housing Bill," *NYT*, 24 April 1958, 27.

52. "Moscow Resigns City Housing Post," *NYT*, 18 May 1957; Charles Bennett, "3 in Housing Office Resign Amid Strife," 21 February 1958, 1; Caro, *The Power Broker*, 724; "Cruise Quits as City Housing Chairman," *NYT*, 25 April 1958, 19; Wayne Philips, "Slum 'Deal' Data Sent to City Hall," *NYT*, 18 June 1959, 16; Charles Grutzner, "Congress Urged to Study Moses's Housing Actions," *NYT*, 20 June 1959, 1; Charles Grutzner, "Wagner Pledges Inquiry in Slum Deals If Justified," *NYT*, 23 June 1959, 1; Charles Grutzner, "Wagner Is Given Title I Findings on Housing Aide," *NYT*, 24 June 1959, 1; Paul Crowell, "Mayor to 'Rein in' on Title I to End Friction," *NYT*, 20 July 1959, 1; Charles Grutzner, "Mayor Proposes a Vast New Plan to End City Slums," *NYT*, 21 July 1959; Charles Grutzner, "Title I Changes Curb Shanahan," *NYT*, 29 July 1959, 1; "Oust Moses Drive On," *NYT*, 17 October 1959, 48.

53. William Reid, *NYT*, 27 October 1965, Box 92B3, Folder 2, NYCHAR. Reid had been city collector (chief tax collector), chairman of the Board of Transportation, and president of the Hudson and Manhattan Railroad.

54. "Top Housing Post Offered to Ex-Deputy Mayor Reid," *NYT*, 18 April 1958, 1; "A New Housing Authority," *NYT*, 2 May 1958, 26; "City Housing Authority Changes Vice Chairmen," *NYT*, 9 June 1959, 27. See also Ira Robbins, "Housing Study Welcomed," *NYT*, 29 March 1957, 20; "New Housing Unit Sworn by Mayor," *NYT*, 2 May 1958, 29; "City Housing Squad Organized to Meet Night Emergencies," *NYT*, 25 June 1962, 31.

55. William Reid to Robert Moses, 4 December 1959, Box 118, Robert Moses Papers, NYPL; Robert Moses to William Reid, 9 December 1959, Box 118, Robert Moses Papers, NYPL.

56. John Sibley, "New Title I Plan Outlined for City by Housing Board," *NYT*, 5 June 1960, 1.

57. William Kirk, "Renewing City Areas," *NYT*, 7 March 1961, 34; Interview of Brian Clarke, director, NYCHA Technical Services Division by the author, 21 July 2006. See also "City Housing Cuts Tenant Red Tape," *NYT*, 2 September 1958, 26.

58. "Statement by the Three Members of the NYCHA," 6 November 1962, Box 65D4, Folder 7, NYCHAR, 4; NYCHA Annual Report, 1962, "A Clearer Focus," Box 100A2, Folder 12, NYCHAR.

59. "30,000 Relocated by City Last Year," *NYT*, 28 May 1961, R16; "23,000 Relocated for City Housing," *NYT*, 23 September 1962.

60. "Housing Agency Report," *NYT*, 20 February 1961, 31; "Statement by the Three Members of the NYCHA," 6 November 1962, Box 65D4, Folder 7, NYCHAR, 1; "Billion in Housing Projected Here," *NYT*, 7 April 1961, 21.

61. Mayor Wagner, Address to the National Conference on Social Welfare, 27 May 1962, Box 68B6, Folder 1, NYCHAR, 3.

62. "Billion in Housing Projected Here," *NYT*, 7 April 1961, 21.

63. Robert Conley, "New City Housing to Cost 83 Million," *NYT*, 26 April 1961, 1; "City Relocated 9,000 During '62," *NYT*, 5 May 1963, 327; Alexander Burnham, "Mayor Cites Need of Housing Funds," *NYT*, 1 May 1963, 1.

64. Alexander Burnham, "Mayor Cites Need of Housing Funds," *NYT*, 1 May 1963, 1.

65. Leo Egan, "Housing Issue Grows," *NYT*, 5 March 1962, 16; Jane Jacobs, *The Death and Life of Great American Cities* (New York: Random House, 1961). Chapter 17, "Subsidized Dwellings," is of particular interest, but Jacobs intersperses critiques of public housing and tower-block development throughout the book.

66. Alexander Burnham, "Mayor Cites Need of Housing Funds," *NYT*, 1 May 1963, 1. See also Douglas Dales, "State Appoints 5 to Study Housing," *NYT*, 9 April 1963, 50; Alexander Burnham, "Rockefeller Asks New Low-Rent Housing Policy," *NYT*, 3 May 1963, 16.

67. Douglas Robinson, "Voters Turn Down 2 Proposals on Housing and Urban Renewal," *NYT*, 5 November 1964, 33; Lawrence O'Kane, "Opposition Rising to Low-Rent Aid," *NYT*, 6 December 1964, 80. See also Tartin Tolchin, "Rockefeller Tours with Mayor in Bid for Housing Vote," *NYT*, 30 October 1965, 1.

68. Martin Arnold, "City Housing Unit Denies Fiscal Crisis," *NYT*, 6 November 1962, 1; Douglas Dales, "State Appoints 5 to Study Housing," *NYT*, 9 April 1963, 50; "Mayor Proposes Bargaining Right for 10,000 More," *NYT*, 5 August 1962, 1; Martin Arnold, "City Bars Pledge Against Rent Rise," *NYT*, 10 November 1962, 21.

69. David Shipler, "The Changing City: Housing Paralysis," *NYT*, 5 June 1969, 1. See also Gonzalez, *The Bronx* (New York: Columbia, 2004) for details on housing abandonment in the South Bronx (126–27). The literature on subsidized suburban growth is vast, but a good starting place, including detailed references, is Thomas Hanchett, "The Other 'Subsidized Housing,'" in *From Tenements to the Taylor Homes*, ed. Rober Biles and John Bauman et al. (University Park: Penn State, 2000), 163–79.

70. "Rent and Rookeries: II," *NYT*, 27 December 1963, 24; Hunt, "What Went Wrong with Public Housing in Chicago?," 31.

71. Lawrence O'Kane, "President's Housing Message Scored by Many Here," *NYT*, 4 March 1965, 19; Joseph Christian to Gerald Carey, 22 November 1965, Box 64B7, Folder 2, NYCHAR. See also Charles Mohr, "President Asks Rent Subsidies to Spur Housing," *NYT*, 3 March 1965, 1.

72. Lesley Oelsner, "City Still Lags in Housing: 14,000–Unit Goal Is in Doubt," *NYT*, 21 March 1971, 64. For bond costs, see John Allan, "Record Rate set on Housing Bonds," *NYT*, 27 February 1969, 55; John Allan, "City Is Paying Record Interest," *NYT*, 17 October 1969, 69. In order to keep building at all the authority occasionally had to borrow money from different programs to make up for high-cost construction. For instance, a project in the South Bronx was paid for out of both federal housing money and Model Cities funds not necessarily earmarked for housing. Barbara Campbell, "Project in South Bronx Begins Under U.S. Model Cities Plan," *NYT*, 14 July 1970, 24. An ambitious reorganization of New York's different housing agencies into a "superagency" known as the Housing and Development Administration reached fruition with one major exception. NYCHA (in part thanks to opposition "by many Housing Authority officials who lobbied against its passage in Albany") opted out of the new agency and thus frustrated Lindsay's hopes of a comprehensive, re-energized, professionalized, cost-saving housing bureaucracy for the city. The NYCHA's chairman, Albert Walsh, would resign as chairman and assume leadership of the new

organization in 1970. See Steven Roberts, "Governor to Act on Rent Aid Bill," *NYT*, 9 April 1967, 49. See also Charles Bennett, "Council Approves City Super-agency," 12 July 1967, 1; Charles Bennett, "Lindsay Signs Bill for a Superagency," 29 July 1967, 1; Steven Robert, "Civic Unit Assails Mayor on Housing," *NYT*, 21 January 1968, 1.

73. Seth King, "Housing Authority Seeking 450 More Policemen," *NYT*, 17 April 1968, 31. See also Jeanne Lowe, "From Shelter to Community, the First Thirty-Five Years of the New York City Housing Authority," Typescript, 26 August 1969, Box 64E4, Folder 1, NYCHAR, 5.

Chapter 7. Designs for a New Metropolis

1. "New Apartments and Civic Developments to Make Harlem a Better Neighbor-hood," *NYT*, 17 November 1946, 201. The estimates on cleared land and the total number of families come from Zipp, "Manhattan Projects," chapter 7, p. 11.

2. Robert A. M. Stern, *New York 1960* (New York: Monacelli, 1995), 40.

3. Caro, *The Power Broker*, 758.

4. Robert Moses, "Housing and Recreation," Robert Moses Papers, MN 22813, Roll 13, Parks Department, MA.

5. Memo, Citizens Housing Council, 3 December 1938, Box 53E3, Folder 14, NYCHAR, 3. Lewis Mumford and Albert Mayer argued that Moses' proposal for ten large projects "would increase the density of population in such neighbor-hoods even beyond the present lower East Side congestion." See Lee Cooper, "Housing Compromise with Outlying Homes Linked to Broad Plan for City of Future," *NYT*, 7 December 1938, 43.

6. "Post-war Project Revealed by Mayor," *NYT*, 9 September 1942, 15; J. Schwartz, *The New York Approach*, 118. The City Planning Commission, rejecting expensive new city services in vacant land projects such as Queensbridge, in 1940 adopted "a map recommending locations of low-rental housing within thirty-two areas roughly coincident with existing slums, generally central areas." Albert Mayer, "So Far, So Good in Public Housing," *NYT*, 15 September 1940, 115. See also City Planning Commission, 3 January 1940, Low Rent Section of Master Plan, Robert Moses Papers, MN 22813, Roll 13, Parks Department, MA, 3–5; Moses to Butler, 4 May 1942, NYC Parks, Robert Moses Papers, MN 22814, Roll 14, MA.

7. "Seven Areas Listed for Future Housing," *NYT*, 9 January 1942, 38. See also Gerard Swope to Commissioner Edwin Salmon, 8 January 1942, Box 68A7, Folder 2, NYCHAR.

8. Robert Moses to Mayor La Guardia, 9 March 1942, Parks Commissioner Pa-pers, MN 22815, Roll 15, MA.

9. Press Release, Office of the Mayor, 13 June 1943, Parks Commissioner Pa-pers, Roll 15, MN 22815, MA. For further details on jurisdiction, see Edwin Salmon to Edward Butler, 12 May 1942, Box 68A7, Folder 2, NYCHAR.

10. "Post-War Public Housing," *NYT*, 4 October 1942, section 9, 1; NYCHA, 13th Annual Report, 1947, Box 98D1, Folder 7, NYCHAR, 13.

11. Henry Churchill, "Housing Plan Disapproved," *NYT*, 31 December 1942, 14; Henry Churchill, "Harlem Site Held Faulty," *NYT*, 6 January 1943, 24.

12. Robert Moses, "Harlem Housing Defended," *NYT*, 2 January 1943, 10.

13. Edmond Butler to Robert Moses, 6 January 1943, Parks Commissioner Pa-pers, MN 22714, Roll 14, MA.

14. Edmond Borgia Butler to Mayor O'Dwyer, 12 June 1946, Parks Commissioner Papers, MN 107880, Roll 35, MA; NYCHA Monthly Report, October/November 1947, O'Dwyer Papers, MN 47035, Roll 35, Subject Files, MA.

15. Robert Moses to Thomas Corcoran, 20 June 1946, Parks Commissioner Papers, 107880, Roll 35, MA. See also Robert Moses to Edmond Butler, 11 July 1946, Parks Commissioner Papers, MN 22817, Roll 17, MA.

16. Robert Moses to the mayor, 15 April 1946, Box 90, Robert Moses Papers, NYPL.

17. William O'Dwyer to Edmond Borgia Butler, 2 August 1946, Parks Commissioner Papers, 107880, Roll 35, MA; Thomas Farrell, Speech at the Building Congress Luncheon, 2 May 1950, O'Dwyer Papers, MN 47035, Roll 35, MA. See also Robert Moses to Edmond Borgia Butler, 11 July 1946, Parks Commissioner Papers, 107880, Roll 35, MA on the issue of vacant land projects. For squabbles between Moses and housing officials, see also Robert Moses to Thomas Corcoran, 1 November 1946, Parks Commissioner Papers, MN 22817, Roll 17, MA.

18. William Farrell, "City Shifts Policy on Housing Sites," *NYT*, 6 April 1947, 14; "Vacant Sites Held Key to Housing," *NYT*, 18 April 1947, 23; "City, State Agree on Housing Plan," *NYT*, 6 June 1947, 25; "City to Spend $200,000,000 for Housing 17,000 Families," *NYT*, 13 March 1948, 1; Interview of Cyril Grossman by Marcia Robertson, 1 August 1990, NYCHA Oral History Project, NYCHAR, 22; Robert Moses to Thomas Farrell, 22 December 1948, Parks Commissioner Papers, MN 107890, Roll 52, MA. Public housing could be used indirectly for displaced tenants and even more directly in clearing rights of ways for highways. Adding a highway right of way to a Williamsburg area project, for instance, would "aid in breaking an impasse in the construction of a very important link of the Brooklyn-Queens Expressway." Progress could not be made in Williamsburg "unless this particular section is included in a slum clearance and vacant land project where site tenants have preference." Moses to Thomas Farrell, 10 February 1949, NYC Parks, MN 22953, Roll 3, MA.

19. Robert Moses to Thomas Farrell, 3 December 1948 Parks Commissioner Papers, 107890, Roll 52, MA. See also "Housing to Precede Clearing of Slums," *NYT*, 8 August 1947, 1; Memo to O'Dwyer, "Federal Program," 12 April 1950, 68B6, Folder 6.

20. "80,000 Apartments in City Projected," *NYT*, 20 November 1949, 76. See also "City Housing Plans Earmark 50 Areas," *NYT*, 21 August 1949, 1; "City Plans Scores of Slum Projects," *NYT*, 15 July 1949, 33.

21. Report on the Program of the New York City Housing Authority in Relation to Mayor Wagner's Platform Proposals," 15 December 1961, Box 68B6, Folder 6, NYCHAR; Joseph Christian to William Reid, 25 June 1964, Box 64B6, Folder 3, NYCHAR; Interview of Raymond Henson by Marcia Robertson, 6 August 1990, NYCHA Oral History Project (LWA), 23; Community Service Society, "The Future of Public Housing in New York City,", *Urban Agenda* 14 (July 1999), www.cssny.org/pubs/issuebrief/no14.htm. For comparisons with more segregated public housing in Chicago, see "Public Housing in Black and White," *Commonweal*, 16 May 1969, 253.

22. Charles Noyes Company, Survey of Unsubsidized Projects, 1958, Box 62A4, Folder 2, NYCHAR.

23. Figures from the NYCHA Development Data Book, 2005. Details of some of the vacant land projects: Edenwald (1953), three to fourteen stories, 16.2 percent ground coverage, and 114 persons per acre; Throgg's Neck (1953), three to seven stories, 16 percent ground coverage, and only 85 persons per acre;

Sheepshead (1950), six stories, 15 percent ground coverage, and 112 persons per acre; Nostrand (1950), six stories, 17 percent ground coverage, and 105 persons per acre; and Glenwood (1950), six stories, 18 percent ground coverage, and 124 persons per acre.

In 1950, the NYCHA also still had to face down federal officials who objected to New York's high land costs. See T. F. Farrell to Mayor O'Dwyer, 13 February 1950, Box 68B6, Folder 6, NYCHAR. See also O'Dwyer to Harry S Truman, 20 February 1950, Box 68B6, Folder 6, NYCHAR. The federal government again complained about high costs and recommended vacant land to cut costs in 1958. See Charles Grutzner, "U.S. Housing Plan Bogs Down Here," *NYT*, 7 October 1958, 1.

24. "'Fact Sheets' List Housing Projects," *NYT*, 7 February 1965, R8.

25. Interview of Cyril Grossman by Marcia Robertson, 1 August 1990, NYCHA Oral History Project, NYCHAR, 22.

26. "159 Slum Acres to Be Condemned," *NYT*, 7 January 1951, 61.

27. Interview of Raymond Henson by Marcia Robertson, 6 August 1990, NYCHA Oral History Project, NYCHAR, 4–5.

28. Randolph White, "Displaced Families Worry about Their Future Homes," *New York Amsterdam News*, 14 April 1951, 21; Gonzalez, *The Bronx*, 111–12.

29. "Wagner Asks Swap of Aid for Taxes," *NYT*, 13 February 1953, 38.

30. Robert Moses to Philip Cruise, 13 March 1953, Box 68C2, Folder 2, NYCHAR.

31. Raisa Bahchieva and Amy Hosier, "Determinants of Tenure Duration in Public Housing: The Case of New York City," *Journal of Housing Research*, (Fannie Mae) 12, no. 2 (2001): 307–48; Interview of Arlene Campana, NYCHA director of applications, by the author, 1 August 2006.

32. Robert Moses to Thomas Farrell, 22 December 1948, Parks Commissioner Papers, MN 107890, Roll 52, MA; Robert Moses, "Rough Memorandum on Slum Clearance," 16 December 1948, Box 68C3, Folder 10, NYCHAR; Robert Moses to Edmond Butler, 22 January 1943, Parks Commissioner Papers, MN 107868, Roll 14, MA. See also Robert Moses to Edmond Butler, 15 May 1945, Parks Commissioner Papers, MN 107873, Roll 23, MA.

33. Robert Moses to Mayor La Guardia, 16 October 1945, Parks Commissioner Papers, MN 22816, Roll 16, MA.

34. "Stichman Critical of Housing Policy," *NYT*, 5 September 1951, 33; "City Housing Units Approved by State," *NYT*, 28 March 1946, 27; Herman Stichman, "New York State Acts to Meet the Housing Crisis," 13 June 1946, O'Dwyer Papers, MN 47035, Roll 35, MA. See also Robert Moses, "Memorandum Suggesting Policy," 14 July 1950, O'Dwyer Papers, MN 47035, Roll 35, MA; William Farrell, "Housing Projects Etch City with Odd Geometric Designs," *NYT*, 10 November 1952, 27; "State Offers Loan for Housing in City," *NYT*, 27 July 1950, 27; Robert Moses, "Memorandum Suggesting Policy of the City of New York," 14 July 1950, NYCHA Papers, Box 68C3, Folder 1.

35. Robert Moses, Speech at the Dedication of Baruch Houses, 19 August 1953, Box 91, Robert Moses Papers, NYPL.

36. "$225,000,000 Plan for Slum Razing in City Approved," *NYT*, 20 April 1955, 1. See also J. Schwartz, *The New York Approach*, 120.

37. J. Schwartz, *The New York Approach*, 120; Martin Arnold, "Harlem Decries 'Ghetto' Housing," *NYT*, 8 June 1962, 33. The twelve paired projects estimate is from Ballon and Jackson, *Robert Moses and the Modern City*, 115.

38. "New Funds to Spur Low-Rent Housing," *NYT*, 5 March 1949, 20. For the

modernist context of this era, see texts such as Mumford, *The CIAM Discourse on Urbanism, 1928–1960*; Anthony Alofsin, *The Struggle for Modernism: Architecture, Landscape Architecture, and City Planning at Harvard* (New York: Norton, 2002).

39. Interview of John Simon by Marcia Robertson, 24 July 1990, NYCHA Oral History Project, NYCHAR, 5; Camilo José Vergara, "Hell in a Very High Place," *The Atlantic Monthly*, September 1989, 72–78.

40. "New Funds to Spur Low-Rent Housing," *NYT*, 5 March 1949, 20.

41. Richard Rosenthal, "The Challenge of Design," in *Fifty Years of Public Housing*, NYCHA, 1985, Box 74E5, Folder 10, NYCHAR.

42. "New York City Public Housing Program," 14 May 1948, Box 68B6, Folder 6, NYCHAR; "City Housing Plans Earmark 50 Areas," *NYT*, 21 August 1949, 1.

43. Jeanne Lowe, "From Shelter to Community; The First Thirty Five Years of the New York City Housing Authority," 26 August 1969, Box 64E4, Folder 1, NYCHAR.

44. NYCHA Monthly Report, October/November 1947, O'Dwyer Papers, Roll 35 (47035), MA. Each development today does have an individual feeling based on factors such as height, the amount and type of open space, the layout, the surrounding community, the tenant body, and the effectiveness of the staff.

45. "General Farrell on Housing," *NYT*, 4 May 1948, 24.

46. "Public Housing Costs Cut 18% in 10 Months," *NYT*, 27 September 1949, 24. For the reference to use of state funds, see NYCHA, 13th Annual Report, 1947, Box 98D1, Folder 7, NYCHAR, 16.

47. The figures are from an excerpt of Robert Moore Fisher's draft dissertation, 21 April 1958, Box 85D2, Folder 5, NYCHAR. A later estimate was that slum clearance added approximately $800 per room. See also Ira Robbins to Simeon Goldstein, 22 January 1963, Box 85D2, Folder 1, NYCHAR.

48. Harry Fialkin to Melvin Feldman, 6 January 1960, Box 85D2, Folder 5, NYCHAR; Marcuse, *Public Housing in New York City*, 144. Bradford Hunt gives the room limit under the 1949 Act as $2,500 per room. He also provides the total development cost figure. See Hunt, "What Went Wrong with Public Housing in Chicago?," 303, 304, 518.

49. Edith Pope, "Background Material," circa 1968, Box 61B4, Folder 21, NYCHAR.

50. Stern, *New York 1960*, 136–39.

51. Louis Pink to Alfred Rheinstein, 16 August 1938, La Guardia Papers, Roll 93, MA. Catherine Bauer, for instance, as early as 1941 began to express doubts: "community parks with all open space landscaped by the management make handsome air photographs. . . . But private gardens, with row houses and flats, are cheaper to keep up and probably more useful and livable for most American families." Bauer, "Large Scale Housing," 97–98. See also her generally positive comments about superblocks in Catherine Bauer, "Housing in the United States," reprint, *National Labour Review* 52, no. 1 (July 1945), CHPC Archive, 8.

52. "Housing Authority Accused of Laxity," *NYT*, 23 September 1945, 39.

53. Mumford quoted in Stern, *New York 1960*, 72–74. Stern reprints a great deal of design criticism over the decades. See also "Reprint of 'The Sky Line' Article and Robert Moses Response," originally printed in the *New Yorker*, 30 October 1948 and 27 November 1948, in Box 36, Robert Moses Papers, NYPLibrary. For earlier criticism of the effect of excessive zoning for future growth on urban land, see Frederick Ackerman, *A Note on Site and Unit Planning*, NYCHA, 1937, CHPC Archive, 54.

54. Wurster, "The Dreary Deadlock of Public Housing," 140–42.

55. Robert Moses to Philip Cruise, 17 August 1951, Box 68C2, Folder 1, NYCHAR.

56. Philip Cruise to Robert Moses, 23 August 1951, Box 68C2, Folder 3, NYCHAR.

57. Edward McGrew to Oscar Kenny, 27 December 1960, Box 68B6, Folder 3, NYCHAR; Charles Grutzner, "Tiled Lobbies, Closet Doors Give a Modern Look to Public Housing," *NYT*, 1 January 1957, 25.

58. AIA Tour, NYCHA, 25 June 1952, Box 59D3, Folder 2, NYCHAR.

59. Annual Report, 1955, NYCHA, Box 98D1, Folder 18, NYCHAR. When the NYCHA tried to build higher cost, "no subsidy" buildings, with balconies and better details, which would rent to the group just above public housing tenants, it found that it had begun to step on the toes of private industry, quickly stopped the program, and eventually sold the buildings to the residents.

60. Alfred Rheinstein to Robert Moses, 15 September 1939, Box 54B4, Folder 6, NYCHAR.

61. Speech by Thomas Farrell to the Building Congress Luncheon, 2 May 1950, O'Dwyer Papers, Subject Files, MN 47035, Roll 35, MA.

62. NYCHA, "Baruch Houses and Playground," Box 100A4, Folder 6, NYCHAR.

63. Harrison Salisbury, "'Shook' Youngsters Spring from the Housing Jungles," *NYT*, 26 March 1958, 1.

64. "More New Housing For Harlem Urged," *NYT*, 14 May 1942, 17.

65. Philip Cruise, "Interracial Housing Succeeds," *Interracial Review*, April 1955, Box 67E2, Folder 12, NYCHAR. See Samuel Zipp, "Manhattan Projects," Chapter 7.

66. Thomas Ennis, "Harlem Changed by Public Housing," *NYT*, 23 June 1957, 225. See also Thomas Ennis, "City Lifting Face of East Harlem," *NYT*, 5 March 1961, R1.

67. See Bauer, *Modern Housing*, 160–67; "Tenants in Project Shun Fancy Stores," *NYT*, 28 November 1938, 5; "City Housing Board Cuts Store Rents 50%," *NYT*, 9 March 1938, 7.

68. Alfred Rheinstein, Address to the Better Housing League of Cincinnati, 2 December 1938, Box 53E7, Folder 7, NYCHAR.

69. "Postwar Housing Includes No Stores," *NYT*, 7 October 1944, 15. Many of Williamsburg's stores have been converted to nonprofit use in order to fill the space, but with the growing popularity of the neighborhood the NYCHA is shifting to market-based rents.

70. Paul Kelley to NYCHA Board, 17 January 1947, Park Commissioner Papers, MN 107888, Roll 42, MA; Charles Grutzner, "Shopping Scarce in City Projects," *NYT*, 16 June 1957, 74.

71. Robert Moses to Thomas Farrell, 13 August 1948, Box 69E4, Folder 7, NYCHAR.

72. Thomas Farrell to Robert Moses, 20 August 1948, Box 69E4, Folder 7, NYCHAR.

73. "Review of Store Renting and Rentals," 28 June 1949, Box 69D7, Folder 4, NYCHAR.

74. NYCHA, Report on Slum Clearance and Relocation, circa 1950, Box 68C2, Folder 1, NYCHAR, chapter 3, 2.

75. "Shops a Problem in East Harlem," *NYT*, 8 May 1955, 46.

76. Peter D'Arpa to John Merli, 11 March 1957, Box 69D7, Folder 3, NYCHAR.

77. Report, East Harlem Merchants Association, 28 February 1957, Box 69D7, Folder 3, NYCHAR, 3–4.

78. Annual Report, 1955, NYCHA, Box 98D1, Folder 18, NYCHAR. NYCHA even listed eighteen hundred businesses condemned for public housing.

79. The South Bronx, for instance, suffered massively in the 1970s from rioting after the blackout. See Gonzalez, *The Bronx*, 122. The NYCHA also faced resistance to bulldozer techniques from working-class blacks in Bedford Stuyvesant. See Alexander Burnham, "Negroes' Protest Puts off Housing," *NYT*, 14 June 1963, 17.

80. Charles Grutzner, "Shopping Scarce in City Projects," *NYT*, 16 June 1957, 74; "23,000 Relocated for City Housing," *NYT*, 23 September 1962; Irving Wise to William Reid, "Stores," 10 May 1965, Box 69D7, Folder 3, NYCHAR.

81. Address of Ira Robbins, Dedication of East Harlem Plaza, 16 May 1960, Box 65D7, Folder 6, NYCHAR.

82. Alexander von Hoffman, "Why They Built Pruitt-Igoe," in *From Tenements to the Taylor Homes*, ed. Roger Biles and John Bauman et al. (University Park: Penn State, 2000), 190, 200.

83. Ibid., 195–96.

84. Ibid., 2000. See also Meehan, *The Quality of Federal Policymaking*.

85. "The Case History of a Failure," *Architectural Forum*, December 1965, Box 92B2, Folder 10, NYCHAR, 22–25.

86. The summary of Chicago is from Hunt, "What Went Wrong with Public Housing in Chicago?"

Chapter 8. The Price of Design Reform

1. Charles Grutzner, "City Will Scatter U.S. Housing Units," *NYT*, 25 February 1956, 1. See also "New York City to Scatter Public Housing Units," *American City*, April 1956, 178; "More Slums, Not Fewer, Made by Bulldozer Plans, Jack Says," *NYT*, 15 February 1959; Charles Grutzner, "Lower East Side to Get 21 Million in Public Housing," *NYT*, 13 July 1956, 1. As early as 1953 the federal government had called for lower-density projects and more attention to the existing urban context. See "The President's Advisory Committee on Government Housing Policies and Programs, a Report to the President of the United States," December 1953, Government Printing Office, CHPC Archives, 269–270.

2. "Setting the Record Straight on Public Housing," WNYC, 12 October 1961, Box 72D5, Folder 2, NYCHAR, 5; Marcuse, *Public Housing in New York City*, 272. The reference to building larger apartments is from Gerald Carey to Milton Mollen, 24 April 1962, Box 85D2, Folder 4, NYCHAR.

3. "City Plans Housing in Small Projects," *NYT*, 8 April 1962, 81; "A Clearer Focus," NYCHA 1962 Annual Report, Box 100A2, Folder 12, NYCHAR; "20% of City Units Going to Elderly," *NYT*, 7 October 1962, R1.

4. Joseph Christian to William Reid, 25 June 1964, Box 64B6, Folder 3, NYCHAR. See also Lawrence O'Kane, "Battle of Frills: A Plea for Help," *NYT*, 25 April 1965, R1 for a description of rising costs.

5. "New York City," *Housing Yearbook*, The National Housing Conference, 1968, 74; David Shipler, "The Changing City: Housing Paralysis," *NYT*, 5 June 1969, 1. See also Albert Walsh for a defense of vest pocket building, "Police Headquarter Dedication Ceremony," 19 June 1968, Box 92 B7, Folder 20, NYCHAR.

6. Richard Miller, Draft Article, *Architectural Forum*, 6 March 1959, Box 73B4, Folder 2, NYCHAR, 1.

7. "Are We Building Vertical Sardine Cans," *Housing and Planning News*, CHPC, April-May 1958, 2.

8. NYCHA Development Data Book, 2005, http://www.ci.nyc.ny.us/html/nycha/pdf/dev_data_book.pdf, 49.

9. "'Village' Is Rising in Bronx Section," *NYT*, 20 August 1962, 25.

10. Martin Arnold, "Harlem Decries 'Ghetto' Housing," *NYT*, 8 June 1962, 33; Algernon Black to William Reid, 15 February 1963, Box 64B5, Folder 1, NYCHAR; NYCHA Development Data Book, 2005, http://www.ci.nyc.ny.us/html/nycha/pdf/dev_data_book.pdf, 35. See also Charles Bennett, "Polo Grounds Doomed to Make Way for Low-Rent Housing Project," *NYT*, 10 March 1961, 1.

11. "One out of 18 New Yorkers a Public Housing Tenant," *Architectural Forum*, April 1961, 7. See also Jeanne Lowe, "From Shelter to Community, The First Thirty Five Years of the New York City Housing Authority," 26 August 1969, Box 64E4, Folder 1, NYCHAR; NYCHA Reports, circa 1965, Guide to Housing Developments, Box 100A3, Folder 7, NYCHAR.

12. "30,000 Relocated by City Last Year," *NYT*, 28 May 1961, R16; "23,000 Relocated for City Housing," *NYT*, 23 September 1962, 1; Joseph Christian to William Reid, 25 June 1964, Box 64B6, Folder 3, NYCHAR.

13. Mayor's Housing Conference, 6 January 1964, Box 68C4, Folder 2, NYCHAR, 3.

14. "Designing Public Housing," Letter to the Editor, *NYT*, 30 November 1961, 30.

15. Max Schreiber and Sam Becker, "Letter from 'Architect,'" 7 December 1961, Box 72D4, Folder 3, NYCHAR.

16. "New Face of Public Housing," 29 November 1962, WNYC Transcript, Box 59D4, Folder 4, NYCHAR, 5. See also "New Face of Public Housing," 13 December 1962, WNYC Transcript, Box 59D4, Folder 4, NYCHAR, 5.

17. Minutes, Advisory Council on the Arts, April 1960, Box 62C7, Folder, 1, NYCHAR.

18. Martin Arnold, "New Design, Managerial Ideas Sought in U.S. Housing Projects," *NYT*, 26 November 1961, 86; William Reid to Congressman John Lindsay, 18 March 1963, Box 85D2, Folder 1, NYCHAR.

19. Lyn Shepard, "New Neighborhoods, Not New Slums," *Christian Science Monitor*, 8 December 1965, Box 92B2, Folder 10, NYCHAR; Martin Arnold, "New Design, Managerial Ideas Sought in U.S. Housing Projects," *NYT*, 26 November 1961, 86. New York was slow to give up its planning style. By the early 1960s other authorities were submitting projects to the federal government that were smaller, contextual, and "less institutional" while New York was still submitting plans for large developments. See "More Housing Aid by U.S. Is Sought," *NYT*, 22 July 1963, 21. The federal government generally sought new models for housing during this time. See "'Livable' Housing Sought in Study," *NYT*, 15 October 1963, 21.

20. Robert Tomasson, "Housing Projects Break Mold," *NYT*, 9 December 1973, Box 59B2, Folder 3, NYCHAR; Carolynn Meinhardt, "Talent Best Housing Authority," *Westsider*, 19 September 1974. The Seward Park Houses on the Lower East Side (1973) and Glenmore Plaza (1968) also received flattering press attention. See Stern, *New York 1960*, 148, 923.

21. NYCHA Annual Report, 31 December 1968, Box 60D8, Folder 11, NYCHAR; "'Model Cities' Housing Respects Neighborhood," *NYT*, 7 September

1969, R1; Martin Arnold, "Dedication Held at Renewal Site," *NYT*, 10 October 1962, 68; "City's First One-Story Public Housing Project Is Rising in Richmond," *NYT*, 11 October 1964, R10. The vanguard of low-cost housing had already passed from the NYCHA to the Urban Development Corporation in the early 1970s. See Alan Oser, "How the U.D.C.'s Reach Came to Exceed Its Grasp," *NYT*, 16 March 1975, R1.

22. Lesley Oelsner, "City Still Lags in Housing: 14,000–Unit Goal Is in Doubt," *NYT*, 21 March 1971, 64.

23. Robert Tomasson, "Housing Projects Break Mold," *NYT*, 9 December 1973, Box 59B2, Folder 3, NYCHAR.

24. Statement of Albert Walsh before the Subcommittee on Housing, U.S. House of Representatives, 30 July 1969, Box 69A7, Folder 7, NYCHAR.

25. Simeon Golar to William Ryan, 6 April 1971, Box 69A7, Folder 6, NYCHAR. The Urban Development Corporation, under the direction of Ed Logue, took the lead in building innovative affordable housing during this period, but also it experienced mixed results, aesthetically and financially, in its projects.

26. Harold Bell and Granville Sewell, "Turnkey in New York: Evaluation of an Experiment," Columbia University School of Architecture, June 1969, CHPC Archive; Interview of John Simon by Marcia Robertson, 24 July 1990, NYCHA Oral History Project, NYCHAR, 12. Similar information was provided in the author's interview of Gloria Finkleman, NYCHA Manhattan Borough Director, 28 July 2006.

27. G. E. Kidder Smith, "Low-Cost Housing Design," *NYT*, 14 August 1964, 26.

28. See Miles Glendinning and Stefan Muthesius, *Tower Block: Modern Public Housing in England, Scotland, Wales, and Northern Ireland* (New Haven, Conn.: Yale, 1994) for details on problems in prefabrication and experimental designs.

29. NYCHA, *NYCHA at 70: Generations of Excellence*, Program, Anniversary Celebration Exhibit, Brooklyn Museum, 1 December 2004, 21; NYCHA, 13th Annual Report, 1947, Box 98D1, Folder 7, NYCHAR, 20.

30. See also NYCHA, "Planning and Designing Public Housing Projects," circa 1956, Box 72D4, Folder 3, NYCHAR.

31. Luciano Miceli to Irving Wise, 12 July 1962, Box 90C5, Folder 21, NYCHAR.

32. William Reid, Annual Meeting of Landscape Materials Information Service, Hotel Manhattan, 14 January 1960, Box 59C6, Folder 10, NYCHAR, 1–5.

33. William Reid, "Parks in City Projects," *NYT*, 11 March 1964, 38; "Report on the Program of the New York City Housing Authority in Relation to Mayor Wagner's Platform Proposals," 15 December 1961, Box 68B6, Folder 6, NYCHAR.

34. William Reid, Annual Meeting of Landscape Materials Information Service, Hotel Manhattan, 14 January 1960, Box 59C6, Folder 10, NYCHAR, 1–5; W. E. Andrews to E. J. McGrew Jr., 6 September 1961, Box 64C, Folder 3, NYCHAR. The system of fines appears to have been initiated in 1945, the year in which reference is made at Red Hook Houses to "vandalistic tendencies" that could be addressed (in the case of those who would walk on the grass or destroy trees) by "summons and fines." See K. Volner to May Lumsden, 11 June 1945, Box 71B7, Folder 3, NYCHAR.

35. NYCHA, Press Release, 8 October 1958, Box 69D5, Folder 6, NYCHAR.

36. Charles Grutzner, "Hopschotch Wins Place in Housing," *NYT*, 8 October 1958, 37.

37. Ibid.

38. Irving Wise to Gerald Carey, "Landscape Design," 28 June 1962, Box 90C5,

Folder 21, NYCHAR; Sam Becker to Irving Wise, 31 July 1962, Box 90C5, Folder 21, NYCHAR.

39. William Reid to Helen Hall, 13 April 1962, Box 62C7, Folder 1, NYCHAR, 2; William Reid, "Toward a Slumless City," November 1965, Box 61B3, Folder 4, NYCHAR, 4–5.

40. William Reid, "Toward a Slumless City," November 1965, Box 61B3, Folder 4, NYCHAR, 4–5.

41. "Landscape Architect Paul Friedberg Creates Handsome Public Spaces for Lower East Side Public Housing," *Architectural Record*, July 1966, 197.

42. Jeanne Lowe, "From Shelter to Community, the First Thirty Five Years of the New York City Housing Authority," Typescript, 26 August 1969, Box 64E4, Folder 1, 36, NYCHAR, 37–38.

43. Ada Louis Huxtable, "At Last a Winner," *NYT*, 24 May 1966, 49. See also "Two Housing Authority Developments Being Planned by Iser for Brooklyn," *New York Construction News*, 29 March 1965, Box 92B5, Folder 12, NYCHAR; Alan Rudolph, "Tenant Reaction to Public Housing" (M.A. thesis, Pratt Institute, 16 January 1970), CHPC Archive, 59–60; Interview of Leonard Hopper by the author, 29 December 2005. Among other problems, the amphitheaters and other grade changes encouraged crime (or fear of it) by eliminating sight lines. All of these landscapes have been redesigned in the last two decades although some elements of the planning remain. Recent renovations at Jacob Riis Houses, for instance, have eliminated walls that blocked visibility, lowered the amphitheater walls, removed a "dark" trellis, and added the variety of landscape elements that now define public housing courtyards: top-notch basketball courts, colorful mass-produced play equipment, extensive seating, and smaller planted areas surrounded by steel fencing.

44. Charles Lewis, "Healing the Urban Environment," Lecture at the AIAP, 30 September 1978, reprinted in the *APA Journal*, Box 76A6, Folder 6, NYCHAR, 330; Interview of Hugh Spence, the NYCHA deputy manager of community operations, by the author, 1 August 2006. See also Alexander Burnham, "Project Dwellers, Young and Old, Take to Gardens," *NYT*, 6 July 1963, 17.

Chapter 9. The Benefits of Social Engineering

1. "Aid Asked in Fight on Bias in Housing," *NYT*, 26 November 1956, 29.

2. Philip Cruise, "Interracial Housing Succeeds," *Interracial Review*, April 1955, Box 67E2, Folder 12, NYCHAR.

3. "New York City Housing Authority: Racial Distribution in Operating Projects All Boroughs," 30 June 1954, Box 63C7, Folder 11, NYCHAR. These figures take into account the fact that projects were added over time.

4. "New York City Housing Authority: Racial Distribution in Operating Projects All Boroughs," 30 June 1954, Box 63C7, Folder 11, NYCHAR. Chicago statistics are from the Chicago Housing Authority, Annual Statistical Reports, Racial Occupancy, 1955–1964, Box 66B6, Folder 3, NYCHAR; "Move-Outs from Operating Projects," Box 63C7, Folder 16, NYCHAR. The relatively small black population in city-aided projects had a nearly identical, and high, income profile compared to that of white tenants, indicating that the black middle class was willing to live in public housing. See "Population by Color: 1950 and 1940," Research and Reports, Box 63C7, Folder 12, NYCHAR. See also "Racial Statistic Sheets" (handwritten), circa 1953, Box 63C7, Folder 14, NYCHAR.

5. Various Data Sheets, circa 1956, Box 66A1, Folder 6, NYCHAR; Sydney Gruson, "Our Changing City: New Faces in the Lower Bronx," 11 July 1955, *NYT*, 25; Charles Abrams (author attribution), "The Relationship between Racial Integration and Site Selection," Draft Manuscript, 8 May 1956, Box 85D3, Folder 8, NYCHAR; "New Tenant Move-Ins Into All Operating Projects," Box 63C7, Folder 16, NYCHAR.

6. "2 Housing Agencies Heal Race Dispute," *NYT*, 20 June 1956, 12.

7. Charles Abrams (author attribution), "The Relationship between Racial Integration and Site Selection," Draft Manuscript, 8 May 1956, Box 85D3, Folder 8, NYCHAR.

8. Willis Jones, "Housing Site Criticized," *NYT*, 18 April 1958, 22.

9. "Bias Issue Stirs Housing Debate," *NYT*, 14 May 1956, 27.

10. "New York's First Desegregation Project a Success," 21 December 1956, Box 65C8, Folder 6, NYCHAR. See also Gould Maynard, "The Bronx Did It for Housing," *Social Whirl* 1, no. 2a (28 March 1955): 12, Schomburg Center, NYPL; "Forest Houses Prove Success," *New York Amsterdam News* 49, no. 10 (8 March 1958): 15, Schomburg Center, NYPL.

11. "City Housing Units Bars Race Quotas," *NYT*, 5 July 1959.

12. Harry Fialkin, "Statement on 'The Integration Problem in Public Housing,'" 7 June 1960, Box 85D3, Folder 8, NYCHAR; "Statement of William Reid," circa 1959, Box 85D3, Folder 8, NYCHAR, 4–7. By 1964 neighborhood preference was eliminated because it had become a barrier to integration. Statement of Ira Robbins, Hearing of the Temporary State Commission on Low Income Housing, 26 June 1963, Box 72D1, Folder 5, NYCHAR, 15; "Resolution Revoking Preference in Admission for Neighborhood Residents," 1 July 1964, Box 70D6, Folder 4, NYCHAR.

13. Charles Grutzner, "City Housing Units Bar Race Quotas," 5 July 1959, *NYT*, 27.

14. Ibid.

15. Intergroup Relations, "NYCHA Procedures for Implementing Policy on Integration," circa 1964, Box 64B5, Folder 1, NYCHAR; Bernard Roshco, "The Integration Problem and Public Housing," *The New Leader*, 4 July 1960, Box 60E7, Folder 10, NYCHAR, 10–13. The authority added Phase IV in 1960 for Puerto Ricans in order to get them into all-black projects or projects already in Phases I and II.

16. Harry Fialkin, Statistics Division, "Phase Program," 27 April 1960, no box, NYCHAR.

17. John Aigner, "The Service Is Lousy," *New York Age* 79, no. 33 (31 October 1959): 1, 3, C5, Schomburg Center, NYPL. See also John Aigner, "Into Each Development Some Disunity Must Fall," *New York Age* 79, n. 35 (14 November 1959): 1, C4, Schomburg Center, NYPL.

18. Bernard Roshco, "The Integration Problem and Public Housing," *The New Leader*, 4 July 1960, Box 60E7, Folder 10, NYCHAR, 10–13. James Gaynor, the commissioner of the Division of Housing, reported that "the operation of the Intergroup Relations' Phase Program has resulted in substantial vacancy losses for the State-aided projects." He found 490 of 1, 1219 apartments vacant in Bushwick Houses and increases in vacancy loses from 80 to 727 percent in five others. See James Gaynor to William Reid, 24 March 1960, Box 72D1, Folder 2, NYCHAR.

19. William Reid to Elmer Carter (chairman of SCAD), 19 July 1960, Box 60E7, Folder 10, NYCHAR; William Reid to Elmer Carter, 19 July 1960, Box 60E7, Folder 10, NYCHAR.

20. Harry Fialkin, "Statement on 'The Integration Problem in Public Housing,'" 7 June 1960, Box 85D3, Folder 8, NYCHAR.

21. William Reid to Elmer Carter, 19 July 1960, Box 60E7, Folder 10, NYCHAR.

22. Summary of the Meeting, N.Y. State Commission Against Discrimination, 11 July 1960, Box 60E7, Folder 10, NYCHAR. Ira Robbins characterized Roscho as "disgruntled. He had drafted an annual report . . . which the Housing Authority had been forced to reject."

23. Press Release, 28 August 1960, Box 89A6, Folder 8, NYCHAR; Earl Brown, "NYC Discrimination," *New York Amsterdam News*, 3 December 1960, Box 89A6, Folder 8. See also Clipping Files, Box 89A6, Folder 8, NYCHAR for responses to the program from leading civic organizations.

24. James Hicks, *New York Amsterdam News*, 16 July 1960, Box 89A6, Folder 8, NYCHAR. See also Editorial, "The City Housing Dispute," *New York Citizen Call* 1, no. 35 (14 January 1961): 10, Schomburg Center, NYPL for a defense of the NYCHA; James Hicks, "Misunderstood," *New York Amsterdam News*, 16 July 1960, 10, Schomburg Center, NYPL.

25. Lawrence O'Kane, "Citizens' Panel Seeks to Settle Racial Dispute in City Housing," *NYT*, 7 January 1961, 1; Bernard Katzen, "Report on Informal Investigation of Tenant Selection Practices and Policies of the NYCHA," 9 April 1962, no box/folder, NYCHAR. See also Lawrence O'Kane, "State to Hold Bias Inquiry on City Housing Program," *NYT*, 7 September 1960, 1; William Reid to Elmer Carter, 20 September 1960, Box 89A6, Folder 8, NYCHAR.

26. William Reid to George Fowler, 11 February 1963, Box 71B5, Folder 2, NYCHAR.

27. William Valentine to Gerald Carey, 30 April 1964, Box 64B5, Folder 1, NYCHAR; Joseph Christian to Gerald Carey, 22 November 1965, Box 64B7, Folder 2, NYCHAR, 6.

28. "Tenant Turnover by Race," Box 64B5, Folder 7, NYCHAR; Joseph Christian, "Internal Review of Intergroup Relations," 27 November 1967, Box 64C5, Folder 3, NYCHAR. See also "Racial Composition of Move-Outs and Move-Ins," January 1967, Box 64B5, Folder 7, NYCHAR for further confirmation of white flight from all the phased projects.

29. NYCHA, Tenant Data, 1969, Box 61B2, Folder 1, NYCHAR. See also NYCHA Annual Report, 1962, "A Clearer Focus," Box 100A2, Folder 12, NYCHAR; Blanco Cedeno to Aramis Gomez, 3 September 1970, Box 71B5, Folder 1, NYCHAR. It should be noted that in *Otera v. New York Housing Authority*, the Second Circuit Court gave the NYCHA permission to select white tenants over minority tenants as part of an integration program. By this point such policies were rather moot. See Martin Schwartz, "Public Housing Developments," *New York Law Journal*, 19 March 1974, Box 88B5, Folder 2, NYCHAR.

30. NYCHA, "Recommendations—Ethnic Characteristics—HA Developments," 3 September 1970, Box 71B5, Folder 1, NYCHAR. Staten Island's phase program remained in modified form until 1990, when a lawsuit challenged white preferences. Legal Aid sued the NYCHA in 1990 and under agreement the NYCHA "set aside three out of every four vacancies in 31 specified projects, up to a maximum of 1,990 apartments, for applicants who may have been denied an equal opportunity to move" from 1985 to 1990. The NYCHA "had ended the policy and most of the practices challenged by Legal Aid" before the suit. The policy was a legacy of local preferences granted "to gain necessary community support for some projects. . . . In neighborhoods where one race predominates, these preferences had a racially discriminatory effect." Some officials were

expediting white applications in the central office at the request of managers and community leaders. "Often these requests favored white applicants who wanted to get into predominantly white projects." On Staten Island, "With little supervision from Manhattan, the Staten Island office departed from Housing Authority policy by allowing white applicants to go into waiting lists for predominantly white projects even though the projects needed no new applicants." The NYCHA closed the Staten Island office after the discovery. Press Release, "NYCHA Discrimination Lawsuit Settled," 1 July 1992, Box 100B2, Folder 15, NYCHAR. NYCHA also settled a suit about Williamsburg and the number of Jews versus other minorities. NYCHA for many years apparently favored Hasidic tenants there. Protests and sit-in by Hispanics forced action. By 1991 the policy was no longer in place. Shawn Kennedy, "For Brooklyn Family, a Rare Find: Public Housing," *NYT*, 6 February 1994, 41. See also Ian Fisher, "Demonstrators Seize Projects in Brooklyn," *NYT*, 2 October 1993, 25; Shawn Kennedy, "Plan to Select City Tenants Is Affirmed," *NYT*, 4 December 1993, 25.

31. "Minutes of Project Security Problems Meeting," 18 October 1967, Box 64B7, Folders 4/8, NYCHAR.

32. NYCHA, "Racial Distribution in Operating Projects," Box 92E1, Folder 12, NYCHAR; Mel Weiss, "Everything You Wanted to Know about Tenant Selection . . . ," January 1973, Box 65C1, Folder 1, NYCHAR; NYCHA Statistics by Project, June 30, 1974, Box 88C6, Folder 5, NYCHAR; William Steinmann to Ruben Franco, "Tenant Data," 13 April 1995, Box 74C5, Folder 1, NYCHAR; NYCHA, Comprehensive Annual Financial Report, 31 December 2005, Author Collection, 72.

33. William Reid, Radio Talk, WMGM, 2 August 1959, Box 62C6, Folder 1, NYCHAR, 4.

34. Barry Gottehrer, "The 30 Hurdles to Public Housing," *Herald Tribune*, 23 March 1965, Box 92B4, Folder 13.

35. Harry Fialkin and Milton Saslow to Alex Moffat, 23 August 1951, Box 71B3, Folder 1, NYCHAR.

36. Ibid.

37. "Income Rule Eased in Low-Rent Homes," *NYT*, 30 June 1953, 25; "Resolution Related to Desirability as a Ground for Eligibility," 25 June 1953, Box 62C6, Folder 4, NYCHAR. The list of factors is from "Proposed Revision of Tenant Selection Policies and Procedures," 14 December 1961, Box 65C8, Folder 12, NYCHAR, 4.

38. "Notes on Meeting Held Monday, 17 February 1958," Box 68C4, Folder 7, NYCHAR.

39. Joseph Fried, "City Easing Rules on Admitting Poor to Public Housing," NYT, Box 60D8, Folder 2, NYCHAR.

40. Interview of Victoria Archibald-Good, the Bronx African American History Project, www.bronxhistoricalsociety.org/journal/afro_american_history.html, 4–7; "The New York City Housing Authority," *The Neighborhood*, Summer 1983, Box 74C6, Folder 5, NYCHAR, 21.

41. See, for instance, Kaplan and Kaplan, *Between Ocean and City*, 102–5, and Ballon and Jackson, *Robert Moses and the Modern City*, 102–3.

42. Philip Cruise to Robert Moses, 26 June 1956, Box 68C1, Folder 1, NYCHAR; Skidmore, Owings, and Merrill, "Harlem Slum Clearance Coordination," 24 March 1955, Box 68C1, Folder 3, NYCHAR.

43. Organization of Housing Managers Report, September 1957, Box 100A4, Folder 13, NYCHAR, 4–91.

44. "Slum Clearance or People Clearance," Manhattan Tenant Councils, June 1955, Box 68C1, Folder 2, NYCHAR; "New Tenant Move-Ins into All Operating Projects," Box 63C7, Folder 16, NYCHAR.

45. The figures are from an excerpt of Robert Moore Fisher's draft dissertation, 21 April 1958, Box 85D2, Folder 5, NYCHAR; Various Data Sheets, circa 1956, Box 66A1, Folder 6, NYCHAR; NYCHA Annual Report, 1955, Box 98D1, Folder 17, NYCHAR, 12.

46. Elizabeth Wood, "Public Housing and Mrs. McGee," Pamphlet of Speech Given 24 October 1956, Citizens' Housing and Planning Council, Box 67E3, Folder 23, NYCHAR, 1–13.

47. Ibid.

48. "Housing Authority Acts to Evict Families . . . ," *NYT*, 31 January 1957, 23.

49. "Evictions from City Housing Protested," *NYT*, 29 March 1958, 20; Grace Bliss to William Reid, "Reply to Mike Wallace," 30 July 1965, Box 62C6, Folder 1, NYCHAR.

50. George Biro to Gerald Carey, 26 February 1960, Box 64C2, Folder 3.

51. Harry Fialkin to Irving Wise, "Addendum to Report on Problem Families," 28 November 1961, Box 65D1, Folder 1, NYCHAR; NYCHA Tables, "Problem Families in Occupancy," 31 December 1965, Box 64B5, Folder 7, NYCHAR.

52. "City to Integrate Welfare Tenants," *NYT*, 14 February 1957, 29. In 1961, for instance, Ravenswood (a city-sponsored project) had income levels of $5,156 while Queensbridge had only $2,880. Howard Marder to Nicholas Bloom, e-mail, 11 April 2006.

53. Alexander Moffat and Percy Frank, "Percentage of Welfare Families . . . ," 17 July 1958, and William Reid to Files, 29 July 1958, Box 64C1, Folder 4, NYCHAR.

54. NYCHA Annual Report, 1962, "A Clearer Focus," Box 100A2, Folder 12, NYCHAR.

55. Mitchell Ginsberg, Speech to the Joint Legislative Committee on Housing and Urban Development, 3 February 1967, Box 68E4, Folder 4, NYCHAR.

56. Hunt, "What Went Wrong with Public Housing in Chicago?," 14, 180, 132.

57. Von Hoffman, "Why They Built Pruitt-Igoe," 201

Chapter 10. Meeting the Management Challenge

1. Edmond Butler to Fiorello LaGuardia, 1 June 1945, La Guardia Papers, Roll 92A, MA.

2. Philip Cruise to the *New York Daily News*, 27 February 1957, Box 65C8, Folder 6, NYCHAR, 4–9.

3. Stern, *New York 1960*, 901; "Fort Greene Houses Will Be Renovated," *NYT*, 10 February 1957, 71.

4. Vandalism is detailed at Williamsburg Houses in 1945. See Mrs. Uffner to May Lumsden, 24 August 1945, Box 71B7, Folder 3, NYCHAR; Robert Moses to Philip Cruise, 17 February 1954, Box 68C1, Folder 1, NYCHAR.

5. Interview of Bernard Moses by Marcia Robertson, 24 July 1990, NYCHA Oral History Project, NYCHAR, 7–9.

6. Charles Preusse, Organization and Management of NYCHA, September 1957, Box 100A2, no folder, NYCHAR, 5; E. W. Kenworthy, "City Housing Unit Faces U.S. Inquiry," *NYT*, 22 August 1957, 31.

7. Interview of Brian Clarke, director, NYCHA Technical Services Division, by the author, 21 July 2006.

8. Ira Robbins, Address to the ADA, 13 September 1958, Box 59D3, Folder 5, NYCHAR, 2, 4; Charles Grutzner, "Tiled Lobbies, Closet Doors Give a Modern Look to Public Housing," *NYT,* 1 January 1957, 25.

9. Thomas Wheeler, "New York Tries a New Approach," *The Reporter,* 17 June 1965, 18–20. See also Lyn Shepard, "New Neighborhoods, Not New Slums," *Christian Science Monitor,* 8 December 1965, Box 92B2, Folder 10, NYCHAR; NYCHA, "Planning and Designing Public Housing Projects," circa 1956, Box 72D4, Folder 3, NYCHAR; NYCHA official to George Winder, 1 April 1968, Box 64C5, Folder 3, NYCHAR.

10. Philip Cruise to the *New York Daily News,* 27 February 1957, Box 65C8, Folder 6, NYCHAR, 4–9; Charles Grutzner, "Tiled Lobbies, Closet Doors Give a Modern Look to Public Housing," *NYT,* 1 January 1957, 25.

11. Elizabeth Lyman, "Tenant Response to a Series of Family Life Discussion Groups in a Public Housing Project," Community Service Society, December 1966, Box 61C5, Folder 8, NYCHAR.

12. AIA Tour, NYCHA, 25 June 1952, Box 59D3, Folder 2, NYCHAR.

13. Philip Cruise to the *New York Daily News,* 27 February 1957, Box 65C8, Folder 6, NYCHAR, 4–9.

14. Interview of Cyril Grossman by Marcia Robertson, 1 August 1990, NYCHA Oral History Project, NYCHAR, 28, 45.

15. Interview of Cyril Grossman by Marcia Robertson, 1 August 1990, NYCHA Oral HistoryProject, Box 1, NYCHAR, 15, 23, 27. The NYCHA official Raymond Henson in oral history interviews also relates that apartment inspections continued into the 1960s but noted that the inspections tended to be undertaken only after painting apartments, so that inspections affected only about 10 to 20 percent of the apartments per year. He relates that "90%" of apartments were in good shape at that time. Interview of Raymond Henson by Marcia Robertson, 6 August 1990, NYCHA Oral History Project, Box 1, NYCHAR, 18. See also Project Survey Report, Taft Houses, 6 December 1974, Box 66E8, Folder 5, NYCHAR.

16. "Setting the Record Straight on Public Housing," WNYC, 8 February 1962, Box 70D6, Folder 4, NYCHAR. See also Management Department, General Memo, 21 February 1967, Box 90C4, Folder 11, NYCHAR.

17. Charles Rutter, Memo, 6 April 1950, Box 71B7, Folder 3, NYCHAR.

18. Interview of Raymond Henson by Marcia Robertson, 6 August 1990, NYCHA Oral History Project, Box 1, NYCHAR, 14–15.

19. William Reid to James Gaynor, 27 April 1959, Box 64E1, Folder 5, NYCHAR, 5.

20. "New York City Housing Authority—Monthly Housing Report," Transcription of a WNYC Tape Recording, 10 August 1961, Box 72D4, Folder 3, NYCHAR; "Residential Security Program," NAHRO Conference, 15 September 1978, Box 92D7, Folder 12, NYCHAR. The figure for resident employment in 2004 is now 29 percent, or approximately four thousand employees. See "Resident Life" in *Celebrating Seventy Years,* 1934–2004, NYCHA Publication, 1 December 2004, Author Collection.

21. Interview of Roy Metcalf by Marcia Robertson, 6 August 1990, NYCHA Oral History Project, NYCHAR, 20.

22. Report by Ford, Bacon, and Davis for the NYCHA, 1 July 1952, Box 74A5, no folder, NYCHAR, 22–29.

23. Joseph Martin and Douglas Sefton, "Public Housing Scandal: Vast 'Waste' Land of Fouls and Faults," *New York Daily News,* 6 April 1965; Joseph Martin and

Douglas Sefton, "Public Housing Scandal: Chronic Woe: Poor Painting," *New York Daily News*, 7 April 1965; Tom Collins, "Painter Tells Cheatin' Ways Used by Corrupt Contractors," *New York World Telegram and Sun*, 10 June 1965, Box 92N1, Folder 4, NYCHAR; Charles Grutzner, "City Paint Inquiry Widened to Cover 7 Public Agencies," *NYT*, 13 June 1965, Box 92B1, Folder 4, NYCHAR; Barry Gottehrer, "Unusual Agency," *New York Herald Tribune*, 2 September 1965; Jack Roth, "City Aide Accused of Taking $400,000 in Bribes from 15 Painting Contractors," *NYT*, 2 September 1965; Samuel Kaplan, "Housing Agency Changes Methods," *NYT*, 3 September 1965, 29.

24. Edgemere Tenant's Association, Percy Frank to Rachel Benson, 29 August 1961, Box 90C4, Folder 6, NYCHAR.

25. Abrams, *The Future of Housing*, 33.

26. "Police Department," January 24, 1944, Box 57D4, Folder 1, NYCHAR; Albert Mayer, "So Far, So Good in Public Housing," *NYT*, 15 September 1940, 115.

27. "The New York City Housing Authority Police," FBI Law Enforcement Bulletin, November 1966, Box 76B4, Folder 89, NYCHAR, 2.

28. "NYCHA-Housing Police," Comprehensive Review, NYCHA, HUD, Region II, September 1983, Box 91C4, Folder 1, NYCHAR, xiv–3.

29. K. Volner to May Lumsden, 11 June 1945, Box 71B7, Folder 3, NYCHAR; Uffner to May Lumsden, 24 August 1945, Box 71B7, Folder 3, NYCHAR.

30. "Crime Kept Down by Housing Police," *NYT*, 11 December 1949, 120.

31. William Reid to James Gaynor, 5 May 1959, Box 64C1, Folder 3, NYCHAR; "The New York City Housing Authority Police," FBI Law Enforcement Bulletin, November 1966, Box 76B4, Folder 89, NYCHAR, 2; "New Force Will Patrol City Housing Projects," *NYT*, 14 November 1952, 10.

32. Annual Report, 1954, NYCHA, Box 98D1, Folder 16, NYCHAR, 14–15.

33. Joseph Martin, ". . . Creates a Juvenile Jungle," *New York Daily News*, 1957 (NYCHAR).

34. "More Policemen Asked in Housing," *NYT*, 30 March 1957, 39.

35. Charles Preusse, "Police Protection in the New York City Housing Authority," May 1957, Box 71E4, Folder 5, NYCHAR, 1–5. See also "City Asked to Add to Housing Police," *NYT*, 20 May 1957, 27.

36. Public Housing Managers of NYCHA, "A Look at New York City's Public Housing Today," January 1958, Box 64C3, Folder 5, NYCHAR, 1–12.

37. Ibid.

38. John Mitchell to All Members of the NYCHA Police Force, 29 August 1958, Box 64C3, Folder 4, NYCHAR; William Reid to James Gaynor, 5 May 1959, Box 64C1, Folder 3, NYCHAR.

39. John Mitchell to William Reid, 30 September 1958, Box 64C3, Folder 4, NYCHAR.

40. John Mitchell to William Reid, "Activity Report," 26 March 1959, Box 64 C1, Folder 3, NYCHAR.

41. Irving Wise to Reid, Madigan, Robbins, and Carey, 6 December 1960, Box 70D3, Folder 4, NYCHAR. In 1963, Governor Rockefeller also signed into law a bill demanding that city governments "provide police and other protective services in public housing projects." The bill had emerged "as a result of crimes and other incidents involving housing developments in New York City and Albany." Rockefeller reminded city officials that "a security force employed by a municipal authority . . . is not a substitute for the municipal police force." Prompting the legislation had been statements by high-ranking police officials in New York City who "contended that the force was not large enough

to give special attention to housing projects." See Leonard Ingalls, "State to Require Police for Homes," *NYT*, 6 April 1963, 7.

42. Finance and Audit Department, NYCHA, 11 May 1964, Box 70D3, Folder 2, NYCHAR.

43. NYCHA Annual Report, 1962, "A Clearer Focus," Box 100A2, Folder 12, NYCHAR.

44. "NYCHA-Housing Police," Comprehensive Review, NYCHA, HUD, Region II, September 1983, Box 91C4, Folder 1, NYCHAR, xiv–2; Lyn Shepard, "New Neighborhoods, Not New Slums," *Christian Science Monitor*, 8 December 1965, Box 92B2, Folder 10, NYCHAR.

45. "The New York City Housing Authority Police," FBI Law Enforcement Bulletin, November 1966, Box 76B4, Folder 89, NYCHAR, 2; Joseph Weldon and Robert Ledee, "High Rise Policing Techniques," publication unclear, circa 1966, Box 60E7, Folder 4, NYCHAR, 755–761. The estimate of 75 percent is from "Minutes of Project Security Problems Meeting," 18 October 1967, Box 64B7, Folder 5, NYCHAR.

46. "Elliott Chelsea Tenants Seek Guards at Night," *Chelsea Clinton News*, 11 February 1965, Box 92B2, Folder 22, NYCHAR.

47. "Meeting on Conditions at Van Dyke Houses," 13 April 1966, Box 66E8, Folder 13, NYCHAR.

48. Mary O'Flaherty, "Tenants Form Patrols to Combat Crime," *Sunday News*, 1 December 1968, B2. For security concerns in large projects, not just the NYCHA, see Thomas Ennis, "Bill Would Put Armed Guards in All Large Apartment Houses," *NYT*, 29 March 1964, R1.

49. Annual Report, 1968, Arrests for Index Crimes, All Crimes, NYCHA Police Department, Box 64C3, Folder 3, NYCHAR.

50. Joseph Weldon and Robert Ledee, "High Rise Policing Techniques," publication unclear, circa 1966, Box 60E7, Folder 4, NYCHAR, 755–61.

51. Ira Robbins, Speech, 27 October 1960, Box 69D3, Folder 2, NYCHAR, 1–3; "Resident Life" in *Celebrating Seventy Years*, 1934–2004, NYCHA Publication, 1 December 2004, Author Collection; Survey, NYCHA Community Affairs, 1949, Box 72D5, Folder 5, NYCHAR, 1–3.

52. NYCHA, 13th Annual Report, 1947, Box 98D1, Folder 7, NYCHAR, 21; "Report on Community Facilities," United Neighborhood Houses of New York, 27 September 1945, Box 72D5, Folder 4, NYCHAR, 1–7.

53. Report, Jacob A. Riis Neighborhood Settlement, 1950 and 1951, Box 71D2, NYCHAR Folder 1, 1–2; "The Functions of the Community Activities Division," 17 October 1955, Box 69D3, Folder 3, NYCHAR; Survey, NYCHA Community Affairs, 1949, Box 72D5, Folder 5, NYCHAR, 1–3. See also "Good Relations Sought in Harlem," *NYT*, 24 September 1948, 30; Milton Levenson, "Low Rentals Grow a Good-Will Crop," *NYT*, 6 December 1948, 21; "Program for All at Lincoln Houses," *NYT*, 11 February 1949, 44; Mary Roche, "Housewives' Ideal in Model Kitchen," 13 March 1946, 26.

54. Ira Robbins, Statement, Hearing of the Temporary State Commission on Low-Income Housing, 26 June 1963, Box 72D1, Folder 5, NYCHAR.

55. NYCHA, Minutes of the Committee on Health, Welfare, and Recreation Services, 18 May 1950, Box 71C7, Folder 6, NYCHAR.

56. "The Functions of the Community Activities Division," 17 October 1955, Box 69D3, Folder 3, NYCHAR; Memorandum for Mayor Wagner, Assorted Authors, circa 1954, Box 68B6, Folder 3, NYCHAR.

57. "More Play Areas Planned for City," *NYT*, 14 September 1954, 22.

58. "First Year's Program," Office of the Mayor, News Release, 14 September 1954, Box 68C1, Folder 3, NYCHAR, 1. By the mid-1960s this policy would come to anger certain city officials, including the assistant director of the budget for the city of New York, who lamented the policy that started "about ten years ago" when "it was the practice of the Housing Authority to design and construct housing projects which included areas for community activities . . . in many instances without approval by the Board of Estimate." He remarked that the "result was that after the project was completed, requests were made for funds to operate libraries, health centers, recreation centers, etc. in these buildings." James D. Carroll to Gerald Carey, 9 May 1963, Box 72D5, Folder 2, NYCHAR.

59. Gerald Carey, "Statement to the Senate Sub-Committee to Investigate Juvenile Delinquency," circa 1957, Box 72D5, Folder 3, NYCHAR, 1–10. Carey estimated that a decent community center occupied ninety-five hundred square feet, "four thousand square feet more than the rules usually allow." He did note, however, that New York had gotten around strict federal rules on total square footage and hoped "that they [the federal government] will make allowances as they sometimes have in other special situations in the past."

60. Charles Preusse, Organization and Management of NYCHA, September 1957, Box 100A2, no folder, NYCHAR, 41; Philip Benjamin, "Housing Tangles Face New Board," NYT, 4 May 1958, 1.

61. Address of Ira Robbins, Dedication of East Harlem Plaza, 16 May 1960, Box 65D7, Folder 6, NYCHAR.

62. "Housing Staffs Expand," NYT, 24 July 1961, 41.

63. "Recreation Staff Augmented," NYT, 2 July 1962, 23; Interview of Victoria Archibald-Good, The Bronx African American History Project, www.bronx historicalsociety.org/journal/afro_american_history.html, 3.

64. Charles Grutzner, "Shopping Scarce in City Projects," NYT, 16 June 1957, 74.

65. J. Schwartz, "Tenant Unions in New York City's Low-Rent Housing, 1933–1949," 428–29; "Program of the Inter-Project Tenants Council of New York," 19 October 1949, O'Dwyer Papers, MN 47035, Roll 35, MA; quotations are from Joel Schwartz's article on tenant activism in New York housing, http://www.tenant.net/community/history/hist04b.html. See also J. Schwartz, "Tenant Unions in New York City's Low-Rent Housing, 1933–1949" for his descriptions of the important role of communists in housing activism during this time. Schwartz notes that HUAC "informants later alleged that the CP had 'colonized' projects like Fort Greene." Unfavorable red-baiting newspaper coverage and evidence of strong communist-ALP support in public housing had the potential to destroy the housing movement in New York, although Schwartz does not see it that way (430).

66. "Blocs Held Peril in Public Housing," NYT, 3 May 1950, 34.

67. James Gaynor, Director of Management, to All Housing Managers, 16 March 1950, Box 69D7, Folder 1, NYCHAR; Memo to Ellen Lurie, 22 April 1959, Box 69D7, Folder 1, NYCHAR.

68. Interview of John Simon by Marcia Robertson, 24 July 1990, NYCHA Oral History Project, NYCHAR, 7. On NYCHA encouragement of participation, see "Students Create Tenant Civic Zeal," NYT, 28 May 1961, 64.

69. Preston David, "Social Casework at Lillian Wald Houses," circa 1965, Box 61B3, Folder 4, NYCHAR, 10.

70. Alan Rudolph, "Tenant Reaction to Public Housing" (M.A. thesis, Pratt Institute, 16 January 1970), CHPC Archive, 68.

71. Mamie Jackson is quoted in "A Transformed Public Housing Program,"

Panel Discussion, Metropolitan Council on Housing, 16 November 1962, Box 64B6, Folder 3 (NYCHAR).

72. Lisa Hammel, "Household Tips One of Services in City Housing," *NYT*, 22 August 1964.

73. Hunt, "What Went Wrong with Public Housing in Chicago?," 144, 16, 146, 18, 449–51, 367–68.

74. Meehan, *The Quality of Federal Policymaking*, 63.

75. Vail, *Reclaiming Public Housing*, 26.

76. Ibid., 26.

77. Ian Cole and Robert Furbey, *The Eclipse of Council Housing* (London: Routledge, 1994); Anne Power, *Estates on the Edge: The Social Consequences of Mass Housing in Northern Europe* (London: Macmillan, 1997), 41; Glendinning and Muthesius, *Tower Block*; Ian Colquhoun, *RIBA Book of 20th Century British Housing* (Oxford: Butterworth, 1999); Anthony Quiney, *House and Home: A History of the Small English House* (London: BBC Press, 1986); Anne Power, *Hovels to High Rise: State Housing in Europe since 1850* (London: Routledge, 1993). The section on the well-run Danish system is particularly hopeful.

Chapter 11. Surviving the Welfare State

1. Homer Smith, "Hits CHA," *New York Amsterdam News*, 8 June 1968, Box 60E1, Folder 8 (NYCHAR).

2. Lowe, "From Shelter to Community, the First Thirty Five Years of the New York City Housing Authority," Typescript, 26 August 1969, Box 64E4, Folder 1, NYCHAR, 8.

3. Mayor's Housing Conference, 6 January 1964, Box 68C4, Folder 2, NYCHAR, 11; William Stewart to William Reid, 9 September 1965, Box 64B5, Folder 1, NYCHAR; "Black Housing Officials Report to NYCHA," circa 1976, Box 88A6, Folder 2, NYCHAR; "Mayor Puts Negro on Housing Board," *NYT*, 17 June 1942, 11. A. Philip Randolph had declined the position first.

4. "Introducing Our New Chairman," NYCHA, Box 92B7, Folder 21, NYCHAR.

5. "Low Rents, But Where?" *Housing and Planning News* 24, no. 7 (June 1966), Citizens' Housing and Planning Council, Box 87B5, Folder 1, NYCHAR, 2.

6. "'Fact Sheets' List Housing Projects," *NYT*, 7 February 1965, R8; Walter Goodman, "The Battle of Forest Hills," *NYT*, 20 February 1972, SM8.

7. Robbins and Tyler, *Reminiscences of a Housing Advocate*, CHPC Archive, 113. New York's ability to build public housing outside traditional minority ghettos may not have been all that activists desired, but it compared favorably with Chicago, where fifty of fifty-four developments were by 1969 "located in black neighborhoods, and 99 percent of their tenants [were] black." The four projects in white areas were over 90 percent white. See "Public Housing in Black and White," *Commonweal*, 16 May 1969, 253. See also Hirsch, *Making the Second Ghetto*.

8. As early as 1947 the NYCHA had encountered resistance to public housing in the predominantly middle-class area of Jackson Heights. "Moses Proposal Snarls Authority," *NYT*, 13 August 1947, 2; "Deadlock Broken on City's Housing," *NYT*, 16 August 1947, 15; "Board Shuffles Plans on Housing," *NYT*, 19 September 1947, 48. Bensonhurst community members tried to stop construction of the Marlboro Houses in 1958. The authority claimed that the project had actually helped the upgrading of the neighborhood. See Thomas Ennis, "Housing

Project Spurs Community," *NYT*, 19 October 1958, 1. There seems to have been some racial objections to the Clason Point project allowing black tenants. See a threatening letter from Simon Porteus to Gerard Swope, 5 September 1941, Box 54D5, Folder 10, NYCHAR. Significant protests surrounded public housing in the Bronx in the 1950s. See Sydney Gruson, "Our Changing City: New Faces in the Lower Bronx," 11 July 1955, *NYT*, 25; and Richard Amper, "Our Changing City: Conflicts in the Upper Bronx," *NYT*, 15 July 1955, 23; Charles Bennett, "Housing Is Voted for Castle Hill," *NYT*, 11 March 1954, 33.

9. "Bias Issue Stirs Housing Debate," *NYT*, 14 May 1956, 27.

10. Memo to Gerald Carey, "Housing Needs and Problems," 22 November 1965, Box 64B7, Folder 2, NYCHAR, 3, 7.

11. David Shipler, "The Changing City: Housing Paralysis," *NYT*, 5 June 1969, 1.

12. Joseph Christian to Ralph Goldberg, 25 June 1968, Box 64B7, Folder 1, NYCHAR. The list of cities that had retreated from public housing by the early 1960s is from Gelfand, *A Nation of Cities*, 337.

13. John Herbers, "City Accused of Failing to Disperse Housing for the Poor," *NYT*, 4 November 1971, 22. Eleven is the number cited by Herbers, but thirteen is more frequently given. Although the project was technically located on the border of Rego Park and Forest Hills, it has become known as the Forest Hills development.

14. Joseph P. Fried, "Simeon Golar's City-Within-a-City," *NYT*, 30 April 1972, 16; Marcuse, *Public Housing in New York City*, 323; David Shipler, "Golar Criticizes Nixon on Housing," *NYT*, 8 May 1970, 9; Martin Tolchin, "Lindsay Attacks U.S. Housing Bill," *NYT*, 26 July 1969, 52; Edith Asbury, "Lindsay Reports Gains in Housing," *NYT*, 15 January 1972, 36.

15. Walter Goodman, "The Battle of Forest Hills," *NYT*, 20 February 1972, SM8.

16. Ibid.

17. David Shipler, "Housing for the Poor: A Typical Reaction," *NYT*, 19 November 1971, 49; "Typical Queens Ethnic Mix Vowed for Project," *NYT*, 5 December 1971, A16. Walter Goodman carefully calculated the impact of the project and found that only the high school would be taxed, and that slightly, by the housing project. Walter Goodman, "The Battle of Forest Hills," *NYT*, 20 February 1972, SM8.

18. Murray Schumach, "City Places Sign on Site of Forest Hills Projects," *NYT*, 24 December 1971, 23.

19. "Golar Assails Washington," *NYT*, 4 December 1971, 21.

20. Interview of Roy Metcalf by Marcia Robertson, 6 August 1990, NYCHA Oral History Project, NYCHAR, 4.

21. Joseph Fried, "Simeon Golar's City-Within-a-City," *NYT*, 30 April 1972, 16; Murray Schumach, "Forest Hills Project Is Upheld on Appeal," *NYT*, 5 May 1972, 1; Martin Tolchin, "Forest Hills Site May Be Cut 50%," *NYT*, 15 July 1972, 1; Francis Clines, "Lindsay Accepts Compromise Plan for Forest Hills," *NYT*, 20 August 1972, 1. The change would cost the city approximately $9 million more because the price per unit would increase but the federal government would not cover costs above the established formula. See also Interview of John Simon by Marcia Robertson, 24 July 1990, NYCHA Oral History Project, NYCHAR, 10; Edith Asbury, "Golar to Oppose Manes on Housing," *NYT*, 26 October 1972, 44.

22. Paul Montgomery, "Forest Hills Project Rising, But the Controversy Lingers," *NYT*, 27 March 1973, 99; Jill Gerston, "Bronx Scatter-Site Project Welcomed by Its Ex-Foes," *NYT*, 14 February 1975, 41; "The Future of Public Hous-

ing in New York City," Community Service Society, *Urban Agenda* 14 (July 1999), www.cssny.org/pubs/issuebrief/no14.htm.

23. "President Finds End of City Crisis, with Dip in Crime," *NYT*, 5 March 1973; Editorial, "The Urban Losers," *NYT*, 27 April 1973; "New York City Public Housing Construction: The Ups and Downs of the Federal Freeze," *New York Construction News*, 30 April 1973, Box 59B3, Folder 39, NYCHAR; "'No' to the Old, 'Maybe' to the New," *NYT*, 23 September 1973; "Is the Government Putting Up 'Instant Slums'?" *U.S. News and World Report*, 11 September 1972, 66; "Public Housing in Trouble: No Room for the Poor," *Commonweal*, 5 January 1973, 292.

24. Edith Asbury, "City Fears U.S. Freeze . . . ," *NYT*, 11 January 1973; John Kifner, "Nation's Cities Brace for Major Financial Problems Resulting from Nixon Budget," *NYT*, 30 April 1973; "'No' to the Old, 'Maybe' to the New," *NYT*, 23 September 1973. See also Interview of Roy Metcalf by Marcia Robertson, 6 August 1990, NYCHA Oral History Project, NYCHAR, 4.

25. Alan Oser, "New York Housing Agency Is Mastering Subsidies on U.S. Units," *NYT*, 10 September 1976, 22; "Major Accomplishments," NYCHA, 1977, Box 92E5, Folder 11, NYCHAR. See also Joseph Fried, "City Begins New Rent-Subsidy Program," *NYT*, 22 January 1976, 20.

26. Gail Radford formulated this "two-tier" concept. See Radford, *Modern Housing for America*.

27. Barry Gottehrer, "The Public Housing Problem . . . ," *Herald Tribune*, 26 March 1965, Box 92B4, Folder 13, NYCHAR.

28. Eric Pace, "City Aide Says Unwed Mothers Are Kept from Public Housing," *NYT*, 10 December 1965, Box 92B2, Folder 10, NYCHAR.

29. Edward Burks, "Housing Agency Upheld on Screening," *NYT*, 11 August 1966, 30. See also Homer Bigart, "City's Welfare Rolls Soar Despite National Prosperity and Decline in Unemployment," *NYT*, 30 July 1967, 66.

30. Mitchell Ginsberg to Walter Washington, 15 December 1966, Box 68E4, Folder 4, NYCHAR.

31. Mitchell Ginsberg, Speech to the Joint Legislative Committee on Housing and Urban Development, 3 February 1967, Box 68E4, Folder 4, NYCHAR.

32. Mitchell Ginsberg to Walter Washington, 23 February 1967, Box 68E4, Folder 4, NYCHAR.

33. Homer Bigart, "City Welfare Rolls . . ." *NYT*, 30 July 1967, 66; George Sternlieb and Bernard Indik, *The Ecology of Welfare: Housing and the Welfare Crisis in New York City* (New Brunswick, N.J.: Transaction Books, 1973), 54–72.

34. Fred Siegel, "The Social Democratic City," *The Public Interest*, spring 2000 (internet archive, no page numbers). See also Gonzalez, *The Bronx*, 118.

35. Albert Walsh to Horace Morancie, 19 April 1968, Box 60D8, Folder 2, NYCHAR. See also a stormy meeting during which Ira Robbins confronted unwed mothers. Deirdre Carmody, "Unwed Mothers Complain to City," *NYT*, 23 March 1968, 28.

36. "Housing Authority Amends Rules," *Citizen Housing and Planning Council News*, April-March 1968, CHPC, 3; Glenn Fowler, "Public Housing Helpless to Aid Most Who Apply," *NYT*, 5 September 1971, R1.

37. Roger Starr, "Which of the Poor Shall Live in Public Housing?" *The Public Interest* 23 (spring 1971) (CPHC).

38. NYCHA, "Activities of Management," April-June 1968, Box 64B6, Folder 1, NYCHAR, 2.

39. Association of Public Housing Managers, "Dangers Facing Public Housing in New York City," April 1968, Box 64B6, Folder 1, NYCHAR.

40. Roger Starr, "Which of the Poor Shall Live in Public Housing?"

41. Ibid.

42. Glenn Fowler, "Public Housing Helpless to Aid Most Who Apply," *NYT*, 5 September 1971, R1.

43. Managers' and Superintendents' Meeting, 21 October 1969, Box 58A6, Folder 7, NYCHAR.

44. Ibid.

45. Simeon Golar to John Lindsay, 4 January 1973, Box 66E, Folder 3, NYCHAR; Glenn Fowler, "Public Housing Helpless to Aid Most Who Apply," *NYT*, 5 September 1971, R1. Val Coleman to Mark Drucker, 24 September 1971, Box 65D2, Folder 4, NYCHAR. See also Joseph Fried, "25,000 Welfare Families in Projects Get Rent Cuts," *NYT*, 7 February 1973, 1.

46. Edith Asbury, "Public Housing Income Limit Is Raised," *NYT*, 19 January 1973, 1; Tenant Data, NYCHA, 1 January 1974, Peter Marcuse Personal Collection, Columbia University; Chicago Housing Authority, Annual Statistical Reports, Box 66B6, Folder 3, NYCHAR.

47. Tony Marcano, "Going Home," *NYT*, 7 May 1995, CY1.

48. Grace Bliss, Draft for William Reid, 1 August 1958, Box 62C6, Folder 1, NYCHAR; Ira Robbins, "Setting the Record Straight on Public Housing," 8 February 1962, Box 70D6, Folder 4, NYCHAR. See also "Income Limit up for City Housing," *NYT*, 11 August 1958, 1; "Wage Limit Eased in Public Housing," *NYT*, 5 July 1961, 35. On state limits, see statement of Ira Robbins, Hearing of the Temporary State Commission on Low-Income Housing, 26 June 1963, Box 72D1, Folder 5, NYCHAR, 12. See also testimony by William Reid, Hearing of the State Commission on Low-Income Housing, 29 October 1963, Box 92B7, Folder 24, NYCHAR.

49. NYCHA Information, 8 May 1967, Box 60E5, Folder 1, NYCHAR, 1.

50. Edith Asbury, "Public Housing Income Limit Is Raised," *NYT*, 19 January 1973, 1; Joseph Fried, "New York Raises Ceilings on Income in Public Housing," *NYT*, 16 February 1977, 43. See also Sidney Schackman to District Chiefs, 27 December 1974, Box 66E4, Folder 2, NYCHAR; Joseph Fried, "Top Income Limit Raised in Public-Housing Projects," *NYT*, 22 January 1975, 39; Joseph Fried, "City Increases Income Maximum for Low-Rent-Housing Families," *NYT*, 7 January 1979, 39; Joseph Christian to Alan Weiner, 4 December 1978, Box 93B4, Folder 8, NYCHAR. By 1980 federal income limits ranged from $10,750 to $19,200 for family of eight or more. NYCHA, "New Tier Ranges," 17 November 1980, Box 70D6, Folder 3, NYCHAR.

51. Joseph Christian to Joseph Monticciolo, 26 November 1973, NYCHAR. See also Julius Elkin to John Simon, 12 September 1973, Box 88C6, Folder 5, NYCHAR. Reference to a selection system that would "attract more working families" was made in a report to HUD in 1973. See NYCHA Response to HUD Review of Operations, October 1973, Box 62A4, Folder 3, NYCHAR.

52. NYCHA Bi-Weekly Status Report, 29 June 1979, Box 93B1, Folder 1, NYCHAR.

53. NYCHA, "New Tier Ranges," 17 November 1980, Box 70D6, Folder 3, NYCHAR; John Simon to James Fuerst, 26 September 1984, Box 70D6, Folder 3, NYCHAR.

54. NYCHA, "Interim Report/Staten Island Outreach Programs," May 1980, Box 89E3, Folder 1, NYCHAR.

55. Tim Sullivan to Edward McClendon, 15 December 1980, Box 76A6, FOLDER 6, NYCHAR.

56. NYCHA Monthly Status Report, 15 August 1985, Koch Papers, MN 41077, Roll 77, MA.

57. Anthony DePalma, "Two Cities, Two Results in Housing the Poor," *NYT*, 14 May 1989, E24.

58. Tenant Data, NYCHA, Annual Reports, 1973–85, Peter Marcuse Personal Collection, Columbia University; Lee Daniels, "New York City Fights a U.S. Move Raising Public Housing Rent," *NYT*, 11 August 1982, A1. City projects retained a less than 10 percent welfare tenancy into the 1980s, but this statistic means little in light of how many of these projects had already been federalized under the federal transfer program.

59. Val Coleman to Walter Fried, 14 March 1979, Box 76A6, Folder 2; William Russo, "People Coming Together: Alfred E. Smith Houses," Columbia University National Housing Policy Class, 19 April 1995, 18, Author Collection; Julius Elkin to John Simon, 29 August 1973, Box 66E4, Folder 3, NYCHAR. Chicago statistics are from Hunt, "What Went Wrong with Public Housing in Chicago?," 372.

60. Emanuel Popolizio, Letter to the Editor, *NYT*, 15 March 1986, 26. Vale, *Reclaiming Public Housing*, 6.

61. John Tierney, "Urging Housing Projects for Welfare Angers Tenants," *NYT*, 28 June 1990, A1; "Responses to Dr. Bloom's Questions," NYCHA Statistics Division, Fall 2005, Author Collection.

62. Albert Walsh, Speech, 1968 Workshop in Community Development, Atlanta, Georgia, 6 November 1968, Box 92B7, Folder 7, NYCHAR. For labor issues, see "Housing Authority Employees Threatening Strike in City," *NYT*, 11 December 1968, 41; Peter Millones, "City Speeds Talks with Its Unions," *NYT*, 27 December 1968, 30; "Housing Authority and Union Agree," *NYT*, 1 January 1969, 18. For rent increases, see David Shipler, "Welfare Rents to Be Raised 47%," *NYT*, 1 May 1969, 1. It also might be well to note that the authority had paid to the city, by 1968, $103,894,622 in payments in lieu of taxes since 1934. NYCHA Annual Report, 31 December 1968, Box 60D8, Folder 11, NYCHAR.

63. Roger Starr, "The Decline and Decline of New York," *NYT*, 21 November 1971, SM31.

64. Bruce Lambert, "Roger Starr, New York Planning Official, Author and Editorial Writer, Is Dead at 83," *NYT*, 11 September 2001, C17.

65. Memo to John T. Carroll, 14 June 1976, Box 88A6, Folder 2, NYCHAR; "Below the Bottom Line," NYCHA, April 1975, Box 89C6, Folder 13, NYCHAR, 2. See also Val Coleman to Mark Drucker, 24 September 1971, Box 65D2, Folder 4, NYCHAR.

66. NYCHA, "The Numbers Don't Work Anymore," circa 1974, Box 92D5, Folder 20, NYCHAR. See also Joseph Fried, "25,000 Welfare Families in Projects Get Rent Cuts," *NYT*, 7 February 1973, 81; "Major Accomplishments," NYCHA, 1977, Box 92E5, Folder 11, NYCHAR. For the national crisis related to the Brooke Amendment, see "Public Housing in Trouble," *Commonweal*, 5 January 1973, 292.

67. Joseph Fried, "U.S. Gives $11 Million Subsidy to City Housing for Fuel Costs," *NYT*, 23 December 1974, 31; Joseph Fried, "City Projects Plan 8% Rent Rise to Cover 'Skyrocketing' Costs," *NYT*, 17 May 1974, 36. Joseph Freid, "Rent Increases Averaging 6% Sought by City Housing Agency," *NYT*, 16 March 1976, 59. See also "Below the Bottom Line," NYCHA, April 1975, Box 89C6, Folder 13, NYCHAR.

68. "Below the Bottom Line," NYCHA, April 1975, Box 89C6, Folder 13, NY-

CHAR, 2; Amalia Betanzos, Remarks, 18 February 1977, Box 92E2, Folder 28, NYCHAR.

69. Joseph Kahn, "Carter's HUD Choice Has Explaining to Do," Box 92E4, Folder 4, NYCHAR.

70. Interview of John Simon by Marcia Robertson, 24 July 1990, NYCHA Oral History Project, NYCHAR, 13–14.

71. "Major Accomplishments," NYCHA, 1977, Box 92E5, Folder 11, NYCHAR.

72. Interview of John Simon by Marcia Robertson, 24 July 1990, NYCHA Oral History Project, NYCHAR, 14; Interview of Roy Metcalf by Marcia Robertson, 6 August 1990, NYCHA Oral History Project, NYCHAR, 9; "Responses to Dr. Bloom's Questions," NYCHA Statistics Division, Fall 2005, Author Collection.

73. Comprehensive Review of NYCHA, HUD, Region II, September 1983, Box 91C4, Folder 1, NYCHAR, vii–4; "The New York City Housing Authority," *Neighborhood: The Journal for City Preservation* (summer 1983), Box 74C6, Folder 5, NYCHAR, 11.

74. Comprehensive Review of NYCHA, HUD, Region II, September 1983, Box 91C4, Folder 1, NYCHAR, no page number.

75. Comprehensive Review of NYCHA, HUD, Region II, September 1983, Box 91C4, Folder 1, NYCHAR, vii–17, vii–18.

76. Interview of Raymond Henson by Marcia Robertson, 6 August 1990, NYCHA Oral History Project, NYCHAR, 25; Interview of John Simon by Marcia Robertson, 24 July 1990, NYCHA Oral History Project, NYCHAR, 12.

77. Interview of John Simon by Marcia Robertson, 24 July 1990, NYCHA Oral History Project, NYCHAR, 15–16; Interview of Roy Metcalf by Marcia Robertson, 6 August 1990, NYCHA Oral History Project, NYCHAR, 14.

78. Interview of Raymond Henson by Marcia Robertson, NYCHA Oral History Project, NYCHAR, 23, August 6, 1990.

79. Interview of John Simon by Marcia Robertson, 24 July 1990, NYCHA Oral History Project, NYCHAR, 15–16; Interview of Roy Metcalf by Marcia Robertson, 6 August 1990, NYCHA Oral History Project, NYCHAR, 14.

80. Simon Anekwe, "Ed Koch Tries to Explain His Administration Housing Plan," *New York Amsterdam News*, 24 December 1988, 20, Schomburg Center, NYPL. See also James Barron, "$5 Billion Plan for Apartments Pushed in Bronx," *NYT*, 28 February 1989, B4; Michael Gecan, "A Housing Legacy," in *New York Comes Back: The Mayoralty of Edward I. Koch*, ed. Michael Goodwin (New York: Powerhouse, 2006), 99–103; Janny Scott, "A National Housing Innovator Leads City's Efforts for the Poor," *NYT*, 25 September 2006. Full details on the successful South Bronx redevelopment movement can be found in Gonzalez, *The Bronx*.

81. Executive Management Report, 18 December 1980, Raymond Henson, Box 92A4, Folder 1; Mayor's Management Report, May 1980, Box 92A4, Folder 6, NYCHAR; Emanuel Popolizio, "Public Housing's Needs," *Wall Street Journal*, 26 January 1987; Interview of Roy Metcalf by Marcia Robertson, 6 August 1990, NYCHA Oral History Project, NYCHAR, 8. See also Joseph Christian to Thomas Ashley, 14 February 1980, Box 76A6, Folder 4, NYCHAR; Testimony of Joseph Christian to the House Appropriations Committee, 6 April 1981, Box 76A7, Folder 1; "18 Housing Authorities Sue U.S. over $500 Million in Unpaid Aid," *NYT*, 4 July 1982, 22; Interview of Raymond Henson by Marcia Robertson, NYCHA Oral History Project, NYCHAR, 26; Mayor's Management Report, "NYCHA," 17 September 1982, Box 91B4, Folder 1, NYCHAR; Emanuel Popolizio to Wendell Foster, 20 March 1987, Box 98B1, Folder 11, NYCHAR.

Chapter 12. The Value of Consistency

1. Oscar Newman, "Proposal for a Study to Find Means for Preventing Elevator Accidents," 1 April 1971, Box 88B4, Folder 3, NYCHAR; Virginia Sligh, "Nobody Loves You When You're Down and Out," NYCHA Elevator Study, Fall 1975, Box 93B5, Folder 12, NYCHAR.

2. Max Siegel, "Elevator Crisis in City Projects," *NYT*, 4 July 1973, 1; "Elevator Crisis Worsens in City Housing Projects," *NYT*, 5 July 1973; Robert McFadden, "Elevator Repairmen End Job Action at City Projects," *NYT*, 7 July 1973; Press Release, 1 December 1977, Box 92E3, Folder 21, NYCHAR.

3. "Elevator Maintenance System Report Abstract," 1975, Box 93B5, Folder 12, NYCHAR.

4. Project Survey Report, Stapleton Houses, 25 July 1975, Box 66E8, Folder 1, NYCHAR.

5. Alan Rudolph, "Tenant Reaction to Public Housing" (M.A. thesis, Pratt Institute, 1970), CHPC Archive, 42.

6. Val Coleman to Alfredo Lanier, 17 July 1980, Box 76A6, Folder 5, NYCHAR; Richard Lyons, "A Perilous Play on Elevators," *NYT*, 25 February 1990, R1.

7. Project Survey Report, Samuel Tilden Houses, 13 December 1971, Box 66E8, Folder 8, NYCHAR.

8. Sidney Schackman to Joseph Christian, 1 August 1967, Box 64B5, Folder 7, NYCHAR.

9. Ibid; Sidney Schackman to Joseph Christian, 12 June 1973, Box 65C1, Folder 1, NYCHAR. See also Paul Montgomery, "Killing at Red Hook Houses Makes Many Fear to Go Out," *NYT*, 23 November 1970, 39. The reporter found that a "'crash' repair program" had reverted to dilapidation at Red Hook.

10. Project Survey Report, 16 Van Dyke Houses, 1970–72, Box 66E8, Folder 13, NYCHAR; Ida Posner, Brownsville Public Housing Coordinating Council, Memo, Box 65C2, Folder 6, NYCHAR.

11. "Requests from the Brownsville Community Council, Inc.," 7 April 1970, NYCHA internal document, Box 65C2, Folder 6, NYCHAR.

12. Project Survey Report, 16 Van Dyke Houses, 10 May 1975, Box 66E8, Folder 13, NYCHAR.

13. "New York City Housing Authority Interim Report on Progress of Target Projects Program," 14 January 1976, Box 76A5, Folder 1, NYCHAR. The projects are Carey Gardens (1970, Coney Island), St. Nicholas Houses (1954, Harlem), Langston Hughes Houses (1968, Brownsville), East River Houses (1941, East Harlem), South Jamaica Houses (1940, Queens), Monroe Houses (1961, Southeast Bronx), and Andrew Jackson Houses (1963, Southeast Bronx).

14. Sidney Schackman to Joseph Christian, 22 November 1974, Box 88B2, Folder 6, NYCHAR; NYCHA Response to HUD Review of Operations, October 1973, Box 62A4, Folder 3, NYCHAR.

15. "Broken Glass Replacement," circa 1973, NYCHA, Box 65C1, Folder 1, NYCHAR; K. E. Bush to R. Henson, "Janitorial Standards," 30 January 1974, Box 90C4, Folder 14, NYCHAR.

16. Mrs. Joda to Mr. W. E. Washington, 25 January 1967, Box 69D7, Folder 1, NYCHAR.

17. NYCHA Response to HUD Review of Operations, October 1973, Box 62A4, Folder 3, NYCHAR.

18. Joseph Christian to Sidney Schackman, "Bronxdale Houses Security Program," 30 August 1973, Box 88B2, Folder 8, NYCHAR, 2; NYCHA, Review of Op-

erations, October 1973, Box 62A4, Folder 3, NYCHAR, 22; Oscar Newman to Simeon Golar, 13 January 1971, Box 88B4, Folder 3, NYCHAR.

19. Joseph Christian to Leonard Farbman, 21 September 1977, Box 93A6, Folder 8, NYCHA Papers, LWA; Interview of Leonard Hopper by the author, 29 December 2005.

20. NYCHA, Review of Operations, October 1973, Box 62A4, Folder 3, NYCHAR; Interview of Leonard Hopper by the author, 29 December 2005.

21. Statement by Joseph Christian, "Rehabilitation Funds," 23 February 1977, NYCHAR.

22. Ibid. Kornblum and Williams also report that the NYCHA successfully turned around Martin Luther King Jr. Towers beginning in the 1970s. See Terry Williams and William Kornblum, *The Uptown Kids: Struggle and Hope in the Projects* (New York: Grosset/Putnam, 1994), 242.

23. "Federal Transfer Program," circa 1977, NYCHA Documents, Box 92D5, Folder 28, NYCHAR, 1–25. The authority did note that "as a result of a continuing management effort, these State-Aided projects remain good and decent public housing, doing the basic job they were designed to do." As evidence of this it noted that "98 percent of the rents due are collected" and tenant turnover remained negligible.

24. Marcia Robertson Interview, 24 July 1990, NYCHA Oral History Project, NYCHAR, 14. Approximately five more projects were transferred during the Clinton administration, so that today only fifteen developments remain in the state program and six in the city. "Responses to Dr. Bloom's Questions," NYCHA Statistics Division, Fall 2005. Author Collection. See also H. Carl McCall, State Comptroller, "Public Housing at the Crossroads: Bricks, Mortar and Public Housing at the NYCHA," 11 February 1999, Internet pdf. www.nysl.nysed.gov/scandoclinks/ocm40950150.htm

25. Interview of John Simon by Marcia Robertson, 24 July 1990, NYCHA Oral History Project, NYCHAR, 18–19.

26. Comprehensive Review of NYCHA, HUD, Region II, September 1983, Box 91C4, Folder 1, NYCHAR, vii–4.

27. Charles Seaton, Untitled, *Daily News*, 18 March 1986, Box 100B2, Folder 11, NYCHAR. See also Calvin Sims, "Tenants Assail Conditions, But Fail to Get New Housing Chief's Ear," *NYT*, 26 February 1992, B3.

28. Interview of Cyril Grossman by Marcia Robertson, 1 August 1990, NYCHA Oral History Box 1, NYCHAR, 30–31; "Collecting the Rent," *Housing Authority Reporter* 1, no. 1 (September 1987), Koch Papers, MN 41077, Roll 77, Subject Files, 3–4.

29. Albert Walsh, "Police Headquarters Dedication Ceremony," 19 June 1968, Box 92B7, Folder 2D, NYCHAR. See also "Housing Authority Statistics," NYCHA, Box 60E7, Folder 3, NYCHAR.

30. Albert Walsh, "Police Headquarters Dedication Ceremony," 19 June 1968, Box 92B7, Folder 2D, NYCHAR. See also "Housing Authority Statistics," NYCHA, Box 60E7, Folder 3, NYCHAR.

31. Joseph Weldon to Robert Ledee, "Detective Bureau," 12 December 1968, Box 64C3, Folder 3, NYCHAR.

32. Interview of Raymond Henson by Marcia Robertson, 6 August 1990, NYCHA Oral History Project, Box 1, NYCHAR, 14.

33. Interview of Victoria Archibald-Good, The Bronx African American History Project, www.bronxhistoricalsociety.org/journal/afro_american_history.html, 12.

34. Cyril Grossman to Norman Peterson, 24 May 1968, Box 76B2, Folder 5, NYCHAR.

35. Letter to Jay Kriegal, "Authority's Safety Patrols," 4 November 1968, Box 64C3, Folder 3, NYCHAR; Mary O'Flaherty, "Tenants Form Patrols to Combat Crime," *Sunday News*, 1 December 1968, B2.

36. Samuel Granville to Charles Owens, 1 October 1976, Box 89E6, Folder 34, NYCHAR.

37. Paul Montgomery, "Killing at Red Hook Houses Makes Many Fear to Go Out," *NYT*, 23 November 1970, 39.

38. "Housing Authority Statistics," NYCHA, Box 60E7, Folder 3, NYCHAR, 2; "Arrests by Program," NYCHA, circa 1976, Box 60E7, Folder 4, NYCHAR. The 1975 figure of 2,188 felony arrests is a revised figure based on later reporting protocols. For revised figures, see Benjamin Ward to Joseph Christian, 12 October 1978, Box 92D7, Folder 12, NYCHAR. See also "Arrests by Program," circa 1976, Box 60E7, Folder 4, NYCHAR.

39. NYCHA Resident Advisory Council, circa 1971, Box 65D2, Folder 5, NYCHAR.

40. NYCHA Resident Advisory Council, circa 1971, Box 65D2, Folder 5, NYCHAR.

41. Alan Rudolph, "Tenant Reaction to Public Housing" (M.A. thesis, Pratt Institute, 16 January 1970), CHPC Archive, 44, 78.

42. Harold Pinkney to Joseph Christian, Resident Advisory Council, 22 March 1976, Box 88A6, Folder 2, NYCHAR.

43. Interview of Cyril Grossman by Marcia Robertson, 1 August 1990, NYCHA Oral History Project, Box 1, NYCHAR, 29.

44. "Public Housing Revises Its Approach to 'Problem Families,'" *NYT*, 29 June 1975, 1, 12.

45. NYCHA Response to HUD Review of Operations, October 1973, Box 62A4, Folder 3, NYCHAR, 28.

46. Interview of Cyril Grossman by Marcia Robertson, 1 August 1990, NYCHA Oral History Project, Box 1, NYCHAR, 27.

47. Paul Montgomery, "Killing at Red Hook Houses Makes Many Fear to Go Out," *NYT*, 23 November 1970, 39.

48. Project Survey Report, Stapleton Houses, 25 July 1975, Box 66E8, Folder 1, NYCHAR.

49. "Residential Security Program," NAHRO Conference, 15 September 1978, Box 92 D7, Folder 12, NYCHAR.

50. Joseph Christian, Testimony to Public Safety Committee, 1978, Box 92D5, Folder 12, NYCHAR.

51. "How We Beat the Blackout! Authority Projects Were 'Islands of Calm,'" *The Housing Authority Journal*, August-September 1977, Box 99D2, NYCHAR.

52. Benjamin Ward to Joseph Christian, 12 October 1978, Box 92D7, Folder 12, NYCHAR; Testimony of Joseph Christian, City Council Hearings on Security in Public Housing, 20 September 1978, Box 91D4, Folder 7, NYCHAR.

53. City Council Hearings on Security in Public Housing, 20 September 1978, Box 92E1, Folder 18, NYCHAR. See also Miscellaneous Police Records, May 1983, Box 91D5, Folder 9, NYCHAR; Val Coleman to Joseph Michaels, 25 January 1980, Box 76A6, Folder 4, NYCHAR.

54. City Council Report of the Committee on Public Safety, 20 June 1979, Box 91D4, Folder 7, NYCHAR.

55. "Residential Security Program," NAHRO Conference, 15 September 1978, Box 92 D7, Folder 12, NYCHAR.

56. Ibid.

57. Benjamin Ward to Edward Koch, 9 April 1979, Koch Papers, MN 41076, Roll 76, MA.

Racial tempers flared in 1984, and occasionally since, and were related to tough NYPD tactics in public housing. The most famous concerned the death of an elderly tenant, Eleanor Bumpers. Police Commissioner Benjamin Ward reported that officers had not come to evict Bumpers but to institutionalize her. The police, members of the Emergency Service Unit, found Bumpers armed with a knife and ultimately shot her. Ward characterized Bumpers as "a deeply disturbed individual who harbored psychotic delusions that Castro and Reagan were coming through her walls and windows." "Ward Replies to AM News," *New York Amsterdam News*, 5 January 1985, 12. See also "Tenants Call It Murder," *New York Amsterdam News*, 3 November 1984, 1; "A Mother Died for $447.20," *New York Amsterdam News*, 3 November 1984, 12; Zamgba Browne, "Public Still Angry over Cop Killing," *New York Amsterdam News*, 11 November 1984, 3; Editorial, "Eleanor Bumpers: Suffering Death Silently," *New York Amsterdam News*, 10 November 1984, 12; "Bumpers: The Charade Continues," *New York Amsterdam News*, 8 December 1984, 12.

The black press, in contrast, told the story of "a 66-year-old grandmother" who "lunged" at a police officer at Sedgwick Houses in the Bronx when he demanded she vacate her apartment for nonpayment of rent (she was allegedly $500 behind) and was needlessly shot (twice) by one of the officers on the case. Officers were ultimately cleared of wrongdoing, but the black community viewed the case as yet another example of police brutality and Mayor Koch's insensitivity. J. Zamgba Browne, "Fed May Probe Bumpers Killing," *New York Amsterdam News*, 7 March 1987. See also Wilbert Tatum, "The Boys in Blue and the Ayatolloah Merola," *New York Amsterdam News*, 16 February 1985, 15; Editorial, "Bumpers: Justice Denied," *New York Amsterdam News*, 20 April 1985, 12; Editorial, "Bumpers: Throwing the Case," *New York Amsterdam News*, 31 January 1987, 12.

58. Subsidy figures are from John Simon, NYCHA Symposium, The New School, 28 June 1984, Box 74C6, Folder 6–9, NYCHAR, 45.

59. Martin Gottlieb, "New York Housing Agency Takes a Bow at 50," *NYT*, 25 June 1984, B3; Miscellaneous Police Records, May, 1983, Box 91D5, Folder 9, NYCHAR.

60. Miscellaneous Police Records, May, 1983, Box 91D5, Folder 9, NYCHAR.

61. "Number of Physical Evictions," 1983, Box 88C5, Folder 5, NYCHAR.

62. Neighborhood Preservation Grant Proposal, 1983, Box 60E1, Folder 2, NYCHAR, 1; Martin Gottlieb, "New York Housing Agency Takes a Bow at 50," *NYT*, 25 June 1984, A1.

63. Interview of Roy Metcalf by Marcia Robertson, 8 August 1990, NYCHA Oral History Project, Box 1, NYCHAR, 10–11. See also NYCHA Annual Reports, 1989/1990 Annual Reports, Box 98D1, NYCHAR.

64. Emanuel Popolozio to Charles Rangel, 22 February 1989, Box 98A7, Folder 10, NYCHAR. See also Joseph Treaster, "Agents Take Aim at Drugs in Projects," *NYT*, 14 February 1991, B3.

65. David Pitt, "At Night, Drugs Invade the Projects," *NYT*, 1 September 1988, B1.

66. James McKinley Jr., "Constant Reality in a Project: Fear of Violent Drug Gangs," *NYT*, 15 May 1989, A1.

67. Manuel Quintana to Rudolph Giuliani, 16 September 1987, Koch Papers, MN 41077, Roll 77, MA.

68. Interview of Cyril Grossman by Marcia Robertson, 1 August 1990, NYCHA Oral History Project, Box 1, MA, 38.

69. Arnold Lubasch, "2 Apartments in Projects Are Seized in Drug Cases," *NYT*, 28 April 1988, A1. See also Emmanuel Popolizio, "At Long Last, a Victory over the Drug Dealers," *NYT*, 21 May 1988.

70. Annual Report, NYCHA, 1988, Box 98D1, Folder 32, NYCHAR.

71. James McKinley Jr., "Constant Reality in a Project: Fear of Violent Drug Gangs," *NYT*, 15 May 1989, A1.

72. Interview of Cyril Grossman by Marcia Robertson, 1 August 1990, NYCHA Oral History Project, Box 1, NYCHAR, 42.

73. NYCHA Annual Report, 1989/1990, Box 98D1, NYCHAR; Susan Rasky, "Kemp Asks Repeal of Drug-Related Law," *NYT*, 11 July 1989, A10.

74. Emanuel Popolozio, "Drug Evictions Can't Be Halfhearted Measures," *NYT*, 11 August 1989.

75. Shawn Kennedy, "Tenants Press for Easier Eviction of Drug Deals," *NYT*, 15 August 1994, B1.

76. "The New York City Housing Authority Tenant Programs Come of Age," 1976, Box 90B3, Folder 7, NYCHAR, 2–7.

77. Preston David, "The 'Poverty' Program and Public Housing," 24 June 1965, Box 69D2, Folder 1, NYCHAR, 2–6; Interview of Hugh Spence, NYCHA deputy general manger of community operations, by the author, 1 August 2006.

78. "The New York City Housing Authority Tenant Programs Come of Age," 1976, Box 90B3, Folder 7, NYCHAR, 2–7.

79. Ira Robbins to the Members of the Authority, "Interim Report," 2 July 1973, Box 88C4, Folder 3, NYCHAR, 1–3.

80. "Resident Life" in *Celebrating Seventy Years*, 1934–2004, NYCHA Publication, 1 December 2004, Author Collection.

81. Alan Rudolph, "Tenant Reaction to Public Housing" (M.A. thesis, Pratt Institute, 16 January 1970), CHPC Archive, 56, 57, 62, 63, 67.

82. Joseph Christian to Joseph Hydock, 14 December 1978, Box 93B2, Folder 18, NYCHAR, 4; Recreation Questionnaire, 20 December 1979, Box 93B2, Folder 19, NYCHAR, 7; "Need Assessment," 14 February 1980, Box 91D5, Folder 6, NYCHAR; Program Information Survey, NYCHA, 6 May 1980, Box 91D5, Folder 6, NYCHAR, 6.

83. "Residential Security Program," NAHRO Conference, 15 September 1978, Box 92 D7, Folder 12, NYCHAR. The figure for resident employment in 2004 is now 29 percent, or approximately four thousand employees. See "Resident Life" in *Celebrating Seventy Years*, 1934–2004, NYCHA Publication, 1 December 2004, Author Collection.

84. Nat Leventhal to Joe Christian, 28 April 1980, Koch Papers, MN41076, Roll 76, Subject Files, MA.

85. "Community Activities," Comprehensive Review, NYCHA, HUD, Region II, September 1983, Box 91C4, Folder 1, NYCHAR, iii–11.

86. Alan Rudolph, "Tenant Reaction to Public Housing" (M.A. thesis, Pratt Institute, 16 January 1970), CHPC Archive, 21–23, 33, 76, 78. One of the most surprising discoveries was tenant acceptance of high-rise living, which is perhaps related to the New York context: "Despite the large number of articles written by concerned sociologists deploring the high rise buildings, the tenants seem not to have noticed. 86% of all respondents were perfectly happy to be living on the

floor where God or the Authority had placed them. . . . Though most of these had young children, it had never occurred to these parents that there would be any advantage in supervision from the second or third story" (Rudolph, "Tenant Reaction to Public Housing," 34).

87. Oscar Newman, *Defensible Space*, 8, 20, 38, 41, 42, 55, 57, 58, 65, 66, 70, 92, 98, 99, 104–7, 124, 127, 163, 164, 176.

88. For growing acrimony between Newman and NYCHA, see Paul Crawford to Denis Dryden, 11 January 1971, Box 72D4, Folder 1, NYCHAR; Simeon Golar to Oscar Newman, 22 January 1971, Box 88B4, Folder 3, NYCHAR; Harry Fialkin to Simeon Golar, 18 May 1972, Box 88B4, Folder 3, NYCHAR; Simeon Golar to Oscar Newman, 22 January 1971, Box 88B4, Folder 3, NYCHAR; Oscar Newman to Simeon Golar, 4 December 1972, Box 88B4, Folder 3, NYCHAR; Simeon Golar to John Lindsay, 4 January 1973, Box 88B4, Folder 3, NYCHAR; Tim Sullivan to Val Coleman, "Design Guidelines . . . ," 3 August 1976, Box 60E6, Folder 19, NYCHAR.

89. Harry Fialkin to Simeon Golar, 18 May 1972, Box 88B4, Folder 3, NYCHAR.

90. Camilo José Vergara, "Hell in a Very High Place," *The Atlantic Monthly*, September 1989, 72–78.

91. Terry Williams and William Kornblum, *The Uptown Kids: Struggle and Hope in the Projects* (New York: Grosset/Putnam, 1994), 20–21, 241–42.

92. HUD Review, Management Review, 6 May 1971, Box 90C5, Folder 14, NYCHA, 1. HUD reported in 1973 that NYCHA projects were "generally being adequately maintained with some findings of isolated deficiency." NYCHA Response to HUD Review of Operations, October 1973, Box 62A4, Folder 3, NYCHAR.

93. "Major Accomplishments," NYCHA, 1977, Box 92E5, Folder 11, NYCHAR.

94. Williams and Kornblum, *The Uptown Kids*, 25. See also *NYCHA Journal* 23, no. 6 (December 1993), Box 99D4, NYCHAR. Pritchett, *Brownsville, Brooklyn*, 239–70, also offers an upbeat appraisal of NYCHA management in Brownsville.

95. "HUD Evaluates NYCHA," NYCHA, 1997 Annual Report, Box 98D1, Folder 33, NYCHAR, 8; NYCHA Comprehensive Annual Financial Report, 31 December 2005, Author Collection.

Chapter 13. Model Housing Revisited

1. NYCHA, Agency Report, 2003–5 (internet version), www.nyc.gov/html/nycha/downloads/pdf/agency_report_2003_2005.pdf.

2. Michael Schill and Glynis Daniels, "State of New York City's Housing and Neighborhoods: An Overview of Recent Trends," *FRBNY Economic Policy Review* (June 2003): 11–13. This article demolishes many myths of the New York housing market and is essential reading.

3. Housing First!, "Building for the Future: New York's Affordable Housing Challenge," November 2001, www.housingfirst.net/policypaper1.html, 6; "2005 Overview," The Furman Center for Real Estate and Urban Policy, Web document; George Lockner and Leonard Rodberg, "The Housing Date Deficit: Why We Need a NYC Housing Census," 27 October 2004, www.tenants services.com/ art_data_deficit.html. The ratio of low renters who are severely overburdened comes from Schill and Daniels, "State of New York City's Housing and Neighborhoods;" 6.

4. Joel Rubin, "When Work Isn't Enough: New York City's Working Poor," 2003, Columbia University Graduate School of Journalism website: www.jrn. columbia.edu/studentwork/investigative/2003/workpoor-rubin.asp. Welfare figures are from the NYCHA Comprehensive Annual Financial Report, 31 December 2005, Author Collection, 75.

5. Randy Kennedy, "In Turnabout, Housing Authority Will Begin Favoring Jobholders," *NYT*, 15 December 1997, A1; Kaplan and Kaplan, *Between Ocean and City*, 130. See also Glenn Thrush, "Judge Blocks NYCHA's Bid to Push Poor to Back of Waiting List," *City Limits*, 11 August 1997, www.citylimits.org/contents/articles/viewarticle.cfm?article_id=628.

6. William Steinmann to Ruben Franco, "Tenant Data," 13 April 1995, Box 74C5, Folder 1, NYCHAR.

7. Shawn Kennedy, "Housing Projects to Give Priority to the Employed," *NYT*, 4 February 1995, 1.

8. Alan Oser, "Seeking to Improve Quality in Shelter," *NYT*, 13 December 1992, R3; Kim Nauer, "Rudy's Public Housing Plan Stalls Over Race Bias Test," *City Limits*, 25 November 1996, www.citylimits.org/content/articles/view article.cfm?article_id=727; "Attracting Working Families," NYCHA Annual Report, 1997, Box 98D1, Folder 33, NYCHAR.

9. Randy Kennedy, "In Turnabout, Housing Authority Will Begin Favoring Jobholders," *NYT*, 15 December 1997, A1; see also Glenn Thrush, "Judge Blocks NYCHA's Bid to Push Poor to Back of Waiting List," *City Limits*, 11 August 1997, www.citylimits.org/content/articles/viewarticle.cfm?article_id=628. Tenant activists were concerned that the preference for working families would undermine implementation of racial integration in Staten Island and Queens. The compromise exempted Queens and Staten Island from the working family preference.

10. Interview of Arlene Campana, the NYCHA director of applications, by the author, 1 August 2006; NYCHA Department of Housing Applications, 2005 Annual Report, 3 February 2006, Author Collection, 1–34. The NYCHA can, it should be noted, only accept Tier III as up to 40 percent of admissions.

11. NYCHA Annual Report, 1999, Box 98D1, Folder 34, NYCHAR, 23. See also E. S. Savas, ed., *Managing Welfare Reform in New York City* (Lanham, Md: Rowman and Littlefield, 2005) for more on New York's successful, and controversial, approach to welfare reform.

12. Kathleen McGowan, "The Devil in the Details," *City Limits*, December 1999, www.citylimits.org/content/articles/viewarticle cfm?article_id=2427; NYCHA Website, "The Working Family Preference," 1 July 2004, http://www.nyc.gov/html/nycha/html/workfam.html; interview of Arlene Campana, the NYCHA director of applications, by the author, 1 August 2006.

13. Raisa Bahchieva and Amy Hosier, "Determinants of Tenure Duration in Public Housing: The Case of New York City," *Journal of Housing Research*, 12, no. 2 (2001): 307–48; "Responses to Dr. Bloom's Questions," NYCHA Statistics Division, Fall 2005, Author Collection; NYCHA, "The Plan to Preserve Public Housing," April 2006, NYCHA website, no page numbers.

14. NYCHA, "The Plan to Preserve Public Housing," April 2006, NYCHA website, no page numbers; "Responses to Dr. Bloom's Questions," NYCHA Statistics Division, Fall 2005, Author Collection; Interview of Gloria Finkelman, the NYCHA Manhattan Borough director, by the author, 28 July 2006; NYCHA, "Budget Summary," April 2006, NYCHA website, no page numbers. Income figures should at this point be viewed with some skepticism as "anecdotal evi-

dence abounds as to the type and scope of unreported activities (legal and illegal) undertaken to produce income." Bahchieva and Hosier, "Determinants of Tenure Duration in Public Housing," 307–48. Maximum income limits for admission range from $35,150 for an individual to $82,400 for a (rare) twelve-person family.

15. Rubin, "When Work Isn't Enough." Roger Starr also describes a 40 percent rejection rate of applicants in 1995. See Roger Starr, "An Ounce of Prevention," *City Journal* (Autumn 1995), www.city-journal.org/html/5_4sndgs05.html.

16. NYCHA, Department of Housing Applications, 2005 Annual Report, 3 February 2006, 1-34, author collection. David Chen, "In Public Housing, It's Work, Volunteer or Leave," *NYT*, 15 April 2004, A1. See also Ron Feemster, "Work in Projects," *City Limits*, July/August 2003. NYCHA had reinstated home visits for about a decade but now simply runs criminal checks and contacts previous landlords.

17. Gonzalez, *The Bronx*, 132.

18. The importance of NYCHA housing as affordable housing is documented in Bahchieva and Hosier, "Determinants of Tenure Duration in Public Housing," 307–48.

Mayor Koch appointed Emanual Popolozio (a longtime Koch supporter in Greenwich Village) as chairman in 1986 and he initiated a tough anti-drug campaign. Wolfgang Saxon, "Emanuel Popolizio, 74, Dies," *NYT*, 27 August 1992, D20. See also Edward Koch to Joseph Christian, 26 March 1979, Koch Papers, MN41076, Roll 76, MA. Laura Blackburne, an attorney, was appointed in 1990 by Mayor David Dinkins as the NYCHA's first woman chairman, but she resigned under pressure in 1992 after questionable expenses were revealed. Under Blackburne's leadership NYCHA nevertheless received $375 million in modernization funds. Blackburne had extensive public service, had once served as a housing assistant, and had spoken out against a high-profile police shooting, that of Eleanor Bumpers, in public housing during the Koch administration. "Laura D. Blackburne, a Profile," 1992, Box 100B2, Folder 10, NYCHAR; Calvin Sims, "Housing Chief Gets Rebuke from Dinkins," *NYT*, 19 February 1992, B1; Calvin Sims, "Housing Chief Quits Her Post Under Pressure," *NYT*, 23 February 1992, 1. See also Simon Anekwe, "New Housing Chief Takes Post with Determination for Change," *New York Amsterdam News*, 13 October 1990, 4, Schomburg Center, NYPL; Editorial, "Laura Blackburne to Housing Authority," *New York Amsterdam News*, 22 September 1990, 14, Schomburg Center, NYPL; Editorial, "Eleanor Bumpers: Coalition Aborning," *New York Amsterdam News*, 24 November 1984, 12; Calvin Sims, "200 Rally to Support Housing Aide," *NYT*, 20 February 1992, B4.

Sally Hernandez-Pinero came in as a reformer and promised "to adopt new spending guidelines" as a "fiscal conservative." Calvin Sims, "New Housing Chief Plans Stricter Rules on Spending," *NYT*, 25 February 1992, B3. Ruben Franco, who was appointed in 1994, was credited by Mayor Giuliani with turning "buildings . . . riddled with crime and vandalism" back into "by far the best public housing in the United States." Dan Barry, "Head of Housing Authority Quits Under Rising Scrutiny," *NYT*, 8 January 1999, B3.

19. NYCHA, Agency Report, 2003–2005, www.nyc.gov/html/nycha/html news/publications.shtml. In one of the more original financing schemes, HUD permits housing authorities such as NYCHA to use future federal funds as collateral for capital fundraising (bonds). This program has contributed hundreds of millions of dollars to the capital funds. Interview of Felix Lam, NYCHA chief financial officer, by the author, 3 August 2006.

20. Clifford Levy, "Housing Projects in New York City Face Big Changes," *NYT*, 24 February 1997, A1; David Chen, "U.S. Deepens Planned Cuts in Housing Aid," *NYT*, 8 April 2005, B1. See also Martin Tolchin, "New York Area to Gain," *NYT*, 9 April 1993, A1.

21. NYCHA, "The Plan to Preserve Public Housing," April 2006, NYCHA website, no page numbers; NYCHA, "Budget Summary," April 2006, NYCHA website, no page numbers.

22. Congressman Anthony D. Weiner, "Impact of the Bush Budget on New York City, FY 2004," www.house.gov/weiner/repot10.htm; NYCHA, Agency Report, 2003–2005; NYCHA, "The Plan to Preserve Public Housing," April 2006, www.nyc.gov/html/nycha/downloads/pdf/ppph-eng.pdf.

23. Kathleen McGowan, "Clean-up Project," *City Limits*, 15 February 1999, 163, www.citylimits.org/content/articles/viewarticle.cfm?article_id=458; H. Carl McCall, State Comptroller, "Public Housing at the Crossroads: Bricks, Mortar, and Public Housing at the NYCHA," 11 February 1999. See also H. Carl McCall, "Deterioration of Public Housing in the State and City Projects Operated by the NYCHA," July 1999, www.osc.state.ny.us/osdc/rpt200/ad200.pdf.

24. Interview of Leonard Hopper by the author, 29 December 2005. See also Jayne Merkel, "Fine Tuning: How the New York City Housing Authority Makes Housing Work," *Architectural Design* (July/August 2003).

Nor was the NYCHA scandal free in recent history. In the 1980s, for instance, Mafia "skimming of millions of dollars" on window contracts came to light. The windows had been replaced, however, and a number of the guilty were convicted. John McQuiston, "Window Case Figure Shot and Wounded," *NYT*, 9 May 1991, B5. See also Arnold Lubasch, "Windows Jury Finds 3 Guilty and Acquits 5," *NYT*, 19 October 1991, 25. See also Jeffrey Schmalz, "14 Charged in Kickbacks in City Housing Projects," *NYT*, 20 September 1985, A1; Joyce Purnick, "Koch Picks a Supporter for Chief Housing Post," *NYT*, 13 December 1985, B7.

25. NYCHA, Agency Report, 2003–2005; Interview of Chairman Tino Hernandez by the author, 11 March 2006.

26. E-mail communication with Xiomara Carcamo, NYCHA staff member, 25 July 2006.

27. NYCHA, Agency Report, 2003–5.

28. Interview of Chairman Tino Hernandez by the author, 11 March 2006. In some cases the office administration of some adjacent developments is being merged in order to maximize efficiency.

29. See "Resident Life" in *Celebrating Seventy Years, 1934–2004*, NYCHA Publication, 1 December 2004, Author Collection. Author discussion of resident employees with Xiomara Carcamo, 19 July 2006.

30. Popolozi to Robert Esnard, "New Initiatives," 30 September 1988, Koch Papers, MN 41077, Roll 77, MA, 3; NYCHA Annual Report, 1989, Box 98D1, NYCHAR.

31. H. Carl McCall, State Comptroller, "Public Housing at the Crossroads: Bricks, Mortar, and Public Housing at the NYCHA," 11 February 1999, 6.

32. Interview of Robert Podmore, the NYCHA deputy general manager, by the author, 21 July 2006.

33. Interview of Cyril Grossman by Marcia Robertson, 1 August 1990, NYCHA Oral History Project, Box 1, NYCHAR, 35.

34. Interview of Leonard Hopper by the author, 29 December 2005.

35. Ibid.

36. Hopper considers Red Hook a model renovation, for instance, but drug

crime has been impervious to landscape redesign. In the late 1980s, Red Hook had become a poster child for disorder related to the crack epidemic. At Red Hook, Hopper began by patrolling with police officers and studying COMP-STAT data to identify hot spots on projects' grounds. Residents eventually "developed models, chose types of pavement, benches and color schemes and presented them to their neighbors in the community." Play areas near entrances were added and designed to be difficult to reach from the street. Crime in Red Hook, according to Hopper, has fallen dramatically since the redesign, but it has not disappeared. In a massive raid in 2006, not the first, the police arrested 153 suspected drug dealers on Red Hook grounds, which the *New York Times* called "a drug dealing cooperative" because "the dealers fostered a peaceful coexistence" even though "the drugs were sold at every corner of the development, day and night." Interview of Leonard Hopper by the author, 29 December 2005; NYCHA, *NYCHA at 70: Generations of Excellence*, Program, Anniversary Celebration Exhibit, Brooklyn Museum, 1 December 2004, 21; Andrew Jacobs, "153 Arrests, and Climbing, after Big Brooklyn Raid," *NYT*, 11 May 2006, select.nytimes.com/search/restricted/article?res=F5061EFF3C5AOC72800DAC 0894DF404482.

37. NYCHA, *NYCHA at 70: Generations of Excellence*, Program, Anniversary Celebration Exhibit, Brooklyn Museum, 1 December 2004, 21.

38. Ibid.

39. Ibid.

40. Elaine Louie, "A Community Center That Is Inviting to Its Young Guests," *NYT*, 17 December 1998, F3. See also Jayne Merkel, "Fine Tuning: How the New York City Housing Authority Makes Housing Work," *Architectural Design* (July/August 2003); Fred Bernstein, "David Burney: Architecture/Urban Planning," *Metropolis*, 19 December 2005, www.metropolismag.com/.

41. Interview of Hugh Spence, NYCHA deputy general manger of community operations, by the author, 1 August 2006.

42. Ibid.

43. Interview of Diedra Gilliard, NYCHA assistant deputy general manager, by the author, 19 July 2006.

44. "Historic Housing Complex Expands Amenities," *American City and County* 118, no. 9 (August 2003), 58. See also "Resident Life," in *Celebrating Seventy Years, 1934–2004*, NYCHA Publication, 1 December 2004, Author collection.

45. In 1956, the housing expert Elizabeth Wood initiated, with the Welfare Department (a source of troubled families), a program to raise "the level of everyday living" for forty-nine targeted problem families. A "welfare investigator would visit patiently, frequently, would make available the minimum equipment for this job—cleaning materials, a minimum of dishes for family meals, cooking equipment. This was not to be casework—just friendly, firm, paternal if you wish, visiting, unrelenting in its persistence." Elizabeth Wood, "Public Housing and Mrs. McGee," Pamphlet of Speech Given 24 October 1956, Citizens' Housing and Planning Council, Box 67E3, Folder 23, NYCHAR, 1–13. See also Elizabeth Wood, *The Small Hard Core*, CHPC, 1957, 19. Although quite a few families made some progress in housekeeping and so forth, management still thought that "the families were not 'rehabilitated.'" Elizabeth Wood, "Report on the Harlem Welfare Center—St. Nicholas House Experiment," Citizens' Housing and Planning Council, 1958, Box 62B6, Folder 22, NYCHAR, 3–13.

In the 1970s the NYCHA sent some of its evicted families to the Urban Family Center run by the Henry Street Settlement at Lavanburg Houses to receive intensive social service intervention. Wendy Schuman, "Public Housing Revises Its Approach to 'Problem Families,'" *NYT*, 29 June 1975, 209. Success in this program led to a modest expansion of the program in East Harlem and the Bronx. Emanuel Popolizio, Letter to the Editor, *NYT*, 15 March 1986, 26.

46. Preston David to Joseph Loncheim, 24 February 1969, Box 65A7, Folder 1, NYCHAR, 2; Interview of NYCHA Legal Department by the author, 1 August 2006.

47. Interview of Jenelle Mitchell, deputy director, Social Services Department, by the author, 19 July 2006. The ratio of housing assistants to units is from an e-mail communication with Xiomara Carcamo, 25 July 2006. Author's visit to Red Hook Houses, 31 July 2006. NYCHA also aims to stabilize developments by sponsoring career-oriented training programs that can lead to permanent NYCHA employment.

48. Interview of Raymond Henson, by Marcia Robertson, 6 August 1990, NYCHA Oral History Project, NYCHAR, 4; "The Future of Public Housing in New York City," Community Service Society, *Urban Agenda* 14 (July 1999): www.cssny.org/pubs/issuebrief/no14.htm; Interview of Deidre Gilliard by the author, 19 July 2006.

49. Deanna Fowler, "Fighting for Public Housing in New York City," Huairou Commission, Advisory Group on Forced Evictions, World Urban Forum, 16 September 2004, Barcelona, Spain, internet resource; Interview of Victor Bach by the author, 17 February 2005.

50. Interview of Hugh Spence, NYCHA deputy general manger of community operations, by the author, 1 August 2006; the NYCHA statistics were reported to City Hall, 2006 (Source: Howard Marder, NYCHA); Interview of Felix Lam, NYCHA chief financial officer, by the author, 3 August 2006.

51. Jan Hoffman, "Process Eased for Evicting Drug Dealers," *NYT*, 20 April 1996, 26. See also Emanuel Popolozio to Edward Koch, 18 August 1989, Koch Papers, MN41077, Roll 77, MA.

52. Naush Boghossian, "High-Rise Hellraiser," *City Limits* (October 2000). In order to enforce the permanent exclusion rule, members of the investigative unit may make unannounced visits to make sure that the excluded family member is not there. Interview of Robert Podmore, NYCHA deputy general manager, by the author, 19 July 2006.

53. Interview of Robert Podmore, NYCHA deputy general manager, by the author, 19 July 2006.

54. Interview of Roy Metcalf by Marcia Robertson, 8 August 1990, NYCHA Oral History Project, Box 1 (LWA), 14; Interview of Victor Bach, by the author, 17 February 2005.

55. "The Police Merger, Act III," Editorial, *NYT*, 22 October 1994, 22. See also Lawrence Gelder, "7 Chiefs Retire from Housing Force as Police Merger Nears," *NYT*, 26 August 1994, B3; Jonathan Hicks, "Council May Force Its Approval for Police Merger," NYT, 15 September 1994, B2. For further background, see also Benjamin Ward to Edward Koch, 9 April 1979, Koch Papers, MN41076, Roll 76, MA. Ward wrote to Koch that "serious consideration should be given to absorbing the housing police into the New York City Police Department" and a shift to guard service with NYPD support. This, he said, would render NYCHA projects similar to middle-income cooperatives.

56. Alison Mitchell, "Giuliani Signs Police Merger Memorandum," *NYT*, 17 September 1994, 27; Clifford Kraus, "Judge Blocks Police Merger in New York," *NYT*, 20 October 1994, B1; Clifford Kraus, "Giuliani May Try a New Merger Strategy: Dismissal," *NYT*, 21 October 1994, B1; "Bringing Cops to Public Housing,"

Editorial, *NYT*, 17 January 1995, A18; "Police Merger, Public Fears," Editorial, *NYT*, 28 January 1995, 18;

57. The Council of the City of New York, "Oversight: Public Safety in Public Housing," 29 April 2004, http://webdocs.nyccouncil.info/attachments/60779.htm.

58. The Council of the City of New York, "NYCHA Housing: Access Granted," June 2004, www.nyccouncil.info, 1–13. Funding had become increasingly tight with the loss of HUD's drug-elimination funding as well as just a general tightening of belts at the NYCHA (city funds have also been cut). Costs in policing have been exceeding operating costs of security and seem to have been absorbed by the NYPD.

59. The Council of the City of New York, "NYCHA Housing: Access Granted," June 2004, www.nyccouncil.info, 1–13; "Mayor Michael R. Bloomberg Announces Operation Safe Housing . . . ," Press release, 24 June 2004, www.nyc.gov; The percentage of families headed by a person sixty-two and over was 30.6 in 1995; see the Council of the City of New York, "NYCHA Housing: Access Granted," June 2004, www.nyccouncil.info, 1–13, NYCHA statistics reported to City Hall, 2006 (Source: Howard Marder, NYCHA). See also Ruben Franco to William Steinman, 13 April 1995, Box 74C5, Folder 1, NYCHAR.

60. Bahchieva and Hosier, "Determinants of Tenure Duration in Public Housing," 307–48.

61. The Council of the City of New York, "NYCHA Housing: Access Granted," June 2004, www.nyccouncil.info, 1–13. These problems with doors are old ones. See also Emanuel Popolizio to Edward Koch, 18 April 1989, Koch Papers, MN41077, Roll 77, MA.

62. The Council of the City of New York, "NYCHA Housing: Access Granted," June 2004, www.nyccouncil.info, 1–13; Randy Kennedy, "Police Cameras Planned for More Housing Projects," *NYT*, 13 November 1997, B3; Interview of Howard Marder, NYCHA public information officer, by the author, 15 September 2006.

63. For crime problems in low-rise public housing, and a powerful discussion of the cost and benefits of high-intensity policing, see Neil Websdale, *Policing the Poor: From Slave Plantation to Public Housing* (Boston: Northeastern, 2001). See also David Garland, *The Culture of Control: Crime and Social Order in Contemporary Society* (Chicago: Chicago, 2001) for an insightful overview of policing strategies in the twentieth century. The problems encountered trying to restore order to public housing projects are documented in Popkin and Gwiasda, *The Hidden War*.

64. Vale, *Reclaiming Public Housing*, 5

65. Hunt, "What Went Wrong with Public Housing in Chicago?," 1, 14, 16, 18, 132.

66. Vale, *Reclaiming Public Housing*, 31.

67. Although NYCHA planners "concluded Beach 41st Street Houses had little of the physical deterioration and abandonment that marked so many other Hope VI projects nationwide" and was nearly full, it did have problems of "crime, chronic poverty, and isolation." New community services and security updates would be introduced, but the authority also planned to reduce project density by "reconfiguring" apartments "to house fewer people" and the lowering of building heights. This initial plan failed in the face of fierce tenant resistance. Kim Nauer, "Demolition Derby," *City Limits* (January 1997). See also Charlie LeDuff, "Grant Fizzles at a Housing Project," *NYT*, 30 March 1997, CY8.

68. The NYCHA website, http://www.nyc.gov/html/nycha/html/hopeocean bayapt.html.

69. Housing Research Foundation website, http://www.housingresearch. org/hrf/hrf_SiteProfile.nsf/0/e561ded513eeeea0852569d5004d16e1?Open Document. Prospect Plaza Townhouses in Brooklyn has replaced a high-rise tower with low-rise housing. Oddly enough, a complex recently slated for complete demolition and reconstruction is Markham Gardens in Staten Island, a low-rise complex built with cheap materials during the war years. See "Oversight Hearings on Markham Gardens," New York City Council, 9 June 2005, Pratt Center for Community Development, www.prattcenter.net/test-mgcitycouncil.php.

70. Housing First!, "Building for the Future: New York's Affordable Housing Challenge," November 2001, www.housingfirst.net, 11.

71. http://www.nyc.gov/html/hpd/downloads/pdf/10yearHMplan.pdf.

Index

Acknowledgments

My family has lived and worked in the shadow of high-rise public housing. My grandfather, Irvin Dagen, was acting chairman of the St. Louis Housing Authority during the 1960s when all hell broke loose. He struggled, without success, to right the miserable high-rise public housing complex known as Pruitt-Igoe. A rent strike and decades of poor management policies smashed his efforts, and he begged the federal government to permit its destruction. Irvin resigned his position before demolition began on Pruitt-Igoe in 1972, but the dramatic implosion of the towers gave rise to the most enduring image of failed urban policy.

My parents' retirement to New York City sealed the strange family connection to public housing. They exchanged a suburban-style existence in a leafy Baltimore neighborhood for an apartment in the middle-income high-rise cooperative complex in Harlem known as Morningside Gardens. From their twenty-first-floor apartment they gaze, somewhat nervously, upon the New York City Housing Authority's massive public housing development, Grant Houses, across the street. During my visits I was impressed with how well managed Grant Houses seemed by comparison to public housing elsewhere and even more impressed that middle-class housing could coexist next door. My parents' new situation presented a host of provocative questions about public housing, some of which I have tried to answer here.

The chief data for this book are drawn from the extensive and well-organized records of the New York City Housing Authority now held at the La Guardia-Wagner Archive at LaGuardia Community College. The director, Richard K. Lieberman, and staff members Steven A. Levine, Joe Margolis, Douglas DiCarlo, Aida Figueroa, and Maureen Drennan abided my detailed approach to the NYCHA papers—and my distracting comments. NYCHA has immeasurably improved the lives of researchers by generously depositing its papers in such capable hands. The Citizens Housing and Planning Council, the New York City Municipal Archive, and the Research Library of the New York Public Library, among other institutions, also supplied essential materials. I benefited from research assistance by Seth Knudsen, who is soon to be one of America's great urban planners.

Professors Peter Marcuse, A. Scott Henderson, and Joel Schwartz provided early encouragement. I had long admired the work of Professor Schwartz and was saddened by his passing. Gail Radford penned a thoughtful reader report of a manuscript in most respects quite different from the one presented here. Research undertaken by these scholars, and others before me, proved essential in setting the context for this comprehensive study. My editor, Robert Lockhart, of the University of Pennsylvania Press, has provided excellent and timely direction.

The administration and faculty of the New York Institute of Technology have been unflagging in their support. The growing emphasis on research has provided course releases as part of an annual, internal grant competition. I would like to thank the Office of Academic Affairs, the ISRC grant committee, Dean Roger Yu, and Social Science Department members Luis Navia, Leslie Schuster, King Cheek, Eugene Kelly, and Gerri Brown. I hope that this book appears worthy of the resources committed to my release time.

I have visited many NYCHA developments officially and unofficially and would like to thank the staff, notably Xiomara Camara, for hosting me in a round of sweltering summer visits. NYCHA public information officer Howard Marder has been a likable guide to the inner workings of the authority. Sheila Green, the director of the Department of Communications, and NYCHA chairman Tino Hernandez graciously allowed me access to people and places.

This book represents, I hope, the beginning of a new era of research into New York's public housing system. I have been able to draw on rich archival materials, secondary sources, and interviews to create an institutional and social history of these tower block communities. All researchers would benefit, however, from a large-scale sociological study of life today for the 420,000 tenants of New York public housing. In light of how many studies have focused on mismanaged public housing, the time is right for detailed consideration of a system that functions adequately. Such an undertaking exceeded my budget and skills, but it would be of incalculable value to future researchers.